INSIDE
ORGANIZATIONS

INSIDE ORGANIZATIONS
UNDERSTANDING THE HUMAN DIMENSION

EDITED BY

Michael Owen Jones
Michael Dane Moore
Richard Christopher Snyder

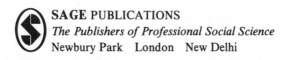

SAGE PUBLICATIONS
The Publishers of Professional Social Science
Newbury Park   London   New Delhi

For information address:

SAGE Publications, Inc.
2111 West Hillcrest Drive
Newbury Park, California 91320

SAGE Publications Ltd.
28 Banner Street
London EC1Y 8QE
England

SAGE Publications India Pvt. Ltd.
M-32 Market
Greater Kailash I
New Delhi 110 048 India

Library of Congress Cataloging-in-Publication Data

Inside organizations.

Bibliography: p.
1. Corporate culture. 2. Organizational change.
I. Jones, Michael Owen. II. Moore, Michael Dane.
III. Snyder, Richard Christopher.
HD58.7.0692 1988   302.3'5   87-26608
ISBN 0-8039-3198-0
ISBN 0-8039-3199-9 (pbk.)

SECOND PRINTING, 1989

Contents

Foreword

Studies of corporate culture probe more deeply into the behavior and internal workings of organizations than past research has done. As a result, they help us to get at deeper factors which block productivity and the internal well being of a firm and its members. A number of recent examples come quickly to mind of the need for organizations to be aware of their own internal culture. These include the disaster in Bhopal, India and the Challenger catastrophe.

Because all problems, not just those involving business, are now global, the study of corporate culture may be even more important as a necessary step in analyzing larger issues. For instance, to truly understand the behavior of Japanese versus American firms, it is not enough merely to study the internal corporate cultures of companies within both countries: It is necessary to study national culture as well.

In order to undertake such studies, it is becoming clearer that greater collaboration among disciplines is essential. If culture is so important to business organizations, it must be an equally important factor in the running of universities. Universities, as we well know, are beset by a fundamental problem, that of fragmentation. The representatives of different disciplines tend to exhibit contempt if not severe misunderstanding of one another; as a result, they achieve only marginal amounts of cooperation. This is unconscionable at any time, but especially now, when organizational issues are of a global scale and hence are in need of attention from as many perspectives as possible.

The present volume is unique in collapsing the barriers between academic disciplines, and thereby helping to bridge the gap between them. One editor is a historian and ethnographer, another teaches business communications, and the third is trained in organization behavior. Authors include humanists and social scientists, academics and practitioners, ethnographers, museologists, management theorists, and so on. Several of the articles grow out of a conference composed of managers, folklorists, and organization behaviorists.

Together the authors and editors have produced an interesting volume with an array of articles that are both theoretical and practical. Above all, the volume is eminently useful. It provides a deeper insight into this thing called culture (whether it exists or not), what it is, how it is shaped and manifested, and what some of its consequences are.

One of the most interesting ways in which the present volume gets at culture is through the notion of stories, those which shape the founding, the history, and the current behavior of organizations. It shows if anything that a rich array of characters—real, imaginative, symbolic, and archetypal—inhabit the realms about which organizational stories are told.

No one is likely to break down all the barriers in the university in one single volume, however good it may be. To change the culture of universities we need to alter the reward system that now promotes working in isolation and, as a result, encourages divisiveness and name calling—a situation that is not only boring and dysfunctional, but presumably something that we should not expect of educated people. Such collaborative efforts as those represented by the preparation of this volume are to be encouraged.

—Ian Mitroff

Prologue

What we call the beginning is often the end
And to make an end is to make a beginning.
The end is where we start from.

—T.S. Eliot, "Little Gidding"

This book concerns symbolic behavior, aesthetic issues, and communication in a variety of organizations. It presents essays on organizational culture and folklore contributing to the growing body of literature on the cultural and symbolic aspects of management and work life, and in so doing offers some guidance and direction to this emerging field.

The volume differs from others on organizational culture and symbolism in several ways. First, it combines these topics rather than treating them separately. Second, it is the only work recognizing that much of what recently has been called "symbolism" in organizations is "folklore," those expressive forms and communicative processes that have been documented and studied for centuries as "lore" and "traditions." Third, this book consists largely of field studies in a variety of organizational settings. Using ethnographic techniques of documentation and analysis, authors describe real situations and actual behavior they have observed in order to derive principles about leadership, culture change, and the social and psychological functions of symbolic behavior.

Some of the questions the book as a whole addresses are the following:

Author's Note: The quotation is from "Little Gidding," in *FOUR QUARTETS* by T. S. Eliot, copyright 1943 by T. S. Eliot; renewed 1971 by Esme Valerie Eliot. Reprinted by permission of Harcourt Brace Jovanovich, Inc.

- How do organization members confront and resolve uncertainty, conflict, and stress through symbolic behavior?
- Does symbolic expression among subgroups that deviates from the norm necessarily weaken the larger organization?
- What are the roles of aesthetics, craftsmanship, and play in organizational life?
- What is "organizational ethnography," and when, why, and how do you use the methods of ethnography in research and practice in organizations?

Authors explore how and why subcultures are created. They examine ways in which organization members cope with tensions and stress as well as deal with ambivalence and ambiguity. Writers explain meanings of symbolic behavior, how subcultures can contribute to the overall functioning of organizations, and why organization members need to understand culture and the symbolic in the work place.

WHO SHOULD READ THIS BOOK

We have directed this book at those wanting to understand organizational culture and symbolism from a practical and theoretical point of view. Although a single volume cannot provide field studies on every kind of organization, process or situation, essays in this book offer a sampling sufficient to suggest some universal principles and applications. Represented here are manufacturing, health care, religious, university, and military organizations. There are situations involving interorganizational cooperation, mission statements, leadership behavior, training, motivation, layoffs, the power paradox, stress, and conflict resolution. Authors describe naturally occurring processes as well as interventions and directed change efforts. A picture emerges of both culture and symbolism at work in varied contexts. We expect a variety of practitioners and academics to benefit from these essays. Many managers, especially those at higher levels in organizations, should find these field studies helpful in understanding their own and others' behavior and in anticipating the need for, or consequences of, different actions. Consultants who advise leaders ought to derive from these articles both insights and practical tools for professional application. Faculty and students specializing in behavioral and organizational science, organizational development, human systems development, folklore studies, anthropology, and similar fields can relate the approach here to their own areas of expertise.

The editors are excited about the prospects of sharing the principles in this volume with others wanting to understand organizations more fully as well as develop and administer them more effectively and humanistically. Their fields of specialty or organizational roles scarcely matter as long as readers are intrigued by the interdisciplinary perspective of organizational ethnography with its emphasis on culture, symbolic communication, and methods of documenting and analyzing traditions and lore.

What appeals to many people about the metaphor of culture is that it emphasizes organization as a complex pattern of human activity. This metaphor helps us comprehend how values and attitudes affect actions while symbolic acts influence beliefs, a fact not accounted for by a mechanical or machine model of organization. Moreover, it becomes abundantly clear that the social, aesthetic, and symbolic are just as important as the instrumental and utilitarian. Not only is much of behavior in organizations symbolic, but also organizations themselves in their structure and functioning stand for intangible ideas about how things should be done, by whom, and for what reasons. In addition, the process of organizing or the experience of organization may generate expectations of meaningfulness and, if conditions are right, feelings of community and personal satisfaction.

The instrumental aspects of organizational administration gain in effectiveness when attention is given to the aesthetic and symbolic dimensions of human experience. This may be one of the most fundamental lessons in this book. Using ethnography in organizations to study processes and behavior, or for advocacy and action, can put this lesson to work.

SELECTED ISSUES

All people tell stories. They celebrate, ritualize, play, and use figurative language. They participate in traditions that convey meanings, recall past experiences, and act as symbols. If these expressive forms and communicative processes are manifested in other social settings, then they must also occur in organizations. How do people's experiences at work and as members of organizations shape the stories they tell and their celebrations, ritual, play, and the like? In turn, how do these expressive forms and communicative processes affect perceptions, attitudes, and actions?

Documenting and analyzing organizational folklore can enhance our understanding of human behavior. It can also enrich our appreciation of what it means to be a participant in an organization. We gain insights into ways that people interact, communicate, project anxieties, cope with problems, and solve dilemmas in human relations. We also discover how people view organizations, and what they expect socially, aesthetically, and symbolically (Jones, 1987). Hence, the information and hypotheses have practical application.

As this volume evolved, several issues came to the fore. One was the concept of *organization*. Should organization be thought of as an entity whose character is practical and instrumental? Or is it more appropriately considered the outcome of ongoing activities and the product of human creation in which aesthetic and expressive concerns loom large?

Some frequent complaints about organizations are that goals are unclear, people are not trusted or given authority commensurate with their responsibilities, and individual accomplishments are neither recognized nor rewarded. When participants wax enthusiastic, however, it seems to be because they have a sense of meaningfulness, find fellowship, and enjoy personal satisfaction. What experiences generate these social and aesthetic expectations, and what conditions help fulfill them?

A third issue arose. How can organizations be designed and administered to meet collective requirements on the one hand, and to attend to individual needs and imperatives on the other? The evidence suggests that people conceive of large organizations as *entities*—formal institutions that tend to be impersonal. But they also hold a model of organizing as a *process*, a term that evokes images and feelings of the personal and intangible qualities in human relations. This second model originates in everyday experiences of spontaneously cooperating with others and coordinating efforts to achieve a common goal. It is reinforced by participation in much of folklore: social rituals, celebrations, and even narrating exemplify organizing in its most basic form. Is it possible to manage people in a *formal*, enduring *organization* according to the model of *spontaneous organizing*?

In the following pages of this prologue we discuss the two models of organization (tensions between which are reflected in and give rise to a large amount of folklore). We outline the development of the transdisciplinary field of organizational ethnography that is emerging, suggest some areas of application, and describe the arrangement of essays.

Authors of articles in this volume have used ethnographic methods of research in order to discover the *meaning* of what people do and say. Having been participants or participant observers in the organizations they write about, they are able to present richly detailed portraits from "the inside." By focusing on those expressive forms and communicative processes that are fundamental to being human, the authors offer a new perspective on management and work life that adds to the understanding of organizations and appreciation of what people seek and can accomplish by organizing.

ON THE CONCEPTS ORGANIZATION *AND* ORGANIZING

What is organization? This question has inspired extensive research and theorizing among scholars, it is implicit in much of the advice literature on how to manage businesses and nonprofit corporations, and it dominates our thoughts sometimes when we reflect on our work experiences, anticipate joining a special interest group, or ponder an encounter with some institution or agency.

If we contemplate designing, developing, or managing organizations as an abstract problem, then we are likely to consider organizing largely a practical—even "mechanical"—matter of designating roles, assigning tasks, allocating resources, establishing chains of command and channels of communication, and ensuring control through systems designed to motivate, discipline, and reward. Many textbooks begin with these assumptions.

Reflecting on day-to-day experiences with organizations and their representatives, policies, procedures, and products or services, we might view organization as a monolithic entity with its own will and volition, beyond the power of any one of us to alter, shape, or influence. Whether we speak of ourselves as "employees," "members" or "customers," *the* organization looms large, seeming to have physical presence and perhaps a life principle.

Perusing the scholarly literature, we find remnants of both the bureaucratic model and of scientific management insisting that organizations can be objectively and rationally designed and should be explicitly regulated, rule driven, and purposely impersonal and, therefore, "efficient."

There is another side to organization, however. The human dimension becomes obvious when we recall instances of spontaneous organization, or occasions of immediate, "small-scale" organizing activities among colleagues, friends, or family. Characterizing these situations is the fact that people combine efforts in pursuit of agreed upon objectives that no one individual could attain alone or as well. The act of striving to achieve clearly defined, common goals tends to generate a sense of larger purpose to our lives. Through repeated interactions with others in the enterprise, we are likely to develop a sense of identification with some people—perhaps a feeling of fellowship. This is especially so when the ambience is pleasant; it happens also when we have had an aesthetic response to an event, object, or activity a frequent result of which is a sense of well being and even unity with other participants. Having contributed time and toil to a group endeavor dependent for its success on our unique skills and capabilities, we typically experience a degree of personal satisfaction when the goals are attained.

The word "organizing," therefore, connotes active participation in a process of bringing something into existence; it may precipitate expectations of meaningfulness, fellowship, and self-fulfillment. In this respect, then, organizations as the products of participants' efforts are not mere mechanically designed structures, nor do they exist as superorganic entities. *They are human creations, and therefore partake of aesthetic concerns.*

Moreover, because organizations are composed of and created by people, symbolic behaviors, expressive forms, and communicative processes that distinguish us as a species and that are manifested in other realms of life are evident in organizations. In organizational settings we tell stories, ritualize, play to relieve boredom or stimulate creativity, formulate assumptive frameworks and act on beliefs, employ proverbial expressions, personalize space, and celebrate. As in other surroundings, these activities at work may provide, variously, a basis for interaction, a means of communication, instruction, persuasion, a way of coping, a method of marking transition, closure, enhancement of status, reinforcement of values or norms of behavior, a source of pleasure and joy, a device for preserving a sense of self-worth and self-esteem, and so on.

One way to increase understanding of management and work life and appreciation of what organizing entails is to employ methods of organizational ethnography. This requires carrying out long-term observation and in-depth interviewing that focus on expressive forms, sociability, and the symbolic. Such a richly descriptive, inside view of organizations can reveal much about the human element in enterprise, informing us of this component of organization.

CULTURE, SYMBOLISM, AND FOLKLORE

Searching for ways to study organizations as human phenomena, rather than as merely mechanical systems, many practitioners and researchers of organizations have drawn upon symbolic interactionism in sociology as well as two other disciplines whose methods, concepts, and bodies of data and hypotheses had once been ignored. One is anthropology, from which is derived the notion of *culture*. This concept provides a single term with which to refer to assumptions, values, and ways of doing things thought to characterize an association of individuals. Conceptions of culture vary from allegedly shared beliefs and customs on the one hand to deep meanings and the projection of the unconscious at the other extreme (Smircich, 1983a). Its appeal lies in its use as an analogy, because to most researchers "culture" implies organization: A society seems to have a "system" of beliefs and practices giving it internal coherence and distinguishing it from all other collectivities of people.

A basis for inferring patterns in culture is found in symbolic behavior and expressive forms like stories, rituals, and ceremonies. Perceiving striking parallels between the rites and rituals of so-called "primitive" people or folk societies studied by anthropologists in the past, and symbolic behavior in organizations in contemporary American society, researchers of organizations have been led to a second field, that of folklore and mythology studies. Of particular interest are the qualitative methods of observation and interviewing that reveal the participants' view of organizations, the concepts of "genres" and "traditions," and the hypotheses and inferences about how and why symbolic behavior of various kinds and content is generated, modified, extinguished, or perpetuated.

Among the many kinds of folklore manifested in organizational settings are metaphors and proverbial expressions; argot and jargon; storytelling; jokes and joking relations; rumors and gossip; material forms, such as personal items made at work and decorated work space; recreation, games, and play; celebrations; and ceremonies, rites of passage, and ritualizing. These expressive forms and communicative processes have in common the fact that they "seem, because of the similarities they exhibit, to be frequently imitated or emulated, repeated or reproduced, modified or transformed" and therefore can "be viewed as traditional phenomena or simply as traditions; and they are worthy of documentation and study because they constitute evidence of continuities or consistencies in human thought or behavior through time or space respectively" (Georges, 1983: 135).

Traditions generated by people in interaction with one another, or continuing through time, may communicate aspirations and concerns, serve as a means of characterizing perceptions, transmit conceptions and interpretations of events, occupy leisure, or teach and reinforce norms and values (Georges, 1983: 135). They can also reveal much about organizing as a fundamental human phenomenon experienced in everyday life.

Celebrations, games, picnics, and family outings, for example, require communication, willingness to participate, and common purpose. These are the principal elements of organizing according to Chester I. Barnard in his classic study *The Functions of the Executive* (1938: 82). They entail the clarification of and agreement on goals, the channeling of resources, and the distribution of roles and activities. It scarcely matters that they are instances of spontaneous or impromptu organization, or that their goals are social and aesthetic rather than pragmatic. But what does matter is that they tend to evoke feelings of enjoyment, meaningfulness, and fellowship, while all too often the experience of formal organization results in the desire for such feelings and frustration in not having them.

In addition to exemplifying organizing as it occurs naturally and spontaneously, much of folklore provides information about individuals' values and concerns, serves important functions for social and spiritual well being, and affects attitudes and behavior through the impact of physical interaction and emotional and intellectual participation. It is not surprising, therefore, that a new field of study is emerging among those dissatisfied with their predecessors' use of mechanical and superorganic models to describe or design organizations.

A NEW TRANSDISCIPLINARY FIELD

Focusing on "organizational symbolism" (or folklore) and "organizational culture," a new field is developing. It crosses disciplinary boundaries of organization development and management studies, folklore research, speech communication studies, cultural anthropology, and qualitative sociology, among other specialties. We call this new field *organizational ethnography* (OE). Its origins can be seen particularly in organizational and behavioral science research and occupational folklore studies in the previous decade.

Folklorists have long studied occupational traditions; witness the numerous collections from the early part of this century to the present of songs, tales, and beliefs of miners, cowboys, sailors, lumberjacks, railroaders, and oil field workers (Green, 1978). Research intensified and broadened in scope in the 1970s. It included bartending as artistic performance (Bell, 1976), the lore of hosiery mill workers (Collins, 1978), the initiation rituals of smoke jumpers (McCarl, 1976), "Xeroxlore" (Dundes and Pagter, 1978), stories told in the transportation and communications industries (Santino, 1978), beliefs and rituals of Texas gulf fishermen (Mullen, 1978), and the rodeo as symbolic performance (Stoeltje, 1979).

Paralleling the folklore literature on occupational lore were publications in the management and organization literature on the expressive and symbolic. Among these were essays on stories managers tell (Mitroff and Kilmann, 1975), formal structure as myth and ceremony (Meyer and Rowan, 1977), leadership as a language game (Pondy, 1978), organizational stories as an expression of management philosophy (Wilkins, 1978), organizational cultures (Pettigrew, 1979) and myths in organizations (Westerlund and Sjostrand, 1979).

In 1980 Dandridge, Mitroff, and Joyce published an article entitled "Organizational Symbolism: A Topic to Expand Organizational Analysis," a seminal essay that introduced management specialists to expressive forms and research questions similar to those dealt with in folklore studies (without, however, citing the works of folklorists or using the word "folklore").

The authors' list of "types of symbols," for example, brings to mind one of the textbooks in folklore studies, Brunvand's *The Study of American Folklore: An Introduction* (1978). For Dandridge et al. identify *verbal symbols* (myth, legends, stories, slogans, creeds, jokes, rumors, names) similar to Brunvand's category of *verbal folklore;* they identify *actions* (ritualistic special acts, parties, rites of passage, meals, breaks, starting the day) not unlike Brunvand's section on *partly verbal folklore*; and their *material symbols* (status symbols, awards, company badges, pins) are analogous to Brunvand's *non-verbal folklore*.

Notable, too, is that the research problems the authors discuss overlap those in folklore studies. "Questions arise," they write, "as to the origin of stories, how they reflect the present organization, and how they participate in subsequent growth or stabilization." Are there industry-wide "symbols," they ask; are certain individuals more influential in initiating or modifying them; what happens to these forms of expressive behavior during organizational change; what are the effects of an organization's "symbol system" on the social environment, and vice versa? Although research was carried out separately, with representatives of the two fields seemingly unaware of each other's existence during the 1970s, it is apparent in hindsight that folkloristics and organization studies are frequently complementary.

In March 1983, the UCLA Center for the Study of Comparative Folklore and Mythology and the Behavioral and Organizational Science Group cosponsored the conference "Myth, Symbols & Folklore: Expanding the Analysis of Organizations." Partly funded by the L. J. and Mary C. Skaggs Foundation and the National Endowment for the Humanities, and directed by Michael Owen Jones in History and Folklore at UCLA, David M. Boje in Behavioral and Organization Science, and Bruce S. Giuliano, President of Ponte Trading Company, this symposium was the first to bring together folklorists, scholars in organization and management studies, and corporate personnel (Regan, 1983; Jones, 1983). Objectives included communicating recent findings in folklore studies and organizational science, encouraging joint research between the fields, and developing transdisciplinary methods based in the humanities. During the following year and a half, there were four more conferences.

Since the terms "corporate culture," "organizational symbolism," and "organizational folklore" began to be used with increasing regularity and frequency, numerous articles on the cultural and expressive dimensions of organizational life have been published in management, folklore and speech journals, or in anthologies (e.g., Jelinek et al., 1983; Pondy et al., 1983; Sergiovanni and Corbally, 1984; Kilmann et al., 1985; Frost et al., 1985). Many relevant papers have been presented at the annual meetings of the American Folklore Society, the Academy of Management, the California Folklore Society, the Western Academy of Management, the OD Network, the Speech Communication Association, the International Communication Association, and the American Anthropological Association.

Obviously, sentiment for a new way of studying organizations has long been felt. The development of a field focusing on folklore, culture, and symbolism in organizations owes much to disillusionment with other approaches and preoccupations, and to the excitement and challenge that a new perspective creates. Two conditions in American society in recent years, however, have given greater impetus to finding other ways of conceptualizing and designing organizations and even a sense of urgency. One is the search for self-fulfillment but a dissatisfaction with the workplace. The other is diminished business vitality owing to a recession and foreign competition, and comparative research of management "systems" to restore American industrial vigor.

THE APPLICATION OF RESEARCH

Much has been written about the changing work ethic in America, noting the increase in dissatisfaction with the organizational workplace, the decrease in loyalty to companies, and the growing propensity to seek self-fulfillment, community, and quality of life in other realms (Terkel, 1974; Yankelovich, 1981). By the beginning of the 1980s, nearly half the American population "felt an intense need to compensate for the impersonal and threatening aspects of modern life by seeking mutual identification with others based on close ethnic ties or ties of shared interests, needs, background, age, or values" (Yankelovich, 1981: 85). The traditional institutions of family, religion and community, however, were no longer as viable for many as they had once been in American society. For the largest number of people, therefore, the workplace seems to be the one institutional aspect of life that holds promise of satisfying the needs of the spirit. Attempts in the 1970s to "humanize the workplace" through job rotation, enlargement, and enrichment had mixed results, the failures owing in part, perhaps, to the imposition of these programs within an earlier conceptual framework in which organization was considered a mechanically designed system of various elements and resources, including people, instead of the emerging concept of organization as the output of human creation and expression of symbolic needs.

Participation—a key principle in the emerging conception of organization—has become prominent in recent years, partly as a result of the vicissitudes of increasing foreign competition that led to studies of foreign managerial success (e.g., Ouchi, 1981; Pascale and Athos, 1981) and the search for homegrown models of successful businesses and practices (e.g., Deal and Kennedy, 1982a; Peters and Waterman, 1982). Also, the worst recession in decades forced business leaders to reexamine basic assumptions about organizational design (Tichy, 1983; Kieschnick, 1983).

One reason that participatory decision making often is effective in improving the quality of work life and increasing dedication is that it makes organizational participants "stakeholders" (Mitroff, 1985); that is, they are more inclined to think of themselves as participants in the enterprise of organizing than as simply those who "work for the company." Quality circles, work teams, and participatory management can, *when manifested in the appropriate circumstances,* fulfill some of the expectations that people have about the nature and results of organizing.

Striving to achieve organizational vitality and attempting to satisfy individual needs *can* be complementary goals. The authors of the best-selling book in the history of popular business publications discovered that, contrary to what they had been led to believe by earlier models in the management literature, the expressive and symbolic are important and necessary components of organizations generating "respect for the individual" and accounting for organizational "success" (Peters and Waterman, 1982: 240). Some of the implications of applied research on organizational folklore, therefore, should be obvious (Bronner, 1984; Snyder, 1984; Pauchant, 1985).

One approach to "applied ethnography" might be to carry out an in-depth study of organizational participants, or of a particular work group, that provides them with a "portrait" of their "culture" and perhaps also recommends programs to management to improve conditions and leadership (McCarl, 1984a). Another might be to design major interventions and large-scale "culture change" (Boje et al., 1982; Sathe, 1983; Schein, 1983a, 1983b; Tunstall, 1983).

The most compelling reason to know more about symbolic behavior, expressive forms and communicative processes, however, is to understand oneself and others more fully—that is: to perceive customs and values upon entering a new situation (Louis, 1980); to interpret ritual, metaphor, and narrative for meaning and significance (Santino, 1978; Wilkins, 1984); to realize the impact that traditional wisdom, language, and stories may have on attitude and belief (Shuldiner, 1980; Frost and Krefting, 1983; Ulrich, 1984); and comprehend sources of tension, stress, and conflict (Ice, 1979; George and Dundes, 1978; Wilson, 1981). Having a basis for making sense of the situation, an organizational participant can then act, attending, for example, to the need for closure, celebration, aesthetic experience, participation, cooperation, coordination, and community.

The essays in this volume provide insights into the kinds of situations often experienced in organizational settings, with implications for acting on that understanding. One purpose of doing so is to sensitize organizational participants, management and labor consultants, and researchers to ways of identifying, documenting, and interpreting traditions in organizations.

ORGANIZATIONAL ETHNOGRAPHY:
FIELD STUDIES OF CULTURE AND SYMBOLISM

Many justifications could be given for undertaking studies of narrating, ceremonies, ritualizing, proverbial speech, festive events, joking, aesthetic expression, and play in organizational settings. These behaviors, or outputs of behavior, are a unique source of information from within an organization about the values, attitudes and concerns of participants, the character or ethos that has evolved, areas of tension and stress, and the expectations and needs of people individually and collectively. Symbolic behavior and expressive forms constitute a basis of interaction and communication, having the results variously of persuasion, entertainment, coping, bonding, and so on. Analysis of how and why this is so is essential to understanding why people believe what they do and behave the way they do as well as to finding ways of attending to basic needs or changing conditions.

Research on communicative processes uncovers their qualities of participation, cooperation, and coordination—in other words, their character as organizational phenomena leading to understanding organization as it is experienced often in everyday life, and to appreciating the expectations generated by organizing.

In sum, studies in organizational ethnography provide insights into particular organizations, offer new perspectives on management and work life, and suggest a different way of conceptualizing organization helping to understand changing attitudes toward work and the relationship between satisfying individual expectations of organizing, on the one hand, and organizational success on the other.

Contained in this volume are essays examining in detail various aspects of the process of organizing, expectations of organizational participants, and means by which people deal with individual needs and collective demands. Articles in Part I on doing ethnography address basic questions about how, why, and when to carry out ethnographic research. Two essays illustrate ethnography in use, on the one hand to discover some of the aspects of management and organizational functioning that can be improved through qualitative research on the symbolic and, on the other, to illustrate some uses of ethnography in customer relations. The final essay in this section discusses how to combine qualitative and quantitative methods of research, focusing on ways to assess the extent to which employees are acculturated and socialized into an organization.

Essays in Part II on functions of the "dysfunctional" consider ways in which folklore, including seemingly "deviant" behavior, may help individuals preserve personal integrity and self-esteem, thus attending to psychic needs but also, in some instances, to collective goals.

Implicit in Part III on the arts of organizing is the notion that people in organizations seek meaning, coherence, and positive aesthetic experiences. Symbolic behavior, expressive forms, and communicative processes may provide purpose and direction, alter conditions, or perpetuate aspects of an organization deemed meaningful and worthwhile.

Essays in Part IV on creativity, commitment, and community demonstrate that organizing generates expectations of larger purpose, fellowship, and personal satisfaction. Essential elements of working are creativity and playing. Ceremony and celebration may be precipitated by feelings of satisfaction in the exercise of skills to accomplish a common purpose. A sense of community can lead to feelings of commitment to collective endeavors.

Part V on paradigms and paradoxes is given over to studies of different perspectives among participants in organizations, and to an examination of some of the paradoxes produced by conflicting or competing paradigms.

Each group of essays is preceded by an introduction setting forth the major themes of the section, and summarizing principal issues and findings in the articles.

The volume is unusual in that articles are by practitioners as well as scholars; most of the essays were written by people about organizations in which they were either participants or participant observers, and the articles concern a variety of business, religious, fraternal, and educational organizations and a wide range of expressive forms and communicative processes.

Unifying the volume is the thesis that organizing is a fundamental human enterprise that is social, symbolic, and aesthetic as well as technological and utilitarian. To develop a concept of organization, understand particular organizations, and apply insights to improving organizational life for the benefit of individual needs and collective aspirations, we must undertake studies of how people express their humanity as they endeavor to communicate, cooperate, and coordinate efforts to bring something into existence. *Any theory of organization is incomplete, and any program of change or continuity inadequate, until organizing as a symbolic and expressive activity is understood.*

PART I

DOING ETHNOGRAPHY

The word "ethnography" literally means "portrayal of a people." Culture is an essential construct, of course. Usually culture is defined as the values, customs, and ways of doing things in a community and the beliefs of its members. People infer much of the culture, its nature and existence, from symbolic interaction and communication, that is, forms of folklore: for example, storytelling and myth making, festive events, joking or kidding, the personalization of space, the use of metaphors and aphorisms, and the development of ritualistic encounters and social routines during the workday. Sometimes these forms and processes reflect values and attitudes. They also may project feelings and concerns as well as point to problems.

Ethnography relies on participant observation, in-depth interviewing, and the documentation of traditions. Such techniques enable one to capture the "feel" of the organization from the inside, the perceptions of individual members, and the community of shared symbols, in addition to the subtleties of everyday routines and rituals as these reveal the quality of life and character of the organization. Ethnographic techniques can be used by researchers, consultants, and organization members themselves.

WHAT DOES ETHNOGRAPHY IN ORGANIZATIONS DO?

Ethnography brings to light the values and ways of doing things in an organization long taken for granted by members. Seldom written down or consciously examined, these precepts and practices guide people's actions, inform decision making, and aid or hinder organizational effectiveness (Schein, 1985).

Ethnography detects what works in different situations. Hence it can be used to uncover and communicate the heritage and character of the organization or examples of effective management, helping perpetuate that which functions positively for individuals and the institution (Jones, 1987).

Often an ethnographic portrait of a community will turn up discrepancies between the ideal and the real in what is professed and practiced (e.g., McCarl, 1984a). This too is beneficial. By identifying inconsistencies, ethnography can help correct what has gone awry. By locating areas of concern, it can expose problems before they erupt into major issues.

Ethnography can help unravel the mysteries of how people deal with ambiguity, anxiety and paradoxes. For we see in their story-telling and use of metaphors some of the ways that individuals express what troubles them as well as how they resolve these issues symbolically.

Field studies that result from ethnography—detailed descriptions of actual behavior in particular situations—may present examples of successful leadership serving as models for application in similar circumstances. They can reveal sources of tension for people to anticipate or try to eliminate before they become sore spots. They teach us about cultural and symbolic processes, knowledge of which is essential to understanding how organizations work or why they do not function well.

In sum, ethnography is a method of discovery and interpretation. It is also a tool for action. Therefore, ethnography is ideally suited to understanding organizational behavior and to directing continuity and change, both of which are vital to effective leadership.

METHODS AND EXAMPLES OF DOING ETHNOGRAPHY IN ORGANIZATIONS

In the first essay, Jones characterizes qualitative methods that focus on the symbolic, comparing them to quantitative methods and explaining when they should be used, why they need to be employed, and how to utilize them in research and application. He emphasizes documenting meanings that people attribute to things and events in organizations, uncovering the community of shared sentiments and symbols, and applying insights to assess customer service, improve morale in the workplace, and enhance organizational communication.

As Christensen reports, by using qualitative methods of oral history and ethnography he discovered conflicting cultures in a health-care organization, caused in part by different messages being sent symbolically by the president and the CEO. The stories, rituals, and metaphors of employees express the resulting confusion and tensions. After showing how to use symbolic communication as a diagnostic tool, Christensen then discusses major organizational processes that can be led more effectively through conscious awareness of culture and the symbolic.

Hanford, the author of the third essay, applies ethnographic methods to resolve a paradox. Why are there persistent, vociferous, and numerous complaints about energy bills in Paradise, California? As a company employee who deals with high-bill inquiries, Hanford, who has degrees in anthropology and folklore studies, discovered that his training gave him unique techniques and skills to solve a vexing problem for the company. An understanding of subcultures and symbolism also led to the creation of innovative ways of communicating with the public.

In the concluding essay, Siehl and Martin set forth methods for measuring organizational culture as well as report the results of using these procedures. The authors combine qualitative and quantitative techniques, first by observing off-site training of recently hired employees to determine what seems to be the core language, stories, and concepts espoused by organizational representatives, and then by constructing and administering a questionnaire to determine levels of cultural awareness over time and between this group and an untrained one. Their methods of measuring cultural knowledge and socialization are readily adaptable to other situations.

Essays in the remainder of the volume consist of field studies exploring how organization members cope with stress, why and how they attribute meanings to things and activities, and why the social, aesthetic, and symbolic aspects of organizational life are so important.

1

IN SEARCH OF MEANING

Using Qualitative Methods in Research and Application

Michael Owen Jones

University of California, Los Angeles

> It is not worth the while to go round the world to count the cats in Zanzibar.
>
> —Henry David Thoreau, *Walden*

Many materials are not readily suitable for quantitative research. Autobiographies, for example, are only collected with difficulty, and after hours of interviewing, recording, transcribing, and editing. The variety of circumstances under which autobiographies are elicited, the changing demeanor of the interviewer, and the fluctuation in the moods of the subjects make the comparison of such documents problematic. Unlike questionnaires, which are widely distributed and often require a subject to select from some fixed set of alternative responses, the content and style of autobiographic documents are not easily coded or counted. Data so resistant to quantification and so unyielding to statistical manipulation can have only limited potential in the enterprise of validating or invalidating hypotheses about human behavior and organizations.

Whatever their deficiencies for quantitative ends, however, autobiographies have particular strengths for increasing our understanding of the meaning of people's experiences and beliefs. Consider the

Author's Note: I am greatly indebted to Elliott Oring, Professor of Anthropology and Folklore at California State University, Los Angeles, for assistance in the preparation of this essay.

recollection of a 24-year-old Mennonite male of his Illinois rural childhood (Oring, 1966: 31):

> I remember one time I came home from school and for some reason I wasn't feeling well so I went up to my room and went to sleep. When I woke up I went downstairs. My folks were gone, and none of my sisters were around, and the whole house was deserted. I went out on the street. The whole place was deserted. I thought Christ had come and taken the saved with him. I was in a real panic, because I didn't know what to do.

> Eventually they came home. I think I found somebody else in the street, or saw someone on the street—maybe he was another lost soul; he must have had a secret sin. As soon as they came home everything was okay again. I mean, obviously Christ hadn't come because my mom was back. And if He wouldn't take Mom, who would He take?

Rather than elicit life history information, the researcher could have asked this individual preformulated questions, perhaps giving him a questionnaire to fill out. The respondent might have been requested to rate on a five-point scale (from "strongly agree" to "strongly disagree") statements such as "You believed in God when you were a child," "You thought of yourself as a good Christian," and "You loved and respected your mother."

Tests, measures, and questionnaires impose structures and articulate concerns of the researcher. Often these structures and concerns are those that facilitate the elicitation of data in a form that can be tabulated and correlated, with summaries graphed and charted.

Autobiography is different. In autobiography, the subjects create their own structures and express their own concerns. The beliefs, behaviors, actions, and events that are described modify and amplify one another.

The young Mennonite was not providing the researcher with "data." Rather, he was telling the researcher his life story. It is his story that suggests the immediacy of his childhood religious beliefs, the sense of his own unworthiness, and the nature of his love and admiration for his mother.

This individual's story shows how a belief expresses itself in his life and how ideas and emotions are given shape, substance, and significance. We are allowed a brief glimpse of what "Christian," "sinner," and "mother" may *mean*. Of course, autobiography is only one of the documents for qualitative research. But it is with such questions of meaning and significance, whatever the documents, that qualitative research is most fundamentally concerned.

In this paper I address three issues: (1) What differentiates qualitative methods from quantitative ones? (2) How do you carry out an ethnography of an organization? and (3) Why use qualitative methods in both research and application? The underlying assumption is that quantitative and qualitative methods are not incompatible; they are only concerned with different ends and ways of achieving them, and they may have different "results," defined as outputs that are tangible and impersonal as well as effects that are intangible and personal (Georges and Jones, 1980: 135-152).

WHAT IS QUALITATIVE RESEARCH?

A comparison between features of quantitative and qualitative methods can highlight some of the characteristics of the latter. Quantitative research typically has the purpose of ascertaining general trends in opinions, values, and perceptions. The researcher elicits data, the aim of which is generalizability, and usually does so by operating with detachment from circumstances; the phenomenon studied is considered independent of and unaffected by the researcher, who is likely not even to be present in the situation examined. Categories can be—indeed, to a large extent must be—a priori. Research questions have to be stated clearly and precisely, and hypotheses articulated in advance and tested systematically through the data-gathering "instrument" that stands between researcher and "subjects." Quantitative research tends to look for and to isolate relationships that reside in an organization structure or system, to verify these hypothesized relationships through statistical correlation, and to thereby reduce the complexity to a certain number of forces. Because the purpose is to control and thus limit or discount the particular and individual, such issues as sampling, repeatability, validity, reliability, and level of significance of correlations are vital concerns.

The intent of qualitative research is to understand the particular, the individual, and the unique. Those employing qualitative methods reject none of the goals of quantitative research of seeking correlations or cause-and-effect relationships, but tend to regard the fabric of human life as too complex to reduce to a few independent and dependent variables. Whereas the emphasis of quantitative research is on the structure of the "mechanical" or "organic" system, qualitative research tends to focus upon individual motives and to ascertain the community of shared symbols, sentiments, and meanings. Qualitative research often emphasizes the *emic* orientation—the conceptualization of the organization from within rather than only the *etic*—the view from outside as a detached observer. The qualitative researcher is likely to experience the situation in which others are immersed, whether directly through participation or indirectly through extensive and intensive interviewing. The "instrument" is not a mailed questionnaire, a poll, or a telephone survey: it is the researcher's multiple sensations and holistic appreciation of "what is going on." Answers to research questions seem to evolve or emerge, as people talk about their experiences and perceptions or as the researcher participates in events. Hence a vital concern is that of rapport and trust—the intangible and personal qualities of human relations (see Van Maanen, 1979; Van Maanen et al., 1982; Jackson, 1987).

While there are important differences between them (see Figure 1.1), the two methods are compatible, even complementary. Tentative concepts that emerge from experiencing unique situations can serve as the basis for developing specific hypotheses that can be tested through the use of instruments such as questionnaires (see, for example, Siehl and Martin's essay in this volume). In turn, understanding the reasons for and impact on individuals of general trends discerned through quantitative research can be achieved by means of intensive interviewing, observation, and participation.

The methods also overlap in actual practice. After all, inquiry is inquiry: It entails asking questions, and delaying judgment while seeking answers to them. We are always hypothesizing, and testing beliefs that evolve by marshalling evidence—quantification. To arrive at the universal, we need to examine specific cases for what conditions and forces, despite their seeming uniqueness, might hold true elsewhere.

To give an example, William Foote Whyte reports in his book *Men at Work* (1961: 32) that during the Second World War a particular management had trouble retaining workers. One part of a personnel program to attend to this problem involved setting up an employee library. Stocked with detective stories and other light fiction, the library also had a few technical books as an afterthought, but provided in the event that workers might wish to brush up on some aspect of their jobs. When assessing (i.e., measuring, counting, quantifying) the use of the library a few months later, management people were discouraged: Virtually none of the light fiction books had been checked out. They were surprised, too; the technical volumes were always in demand. Closer inspection revealed, however, that in spite of their being constantly checked out, the technical books remained in extraordinarily pristine condition. Why?

Dimension	Quantitative Research	Qualitative Research
field	social "scientific"	"humanistic"
goal	establish general trends, correlations between dependent and independent variables	uncover meanings in particular settings
assumption	researcher is independent of "subjects" and situation	researcher influences, and is affected by, those studied
categories	a priori, imposed	inherent, emergent, peculiar to situation
techniques	administer tests, measures	interview, observe, experience (directly or vicariously), participate
instruments	polls, questionnaires, surveys	self (multisensory)
understandings	through concise statement of problem, articulation of hypotheses, systematic testing	evolve or emerge as events unfold and evidence mounts
relationships postulated	forces within structure/system	thinking, feeling individuals as active forces in setting
concerns	validity, repeatability, comparability of "data"	uniqueness; effects of researcher and those studied on one another (trust, rapport); meaning and action "in context"
limitations	investigates only what can be readily hypothesized and tested through instruments	not repeatable, not easily comparable across settings
image to critics	atomistic, reductionist, "cold," aloof; with "obvious" or only "common sense" conclusions	"fuzzy" and "unscientific"; findings are supported by "anecdotal" evidence

Figure 1.1 Quantitative Versus Qualitative Research

A consultant was called in to advise management. After developing a relationship of mutual respect with workers, he discovered through interviewing the reasons that light fiction stayed on the shelf while technical volumes were avidly sought (but obviously not used).

Workers were hostile to management. They felt that any friendly act by management must have a manipulative and exploitive intent. In the case of the library, they felt it must be a scheme to discover which workers were serious about their jobs and should be considered for promotion. The library could easily inform management who had checked out which books. Reading light fiction wasn't going to get anyone promoted. Therefore, choose a technical book instead. You don't have to read it; just check it out!

Although management had no intention of using the library for these ends, antipathy among workers had created a distrust of management and generated a constant suspicion about motives and purposes. The workers shared a view that determined to a great extent what actions in the workplace would mean.

By being close to the situation, gaining trust and letting understanding evolve or emerge as he observed and interviewed workers, the consultant discovered a system of "meaning" in which "symbols" loomed large. Hypotheses were tested and confirmed or disconfirmed as they occurred, until ultimately the consultant arrived at some "truth"—and something approaching a "law" of human behavior.

HOW DO YOU DO QUALITATIVE RESEARCH?

Recent years have witnessed an unprecedented frequency and intensity of criticism of methods in the organizational sciences. Many have questioned the relevance of both methods and results (summarized by Thomas and Tymon, 1982), including quantitative research. Some have challenged the seeming preoccupation with survey research to the neglect of other methods that reveal the meanings human beings attribute to the world they perceive (Dubin, 1982). Others have called attention to the value of "inquiry from the inside" rather than "inquiry from the outside" (Evered and Louis, 1981). And an increasing number are heralding the use of qualitative methods (Van Maanen, 1979; Morgan and Smircich, 1980; Pondy et al., 1983; Jelinek et al., 1983).

For all the interest in alternative modes of inquiry, however, the way you go about doing qualitative research is not well described. The many guides to fieldwork clarify how to ask questions, observe, and document. Simultaneously, however, they obscure the process of people studying people by implying after the fashion of quantitative research that there is only one way or a best way to proceed, that the researcher is independent of people and the situation studied, and that understandings best follow from problem statement and hypothesis testing. The image is that of a lab-coated scientist seemingly always "in control" of an experiment. Yet, paradoxically, reports of the actual experiences of fieldworkers engaged in qualitative research suggest a process dominated by the human element, in which much is unanticipated, unexpected, and serendipitous (Georges and Jones, 1980).

Rather than try to prescribe qualitative methods, I shall describe and analyze the way that one individual undertook an organizational ethnography as interviewer and participant observer. Although in many ways unique to this individual, the procedures generally seem to characterize much of qualitative research.

At the annual meeting of the Minnesota Historical Society in 1985, Nicholas C. Vrooman gave a presentation entitled "A Folklorist in the Works." Formerly a "state folklorist" employed by an arts agency in North Dakota, Vrooman formed (with his wife, Patrice Marvin) a private cultural conservation firm to protect and encourage community traditions. He was employed by the Red Wing Shoe Company in Red Wing, Minnesota, for his skills as an ethnographer. One of his tasks on behalf of the Red Wing Shoe Company, he reported, has been to document the customs, symbols, rituals, work ethics, artifacts, stories, special language, humor, and guiding vision or worldview of the organization as a corporate community. These material and intangible things express the nature of the company and its identity; they are crucial, notes Vrooman, "in achieving and maintaining a healthy, equitable work atmosphere and a common sense of direction— therefore, giving productivity its best chance, which is, of course, a paramount desire of corporate existence."

The "folklife history" project was to be not only a mirror of the company but also a reflection of the organization in the community, thus indicating how work life fits into the larger society. "The story of the Red Wing Shoe Company will be told by the workers," that is, all categories of organization members, whether in manufacturing, management, sales, or shipping. "The project hopes to bring recognition and honor to the skills and efforts of the people involved in producing Red Wing Shoes; to show changes in the work process and in the product over time; and to amplify the positive attributes of pride and esteem in work lives, and of quality work in the work place."

To accomplish these goals, the project required documentation of varied sorts: tape-recorded interviews; photographs of the work place and process, as well as of workers; examination of business records and promotional literature; and observation of work processes and worker interaction. The information was be indexed and archived for future retrieval. Some of the materials were to be assembled soon as a publication available to workers and the public.

From the outset, the intentions and nature of the study were stated and agreed upon. "The potential for abuse of information always exists, and an ethical stance is required to determine what is to be presented publicly," writes Vrooman. "We want to be very careful to use nothing that might hurt somebody or jeopardize the company." A factor determining successful working relationships was mutual respect: "To not only look for it in the work place, but to practice it in our strategy for collecting information."

He began his research with retirees—the "elders"—a procedure that gave him historical perspective, taught him the language and process of shoemaking, provided "reflective narratives," and turned up old photos. "This strategy was crucial in that it gave us a general knowledge of the business and it established community ties, so that when we went into the factory and the office for interviews, we could speak and question with an informed view."

Because he wanted to determine what it meant to be a maker of shoes and boots as well as a participant in a particular organization, Vrooman asked a variety of questions, many of which would precipitate descriptions and stories.

> We sought to elicit *talk* [emphasis added] that would clue us in on what it takes to know leather, place a cutting die on the hide, emboss a vamp, stitch a quarter to a gusset, last, make a Goodyear welt . . . , and finish a pair of boots. What are the names of the tools and machines you use? How do you work at the same machine for 40 years? What are the tricks of a good pieceworker? Describe a typical day at your job. How did you pick up the skills? How's your work today different from when you first started? Describe any humor from the work place. What was your involvement with the union? What was work like during the Depression? Tell me about the picnics and retirement parties. Who were the local characters in the company? Who determines the standards for quality in the shoes? What are the highlights of the company's history?

"We asked these kinds of questions in the home, on the factory floor, and in the office," reports Vrooman. When interviewing workers in the factory, he "checked in with the foreman of the department to explain my purpose. Then I just hung around the factory for a while, letting myself be seen, getting into casual, nondocumented conversations, having the word get out as to what I was up to."

"In all of this work we look to find common factors that describe a sense of shared values, concerns, issues, skills, and behavior which are necessary to fulfill the tasks of producing Red Wing Shoes." He continues: "We strive to present the material as it was told to us." Hence, those who view it should feel that they can read a truth in it. "We hope the work will serve as a kind of family album for future generations . . . and as a special record of the company that is so integral to the local community life. We hope the work will promote an understanding of what we must all give—WORK. The more we understand work and how it fits into our lives, the better we'll be able to appreciate the fruits of our labor."

In Figure 1.2 I have identified some of the elements in Vrooman's qualitative research. He had formulated questions for research which could be answered only through interviewing, observation, and experiencing the situation firsthand; some questions were specific (changes in work processes and in products) but others were more general (the feeling of the workplace and the relationships and interactions of people). He made some assumptions on which questions were based and goals predicated: that the expressive and symbolic determine the character and identity of an organization, and that participants must understand aspects of work life in order to more fully appreciate accomplishments and enhance self-esteem. His intentions were clear and both known and agreed to by others: to determine what is unique about this organization and how it relates to the community. He explained his purpose at every opportunity. An overriding concern was to develop trust and maintain mutual respect at all levels in the organization. He learned the language, the processes, the traditions. He employed questioning that resulted in the unfolding of meanings over time, eventually giving him an overall image of the organization. This ethnographic portrait was based on recurrent patterns and commonalities in a particular setting. Because the description unveiled a community of shared symbols, sentiments and meanings, authenticity in documentation and reportage was essential.

By following these procedures, Vrooman was able to observe and to elicit information yielding hypotheses and inferences about many aspects of the organization that gave him insights that he could communicate to others. Some of the results were tangible: an archive of material, a publication, oral presentations, visual displays. Many results were personal and intangible: the relationships formed with others, the mutual respect, Vrooman's growing appreciation of the quality of what people make and do and their increasing understanding of values and assumptions they had long taken for granted, a clearer sense of history and future direction for the organization. Perhaps the most important results of Vrooman's applied research for organizational participants

Feature	Details
research questions	identify traditions and expressive forms; determine changes in work processes and products over time; ascertain what it is like to work here, and why it is this way
assumptions	expressive forms reveal nature, ethos, and identity of the company and contribute to individual objectives and organizational goals; the more we understand the nature of work in our lives, the better we will appreciate our accomplishments
intentions, goals, objectives	construct a mirror of the company and reflection of the organization in community; create a sense of history and community; present tangible results as "family album" showing past and present, answering question of "Who are we?"
procedures	observe and interview in homes, factory, offices; elicit stories, descriptions, and accounts of the personal and intangible; assemble and examine tangible items (old photos, company records, promotional literature); photograph workers, work processes and products, and tape record interviews
concerns	clarification of intentions, participation in activities, trust, authenticity of information and presentation
results	tangible (archive, book, photo exhibits, reports) and personal and intangible (evolving understanding and appreciation, respect, enhanced self-esteem, clarification of identity)—with benefits directly to individuals, the organization, and the community

Figure 1.2 Example of Qualitative Research by Nicholas Vrooman (An Organizational Ethnography of the Red Wing Shoe Company)

are enhancement of self-esteem and also answers to the questions "Who are we?" "Why are we here?" "Where are we going?" This brings up the matter of why undertake qualitative research.

WHY USE QUALITATIVE METHODS?

Qualitative research of organizations need not entail a complete ethnography, of course. Ethnographic methods can be used for action research of much smaller scope (as in the instance described by Whyte). In addition, whether one relies on quantitative methods or uses the qualitative mode of inquiry should depend on what one seeks to discover. Biases intrude, however. Quantitative research seems "scientific" (one is "controlling variables"), while qualitative methods may have a certain "mystique" (how do you "infer meaning"?). And one or the other mode is usually selected owing to the fact that it seems more compatible with an individual's personality, training, values, or assumptive framework.

Some researchers or clients seem to think that quantitative research is cheaper, because it requires less time to distribute questionnaires than to develop trust, interview in depth, and observe surroundings. However, this belief does not take into account the amount of time needed to ascertain the variables, frame questions, pretest and refine the instrument, or code the data and establish the validity and statistical significance of the results. Of course, quantitative research can be inexpensive if the researcher uses preexisting instruments. But the cost may be dear to the client who is given results that do not get at the real problems. It may be a matter of false economy: What is to be gained by having answers to questions that do not address the significant issues in one's own organization?

The example of changing the formula for Coke comes immediately to mind. Tests and measures were not the issue; decision makers failed to understand how Coke was part of a larger fabric of meaning or to even appreciate that this was a significant factor. Public outcry followed the change in formula because the old Coke was a symbol evoking memories and associations; it was fraught with cherished meanings that were disregarded in the decision to alter the flavor. (Ironically, one of the most adamant leaders of a grassroots movement to force Coca Cola to reinstate the old formula failed to identify the old Coke correctly in a taste test involving the new and the old Coke and Pepsi.) The mass media did the qualitative research for the company by reporting the hue and cry and identifying the many meanings and associations people have with the old formula. The company president did the only thing he could: He restored the old formula ("classic Coke")—while maintaining the new: "Now America has a choice," he claimed. The results await evaluation. What is apparent in retrospect is that "context"—the system of sentiment and meaning—was not considered early in the decision-making process.

Because human beings reason analogically as well as think logically, because they express themselves not only directly but in many subtle ways, and because they have aesthetic as well as practical concerns and are given to symbolic behavior, qualitative research is essential. As essays in this volume demonstrate, qualitative methods identify where the sore spots are in organizations and how people cope, they contribute to an ongoing effort to understand particular organizations and thus avoid crises, and they reveal meanings that can aid in the management of cultural differences. These studies from inside organizations uncover ways that individuals affect one another through their expressive behaviors, how cultures emerge or are transmitted both spontaneously and in an orchestrated way, how people manage a crisis, and why participants identify with an organization. They bring to light contradictions, the ways that conflicts are resolved and a sense of community is generated, and how self-esteem is developed and reinforced. In sum, the use of qualitative research provides greater understanding of particular organizations and enhances appreciation of the nature of organizing and organization in general.

Both practitioners and theorists need qualitative research when issues require understanding perceptions, meanings, and social realities. I will briefly characterize four situations in which knowledge of context and systems of sentiment is crucial. As will become apparent, the four situations are related and the issues interrelated.

A recurrent concern to organizations is *customers' perceptions of the product or service.* Polls and surveys are often conducted. Qualitative methods are less frequently employed, paradoxically so, for the questions of ultimate interest are likely to be those of quality, perception, and meaning.

Take as an example the quality of health care received by subscribers of a health maintenance organization. One way to ascertain the nature of patient care is to examine patients' charts to determine whether annotations about allergies and drug sensitivities, symptoms, and current diagnosis have been made and are entered in the appropriate place, to examine manuals and audits for completeness and thoroughness, and so on. This is what "surveyors" do when visiting a site for purposes of accreditation. Results are tabulated and measured against established practices and standards. The committee grants accreditation, or withholds it, on the basis of this "report card."

Accreditation places the organization on a par with many other institutions, implying a certain degree of excellence. But it does not differentiate this organization from the others. The organization's success depends on attracting and retaining enrollees; it must stand out (for all the right reasons), which requires that it be known how patients perceive the care, the care givers, and the organization.

Another measure of quality, therefore, is the way in which patients and their families answer the following questions: "Why did you choose this facility?" "Will you select it in future?" "Will you recommend it to others?"

If given the opportunity, people are likely to illustrate their answers by telling stories of their experiences. Narratives embody and reflect perceptions. Moreover, as forms of symbolic communication, stories dramatize events and actions with vivid imagery and figurative language that engage listener and teller alike. Patients will tell stories to other people about the care they received and the concern they were shown, perhaps many times. When they are told, these stories will shape listeners' opinions, while also reinforcing the tellers' own beliefs and attitudes. The "bottom line" for the organization is not responses on a questionnaire that patients either "strongly agree or "strongly disagree" that care is of high quality, but the stories they tell of their "treatment" (practically and expressively).

Because quality of service or product often is a function of how people feel about themselves and what they do, a second area of application for qualitative methods is *organizational participants' perceptions of the work place.* Surveys of "climate" are a useful beginning. They suffer in two major respects, however. One is that since they must restrict responses to a range of a priori considerations, they are not likely to get at the unexpressed, the implied, or the taken-for-granted character of this particular setting. The other is that attempts to change conditions and attitudes are likely to be resisted, because they entail programs designed at a distance and imposed from above; this is owing to the fact that categories of meanings inherent in the situation and peculiar to it are not known or fully appreciated.

Another approach is to ask such questions as the following (Sonduck and Perry, 1983): "What is it like to work here?" "Why is it this way?" "What happens, or fails to happen, because of this?" These questions elicit description and narrative, which reveal meaning and also are likely to suggest alternatives in the event that conditions need improvement—or means of reinforcement—in instances in which circumstances are considered satisfactory. Through qualitative research, the practitioner or theorist gains immediate understanding of the effects of rewards, organizational functioning, and work life and how they are perceived, appreciation of why they are perceived this way, and insights into what participants feel should be perpetuated or changed and how to do this. Hence, results are multidimensional.

The need for both continuity and change is felt especially *during times of major change* brought about by unprecedented success, a sudden downturn, rapid growth, unexpected retrenchment, and mergers or acquisitions. A good deal of energy is expended doing economic forecasts, conducting financial audits, and carrying out other quantitative measures—particularly when acquisitions or mergers are contemplated. Strangely, despite all this research, something like 75% of mergers and acquisitions fail. What is missing?

Much of what occurs in an organization is expressive, communicative, symbolic. It is "folklore," "mythology," or "myth making" in the best sense of these terms: the creation and expression of systems of meanings and social realities. An organization develops a certain character and evolves an ethos. Hence, when change efforts are planned (or change is experienced) several questions become crucial. Three are the following: "What is the collective reality of the organization now?" "What should the social reality become?" "How do you preserve and perpetuate some attitudes, values, and beliefs while altering or creating other traditions?" Attention must be paid not only to the stories that people tell and the figurative language they use but also the rituals, ceremonies, and material culture that evince, communicate, reinforce, and perpetuate the character of this particular setting.

Growth is often attended by loss (or fear of loss, or belief that loss has already occurred) of the social and symbolic or other benefits enjoyed in the past. Mergers and acquisitions are analogous to the model of culture contact and resultant acculturation or cultural pluralism (or conquest, colonization, exploitation, and cultural extinction, as the case might be). Sometimes "success" is measured by the riches plundered. But assuming that success is considered a function of organizational and personal integrity, then it behooves those planning policy and strategy to identify, document, and even perpetuate traditions that characterize the organization. Obviously, this is a task appropriate to qualitative rather than quantitative research.

A fourth area is that of the *ongoing concern* of individuals and organizations *with matters of identity, values, goals, and action.* It is difficult to imagine quantitative methods being relied upon, since by nature they place the researcher at a distance from the setting. Questions within a qualitative orientation would include the following: "Who are we?" "What should we be doing?" "Why should we be doing these things?" Answers are to be found not only in what people state explicitly but also in their stories, figurative language, decoration of work area,

Concern	Questions
customer perceptions of service or product	"Why did you choose this facility?" (or product)
	"Will you select it in future?"
	"Will you recommend it to others?"
	(and note stories people tell)
organizational participants' perceptions of the work place	"What is it like to work here?"
	"Why is it this way?"
	"What happens, or does not happen, because of this?"
	(and note stories people tell, figurative language employed)
change (rapid growth, merger, acquisition)	"What is the collective reality of the organization now?"
	"What should the social reality become?"
	"How do you preserve and perpetuate some attitudes, values, and beliefs while altering others?"
	(and note stories, figurative language, rituals, ceremonies, and material culture)
ongoing concerns of identity, philosophy, goals, planning, quality	"Who are we?"
	"What should we be doing?"
	"Why should we be doing these things?"
	(and note stories, figurative language, rituals, decoration of work area, ambience of interaction, ceremonies, festive events, heroes and history, mission and mottos, slogans and self-awareness)

Figure 1.3 A Sampling of Issues Appropriate to Applied Qualitative Research

ceremonies, festive events, customs, heroes and history, mission and mottos, and slogans and self-awareness.

Although not intended to be exhaustive, the list of four issues appropriate to applied qualitative research consists of interrelated elements having an internal consistency (see Figure 1.3). Customer perceptions of the quality of service or product are likely to be affected in subtle ways by the attitudes and behavior of organizational participants whose perceptions of the work place are influenced by conceptions of the organization's character determined in part by on-going concerns about identity. Ultimately the answer to the question of "Who are we?"—the fourth issue—has a bearing on the stories that customers or clients will tell—the first consideration.

CONCLUSION

Those undertaking so-called pure research in an organization using qualitative methods may confront a dilemma. Practitioners might want to use the results for some specific purpose, whether in keeping with the researcher's intentions or not. As Vrooman notes in his paper "A Folklorist in the Works," however, and as I quoted earlier but repeat here because of its importance, "The potential for abuse of information always exists, and an ethical stance is required to determine what is to be presented publicly. . . . We want to be very careful to use nothing that might hurt somebody or the company." On the other hand, while conducting pure research the investigator may become motivated to communicate the meanings uncovered because of their relevancy only to have the report rejected or precipitate the wrong kind of response because the results challenge long-standing assumptions. Both dilemmas demonstrate, paradoxically, how crucial to application are the understandings that qualitative methods can provide.

Qualitative methods are distinguished by the search for meaning in particular settings in which human beings are considered active forces. Qualitative research is carried out using extensive interviewing and observation in order to experience indirectly or directly the circumstances in which participants are immersed. The reasons for employing qualitative methods are that this mode of inquiry addresses some fundamental issues recurrent in organizations that quantitative research alone is unable to deal with or even recognize. The in-depth knowledge of situations resulting from qualitative studies more directly serves practitioners' needs (Evered and Louis, 1981: 392).

Because they observe and interview at firsthand, are physically and psychologically close to the situations studied, and consider the participants as thinking and feeling individuals who are active forces in the setting, qualitative researchers are concerned with matters of trust, mutual respect, validity of information and authenticity in its presentation, and results conceived of in highly personal and intangible forms. Several commentators on methods have observed that the norms of scientific detachment characteristic of much of quantitative research encourage researchers to view and treat organizational members as "reactive entities to be manipulated" (Thomas and Tymon, 1982: 347; Susman and Evered, 1978). By contrast, qualitative research can "most help a practitioner collaborate with other organizational members as thinking individuals" (Thomas and Tymon, 1982: 347).

In sum, qualitative methods are part and parcel of the growing trends to explore the cultural, expressive, and symbolic aspects of organizations and to practice more participatory decision making and collaborative management. Qualitative methods are not simply a few techniques to gather data; they encompass a whole host of assumptions, concepts, questions, and hypotheses as well as an orientation—a way of looking at the world, ascertaining what is significant, seeking meaning, and creating understanding. Writing in *Walden*, Henry David Thoreau suggested that the value and meaning of a culture are not to be found in mere counting, computation, and correlation. An increasing number of organization theorists and practitioners appear to agree.

2

MIRROR, MISSION, AND MANAGEMENT

Reflections on Folklore and Culture in a Health Care Organization

Don Christensen

University of California, Los Angeles

During 1984 I spent over six months as a part-time observer and fieldworker at Global Medical Group (pseudonym), one of the largest health care organizations in the country, as part of a project for a graduate seminar in Corporate Culture and Organizational Symbolism offered by Michael Owen Jones at UCLA. Most of my research was conducted at Global Medical's corporate offices in Los Angeles, although I also spent time at some of their other offices in the Los Angeles area. I am a folklorist and historian, among other things, and my chief research interests involve oral and written personal narratives, but I tend to be an incurable generalist and had become intrigued with the study of organizational folklore at a 1983 conference, Myth, Symbols, & Folklore: Expanding the Analysis of Organizations, which was directed by Jones and others in Santa Monica, California. Early in 1984 I learned that certain individuals at Global Medical were interested in having a graduate student conduct qualitative research within their organization, and I decided to give it a try and see what developed.

Traditional behavior and thought are apparent everywhere, including in modern organizations. All individuals, even those who assume the role of corporate personnel, repeat stories and jokes, rumors and gossip; use jargon, slang, metaphors, proverbial expressions, and nicknames; create and perpetuate rituals, ceremonies, celebrations, and rites of passage; and adapt and use material forms of expression such as graffiti, cartoons, costume, and the personalization of space. These processes and behaviors, as well as many others, which have been identified as *folklore*, have been the focus of research by folklorists for many years.

We can infer a great deal about human beings, both as individuals and as members of groups and organizations, from the presence or absence of various forms of folklore in their everyday lives. Folklore both reflects and refracts people's hopes, fears, aspirations, repressions, fantasies, beliefs, world view, and more, and allows people a way to express them (Wilson, 1981; Toelken, 1976). In addition, some understanding of the use and function of various forms of folklore should be valuable to those interested in understanding their own organizations, since decisions and actions that influence all members of an organization may be based on folklore—for example, stories, beliefs, and rumors.

ON THE HISTORY, PHILOSOPHY, AND MISSION OF GLOBAL MEDICAL GROUP

One of my first meetings at Global Medical was with Joan Simmons, who is Group Vice President of Management Development. She was looking for a better way to articulate and disseminate what she saw as the history, mission, and philosophy of Global Medical to its employees, including its executive directors, while I was curious to see what a folkloristic approach would reveal about organizational life. We decided that given my interest and experience in personal narrating and oral history I might be able to interview various individuals in the organization and identify people who told stories exemplifying the history and mission of Global Medical and its uniqueness in the health-care field. Joan Simmons wanted to be able to make a videotape of various narrators to be shown in training in order to establish a better sense of tradition and mission among members of the organization. I was not particularly interested in helping Global Medical to become a "better" organization, but this looked like a fair trade-off and a reasonable way for me to explore my own interests and curiosity.

Joan had many stories to tell, through which she expressed a strong sense of the philosophy and mission of her organization. She told me how she began working as a nurse in a hospital in Kentucky and in time became head nurse, then director of nursing, assistant administrator and eventually administrator, which was her position when the hospital was acquired by Global Medical in the 1970s. With fervor in her voice she told me that "the greatest example of what Global Medical represents can be seen in the hospital and community from which I came." She went on to tell me that her hospital was old and deteriorating and that she was struggling to enable it to serve the needs of the community more fully when Global Medical took over and gave her the resources to make it into a large regional medical center with services that patients formerly had to travel over 65 miles to find. She called it "Southern hospitality at its finest," and added that it required a great deal of entrepreneurism because, "in the midst of all that expansion you can rest assured there was a great deal of risk taking, and Global Medical backed us all the way." She told several stories about individuals whose lives were spared or who were given a new sense of purpose through their contact with this upgraded hospital. It was this concern for people and the emphasis on humanitarian goals that she saw as part of the real mission of Global Medical, and she added,

> That's what excites me about Global Medical. It's not that they are nice to employees—because they are—or because they have a wonderful benefit package—because they do—it is that the mission you can accomplish as a manager for Global Medical is above and beyond what most managers ever have the privilege to do, not just fair, but humane and excellent.

She felt that her company had grown so large and rapidly in recent years that it was now important to remind everyone what the organization stood for, and she said,

> As I look back over the years I found that the only way I could successfully lead a group of people forward to work at the level of intensity and under the stress that you have in a hospital, growing at the rate of speed we were, was to articulate for them a mission that was common to all of us, that they could get excited about, that they could belong to, that kept them off the whole idea of pettiness and all the other things that can get in your way. Our motto was "We Care." I felt I had to constantly hold that mission forward to them. And I think that we have just reached a point in our stage of growth at Global Medical where we desperately need to articulate our philosophies, culture, and mission.

When I questioned her more closely about the philosophy of Global Medical, Joan mentioned that the most important matters were a strong commitment to humanitarian goals, encouragement of an ongoing entrepreneurial spirit, and a firm emphasis on decentralization and local autonomy. She said that if I really wanted to find out what Global Medical was all about, I should meet with Bill Lemon, the founder of the organization, who was now retired but who still maintained an office in the building and acted as something of a consultant at board meetings.

She spoke highly of Lemon as the person responsible for the early emphasis on humanitarian ideals, as a man who encouraged a "family feeling" among his associates and employees, and as someone who stressed the need for Global Medical to remain as unstructured as possible and therefore to allow as much individual creativity, entre-preneurism, and autonomy as possible. She definitely wanted to get Lemon on videotape in order to instill some of his philosophy among Global Medical employees, and agreed to arrange for me to meet with Lemon in the following weeks.

Bill Lemon is indeed a warm and interesting person, with the assured air of a self-made millionaire who now spends much of his time sailing and enjoying his retirement. In the late 1950s he and some associates had taken over a decrepit hospital in Los Angeles by merely assuming its debts, and in less than a year they turned it into the black. Bill said that he discovered that doctors did not know how to run hospitals, because they were not trained in sound business practices, and he felt that some of the management principles he had learned in other ventures could apply to hospitals as well. His basic method was to acquire hospitals or hospital-management companies that were in financial trouble and to turn them into cost-effective operations in a short time. "We didn't start with anything great," he said, "but who gets something for nothing? We assumed a lot of debts and had to turn them around right away. We just knew how to do that."

Lemon told me many stories about the risk taking of those early days and the camaraderie that existed among his associates. From the beginning he felt his role was to hire competent people and let them do their jobs with a minimum of interference. "I'm a firm believer in not being a Monday morning quarterback," he stated. "If you put a team together you need to let them make mistakes and learn or you'll never have a successful venture." He stressed the need for "open-door management," and for maintaining a family feeling among employees. To illustrate some of his philosophy, Lemon told me that when he worked in the hotel business his father had one day pointed to a janitor and said, "You see that guy with the broom? If he wants to tell you something, you listen, because it's free, and he may have a good idea." Lemon added, "I've never forgotten that." From the beginning, he said, he and his associates had felt the need to help those who could not normally afford private health care and so there were always several "charity beds" in each Global Medical hospital and a lot of talk about the importance of maintaining human dignity. When I asked him if all of these principles were still a part of Global Medical he looked wistful and said that they try, but it's much harder to maintain such attitudes and practices in a large corporation.

Following these initial meetings, I set out to talk to others at Global Medical to see what kinds of stories they had to tell about the history of the company and what sorts of ideas they had about its philosophy and mission. I also wanted to keep my eyes open and to ask a lot of questions about the daily expressive behavior within Global Medical offices. After talking to Simmons and Lemon I certainly anticipated finding a rich and varied folklore within this organization, as well as a shared sense of mission and purpose.

One of my first surprises was to discover that many "top" corporate people were reluctant to meet with me, and my appointments were frequently postponed or broken. I think some were suspicious of an outside observer and were wary of what I would do with my information, while others seemed to feel that since I was not being paid anything for my efforts, then my work must also be worthless. In six months, however, I did manage to interview or speak with dozens of people, and I was further surprised to learn that very few individuals had more than a vague sense of the history or philosophy of their company. In fact, most people were a little uneasy with my questions, and responded with comments such as, "Well, I've only heard about things third hand," or "I haven't been here long enough to know about that," or "You really ought to talk to Mr. Lemon about those things."

This puzzled me, because part of my agreement with Joan was that I would help to locate individuals who could tell "good" stories conveying a sense of Global Medical's history and purpose, and yet I could not seem to locate such persons. When I asked individuals about philosophy or purpose, they frequently grappled with descriptive comments or metaphors in trying to answer me. One person remarked that he could give me a few phrases that he felt epitomized Global Medical philosophy, but he could not put them into a coherent statement. Ideas such as autonomy, quality, integrity, and familial relationships were expressed or implied in some comments like "I don't have to ask if I can go to the bathroom," "The message around here is, whatever you do, do a quality job," "We're willing to do business on a handshake," and "There's something of a family feeling around here." Questions about Global Medical's mission were frequently met with embarrassed silence; even though several individuals had some sense of a mission, they were unable to express it in explicit and succinct form the way Joan Simmons was.

When I asked questions about the kinds of stories, jokes, celebrations, rituals, etc. that existed within Global Medical I got answers like "There's really very little humor around here, except maybe some gallows humor," or "We used to have a lot of celebrations and things when Mr. Lemon was around, but we don't do that much anymore," or "We've gotten too big for much of that sort of thing," or "Now that you mention it, I think we've lost something in recent years." Why were so few people able to articulate anything about the history, mission, or philosophy of their organization? How could I account for the apparent dearth of active folklore? As I implied, a lack of expressive behavior can also reveal a great deal about people; however, inferences based on a lack of folkloric expressions and behaviors are more problematic and open to the interpretation of the observer. Global Medical is largely decentralized, which is part of the philosophy as Simmons stated it, and it has also grown very rapidly in recent years through acquisitions and mergers. Perhaps it is not unusual, therefore, that people do not know much about the larger organization beyond their immediate circumstances and daily concerns. In addition, the second or general-manager generation of leadership that is in control following Lemon's retirement seems much more concerned with being cost-effective than in maintaining either the humanistic mission of the founding generation or a sense of historicity within the organization. But whatever the reasons, this was certainly a different organization from what I expected to find following my initial conversations there.

THE CULTURE CONSTRUCT

While most people had little to say about Global Medical's purpose or its folklore, many people used the term "culture" freely, as if it just rolled off their tongues. Among the comments were "The culture around here is pretty top-heavy, no matter what anyone tells you," "You'll probably find out that each floor has its own culture," and "I think we have an excellent culture in this company." At the time I was visiting Global Medical, Peters and Waterman's *In Search of Excellence* (1982) was on the best-seller list, and it seemed that everyone had a copy on his or her desk or had just read it, often at the request of a superior. It was very trendy to speak of "corporate culture," even though it seemed to mean different things to different people.

In recent years growing dissatisfaction with earlier mechanical and organic models of organizations has led to this shift to "culture" as a model or metaphor, but it has not eliminated confusion. Some of the uncertainty surrounding the concept of organizational culture is well illustrated in a recent story by Terrence Deal and Allan Kennedy, who are themselves authors of a popular book entitled *Corporate Cultures:*

> In one company, we presented the concept of culture—its functions and elements—to the senior executives of a multinational conglomerate. At the end of the presentation the chairman of the board turned to us and with great enthusiasm remarked: "That's the finest presentation I've heard in ten years." Without a pause he turned to his CEO. "George," he said forcefully, "I want a culture installed here next Monday." "With all due respect," we interrupted, "we believe you have a culture here now; that's one of our key points." "Bullshit!" said the chairman. "We don't have one, and as you pointed out, that's the problem. George, I want a culture here and I want it now—by next week. Your butt is on the line." We left [Deal and Kennedy, 1984b].

There are several problems with the "culture" construct, both in the way I heard Global Medical people use it and in the way I read about it in the popular press. In the first place, for many people it implies a stabilizing force and an equilibrium model that helps preserve the status quo. In fact, organizations are seldom static. They are generally dynamic, ever-changing phenomena that are created, influenced, and transformed by *all* members, not simply by a single segment such as management, and therefore are not as susceptible to manipulation and control as many authors and management consultants would have us believe, or as the character in the Deal and Kennedy story thought. Organizations are human creations, and people create and change organizations through their narrating, ritualistic interactions, demeanor, beliefs, and so on. The term "culture" may be useful if we realize that it is a metaphor and not a reality. Organizations are made up of people, not "cultures," but it is the assumptions and values that some people appear to share or have in common in a particular setting that we often refer to as "culture," tying the people in an organization together and giving them common purpose. What we can hope to learn from studying organizational folklore or culture is more about people and their capabilities, not a better way to manipulate them.

Another problem with the culture construct is that many people who use this term seem to feel that each organization has a single, overriding, homogeneous culture when, in fact, most organizations consist of multiple subcultures, and even countercultures or factions that may hold very different or competing views on the nature of situations within the organization. This is clearly the case at Global Medical, which, because of its far-flung and decentralized nature, consists of different "cultures" in different places. Even among the personnel at corporate headquarters there were differing assumptions and values among those who were loyal to the CEO and those who were aligned with the COO. A question I heard frequently was "Are you on Andy's team or Roy's team?" There were even perceptible differences in dress, demeanor, and relationships between members of these different "teams," cultures, or networks.

Probably the most useful way to view organizational culture is to see it as the underlying assumptions and shared meanings and values that individuals and groups assign to their social environments. It might be viewed as a kind of "automatic pilot" that provides direction and focus for activities and decisions in a way that does not require one's full or conscious attention. These basic assumptions, values, concepts, and beliefs are frequently discovered, developed, or invented as people learn to cope with problems both from within and without the organization. These shared notions usually work well enough to be considered valid and to be taken for granted to the extent that they may drop out of active awareness and become almost unconscious, and are thus passed on to new members as "the right way," or simply "the way we do things around here." There usually are, of course, multiple cultures within a single organization (Wilkins, 1983a; Schein, 1983c).

As long as things are running smoothly, the underlying assumptions (or cultures) of most organizations are taken for granted and are seldom questioned or even articulated. It is only when circumstances change, times get tough ("when the manure hits the fan"), or when new competition appears that the basic assumptions are questioned or challenged. At such critical times many organizations falter or fail because their members may discover the lack of shared values or the existence of conflicting assumptions that were not apparent prior to the crisis, and much time and effort are spent trying to come to grips with these discrepancies before the crisis can be addressed effectively.

If members devoted more ongoing effort to understanding their organization instead of waiting until times of stress to become concerned, there would be less chance of surprises, and individual energies could be devoted to dealing with the crisis at hand rather than to going back to try to hammer out the basic assumptions of the organization once again. Perhaps this is one of the reasons that Joan Simmons was so interested in articulating and disseminating the mission, philosophy, and culture of Global Medical, although she did not make that point explicit.

FOLKLORE AND CULTURE
AT GLOBAL MEDICAL GROUP

An interesting example of what can happen at times of crisis occurred while I was observing Global Medical. As I mentioned, part of the philosophy of the organization was to remain decentralized and to allow regional and local leaders as much autonomy as possible. People in general seemed proud of this aspect of the organization and I heard several proverbial or metaphoric phrases to describe the situation, such as "We're really in the trenches making our own decisions," "We want people to take care of themselves and not call home all the time," and "I like the fact that I don't have to ask if I can go to the bathroom." There were, however, certain corporate policies that were potentially in conflict with this notion of autonomy, but that were not intrusive when things were running smoothly.

For instance, as early as 1978 a policy memo was circulated stating that any Global Medical employee who had been with the organization for at least three years could be terminated only with the approval of the COO, and any five-year employee could be terminated only with the approval of the CEO. Most people, instead of viewing this policy as being in conflict with the notion of decentralization and local autonomy, saw it as evidence of the beneficence of the corporate leaders in assuring job security for the 45,000 employees, most of whom were nurses. But early in 1984, Global Medical, along with the health care field in general, experienced something of a crisis owing to changes in Medicare policy, strong criticisms of rising health care costs, charges of unnecessary and expensive treatments, and a drastic decrease in hospital enrollment. This resulted in some noticeable nervousness at Global Medical corporate offices.

By May, regional leaders in various parts of the organization had done little to respond to the situation, so orders went down from corporate headquarters to lay off more than 4,000 employees, mainly hospital personnel. This led to a good deal of tension and misunderstanding. Local leaders felt their autonomy was being undercut; employees who had been led to believe that the purpose of the termination policy was to protect them from the whims of local managers now felt it was being used against them by top management, and some people at corporate headquarters felt perhaps it was time to pull in the reins and to begin to exercise more control from the top. A number of people told me in private that it seemed to them that Global

Medical had "changed its message," and many attributed this to the fact that the organization had grown too large and too fast; members of "Andy's team" seemed resentful and suspicious of "Roy's team," and vice versa. All of this resulted in much confusion, anger, resentment, closed meetings, recriminations, and so on, most of which I was not privy to, but which I could not help noticing. In fact, this may have been one reason some people were not willing to meet with me at this time—they did not like having an outside observer see their "dirty laundry."

Most people at the corporate offices seemed to be caught rather unawares by these developments, but from my vantage point I had been noticing some frustration and dissatisfaction with Global Medical leadership for quite some time. I found it interesting that an organization that at least paid lip service to a "family feeling," and that promoted open-door management and an emphasis on autonomy and egalitarianism, could still show evidence of heavy-handed leadership from above in the metaphors people used and the attitudes they expressed. Employees throughout the Los Angeles area frequently referred to the twelfth (top) floor at the corporate office building, where the CEO and COO had their offices, as "Walnut Heaven," an allusion to the ornate decor and the staid and authoritarian atmosphere there. In response to a question, one person told me that at Global Medical it was "a *sin* to buy expensive office furniture—except for those people in Walnut Heaven." Some joked about directives from the twelfth floor as coming "from God," and one person who was scheduled for a meeting there told me, "*They* like to put the fear of God into you," while an individual who had just come from a meeting said, "There is a sense there of searching for the guilty rather than of solving problems." This use of metaphors about God, heaven, sin, and guilt is significant and revealed a good deal about prevalent attitudes toward Global Medical leadership long before a crisis surfaced.

It was my impression that many top people at Global Medical were completely unaware of the effect that the discrepancies between the stated or implied values and the reality of the situation had upon the morale of their employees or themselves, or were at best puzzled by it.

I observed several other areas where an understanding of organizational culture and folklore could be valuable for members of Global Medical. One is the hiring of new employees and the changing of roles for continuing personnel. This is an area in which a company's assumptions and values are continually being challenged or having to be asserted as individuals seek to find out where they fit in and to learn "how things are done around here." People are usually anxious to know how work is done; how employees are treated, rewarded, and punished; how one is evaluated; what the boss is really like; what the cardinal sins are; and so forth. Only part of what an employee learns about these matters comes from official sources and orientation meetings. Much more is usually learned from the folklore—from the stories, jokes, advice, and gossip people hear, and from other behavioral clues they pick up, such as approval or ridicule from associates and superiors.

Several individuals at Global Medical expressed a sense of frustration that they had received no clear guidelines for their jobs, but had received criticism for what they thought was reasonable behavior. "I only found out where the walls were by running into them," one person told me. Another said that he had been visited by a corporate official who had remarked about one of his decisions, "Don't you know that's against Global Medical policy?" His response to me was, "How the hell could I know? No one ever let me know." In this firm, as in most others, a better understanding of company folklore, its importance, its functions, and how it is perpetuated and transmitted could aid in understanding how employees, including managers, are acclimated and educated, and how they feel about their jobs.

Another issue about which an understanding of folklore and culture is important, and one that confronts Global Medical continually, is that of mergers and acquisitions. Questions that are helpful in contemplating such actions include, Will the new organization fit in with us? Will we be able to understand it? What parts will we be able to incorporate and what parts will need changing? Several people at Global Medical expressed concern in this area with statements like "Some Universal people still seem to feel they belong to someone else," and "It took Wyatt people two years to begin to accept us." Michael Owen Jones (1984b) remarked on this issue,

> Many acquisitions and mergers sink into a sea of red ink. Often the acquiring company installs new officers, forcibly removing top management of the acquired company or accepting resignations en masse. The current officers anticipate the eventual demise of themselves and the firm that will not survive under the command of those who know little or nothing of its traditions and likely do not care about the memories and associations that have built up over the years among the organizational participants who made the company what it is today. . . . One lesson about acquisitions is that attention to the bottom line must include not only a financial audit but also a culture audit—of both the acquiring and the acquired companies.

For the people at Global Medical, another area in which understanding of their company's culture is crucial, and to which they have
not given nearly enough attention, is the changeover from the "founder
generation" to the "general-manager generation." Global Medical
certainly had a strong and successful founder-culture. Bill Lemon and
his associates started a health-care organization based on sound
business practices, but they also introduced many humanistic, social
service, and other noneconomic concerns and values into the organization. Notions about a "family" of Global Medical employees, the
importance of community service and local involvement, concern for
compassionate service and human dignity, the setting up of charity beds
in each hospital, "open-door" management, and an emphasis on quality
care as well as on profits are all part of the legacy of the founding
generation.

In many organizations, and in Global Medical in particular, the role
that the second, or general manager, generation assumes is that of
rationalizing the organization, handling its growth, and making it more
efficient. These managers often find the noneconomic concerns of the
founders to be the very things they want to change in order to do their
job well. However, as changes are made, if these managers are not aware
of the history, the values, and the philosophy of the founder-culture and
the positive effects they have had upon members of the organization and
their patients and customers, they run the risk of throwing out the baby
with the bath water, of attempting to change those aspects of the
organization that should not or cannot be changed (Schein, 1983c).
Many employees at Global Medical are aware that there is a problem in
this area; several people indicated that the company had "lost something" since Lemon's retirement and remarked that they were not
particularly pleased with the more "efficient" direction the organization
had taken recently.

CONCLUSION

Many individuals at Global Medical seemed at least implicitly aware
of problems and inconsistencies in one or another area within the
organization, but no one—especially the top managers—has put it all
together or has a very clear picture of the situation. The video that Joan
Simmons hoped to introduce into her training programs might be a first
step toward understanding the essential character of the organization as

it once existed and as many still desire it, but more is required. Some of those in higher level positions who have joined the organization in recent years appear to be unaware of the ethos of the organization as perceived by long-time members such as Joan Simmons, or perhaps they do not care.

As I mentioned earlier, cultural information about an organization, based on various forms of folklore, does not lend itself to manipulation, but is valuable mainly for gaining a better understanding of organizations. What it reveals in this instance is the desire of many participants to know their organization, to preserve and perpetuate certain elements of the company, and to shape the institution according to their conceptions of what it ought to be and do. Through some of their folklore, a number of individuals are expressing their concerns; they are also trying to cope with rapid expansion, the change from the founder-culture to general manager culture, vicissitudes of the economy, and uncertainties within the organization. Folklore is generated spontaneously to confront a series of crises in organizational life.

Presumably a wise leader would be both interested in and responsive to the feelings expressed in stories, figurative language and other folklore, and the attempts to deal with problems through these expressive forms and communicative processes. But for all the talk about "corporate culture," "excellent companies" and "human resources," I wonder whether a sufficient number of participants—particularly at higher levels—are aware and appreciative of the meaning and significance of the traditions and symbolic behavior within their organizations. Folklorists, anthropologists, and sociologists have a great deal to offer toward a better understanding of organizational life and behavior, but unless members of organizations are informed of and receptive to these observations they will not benefit from the inferences and insights.

At Global Medical, some of the folklore reflects everyday experiences and mirrors elements of a culture of management—the negative themes in rumors, stories, and language characterizing situations and expressing reactions to them. Some of the expressive forms and communicative processes are also a screen on which are projected images of what the circumstances ought to be but are not. And some of the symbolic behavior is an active attempt to cope with the situation or change it. Reflecting on folklore and culture, we realize there is a message about management's mission. Communicated daily in a multiplicity of ways, this message only needs someone to hear it.

3

COMPLAINTS IN PARADISE
Using Ethnography in Customer Relations

Rob Hanford
Pacific Gas and Electric

Upon completing my studies in anthropology and folklore at the University of California, Berkeley, I was hired as a clerk and meter reader for Pacific Gas and Electric Company, the largest investor-owned utility in the country. After a year of reading meters in the farm communities of Glenn County, I took a permanent position as a clerk/meter reader in the foothill retirement community of Paradise, California. It is proving to be an ideal place to study how people are weathering the energy crunch that began with the oil embargo of 1972 and is likely to continue.

This report suggests some of the kinds of ethnographic research that can be conducted at a public utility company, and indicates the value of such research. It also explains how a service representative, in order to satisfy the needs of his or her customers, must be very proficient in the art of informal interview and other ethnographic skills. Exposure to the

Author's Note: This essay reflects the direction and support of several people. Tom Johnson of California State University, Chico (CSUC), was the person who first planted the seed of "corporate folklore" in my imagination, and has subsequently guided the events that lead to this fruition. The paper was originally prepared for a class on ethnographic methods given by Jim Meyers of CSUC, an experience that fully awakened me both to the need for doing an ethnography in a workplace and to the career possibilities that could be created with my present employer (credit is also due each member of the class). I am deeply indebted to Monty East, former manager of PG&E's Paradise District, for the trust and confidence he had in the project despite the sensitivity of the issue and the temperament of the community. Thanks also to Mike Jones of the University of California, Los Angeles, for his interest in and refinement of the issues and opportunities that surround the process of the High Bill Inquiry.

techniques that have been systemized by folklorists and anthropologists would no doubt enhance these abilities. At the same time, the occupational "know-how" of these professionals offers scholars not only a rich source of data on American energy habits, but some much-needed insights into how ethnographic skills can be applied in the workplace.

The central issue of my research, and the most problematic aspect of my work as a meter reader and service representative, is the "H.B.I."— the acronym for a form titled the High Bill Inquiry Investigation. Coming into such a job with a background in folklore made for two general kinds of observations: service representatives act as ethnographers from the moment they begin the H.B.I. process; ethnographers can become service representatives and enter the fascinating world of energy demand and supply.

I should state at the outset three beliefs that influence my work. First, it seems to me that what we have been calling an energy crisis is, in fact, a crisis in worldview. The notion of cheap energy was and continues to be surrounded by assumptions about how North Americans should properly live in the world: how we should arrange our communities, design our homes, grow and distribute our food, wear our clothes, rear our children, treat our environment, view our neighbors, and see ourselves.[1] As the price of oil soared during a decade that witnessed a ten-fold increase, Americans found themselves reexamining some of their assumptions; this, I think, is a source of great anxiety and is what lies behind some people's anger about the cost of energy.

My second assumption is that utility companies are increasingly becoming organizations that coordinate energy from many sources— windmills, cogeneration plants, small-scale hydroelectric facilities, photovoltaic cells—rather than a few, as in the past. The public will own many of these sources, and therefore has a much greater stake in the business of energy supply. The change is already under way, and affecting much about the way we live.

Third is the belief that the prime mover of this change in the way we view our world, and in our behavior, is the rising cost of energy consumption. In today's world, logic and pathos follow suit. For example, the summer following the rate restructuring of 1982 a physician contacted the Chico office because he was enraged by his $1,300 electric bill for the previous month. An energy auditor visited his lovely and spacious home, with close to 3,600 square feet of west-facing and unshaded glass, which afforded a marvelous view of the valley and setting sun. In effect, however, the architect had designed a huge solar oven that collected heat within the building as fast as the two air conditioning systems could put it back outside. The interesting point is that the customer had lived in the same house the summer before when the rates were much lower, but at $600 per month the inefficiency of this "heating and cooling" system was not perceived, or at least it was not considered a big enough problem to warrant a complaint, much less a redesign.

The case of the doctor is an extreme one, but it displays an attitude that permeates our culture. Even my most liberal friends who have long argued for conservation didn't get around to wrapping their own water heaters with insulating material until 1982. Consider also that today we have the technology and know-how to construct moderately priced homes that would require 50 to 70% less energy for space heating and cooling than even the modern "conservation" homes being built today. The Anasazi were doing it on this continent 900 years ago! One wonders how expensive energy will have to get in order for us to see the wisdom of combining our technology with these concepts.

Or is there a way to assist the growing appreciation of this new view, perhaps by using ethnographic techniques, which would circumvent the need for Americans to get the picture only by first making things so collectively hard on themselves? I am not sure that there is, but this is the question that guides my interest and gives me the patience to serve the steady stream of customers inquiring about their bills.

THE SERVICE REPRESENTATIVE AS ETHNOGRAPHER

The dramatic increases in gas and electric rates in the early part of this decade have meant that the local offices of public and private utilities have been besieged by angry and befuddled customers demanding an answer to the question, "Why is my bill so high?" Although service representatives hear this same question several times every day, the answers they give are very different.

People's bills represent the sum total of their energy lifestyle, a unique and complex blend of (1) their dwelling, its contents and state of repair; (2) the environment, climate (especially seasonal variations) and topography of the site; and (3) the inhabitants themselves: their age, income, health, family status, and social position as well as their special needs, habits, and tastes. When service representatives "take an H.B.I. from a customer," they in effect encourage that person to tell his or her story, carefully noting any data that will help reconstruct the situation in which the customer feels trapped. One might posit that "not all ethnographers are service reps, but all service reps are ethnographers"; both roles require the ability to interview people who may be reluctant if not hostile informants, and both require knowing how to find out things without making people feel defensive.

There are several techniques that a clerk might use to conduct a High Bill Inquiry, or an ethnographer an interview. (Many of the concepts discussed in Whyte, 1960; Agar, 1980; and Georges and Jones, 1980, should be worked into the customer services training for PG&E as well as other companies.) The least directive is simply to utter such responses as "Uh-huh," "That's interesting," "Hmmmm," in order to encourage the interviewee to continue. Such responses are classically used when a customer is expressing much anger, or an informant is talking about a delicate subject or one about which the ethnographer deems it appropriate to avoid direct comment.

A response further up the scale of directness is that of a clerk repeating the last phrase of sentence with rising inflection, thereby directing attention to something of particular interest. For example, the clerk may ask, "Your thermostat was set at sixty-eight degrees the whole time you were gone?" Or, "You have three waterbeds?" (An uninsulated waterbed is just another form of electric space heating.)

More directive still is probing the preceding remark by raising a question. "Was your thermostat turned off, or was it turned down to the lowest setting?" "You were gone the whole time, but your bill didn't go down? What day did you leave?" "How long has the hot water faucet been dripping?"

Fourth on the scale of directness in carrying out a high bill inquiry (or ethnography) is suggesting a different conclusion that could be drawn based on the evidence as testified to by the interviewee. "You left on the thirtieth, and we read your meter on the following fifteenth. You were gone only half of the billing period, which is why your bill was cut only in half." Or, "It may be that we misread your meter, and we'll read it again if you want, but with that leak in your bathtub faucet I can tell you that your water heater won't shut off till it's heated the Paradise reservoir, and I would not wait for the reread to get busy fixing it."

Finally, there is the introduction of a new topic. "It may be that your neighbor's bill is half of yours, but there are so many variables that we are really talking about apples and oranges. We need to focus on your household habits if we are to get anywhere with your bill."

The art of the interview, of course, is knowing which level of directness to use in which context. Both the ethnographer and service representative have to rely on body language, voice tone, eye contact, and their own intuition. I remember one customer inquiring about his bill; there was something in the tone of his denial that made me suspect his electric space heater. I asked him if he had one in his bathroom, but the question only increased his anger, so I dropped the issue and asked about his water heater. This piqued his interest, and soon I sensed that we were gaining rapport. After a brief chat, which ranged in subject matter from my family to his granddaughter, I asked him if he had turned the heat on for any visitors last month. "Oh, that's right," he said, half apologetically, "we had the kids up for Christmas, and Tracy had a cold. I'll bet that's it. I had forgotten about that."

The essential point about the experience is that the customer was not deliberately trying to mislead me when he began our exchange with the statement, "My bill has more than doubled this month, but I haven't done a damn thing different than I did the month before!" He was telling me what in his mind was the absolute truth, having simply forgotten about his grandchildren's visit, or having been preoccupied with Tracy's illness rather than with the effect on his bill of turning up the heat. It might have been any one of a hundred other things about his daily routine that had slipped his mind or of which he had never been aware. The job of the clerk is to ask the right sequence of questions in order to jog the person's memory or bring awareness about a possible cause. This is what ethnographers do. They probe for the beliefs and ways of thinking by which people actually live and function, but of which they may be unaware or which they may deny.

THE ETHNOGRAPHER AS SERVICE REPRESENTATIVE/METER READER

In the process of moving to the inside of a culture, it is commonplace for the researcher to be regarded as a little strange by the chosen group of study (Georges and Jones, 1980: 43). While this does not speak for the whole of my reputation with the company, I have come to appreciate why such a perception is an inherent part of our trade. For example, most of the company employees from bottom to top consider the H.B.I. to be a negative and unpleasant aspect of their job. As it became obvious to my fellow employees that I was fascinated by people who were angry about their bills, I realized that folklorists appear odd because we delight in the commonplace and therefore display "unnatural" exuberance over the "wrong" kinds of experiences (Berreman, 1968: 343). The effect of this on my acceptance has been varied, accelerating it with some groups and retarding it with others.

The sense of being an insider begins with the first moments of employment. There is a certain stigma attached to working for any controversial industry, a coldness and resentment that is heightened in Butte County by the fact that there are few jobs that pay as well as those at PG&E. The new employee soon learns through conversations at work, cocktail parties, and the grocery store that he or she has been thrust into a world where there seem to be two kinds of people: those who have high bills, and those who are expected to know why. The energy complaint, then, serves as a common bond and source of identity for the employees, who must develop some degree of proficiency and a repartee in order to conduct their daily lives. (During the furor over the recent rate hikes, many employees chose to conceal their place of employment because of stories about ugly scenes at restaurants and other places of public gathering.)

On January 1, 1982, PG&E set up a new rate structure that meant as much as a 100% increase for some of its all-electric customers. On January 2, the worst snowstorm in recent memory hit the Paradise ridge, and people found themselves in the freezing cold without electricity for up to five days. And so it continued through April: snow storms, rate hikes, more snow storms, more rate hikes. One minute people were realizing they couldn't live without energy, the next minute they couldn't live with it. Throughout this period, our office was filled with angry people standing in line wanting to discuss their bills (I was a cashier at that time). As the customers talked to each other while waiting, there were two or three occasions when we PG&E employees at the counter were on the verge of knowing how it is that a room full of good people can turn into a lynch mob. To make matters worse, if ethnographers are delighted with the commonplace, many of us are ecstatic when a culture is in chaos: during this period the veil of complacency that normally surrounds Americans' energy habits was dropped.

My interests in the H.B.I., then, simultaneously strengthened my ties with my coworkers, yet made me appear strange, a pattern that repeated itself in my enthusiasm for reading meters. A meter reader position is thought of as an entry-level job, a kind of boot camp that people have to endure in order to get to better things. I confess that in the early months there were many moments when I disliked it intensely, but again the anthropological background converted what is a distasteful job to many into a golden opportunity for me.

While taking H.B.I.s over the counter or on the phone is a rich and vital source of insight into American energy habits, there would be serious limitations and distortions in a study based on these experiences alone. For one thing, not everyone has an energy complaint; nor does everyone contact the office if he or she becomes upset. For another, it is important to actually see the customers in their homes in order to study the symbiosis of structure, site, and inhabitant. (In fact, service representatives make home visits on difficult H.B.I.s.) Furthermore, there is no way to compare the consumption patterns and attitudes of different neighborhoods, or houses within the same neighborhood. And finally, people in the office get less exposure to the many innovations and ideas that Paradise ridge residents are developing on their own.

Ethnographers begin their research by surveying the population and terrain; there is perhaps no better way to gain an overall impression of the area I am reporting on than from the cab of a meter reader's pickup truck. The Paradise district covers approximately 400 square miles, extending from Cherokee and the Mesilla Valley at the lower elevations to the south up to Stirling City, a logging community at 3,500 feet. The western boundary is the steep cliffs along Butte Creek canyon, while to the east we serve PG&E's hydroelectric facilities along the North Fork of the Feather River. Every structure or business enterprise using electricity within this area has an electric meter, and every meter has its own page in the log book that is carried on each route. On each page is recorded a two-year meter history, an account number (computerized identification number), name and address of the occupant, location of the structure, location of the meter on the structure or grounds, and information about the pitfalls one might encounter when "egressing and regressing" the premises. In other words, not only are the field notes in place, but the collecting is systemized and ongoing.

Currently, Public Utility Commission (PUC) regulations state that every meter *must* be read not fewer than 28 nor more than 33 days apart. The approximately 40,000 customers of our district have been divided into roughly 63 routes to be read in the same sequence by three meter readers (21 routes each). As the relief meter reader I had to learn all 63 routes, which meant that I frequented every domestic structure and place of business in our district several times a year. The meter reader/ethnographer has no choice in this matter (never mind the weather).

Each full-time meter reader has the opportunity to visit 5,000 sites a month, 12 months a year, at roughly the same hour of the day, and precisely record the rise and fall of the energy consumption. These figures determine the size of each person's bill. One must be alert and careful to observe the courtesies and proprieties unique to each situation along the route. I did not know, for example, that the dust kicked up by a pickup truck spreads spider mites onto walnuts and alfalfa, a lesson I was thankful for having learned in training instead of at the top of some farmer's voice. Part and parcel of doing the job is noting each person's name, work, character, attitudes toward home security, dates of annual vacation, name of dog, and of course, history of energy habits. I have recorded figures that mean $10 a month for some, and $2 million a month to others (a fiberglass insulation plant in Willows). I have walked through tracts of identical homes with incredible discrepancies in energy consumption among them. I have been to houses with manicured front yards but back yards that are trash dumps. I have seen the hot tubs go in, the swimming pools get filled with rocks, and the faucets drip month after month. I could write a treatise on ways not to latch a gate.

It is estimated that in our district 2.4 persons reside at every meter. Therefore, the average set of routes provides the opportunity to talk to the same 12,000 people every month. It is not difficult to turn any of these encounters into an interview situation, made all the easier by the public's perception of the employee as that kind of person "who knows why." In jotting down bits of personal information from each encounter I find myself developing a growing sense of intimacy and trust with a very great number of people. I could not have gained this rapport in any other way.[2]

UNDERSTANDING THE NATURE AND TONE OF CUSTOMERS' BILLING COMPLAINTS

Knowing these techniques of interviewing and applying them in the appropriate context is not always sufficient to resolve the issue immediately. A case in point is the vexing problem of why the population in any area is notorious for its complaints about energy bills, while people in an adjacent area are less vociferous. The answer has much to do with values, worldview, and expectations. By studying the behavior of people in Paradise and Magalia, one comes to realize that it is the rising *price* of energy more than it is social consciousness that is forcing a change in attitudes toward and assumptions about the use of energy and the way we live.

Paradise and Magalia lie on the "ridge" that separates the West Branch of the Feather River Canyon (to the east) from the Big and Little Butte Creek Canyons (to the west). The cliffs on each side are beautiful and abrupt, making the city limits of these communities distinct. The spine separating the two canyons is most narrow at the northern boundary between Paradise and Magalia; it is here that the natural gas supply line also ends. This means that all those who live above the boundary and the end of the gas line have only electricity, propane, and the alternatives of wood and sun to choose from for heating. At present rates it is up to three times as expensive to heat a room with electricity as it is with natural gas. To be able to retire to this area "comfortably" will require new attitudes about what it is to have a home. Contrasting rate structures may motivate some people to make changes in attitudes and behavior.

A second feature of the terrain is the elevation. While the Paradise office serves some customers on the valley floor, most of our customers have "taken to the hills" and are residing in the area between 1,500 and 2,700 feet elevation. Promoters have extolled the settlement's virtues as being "above the fog and below the snow." (The wise resident quips, "Yeah, three feet below the snow.") The community enjoys cooler weather in summer than the valley below, and in winter it tends to be warmer at the higher elevation, above the fog. Because of the (usually) moderate climate, the scenic beauty, and the fact that a low-maintenance yard is possible just by adding a little gravel and a metal shed to what is already there, this is an attractive place for retirement—except when it snows, the effect of which is all the more severe owing to its infrequency. Oaks and other deciduous trees have grown tall and thick; when snow does come down, so do branches and sometimes trees. At these lower and warmer elevations, snow is wetter and therefore heavier. The result is that electrical outages are a virtual certainty. Installing "heavier wire," "putting everything underground," or "cutting down more trees" does not really solve the problem.

After the winter of 1982, ridge dwellers began taking advantage of the Residential Conservation Service (RCS) audits and Zero Interest Program (ZIP) loans offered by the utility company at the highest rate per capita of any district in the entire system (PG&E serves customers from Bakersfield to the Oregon border). They also began buying wood stoves and kerosene heaters for emergency use—actions precipitated by the weather's challenge of their beliefs about how to live. Before the snowy winter of 1982, I heard many express their hope for "a white Christmas"; the next year, not a word. In sum, the terrain of the Paradise/Magalia area exacerbates the effects of the energy crunch. No other consumers in the region have suffered as much as the all-electric customers residing in the foothills, nor have their lifestyles and beliefs been so rudely challenged. The area thus serves as a prognosticator of how other Americans may react to similar challenges in energy supply.

Another factor to consider in attempting to account for unprecedented customer complaints about bills is the population of the area. According to the 1950 census, Paradise had a population of only 4,426; during the next decade it nearly doubled to 8,268, partly because of the bomb shelter craze that swept the nation; many people picked out Paradise as a "safe" place, according to an oral history that I have pieced together at the counter as I talk to customers. In 1970, the population was 14,539, and in 1980 it was 22,571, largely, it seems, because of the area's growing reputation as an ideal place to retire. These figures are for Paradise only; they do not tell us of the upsurge pushing gravel roads into the plateaus and canyons of Cherokee, Concow, Del Oro, and Toadtown.

This population has a bad reputation among local PG&E employees, most of whom prefer not to work in the Paradise office. It is not just a matter of the greater number of High Bill Inquiries per capita; rather, their nature and tone are particularly distasteful. The extreme to which a customer may take an H.B.I. is the Public Utilities Commission; an unusually large number of people on the ridge do so. One employee who transferred from another area to Paradise was accustomed to seeing three or four PUC complaints a year, but witnessed that many added to his basket in a single day. Another employee who transferred from Paradise to Chico told me, "Rob, you just can't believe the difference in public attitude down here."

Trying to explain the region's temperament has taken much of my attention since I started work here five years ago. Chico has natural gas, which is cheaper and therefore might account for the difference in the number and tone of H.B.I.s, but Paradise has natural gas available, too. Clerks who have worked in both places insist that there is a marked contrast in the temperament of customers; their explanations for the differences are consistent, but whether singly or taken together, do not satisfactorily account for the number and tenor of complaints in Paradise.

The first point always mentioned when we try to fathom "what's going on out there"is the age of residents of Paradise. The median age is actually 46.2. The clerks, however, perceive most complainers to be over 60 years of age. While many of the people who come into the office are older, it is not certain to what extent they represent the population as a whole, nor do we know much about the people who pay their bills without complaint.

A second reason often suggested is that so many are retired and on (often very low) fixed incomes,[3] but this ignores the fact that while some complain, others do not. Some employees contend that retirees have the time to complain. Some complainants do seem to be fighting off loneliness and boredom by arguing about their bill, or at least they come into the office to pay their bills largely so they can have the chance to visit. These customers may say it is because they want a stamped receipt or to save the cost of mailing the bill, but is in fact an outing providing exercise and the occasion for socializing. Some employees insist that not only are residents retired, but also that "they're retired big shots. They are used to treating people this way; it's all they know." This contention has some basis in fact. For example, one woman who had just moved to Paradise from Newport Beach wanted the utilities turned on in her name, but did not know her address. In response to being told that this was a bit of a problem, she said, "This is a small town, young man. You live here; I just moved here. It's your job to know my address—not mine." During the snow of 1982, some people demanded to speak to the district manager because their power had been off longer than others' had been, as if the work to restore power was being done in a boardroom somewhere and knocking on the right door would result in quicker action.

Finally, the staff attribute the town's temperament to the fact that many people moved here to get away from something: pollution and crime, among other urban problems. Indeed, many homes seem overly secure. Chain link fences abound, which are in part necessary to keep out the deer (a ridge gardener's biggest headache), but three strands of barbed wire along the top all the way around? And a plethora of gates, lights, and locks? And dogs that would stretch even early man's notion of a pet?

There is much to be said for the likelihood that the larger number and more spiteful tone of complaints about utility bills in Paradise is because of the older age of residents and the conditions that this implies, or because residents moved here to escape the vicissitudes of urban life. But there seems to be more. In their beliefs and expectations, the population might constitute a microcosm of values and worldview characteristic of our society as a whole; the confusion and anger expressed by those living in Paradise about their energy bills may be symptomatic of a shift in American values away from the formerly dominant ethos of extreme individualism, and the outlook that this entails.

Consider the actions and implicit assumptions of some residents. A number of people come to the counter to complain about what is happening to "their" hydro power. The belief seems to be that if you live by the water, then it is yours and yours alone. The fact that the rates paid by metropolitan customers subsidize rural consumers who are more costly to serve is ignored. "Let them burn the oil; we'll use the water and see who has the lower rates!" Regionalism is narrowly defined, with self-interest paramount. A case in point is the ZIP program, through which PG&E will loan customers up to $3,500 to install specific energy-saving measures that cut costs in the person's home. Low-income families who cannot afford even a no-interest loan may qualify for "direct" weatherization paid for by the company. To many residents, this merely adds another charge to their bill; it's "somebody else's problem." But the pennies in cost added are small compared to the cost of new power plants, or to the higher energy costs demanded of current sources with increased usage. Utility companies are investing one person's dollar in another individual's home because it is profitable for both the utility and the rate payers—one of those rare solutions whereby everybody wins. The irony is that our culture's sacred cow of profitability is blazing a new trail of communalism.

The shift from self-interest to commonweal, from rugged individualism to communalism, is upsetting. It is especially problematic for a generation of Americans whose wisdom of the world and whose dreams for the future were forged by the Great Depression, the Second World War, and the postwar boom that could only be their reward for having suffered through the first two events. It is among them that the expectation of cheap and plentiful energy (and the worldview and life-style this breeds) is most firmly entrenched. Now in their sixties, they are retiring by the hundreds to the foothills of Paradise. The following letter may speak for many:

I am a disabled WWII combat veteran who was wounded in action in Germany while serving with General Patton's 3rd Army. I sustained wounds which forced me to spend 16 months of my young life in an Army hospital. At the time I thought what I was doing for my country, its people, its corporations, etc., was the right thing to do. But progressively, as time passes, and I see PG&E dipping into my disability compensation check to the point where I have to sit in the dark and in the cold I somehow have my doubts that all the suffering that me and my buddies went through on the battlefield . . . was worth it. I thought my being cold days were over when I left the cold foxholes of the 1944 winter in Germany! But maybe in the next war (God forbid) the PG&E PUC officials can spend some time in them cold foxholes and find out what being cold is. Then when they come home they may not be so eager to get right at the expense of those who have to sit in the dark and the cold . . . !

I think it's time that you forget fattening your pocketbooks. I think it's time that PG&E rates are reduced. Look what we done for you in an emergency. Now how about doing something for us by reducing these PG&E rates to the point where we disabled can again afford to stay warm!

The point of view and the values and concerns expressed by this man are more prevalent in Paradise and Magalia because these communities are home to a large number of retirees who hold an older worldview about energy and lifestyle. The changing world that some must have thought they were escaping caught up with them in the winter of 1982. First, the all-electric rates rose to incredible heights—to the point that people felt they could no longer afford heating—and then the snows came, to remind everyone just as convincingly that they cannot live without it. Had these individuals retired elsewhere, perhaps they would have escaped this dramatic combination of events, at least in 1982. During the winter of that year, the Paradise office processed more than 400 H.B.I.s each week for four months, as did other foothill retirement areas within the system serviced by PG&E.

CONCLUSION

When I started work in Paradise, one of the first routes I read included Apple Tree Village, a large mobile home park consisting of single- and double-wide trailers, each of which has a carport to one side and gravel everywhere else. Most residents have been retired for many years, meaning that their incomes are very low, and so by necessity is their energy consumption. The margin of economic comfort is slim to nil. I remember a woman who came to the window wrapped in a blanket as I read her meter. She said frankly and without malice, "Tell your bosses I'm cold." A sad commentary—the situation was made the more poignant because part of the reason she was so cold on that January morning was that her carport shaded her from pleasant sunshine. I was working in my shirtsleeves.

There is a ray of hope. I continued on my way that day, feeling the cold each time I ducked into a carport to read a meter, thinking all the while that the only rationale for shading a building from a source of heat that is free in order to supply it with another was if that "other" was very cheap—which the "other" no longer is. I noticed, by contrast to the woman who complained of the chill, that a man in the same park had built two small preheaters to let the sun warm his water supply as much as possible before he had to pay the utility company to do it. It was not until recently, when I began systematically conducting an ethnography, that I had a chance to ask for details. One "breadbox" preheats the water to the water heater and another pipes the water directly to the kitchen sink, providing water sufficiently hot for washing hands and rinsing dishes on any sunny day of the year. He was proud of what he had done, and so pleased with the results that he went to his den to pull out three old bills to show me the contrast in costs. He said, "Put a picture of it up in the office with my name and phone number, and anyone who wants to come and talk about it is more than welcome. We could even organize a little class."

I sense a new regionalism, one that has something to do with neighborliness, independent thinking, and the effect that taking personal initiative seems to have on feelings of being victimized. These are traditional concepts, but seemingly they are being combined in new ways to meet changing conditions. This is apparent inside the utility company as well. A couple of years ago there emerged a new public relations program replacing the this-is-your-utility-speaking approach with the actual faces and voices of the local meter readers, office staff, and linemen.

While ethnographic techniques seem essential to carrying out the role of service representative in understanding the reasons for people's complaints, and concepts such as that of "worldview" help us realize that concerns are not isolated from values and lifestyles, an ethnographic approach contributes in other ways.

Having obtained permission to carry a camera on my routes, I had been photographing causes of increased energy consumption and also devices and procedures used by some residents to reduce their heating bills. It is not uncommon for ethnographers to show photographs to others to stimulate conversation, jog the memory, elicit explanations, or get people to think about a subject in a new way. A slide show at the staff's traditional meeting place seemed a promising experiment.

One Friday evening after work, a meter reader, a service representative, a home energy auditor, and I sat around a table eating pizza and looking at pictures. Everyone talked about the circumstances depicted, adding insights and understanding. The others came to me independently the following day, commenting on how much they had learned that night and expressing the hope that we could do it again with others. Ethnographic data, then, can be used in training sessions and for brainstorming, something that had not occurred to me earlier.

If a review of ethnographic documentation of customs, traditions, and material culture is useful for the staff in understanding consumer values and behavior, then it may be of benefit to the public as well. One might give demonstrations at luncheon meetings, dwelling on matters of particular interest with visual and narrative accompaniment. For example, a presentation could be developed on the question, "Why is the power across the street on, but ours has been off for 12 hours?" One way to answer this is to fly over Paradise and to photograph the neighborhoods as they relate to the grid. By adding some images taken by crews of tree limbs through power lines, and some stories about what it is like to work in the snow or a storm, some of the questions about outages could be answered in an effective way. In other presentations people could be prepared in subtle ways for the changes that must inevitably affect their lives and beliefs about lifestyles.

In sum, my training in the use of ethnographic methods, and in particular concepts and ways of interpreting patterns of behavior, lends itself to dealing with the public in a role seemingly removed from that of ethnographer: that of a service representative for a utility company. The same training provides ways of dealing with a long-standing issue regarding why Paradise residents are particularly disgruntled—their beliefs, expectations and ways of doing things having suddenly been challenged by a very different kind of world and the need for a new worldview. Finally, developing presentations for PG&E staff and the public involving the documentation of customs, habits, stories, and material culture holds great promise for increasing understanding of the causes of problems and of enhancing appreciation of likely solutions. Fortunately, I do not have to convince the utility company of the verity or value of any of this. All I have to do is apply my ethnographic skills to the tasks and projects assigned to or expected of me as a service representative and meter reader.

NOTES

1. Schurr points out that Americans have long used excessive amounts of energy in heating their homes because they favored the open fireplace to the cast iron stove. "Conservative estimates indicate that around 1850-1860 an American family used on the average some 17.5 cords of wood per year to keep comfortably warm according to their standards. . . . It has been estimated that the same quantity of wood, burned in a well constructed stove, would supply about four times as much heat as when used in an open fireplace" (Schurr, 1960: 50). He accounts for this preference for inefficiency to the abundance of the natural resource, "fueled" by the fact that the forests had to be cleared for farmland.

2. Berreman (1968: 63) says that "the only way [for a culture] to feel sure that such dangers do not inhere in a person is to know who he is, and to know that he must fit somewhere into the known social system. Only then is he subject to effective local controls so that if he transgresses, or betrays a trust, he can be brought to account."

3. In relating this anecdote to schools, service organizations, and anthropological conferences I am invariably reminded by several in the audience that viewing the rising price of energy as the catalyst for social change places an undue burden on the elderly and the poor. I couldn't agree more, and no doubt the various forms of energy assistance programs will be increased as the prices climb. However, given the fact that the elderly are more susceptible to the cold and less able to afford heat, it only underscores the need to build dwellings that maximize passive solar principles so that every customer gets the widest margin of comfort for his or her energy dollar.

4

MEASURING ORGANIZATIONAL CULTURE

Mixing Qualitative and Quantitative Methods

Caren Siehl

University of Southern California

Joanne Martin

Stanford University

Studies of organizational culture have relied almost exclusively on qualitative methods, such as ethnographic observation or in-depth, open-ended interviewing. There are good reasons for these choices. Qualitative methods produce richly detailed data which can be used to generate "thick descriptions" (Geertz, 1973) of cultures. Such data allow ambiguities, contradictions, and paradoxes to be explored with relative ease. In addition, many would define culture in terms of a socially constructed reality, and qualitative methods are usually considered epistemologically congruent with this approach (see Berger and Luckmann, 1966; Burrell and Morgan, 1979).

Some have stated a preference for these methodological choices in even stronger terms, arguing that culture must be, or is best, studied

Authors' Note: Portions of an earlier version of this article were presented in invited addresses at the meeting of the Western Academy of Management, Colorado Springs, Colorado, April 1982 and at the NATO International Symposium on Managerial Behavior and Leadership Research, St. Catherine's College, University of Oxford, July 1982. We wish to thank the following people for their helpful comments on earlier drafts of this paper: Robert Faulkner, Peter Frost, Harold Leavitt, Meryl Louis, Nigel Nicholson, Jeffrey Pfeffer, Lee Sproull, and Andrew Van de Ven.

using qualitative methods (e.g., Geertz, 1973; Morgan and Smircich, 1980; Smircich, 1983a). For example, Daft (1980: 632) categorizes culture as a topic of the highest order of complexity. He then states that "low-variety" methods, such as quantitative approaches, would be inappropriate for the study of such a topic because of the dangers of oversimplification.

THE NEED FOR SYSTEMATIC COMPARISONS

The advantages of qualitative approaches have been bought at a cost. It is exceedingly difficult to make analytic comparisons on the basis of the data available. There are many centrally important theoretical questions which cannot be answered until culture can be measured with repeatable, easily administered instruments that permit systematic comparisons.

For example, culture is generally defined in terms of the values and interpretations that organizational members share (e.g., Gamst and Norbeck, 1976; Pettigrew, 1979; Van Maanen and Schein, 1979; Baker, 1980; Pondy et al., 1983). In order to determine the extent to which values and interpretations are shared, the responses of individual organizational members must be compared. In order to learn if an organization has subcultures with distinctive values (e.g., Gregory, 1983; Louis, 1983; Martin and Siehl, 1983; Van Maanen and Barley, 1984), it must be possible to identify and compare groups that share values. In order to study culture as a dynamic process of learning and change (Schein, 1981), systematic comparisons across time must be possible. In order to test speculations about a relationship between type of culture and levels of productivity or profitability, it would be helpful if entire organizations could be compared. It is difficult to make these types of comparisons systematically, when only qualitative data are available. Without quantitative measures, important blind spots in our knowledge about culture are inevitable.

Given the potential benefits, it is not surprising that a few studies have used quantitative approaches to the study of culture (e.g., Cooke and Rousseau, 1983; Kilmann and Saxton, 1983). These studies have usually relied upon direct questions about employees' values, such as: "Does it help people in your organization to 'fit in' and meet expectations if they: Please those in positions of authority? Work for a sense of accomplishment? Maintain their personal integrity?" Answers to such direct questions are likely to be biased by social desirability concerns. For example, employees may be reluctant to admit departures from their personal values or the values espoused by top management. If employees are given guarantees of anonymity, and if they respond to such questions with reference to generalized others, rather than themselves personally, these social desirability biases can be reduced, but they will not be entirely removed.

In this essay we present a hybrid approach that combines qualitative and quantitative methods for studying organizational cultures. The methodology minimizes social desirability biases, while permitting systematic comparisons across individuals, groups, organizations, and time periods. Before describing the methodology, it is important to specify the aspects of culture that will be measured.

A CONCEPTUAL FRAMEWORK

A few definitions make the task of measuring cultural content more manageable. In accord with previous research, we define culture in terms of shared values and interpretations. It is important to distinguish espoused values from values-in-use, as these may differ (Argyris and Schoen, 1978). Espoused values are the values that people say they believe in. Espoused values are communicated directly, for example, in statements about one's philosophy of management. Values-in-use are those that are actually enacted.

Values-in-use surface in two types of cultural manifestations: practices and forms. Practices may be formalized—for example, a training program or a structured performance appraisal procedure. Practices may also be informal, such as unspoken norms about the deference due superiors or the desirability of smoothing conflicts.

Other cultural manifestations, which we label "forms," reflect values-in-use more indirectly. Cultural forms include jargon or special language (e.g., Edelman, 1977; Pondy, 1978; Hirsch and Andrews, 1983); humor (Boland and Hoffman, 1983); organizational stories (e.g., Clark, 1970; Wilkins, 1978; Martin, 1982); and ceremonies and rituals (e.g., Gephart, 1978; Moch and Huff, 1983; Smircich, 1983b). Forms may be embedded in practices and one form may be embedded in another. For example, a training program may include award ceremonies where organizational stories are told.

Until recently, organizational members and researchers have focused most of their attention on formal and, to a lesser extent, informal practices. In contrast, organizational culture research has drawn attention to what can be learned from cultural forms. Although employees are often reluctant to admit it, practices are often implemented in a manner that differs from formal rules and procedures. Cultural forms are less subject than practices to managerial control and therefore are less susceptible to social desirability biases. For these reasons, cultural forms, in contrast to practices, offer a clearer reflection of what values are in-use and whether employees are committed to them. For example, a shared organizational story about a "fast-track," frequently promoted employee may give more accurate information about a company's values-in-use than could be obtained from descriptions of official promotion criteria. For this reason, in the study described below particular emphasis was placed on values-in-use as they were reflected in cultural forms such as stories and jargon.

A HYBRID MEASURE OF CULTURE

The present study uses these conceptual distinctions in a two-stage approach to measuring organizational culture. The first of these stages uses qualitative methodology to gain an understanding of the content of a culture or a subculture. Ethnographic observation, in-depth interviews, and archival data are used to determine espoused values and values-in-use, particularly as the latter are reflected in cultural forms. These qualitative data are then used to construct a questionnaire, responses to which can be coded quantitatively. In the second stage, the questionnaire is administered to any set of present or potential organizational members to measure quantitatively their levels of cultural awareness and commitment. If the questionnaire is administered for comparison purposes at two or more points in time, qualitative data collection can be continued during this second stage.

This hybrid methodology retains some of the richness characteristic of exclusively qualitative approaches. The questionnaire focuses on the specific values, practices, and forms that have evolved in the particular organizational setting. However, the questionnaire items are structured to permit statistical analyses, producing data useful for comparisons within and across organizations at various points in time. Because the items measuring awareness and commitment are indirect and subtle, and because anonymity of questionnaire responses can be guaranteed, social desirability biases are minimized. This methodology for studying culture is illustrated below, in a study that focuses on the socialization of newcomers.

SOCIALIZATION: OPENING THE BLACK BOX

The process of socialization often appears to be as mysterious as a black box. New employees enter the organization and, some indeterminate time later, emerge as socialized organizational members. Part of what is in the black box of socialization is an enculturation process, whereby newcomers become aware of and, to some extent, committed to the shared interpretations and values of "old-guard" organizational members (e.g., Louis, 1980; Van Maanen and Schein, 1979).

Some critical questions about this enculturation process are currently unanswered. When do newcomers become aware that particular values and interpretations are shared? At what point, if ever, is that awareness transformed into commitment? Can important parts of this enculturation process be completed within a few months on the job? Are some manifestations of culture predictably learned first? Are others absorbed later, perhaps because they are more difficult to communicate or less essential for survival on the job? Answers to these questions would help demystify the enculturation process.

The hybrid methodology is particularly well suited to address these issues. The first stage of the methodology can be used to gain a preliminary understanding of the culture, especially as it is perceived by longer-term employees.[1] The second stage then can be used to determine the extent to which newcomers share these cultural perspectives. This second stage of the process can include the collection of comparative data. If a company has a training program for newcomers, trained and untrained employees can be compared to determine if the training facilitates enculturation. Comparisons can also be made across time, perhaps soon after an employee starts work and again a few months later, in order to address questions about the sequence in which cultural information is learned.

A BUILDING-BLOCK CONCEPTUALIZATION
OF THE ENCULTURATION PROCESS

Even after a short time on the job, new employees should be aware of and, to some extent, committed to espoused values. This kind of cultural knowledge is likely to be absorbed during the hiring process, assuming that the new employees have some choice in the selection of the company and at least a minimal level of interest in learning about it. In addition, job applicants who espouse the same values as current employees may be more likely to be hired.

Familiarity with values-in-use should develop more slowly than knowledge of espoused values, in part because values-in-use must be inferred indirectly from cultural forms and practices. In addition, the various cultural forms may usually be learned in a predictable sequence.

The information carried in some cultural forms is essential for a new employee's survival. For example, if new employees do not understand company jargon, they will find it difficult to learn the technical requirements of their jobs and they will have problems deciphering the meaning of other cultural forms, such as stories or rituals. Thus, learning jargon is a fundamental building block, essential for comprehending the rest of organizational life. For these reasons, new employees should be familiar with much of a company's jargon soon after starting work and should master most of that jargon relatively quickly.

Having become fairly proficient with jargon, new employees can then use this knowledge to interpret other cultural forms. For example, when new employees start work they probably will be unfamiliar with most organizational stories, but after a relatively short while they should be aware of the stories that figure centrally in the organization's culture.

Organizational stories are ambiguous stimuli. It is difficult to infer values-in-use from a story. Many alternative interpretations are logically plausible. When new employees start work, they should be unable to interpret the value messages of stories in the same manner as longer-term employees. After some time on the job, this type of cultural learning should be better developed.

Although meanings and interpretations of a jargon word or a story may vary, at least the word or the story itself can be articulated. Other cultural forms tap tacit knowledge that is more difficult to articulate. For example, it may take a relatively long time for employees to be able to recognize and anticipate the ways top executives use language to express their values. Employees who have developed this skill would probably find it difficult to articulate exactly what rules are guiding their judgments about language use. This type of tacit knowledge should be difficult to acquire, and even rudimentary traces of it should emerge slowly, relative to the other types of cultural knowledge discussed above. The design of the study described below includes comparisons between groups and across time, thus permitting examination of this building block conceptualization of the cultural learning process.

An analysis of beliefs about practices can be used to assess whether the newcomer is becoming ideologically committed to the organization. New employees starting work should be only vaguely familiar with most company practices. Their guesses about the exact nature of those practices may reflect their current beliefs about shared values-in-use. To the extent that those guesses are wrong, the direction of the errors (pro- or anticompany) is an indication of the level of their personal acceptance of and commitment to these shared values. For example, estimates of the company's willingness to fire employees may underestimate (pro- company) or overestimate (anticompany) actual involuntary turnover rates. If new employees are successfully enculturated, the number and magnitude of procompany errors should be greater after a few months than at the start of employment. This measure of commitment is subtle enough that it should minimize social desirability biases.

METHOD

Stage One: Observation, Interviews, and Archival Study

The study was conducted at a Fortune 500 company in the electronics industry. During the first stage of the study, the first author collected qualitative data for a period of three months. Three methods were used: observation; open-ended, in-depth interviews; and archival study.

The first author began by observing, for 20 days, the daily activities of five employees, representing five functional areas, at a branch office of the firm. She then attended a one week, off-site retreat. Invitees included the organization's top management team, middle managers labeled as "rising stars," and exceptional sales people who had met preestablished performance criteria during the previous year. A series of interviews were conducted with approximately 50 of these and other, lower-ranking employees, during the retreat and subsequently in various field settings. Finally, written documents were studied, including sales reports, personnel records, company newspapers, correspondence, memoranda, and ten years of annual reports.

During all aspects of this data-collection effort, field notes were kept, focusing on espoused values and on cultural forms and practices that supported or refuted those values. In the context of this volume, the qualitative aspects of this study are not distinctive, so further description of these procedures and results will be held to a minimum. Appendix A contains more details about the qualitative data collection effort.

The Questionnaire

Data collected during the first stage of the study were used to construct a questionnaire for use in the second stage of the study. The questionnaire had five sections: espoused values, company jargon, organizational stories, tacit knowledge, and beliefs about practices. The content of the questionnaire items was tailored to fit the specific culture of the company. Because this questionnaire is the crux of the hybrid methodology, the structure of each section of the questionnaire is described in detail below. Examples of each type of questionnaire item are also presented.

Espoused values: In stage one of the study, five values were espoused by almost all members of the top management team and were mentioned by a majority of the other company employees interviewed. Most of these values were also mentioned in the company's annual reports. For example, one espoused value concerned the importance of meeting social and environmental commitments to communities surrounding corporate facilities. The questionnaire asked respondents to rate the importance of each of these five values to the company and to themselves personally. (On these items, and on all subsequent items unless otherwise mentioned, employees responded on 11-point scales.) This provided a measure of whether the questionnaire respondents were aware that these values were espoused by many organizational members and whether the respondents had a personal ideological commitment to these espoused values. Because these items directly asked respondents' opinions about values, the data from this section of the questionnaire, in contrast to other sections, may be open to social desirability biases.

Jargon: This section of the questionnaire consisted of a vocabulary test. Respondents were asked to define 20 words or phrases. These examples of company jargon were selected because they were particularly relevant to the company, rather than to the industry as a whole, and because they had been used by employees in a wide variety of circumstances. Twelve of the words or phrases had technical meanings, such as MOF (Master Order Form), while eight referred to more value-laden aspects of the corporate culture, for example, "working the issue" (confronting disagreement and continuing the discussion until genuine consensus is reached). Definitions were coded as correct or incorrect. (Inter-coder reliability on this and subsequent coding tasks was perfect, with one of the authors and a graduate student reaching 100% agreement after a brief training session.)

Organizational stories: The questionnaire focused on four stories, selected because they had been recounted without prompting by many different types of employees during the in-depth interviews and informal conversations. This section of the questionnaire asked respondents how much of each story they had heard. Three morals to each story were then presented. Although all three morals for each story were logically plausible, data from the first stage of the study indicated that longer-term employees generally considered one of the morals to be the "correct" interpretation, another moral was obviously "incorrect," and the third moral was ambiguous. Respondents were asked to assess the appropriateness of each moral on an 11-point scale. The endpoints of this scale were labeled "correct" and "incorrect" and the midpoint was labeled "ambiguous." To the extent that newcomers evaluated the morals in the same way as the longer-term employees, the newcomers were demonstrating knowledge of the shared interpretations of meaning prevalent in this organizational culture. For example, the star of one of those stories was a secretary of a sales unit in Northern California:

> Susan Sanders had been working for the company for about two years. She was well respected by everyone—her manager, the sales people, and other secretaries. She was extremely skillful, and her performance had been rated as excellent. Due to her efforts, Susan's manager did not need to direct his attention to proofreading or correction tasks. Susan also had a pleasant personality. In fact, she was one of those people who was generally cheerful, even on bad days. During her second year with the company, Susan's husband, who worked for another company, was promoted to a new job in Arizona. Although he would be losing a valued employee, Susan's manager approved her request for a transfer to a branch office of the company in Arizona. This office was not hiring at the time, but gladly accepted her transfer, knowing that her skills would be helpful in some capacity in the future.

The possible three morals to this story were: "We believe that people are clearly our most important asset and we take pride in treating our employees well" (Correct); "Employees are one part of the financial structure of the company and are as important as their contribution to the bottom line" (Incorrect); and "Because good employees are hard to find, we feel it is to the company's advantage to try to meet the needs of such people" (Ambiguous: logically plausible, pragmatic rather than humanistic, an interpretation not offered or considered appropriate by longer-term employees).

Tacit knowledge: This section of the questionnaire contained extracts from the company president's letter to stockholders, published in the company's annual report. Two paragraphs from the letter, counterbalanced across versions of the questionnaire, were reproduced with every fifth word left blank. Respondents were asked to supply the ten missing words. Their responses were coded as +2, totally correct (exactly the same words as in the president's letter); +1, partially correct (a synonym or more abstract version of the word); or 0, incorrect. Accurate performance at this task indicates knowledge of the subtleties of language used to communicate this company's corporate objectives and philosophy of management.[2]

Practices: Five statements describing managerial practices were taken from published material about the company. A key numerical fact in each statement was left blank. A multiple choice test format required the respondents to fill in the blank with one of two predesignated alternatives. Respondents were not aware that both alternatives were incorrect. Because the missing information was numerical, the incorrect alternatives could be equally incorrect. One alternative made the company look better than in fact it was; the other was biased against the company. For example, one item estimated the company's market share as 35% or 45% (the true figure at the time was 40%); another item calculated sales force turnover to be either 12% or 16% (the correct figure was 14%). Ideological commitment to the company should be reflected in a disproportionate preference (greater than the 50% expected by chance) for the positively biased, procompany alternatives.

Stage Two: Sample Selection and
Questionnaire Administration

Respondents: The employees who participated in the second stage of the study were entry-level, newly hired sales people. The sample included all 20 sales people hired by the company during a two-month period. (Preliminary data analyses produced significant results with this small size, so a larger sample size was unnecessary.)

Design: Versions of the questionnaire, appropriately counter-balanced, were administered to the new employees at two times: within one week of starting work and eight weeks later. The responses of two groups of employees (trained and untrained) were contrasted at each of these times. Thus the design of the study illustrated two kinds of comparisons (across time and across groups) that can be made using this hybrid methodology. Below, reasons for these comparisons are given and a chronology of the new employees' activities is presented.

The comparisons across time permit an examination of the building block conceptualization of the enculturation process. Given the particular circumstances of this organizational setting, we expected that new employees at the company would already exhibit some types of cultural knowledge within one week on the job. New employees at this firm could exhibit considerable self-selection, as sales positions in the high technology industry were plentiful at the time this study was conducted. Furthermore, managers at the company exercised considerable selectivity in the recruitment and hiring processes. Both of these factors should facilitate shared values and interpretations before and during the initial days of employment.

During the next eight weeks all 20 new employees studied orientation material and attended a one-day orientation session. In addition, these employees interacted on the job with their peers and immediate managers. Because these new employees were to join the sales force, they devoted most of this time to learning about the company's products and different potential markets. Thus it was expected that, at the end of the eight-week period some, but not all, of the cultural information described in the questionnaire would have been learned, tacit knowledge being the most difficult to absorb.

During the last two of the eight weeks, half of these new employees participated in a 10-day technical training program at regional head-quarters. The training of the other 10 employees was deferred until after the present study was completed, owing to scheduling reasons that had no relationship to the topic of this study. Thus responses of the trained and untrained groups could be compared to determine what, if any, impact the training had on the content, sequence, or speed of cultural learning.

During the last two weeks of the study, the new employees who did not attend the training class continued to interact with coworkers, learning product and market information on the job. During this time their activities were the same as they had been the preceding weeks. In contrast, the other group of employees had been taken off-site to regional headquarters to attend the training class. Their training was designed to be exclusively technical, as were the formally and informally stated objectives of the trainers. In spite of this technical focus, participation in an off-site training program should have freed the new employees from the time pressures and cognitive demands of performing an unfamiliar job, giving them slack for learning nontechnical information. For these reasons, we expected that participation in the training process, in spite of its technical focus, would facilitate the learning of cultural information. Thus, in contrast to the untrained group, the trained employees were expected to have learned more of the material included in the questionnaire.[3]

During the entire eight weeks of this second stage of the study, collection of qualitative data continued. The first author attended the orientation session, observed employees on the job, and attended eight of the ten days of the training program, including several after-hours events such as a tequila party and a graduation dinner.

RESULTS AND DISCUSSION

Observation, Interview, and Archival Data

Space limitations preclude a detailed description of the qualitative data, so highlights, relevant to the conceptual framework outlined above, are presented. These highlights are drawn from both the stage one data and the qualitative data collected during stage two of the study. Five espoused values recurred frequently in the speeches, interviews, informal conversations, and written documents of the company's top executives. These espoused values included a focus on the quality of the firm's products, the importance of the financial prosperity of the firm, the company's social responsibility to maintain the environment and to be a good neighbor to the surrounding community, and, to a lesser extent, two values related to humanitarian concerns for employees.

The employees' values-in-use, as inferred indirectly from cultural forms and practices, had a somewhat different emphasis. The importance of a humanitarian approach was accentuated, while less stress was placed on other types of values.[4] Specifically, a core of four values-in-use repeatedly surfaced: first, "The family of an employee is an integral part of the company"; second, "The company doesn't undercut the future by considering only the short-term consequences of decisions"; third, "The company believes that people are clearly the most important asset of the company"; and fourth, "We are different. We build a unique product and our people are unique also." A sampling of forms and practices, from which the employees and researchers inferred these values, is presented below. Many of the examples are taken from the orientation session and the training program, in order to illustrate ways in which the new employees were exposed to these aspects of the culture.

The first of the values-in-use, which emphasizes the company's concern for the families of its employees, is illustrated by the story of the secretary whose request for a transfer was granted so she could remain near her husband and stay with the company. This story also illustrates the second value-in-use. The branch office, to which she was transferred, did not immediately need her services, although it was likely that her superlative skills would be useful in the longer-term future. In this story, the company did not undercut the future by considering only the short-term consequences of decisions.

The company's third value-in-use, that the company cares about its employees, was manifested in the ritualistic orientation session. The coordinator of the orientation session described its objective as follows: "Most employees go through buyer's remorse. They aren't totally confident they made the right decision. All we want to do today is let them know that we are really happy to have them on board. We want them to share our ideal of giving 100% to each other and to the company." As the last part of this statement indicates, the company's emphasis on caring about its people was not totally altruistic.

Another illustration of this third value-in-use was observed during the technical training program. Trainees had been told to prepare for a test to be administered during the afternoon of the second day. Just before breaking for lunch, the instructor held an "impromptu" review session. She asked several sample exam questions of each individual, beginning with the last person in the last row and moving sequentially through the class. One trainee appeared to be completely unprepared, and failed to answer a single question correctly. Rather than reprimanding this individual publicly or privately, the instructor was encouraging and offered additional study help during lunch. Later that afternoon the trainer said to the researcher, "We believe that if an employee is failing to perform, we owe that person assistance." This statement is clearly consistent with caring about the company's employees and considering them a primary asset.

The company's fourth value-in-use emphasized the organization's uniqueness. This value was primarily communicated through jargon and humor. Jargon is understandable only to company insiders, so by definition this cultural form emphasizes something unique about an organization. At this particular company, for example, "company ethic" was a phrase used to characterize the organization's pride in its supposedly unique emphasis on quality and service.

As employees remained longer at the company, their humor also began to reflect a concern with the company's uniqueness. For example, at the beginning of the training program laughter was scarce. The few jokes told contained little jargon and were understandable to an outsider. Rather than focusing on the unique attributes of the company, these early jokes were relatively universal: foolish mistakes, sexual innuendoes, and so on. By the end of the training program, laughter occurred frequently. Understanding these jokes required more knowledge of the unique attributes of the company, and more familiarity with its jargon. These later jokes were not funny to an outsider. The targets of the jokes were out-groups: either competitive companies or employees who were not members of the sales division. These changes in joking behavior suggest that jokes, like humor, may be a cultural form particularly well-suited to communicate the value placed on uniqueness.[5]

These examples can only suggest the richly detailed portrait of the corporation's culture that emerged from the first stage of the study. The descriptions of the examples do, however, illustrate the kinds of material subsequently integrated into the questionnaire.

Questionnaire Data

At time 1, the new employees scheduled to receive training, and those whose training was to be deferred, were not expected to respond differently to the questionnaire. Two-tailed t-tests revealed that the two groups responded significantly differently ($p < .05$) to only three of the 57 questionnaire items. Since this proportion of the responses would be significantly different simply by chance, the data from the two groups at time 1 was pooled for the first part of the discussion below.

At time 1 the new employees were already aware of, and personally committed to, the espoused values of the management of the company. At time 1 the new employees rated the five values espoused by top management as highly important to the company (mean of 8.8 on an

11-point scale, averaging across the five values) and to themselves personally (mean of 8.8, again averaging across the five values).

At time 1, the new employees had also begun to learn the jargon of the company. At this time, the new employees correctly defined a mean of 7.1 of the 12 technical words or phrases (59%) in the vocabulary test and a mean of 3.9 of the 8 more value-laden words or phrases (49%). The technical jargon may have been learned somewhat faster than the value-laden jargon because the former may have been more essential for performance on the new job. It may also be normatively appropriate to teach definitions of technical terms explicitly, while value-laden jargon may be transmitted in a more tacit manner (Goffman, 1963).

At time 1 the new employees were partially familiar with two organizational stories (means of 5.3 and 4.8, respectively, on 11-point scales). The other two stories were essentially unfamiliar (means of 0.8 and 1.5, respectively). The new employees showed only a rudimentary ability to interpret the story messages in the same manner as longer-term employees. On the 11-point scales rating, the messages' "correct" morals should have received high ratings, "neutral" morals should have been rated near the midpoint of the scale, and "incorrect" morals should have received lower ratings. At time 1, averaging across the four stories, the new employees showed a weak trend in the predicted direction, giving the "correct" morals a mean rating of 8.3, "neutral" morals a mean of 7.8, and "incorrect" morals a mean of 5.6. At time 1, tacit knowledge was less well developed, as indicated by the new employees' inability to fill in the blanks in the president's letter correctly (mean of 7.1 correct out of a possible score of 20.0).

The multiple-choice test, measuring values-in-use inferred from company practices, was scored by assigning +2 for each selection of a procompany error and +1 for each anticompany error chosen. Summing across the five items in this test, employees showing no bias should, on the average, score 7.5. A score of +10 indicates the maximum procompany bias and +5 is the lowest possible score, indicating maximum anticompany bias. Using this scoring method, the new employees at time 1 showed virtually no evidence of pro- or anticompany bias (mean of 7.6).

The next step in the analysis examined the changes in cultural knowledge that occurred between time 1 and time 2. Differences between these two time periods are referred to as cultural learning scores. These scores were calculated, separately for the trained and untrained groups, for six types of cultural learning: espoused values,

**TABLE 4.1   Mean Amount of Cultural Knowledge for
Trained and Untrained Employees Combined**

Type of culture knowledge	Maximum possible	Mean at time 1*	Mean at time 2*	t-value (time 2- time 1)	Probability**
Epoused values					
Importance of goals to the company					
Financial	11	7.2	8.0	2.12	.024
Quality	11	10.0	10.1	0.24	n.s.
Products	11	9.2	9.2	0.20	n.s.
Social responsibility	11	8.3	8.5	0.55	n.s.
People	11	9.1	9.6	1.63	n.s.
Importance of goals to subject					
Financial	11	7.1	7.7	1.67	.054
Quality	11	10.0	10.2	0.94	n.s.
Products	11	9.1	9.6	1.63	n.s.
Social responsibility	11	8.3	8.1	−0.52	n.s.
People	11	9.8	10.0	0.96	n.s.
Jargon					
Technical	12	7.1	9.5	5.79	.0001
Cultural	8	3.9	6.2	6.57	.0001
Both	20	11.0	15.7	8.81	.0001
Tacit knowledge	20	7.1	8.5	1.23	n.s.

NOTE: N = 20.
*Higher scores indicate greater cultural knowledge; **One-tailed.

jargon, stories, story interpretation, tacit knowledge, and beliefs about
practices.

The magnitude of the cultural learning scores of the trained and
untrained groups was then compared using one-tailed t-tests. These
tests revealed no significant differences between the two groups in three
areas of cultural knowledge acquisition: espoused values, jargon, and
tacit knowledge. In the discussion below, data from the trained and
untrained groups are pooled for these variables. In the remaining three
areas of cultural knowledge (story familiarity, story interpretation, and
beliefs about practices), the trained group learned significantly more
than the untrained group, so these data are discussed separately for the
two groups.

Table 4.1 presents the mean espoused value scores for the combined
groups (trained and untrained employees). By time 2 the new employees
showed very high levels of awareness of, and personal commitment to,

the values espoused by the top management of the company (means of 9.1 and 9.2, respectively, averaging across the five values). Although the ratings at time 2 were higher than at time 1, these differences were significant for only one of the five ratings of awareness ($t = 2.12$, df = 18, $p < .03$) and were marginally significant for only one of the five commitment ratings ($t = 1.67$, df = 18, $p < .06$). For all these measures of espoused values, the same explanation can be offered. Awareness of and commitment to espoused values were already so high at time 1 that a ceiling effect at time 2 prevented the differences from being significantly higher. This ceiling effect is not unexpected, given that these items are more direct, hence more open to social desirability biases than the other items in the questionnaire.

Table 4.1 also contains the jargon data for the combined groups. By time 2 the new employees showed considerable mastery of company jargon, correctly defining a mean of 9.5 of the 12 technical words or phrases (80%) and a mean of 6.2 of the 8 more value-laden words or phrases (78%). For both of these types of jargon, the differences between time 1 and time 2 scores were significant ($t = 5.79$, df = 18, $p < .0001$ and $t = 6.57$, df = 18, $p < .0001$, respectively). Although the newcomers were familiar with some of the jargon at time 1, eight weeks later they had become significantly more adept at understanding the special language of the corporation.

Table 4.2 presents the story data for the trained employees, and Table 4.3 presents the same data for the untrained employees. By time 2 the trained group was quite familiar with two of the stories (means of 9.3 and 7.7, respectively) and was partially familiar with the remaining two stories (means of 4.4 and 3.0, respectively). At this time the untrained group was moderately familiar with two stories (means of 7.2 and 6.6, respectively) and was still unfamiliar with the remaining two stories (means of 2.9 and 1.7, respectively). For the trained group, the differences between time 1 and time 2 were significant for all four stories ($t = 4.81$, df = 18, $p < .001$; $t = 3.13$, df = 18, $p < .006$; $t = 3.84$, df = 18, $p < .002$; $t = 2.68$, df = 18, $p < .02$, respectively). For the untrained group, only one of the four differences between time 1 and time 2 was marginally significant ($t = 2.00$, df = 18, $p < .08$).

Averaging across the four stories, at time 2 the trained employees were appropriately giving the "correct" morals high ratings, rating the "neutral" morals near the midpoints of the scales, and giving the "incorrect" morals low scores (means of 9.5, 7.6, and 3.8, respectively). Again averaging across the four stories, at time 2 the untrained group

TABLE 4.2 Mean Amount of Cultural Knowledge for Trained Employees

Type of culture knowledge	Maximum possible	Mean at time 1*	Mean at time 2*	t-value (time 2- time 1)	Probability**
Story familiarity					
Story 1	11	4.6	9.3	4.81	.001
Story 2	11	0.0	4.4	3.13	.006
Story 3	11	4.3	7.7	3.84	.002
Story 4	11	1.0	3.0	2.68	.02
Story messages rated appropriately					
Correct messages					
Story 1	11	8.1	9.9	5.51	.0001
Story 2	11	7.4	9.7	5.81	.0001
Story 3	11	9.0	10.2	3.67	.003
Story 4	11	5.4	8.1	6.82	.0001
Incorrect messages					
Story 1	11	8.1	4.9	−5.40	.0001
Story 2	11	7.1	5.0	−2.60	.02
Story 3	11	3.3	1.6	−3.43	.004
Story 4***					
Neutral					
Story 1	11	6.6	4.5	−11.70	.0001
Story 2	11	8.9	8.7	−0.48	n.s.
Story 3	11	9.4	7.7	−3.43	.004
Story 4****	11	6.9	6.9	0.00	n.s.
	11	9.2	8.7	−0.83	n.s.
Values-in-use	10	7.1	9.7	4.00	.002

NOTE: N = 10.
*Higher scores indicate greater cultural knowledge; **One-tailed; ***No incorrect message for story 4; ****Two neutral messages for story 4.

also gave high ratings to the "correct" morals (mean of 9.2) and rated the "neutral" messages near the midpoints of the scales (mean of 7.6). However, in contrast to the trained group, the untrained group gave relatively high ratings to the "incorrect" morals (mean of 5.5). The untrained group was less able than the trained group to differentiate story messages considered "incorrect" by longer-term employees.

For the trained group, these differences between time 1 and time 2 were significant for all four of the "correct" messages, for all three of the "incorrect" messages, and for two of the five neutral messages. For the untrained group, no significant differences between time 1 and time 2 message ratings were found, with the exception of the ratings for one

TABLE 4.3   Mean Amount of Cultural Knowledge
               for Untrained Employees

Type of culture knowledge	Maximum possible	Mean at time 1*	Mean at time 2*	t-value (time 2- time 1)	Probability**
Story familiarity					
Story 1	11	6.0	6.6	0.66	n.s.
Story 2	11	1.6	2.9	0.89	n.s.
Story 3	11	5.2	7.2	2.00	.08
Story 4	11	1.9	1.7	−0.29	n.s.
Story messages rated appropriately					
Correct messages					
Story 1	11	9.0	9.1	0.32	n.s.
Story 2	11	8.4	8.8	0.29	n.s.
Story 3	11	10.3	10.0	−1.15	n.s.
Story 4	11	8.3	9.2	1.59	n.s.
Incorrect messages					
Story 1	11	6.0	5.9	−0.10	n.s.
Story 2	11	6.1	7.6	0.29	n.s.
Story 3	11	2.8	3.0	0.12	n.s.
Story 4***					
Neutral					
Story 1	11	6.9	6.1	−0.79	n.s.
Story 2	11	7.6	9.0	1.23	n.s.
Story 3	11	8.1	7.2	−1.65	n.s.
Story 4****	11	5.5	7.3	3.52	.007
	11	8.3	8.6	1.15	n.s.
Values-in-use	10	8.1	8.7	1.96	.09

NOTE: N = 10.
*Higher scores indicate greater cultural knowledge; **Two-tailed; ***No incorrect message for story 4; ****Two neutral messages for story 4.

"neutral" message. Thus after eight weeks of employment the trained employees generally interpreted the organizational stories in the same manner as longer-term employees. After the same time period, the untrained employees also showed some improvement in their ability to interpret the stories, but not to the same degree or with the same consistency as the trained employees.

The tacit knowledge data, for the trained and untrained groups combined, are presented in Table 4.1. At time 2 the new employees received a tacit knowledge score of 8.5 (out of a maximum of 20 points). Although this represented an improvement over their time 1 score, the difference between the two time periods was not significant. Although some improvement in this difficult arena of cultural knowledge was noted, these skills were still quite rudimentary after two months of employment, even for those who had participated in the training program.

Finally, the measure of beliefs about practices showed that at time 2 the trained employees had a strong tendency to make errors that were favorable to the company (mean of 8.7). For the trained employees this bias, indicating commitment, was significantly stronger at time 2 than at time 1 ($t = 4.00$, df = 18, $p < .002$). At time 2 the untrained employees also had a strong tendency to make errors that were favorable to the company (mean of 8.7), a marginally significant increase in comparison to time 1 ($t = 1.96$, df = 18, $p < .09$). The change in the trained employees' procompany bias was significantly greater than that for the untrained employees ($t = 1.99$, df = 19, $p < .03$). However, it should be noted that at time 2, both groups showed strong tendencies to make errors favorable to the company.

CONCLUSION

Comparisons across the two time periods provided support for the building-block conceptualization of the enculturation process. The new employees who had just started work were aware of, and committed to, many of top management's espoused values. At this time they were familiar with much of the company's technical and value-laden jargon and aware of a few organizational stories. However, at this time the new employees failed to interpret the messages of those stories in the same fashion as longer-term employees, showed virtually no evidence of tacit forms of cultural knowledge, and did not exhibit a strong procompany bias in misperceptions of company practices.

After a few months on the job, the enculturation process apparently was successful. New employees had fully mastered the jargon, were thoroughly familiar with the organizational stories, generally interpreted those stories in the same manner as longer term employees, showed a slight improvement in tacit forms of cultural learning, and exhibited a strong procompany bias in misperceptions of company practices.

Although these results provide support for the building block conceptualization of the enculturation process, it is important to note two limitations of the present study. First, the exact amounts of cultural knowledge exhibited at the two time periods are probably particular to the organization studied. For example, in a firm with less opportunity for selection of, and self-selection by, new employees, there should be less evidence of shared cultural knowledge immediately after starting employment. However, the relative mastery of the different categories of cultural knowledge fits predictions based on the building-block conceptualization. If that conceptualization is correct, a similar pattern of relative mastery should be found in other organizational settings.

It is possible that jargon is easier to learn than stories because less information is conveyed in a word or phrase than in an entire event history. It is also possible that the content of the value messages transmitted with jargon is simpler and easier to understand than the complex and ambiguous messages of stories. Both of these explanations may contribute to the results of the present study and are worthy topics for future research.

The results also supported predictions concerning the effects of training expected in this particular company. In contrast to the untrained group, the trained group showed greater mastery of some kinds of cultural information by the end of the eight-week period of the study. These results are consistent with the explanation that attendance at the off-site training sessions may have facilitated cultural learning by removing the new employees from the time pressures and cognitive demands of performing an unfamiliar job. Training primarily facilitated familiarity with, and interpretation of, organizational stories. Perhaps in the first few weeks on the job, learning jargon is essential, mastering tacit knowledge is inessential, and absorbing organizational stories is an intermediate priority, occurring only if a training program or some other stimulus creates slack that permits this kind of deferrable cultural learning.

This explanation for the results, however, must be tentative. Differences between the trained and untrained groups may be attributable to factors other than the training (see Campbell and Stanley, 1963). For example, the two groups may have been differentially exposed to company events that affected the rate at which they absorbed cultural knowledge. Even if differences between these two groups can be attributed to the training, in other organizations the content of training and on-the-job experiences may be different. Future research, testing the slack explanation in other firms, could rule out such alternative explanations for differences between the trained and untrained groups.

This discussion of the issues raised by the present study has led to several suggestions for future research. A general theme underlies these suggestions: In order to understand the results of this study more fully and generalize from them, comparative studies are needed. This need for more comparative research is not particular to the present study. The entire domain of organizational culture is faced with problems that cannot be resolved without comparative data. Although some culture researchers do not aim to construct generalizable theory, others could use comparative data, collected with the hybrid methodology, to address a wide range of theoretical problems.

For example, too many culture studies have assumed the existence of a universally shared organizational culture or subculture. The hybrid methodology can be used to test this key assumption by comparing individual and group differences in perspective. For example, researchers could measure the extent to which top management values and interpretations differ from those of lower-level employees. In a firm with a single dominant culture, pockets of ignorance, resistance, and fanatic enthusiasm can be discovered. Occupational, divisional, and hierarchical subcultures could be located. Congruences and conflicts among groups and individuals could be mapped, providing a complex and detailed picture of what is—and what is not—shared.

With the hybrid methodology, systematic comparisons across time can be made, permitting the study of culture as a dynamic process. For example, researchers can use the methodology to map the spread of a new belief across an organization. The death of an obsolete culture or the birth of a new culture could be studied. In a mature organization responding to a crisis, the process of cultural adjustment could be examined to determine where accretion and adjustment occur easily and where inertia is strongest. If deliberate attempts to manage cultural change were attempted, short- and long-term effectiveness could be assessed.

With careful attention to standardizing data-collection procedures during the first stage of a study, the hybrid methodology can be used to make systematic comparisons across organizations, making a whole domain of previously inaccessible theoretical issues open to empirical examination. For example, potential mergers and acquisitions could be evaluated for cultural "fit." Cluster analyses could determine if distinctive types of cultures exist, for example, with particular orientation towards humanism, innovation, or the importance of the "bottom line." Claims that some types of cultures generate more commitment, productivity, or profitability could be empirically tested.

Perhaps most importantly, if comparisons across organizations are possible, the institutions studied by previous researchers can be classified as deviant or as representative of particular subgroups. One can determine if the frequently mentioned members of the "Culture 500," such as I.B.M., Digital Equipment and Hewlett-Packard, are cultural norms or anomalies. The results of previous studies could be systematically integrated. The existence of comparative data would make it easier to explore relationships between culture and other areas of organizational research, eventually facilitating the integration of culture into the core of organizational theory.

The hybrid methodology retains some of the strengths of qualitative approaches, avoids strong social desirability biases, and permits the generation of comparative data. With variants on this methodological approach, organizational culture researchers could address the centrally important issues described above. If we continue to fail to generate comparative data that address these theoretical blindspots, our interesting speculations will remain speculations and interest in culture may be deservedly evanescent.

APPENDIX:
QUALITATIVE DATA COLLECTION PROCEDURES

The researcher began a typical day of observation at the local branch office by riding to the office with the first-line manager. During the one-hour drive, the manager would dictate his "to-do" list for the day into a hand-held recorder. He would also dictate any correspondence to be typed by his secretary. Of special interest to the researcher were his internal memoranda, which contained numerous examples of company jargon.

Upon arriving in the office the manager made copies of all these documents available to the researcher for subsequent examination. The researcher usually spent the next hour talking informally with employees in the coffee room. She attempted to learn what activities were planned for the day, in order to distribute her observation time evenly across individuals and functions. At the end of the hour, a record was made of the announcements and memoranda posted on the bulletin board in the coffee room.

The remainder of the day was spent observing meetings and discussions. The number of participants in these activities ranged from 10 to 15 employees to 2, for example, between a manager and a subordinate. The researcher joined employees for lunch every day and met with at least one employee at the end of each day to discuss any questions that had arisen. For example, at first much of the jargon and almost all of the jokes were unintelligible to the researcher. Employees provided explanations and definitions of unfamiliar terminology and helped the researcher distinguish jokes and jargon unique to this company. These definitions and explanations were corroborated by asking similar questions of other employees on subsequent occasions. Each night, after leaving the field setting, the researcher expanded field notes and reviewed documents collected during the day.

During the off-site retreat for top management and "rising stars," each morning began with two-hour meetings of small groups. Each group was composed of eight sales representatives and a rotating chairperson selected from the top executive team. The topics of the small group sessions varied each day, and included issues directly relevant to the present study, such as the importance of the company's philosophy of management and its "culture." At the end of each morning, all participants gathered in a large room, where the small group discussions were summarized by one member of each group.

Dinners during this retreat were elaborate. Pre- and postmeal receptions featured top executives as keynote speakers. These speakers emphasized the future of the company, the technical and marketing challenges that faced the firm, and the importance of the talents of the assembled superior performers. Several award ceremonies were also held. The researcher attended all these functions and joined informal conversations and leisure activities, such as tennis, golf, tours of the surrounding locale, and various eating and drinking gatherings.

NOTES

1. A researcher, somewhat like a new employee, "learns" a culture. Particularly if the learning process is a short-term endeavor, the researcher will learn most about the relatively superficial aspects of the culture, which are more accessible to outsiders and new employees. The present study focuses on the short-term enculturation of new employees, with reference to a particular set of cultural manifestations. For a longer-term study, with a need for deeper knowledge of tacitly-held cultural assumptions, it would be helpful to use sophisticated qualitative methods during the first stage of the research process described in this chapter. Particularly useful would be lengthy participant observation (e.g., Van Maanen, 1979; Smircich, 1983a) and/or in-depth clinical interviews (Schein, 1985). However, no length of involvement, clinical skill, or mix of qualitative techniques can guarantee that the researcher has understood the culture in the various ways it is perceived by its members.

2. Karl Weick encouraged us to take an imaginative approach to designing this questionnaire and suggested this measure of tacit cultural knowledge. We are grateful for both his encouragement and this particular suggestion.

3. A cover letter to the questionnaire requested the new employees' voluntary assistance and assured them that the confidentiality of their responses would be respected

and that no one at the company would have access to their individual data. The response rate was 87%.

4. Although a disjunction between the company's espoused values and values-in-use was anticipated, the content of this disjunction was unexpected. In contrast to the espoused values, the values-in-use placed more stress on humanitarian concerns and deemphasized financial, product, and social responsibility values. One plausible explanation for this disjunction concerns the audiences to whom these value statements were addressed. Values-in-use may be primarily oriented toward an internal audience of employees, the primary beneficiaries of humanitarian policies. In contrast, espoused values concerning finances, products, services, and social responsibility should be more relevant to an external audience, such as customers and shareholders. If this explanation is correct, studies of other organizations should reveal similar disjunctions between the content of espoused values and values-in-use.

5. This company is not unique in its focus on the value of uniqueness. Most organizational cultures place strong emphasis on unique accomplishments or distinctive institutional competence (see Selznik, 1957; Clark, 1970; Wilkins, 1978). The claim to uniqueness is often communicated through organizational stories. Ironically, these stories are not themselves unique to a particular setting. Instead, in widely divergent organizations, virtually identical stories transmit the value of uniqueness (Martin et al., 1983). The present study suggests that, in addition to stories, humor and jargon are cultural forms particularly well-suited to transmit claims of uniqueness.

PART II

FUNCTIONS OF
THE "DYSFUNCTIONAL"

In *The Functions of the Executive*, first published half a century ago, Chester I. Barnard writes that informal organizations "are necessary to the operation of formal organizations as a means of communication, of cohesion, and of protecting the integrity of the individual" (Barnard, 1938: 123).

These observations about the nature of organizations by the chief executive officer of the New Jersey Bell Telephone Company serve as the theme of the present section on the functions of seemingly dysfunctional behavior.

Barnard is widely recognized for his treatment of organizations as complex systems of biological, physical, and social components affected by environmental forces. He challenged the notion that economic motivation is primary in generating the cooperation essential to effective organization, emphasizing instead the non-material rewards of honor, status, personal satisfaction, participation, and pride in workmanship. He stressed the intuitive nature of decision making, contending that the executive process is not principally intellectual, but aesthetic and moral (Wolfe, 1974; Pauchant, 1985; Jones, 1987). He is also credited with having introduced the concept of "informal organization," which, as he describes it, includes or produces "customs, mores, folklore, institutions, social norms and ideals" (Barnard, 1938: 116).

According to Barnard, informal organization may be defined as an aggregate of personal contacts and interactions; usually without specific conscious joint purpose, this association has "common results," namely the generation of norms and folkways. The direct effects of organizing, then, include attitudes, understandings, and customs—values, norms, and ideals as embodied, expressed, and perpetuated through traditions or folkways (Barnard, 1938: 114-116). Although he focused most of his attention on formal, enduring organizations and the functions of executives within them, Barnard realized that organizing is a common and frequent endeavor in everyday life. He pointed out that an organization of any kind (whether spontaneous, informal, or formal) comes into being whenever "(1) there are persons able to communicate with each other (2) who are willing to contribute action (3) to accomplish a common purpose" (p. 82).

Informal organization necessarily precedes formal organization, Barnard insisted. This is because "the possibility of accepting a common purpose, of communication, and of attaining a state of mind under which there is willingness to cooperate" demands "prior contact and preliminary interaction" (p. 116). On the other hand, *informal organization compels a degree of formal organization* to persist or become extensive. This is so even when the object of association is social, for people are impelled as a condition of their existence to do something and to seek purpose to their actions.

Hence, there is interdependence: The formal organization is essential to order and consistency, the informal organization to vitality; "there cannot be one without the other," writes Barnard. "If one fails the other disintegrates" (p. 120). Formal organizations arise out of informal organizations, giving the latter structure. When formal organizations are generated, they bring into existence and require informal organizations whose effects are to establish norms and ideals, customs and mores.

What Barnard characterized are not necessarily two kinds of organizations, but perhaps more accurately two aspects of organizational life. One is the structural element, with a formal division of labor (the organization chart and written job descriptions), clearly stated rules and regulations, channels of communication, a chain of command, and so on. The other consists of the daily activities of people that are largely traditional and expressive—the "folkways" that Barnard mentions.

Much is expressed in informal interactions and spontaneous groupings that would not be communicated through official documents. This information (as well as the vehicles by which it is transmitted) affects individuals' experiences, knowledge, attitudes, and feelings. Cohesiveness may result from the socializing and expressive behavior, because narrating, ritualizing, and celebrating are participatory activities in which individual beliefs may be socially reinforced.

Perhaps the most important result of "informal organization" or "workers' culture" (McCarl, 1979, 1984a)—the traditions generated in firsthand interaction—is that of maintaining "the feeling of personal integrity, of self respect, of independent choice" (Barnard, 1938: 122). Although often this function, observes Barnard, "is deemed destructive of informal organization, it is to be regarded as a means of maintaining the personality of the individual against certain effects of organizations which tend to disintegrate the personality."

As they interact, individuals in organizations learn, discover, or invent techniques for carrying out their tasks, participate in and contribute to a system of traditional knowledge, develop customs, generate rituals, and in other ways manage to accomplish objectives through "working relations" within the given structure of an organization (McCarl, 1978). If people imagine and implement better ways to work, if they tell stories communicating and illustrating the larger purpose and mission of the organization, if their ceremonies and customs express and reinforce a general organizational philosophy or set of values, then their activities seem to conform to and support the formal aspects of organization promulgated through policy and official procedure.

But what if they make items at work out of company materials for their own use, play practical jokes, ridicule the image of the organization, undermine the authority of the hierarchy, or engage in forbidden activities? Are these behaviors invariably harmful to self or destructive of the organization? The answer is not always obvious or simple, as essays in this section point out.

RESEARCH ON SEEMINGLY "DEVIANT" BEHAVIOR IN ORGANIZATIONS

In the first essay, Wells considers the "paradox of functional dysfunction" in the behavior of staff personnel at a Girl Scout camp held each summer on Catalina. The official image of the Girl Scouts is that of young women who are "proper" and "decorous." It is difficult for the staff to live up to the image, policies, and professed values of the organization in a work environment that is isolated, stressful, and even hostile. Some respond by engaging in activities that violate the image and proscribed codes of conduct. As survival tools, aesthetic outlets, and expressions of group identity, this seemingly deviant behavior helps individuals do their work and thus contributes to organizational goals. Moreover, such behavior aids in achieving in a "perverse" sort of way exactly those skills, values, and qualities most cherished: imagination, initiative, problem solving, and teamwork.

In the second article, Fine raises the question of whether play is merely a way to let off steam (thus providing a safety value for frustration), or whether play contributes directly to productivity. In his study of the activities of restaurant workers, he finds that time away from work in the form of play may change conceptions of the workplace from that of institutionalized coercion to that of an arena in which one can control the environment. Hence, play may support the values that support the conditions of work.

In the third essay, Runcie examines improvised forms of job enlargement and enrichment on the assembly line that, while contrary to company policy, are often tacitly permitted by supervisors. When seeming "deviant behavior" goes beyond the limits defined by informal rules, then it is conceived of as "bad." Group-defined "bad" deviancy (and even some "acceptable" deviancy) might not exist, contends Runcie, a vice president of human resources, if those with the power to change conditions would cure the boredom and lack of autonomy characterizing many workplaces.

Beyer and Trice address the issue of power in their essay, which examines rites of passage, enhancement, degradation, conflict reduction, integration, and renewal. The elaborately planned, dramatic events that they describe are powerful vehicles presenting and reinforcing values, assumptions, and concepts of status. Whether they are aware of it or not, point out these specialists in organization behavior and labor relations, managers who control organizational rites are in possession of an influential form of communication that can reinforce or change the existing distribution of power.

Together, the essays illustrate ways in which informal organizations, to again quote Barnard, "are necessary to the operation of formal organizations as a means of communication, of cohesion, and of protecting the integrity of the individual." They illustrate some of the many ways in which people, objects, and activities are taken to be symbolic, and what this in turn suggests for management theory and practice.

5

THE PARADOX OF FUNCTIONAL DYSFUNCTION IN A GIRL SCOUT CAMP

Implications of Cultural Diversity for Achieving Organizational Goals

Patricia Atkinson Wells

University of California, Los Angeles

In his article "The Esoteric-Exoteric Factor in Folklore," William Hugh Jansen characterizes expressive culture-based communications generated in interaction both within and between groups of human beings. The "esoteric factor" pertains to what a group thinks of itself and what it supposes others to think of it. It stems from a group sense of belonging and serves to defend and strengthen that sense. The "exoteric factor" relates to what one group thinks of another, and may result from fear of, mystification about, or resentment toward the group to which one does not belong. According to Jansen, the features of groups particularly subject to the esoteric-exoteric factor in folklore include isolation, customary wearing of a uniform, danger of occupation, knowledge or training which is or seems to be peculiar, and being considered by others to be particularly admirable (Jansen, 1965: 46-47, 49-50).

Within any organization, the structure of that organization, the nature of the work environment, and the actual activities of and interactions between people may give rise to multiple folk groups. For those scholars who posit organizational cultures, these groups could be considered subcultures, existing within the greater culture yet to some degree functionally autonomous. Groups of workers may be at a physical remove from the administrative center of an organization, or they may experience environmental isolation because of such things as machine noise, office layout, or reflection of organizational hierarchy in the allocation of personal work space. Strong subgroup identification may result in (or *from*, this being a "chicken or egg" problem) the individual's perception of an organizational or community identity separate from that of the "parent" or larger organization.

For purposes of this essay, one particular work environment, a summer camp operated by the Girl Scouts of America, serves as a metaphor for worker isolation. The work site is not only removed from the administrative offices of the organization but is geographically remote. The organization is, in large degree, *exoteric* to the work group which it generates. As Toelken (1979: 12) observes about symbolic forms,

> all folklore is phrased in terms appropriate to—and usually demanded by—the group in which it is performed. *Often* these particular manners of expression are *registered as inappropriate* when they are heard by outsiders, when they are presented out of their normal context, when their audience is expanded beyond the usual local group for which and in which the performance makes sense [emphasis added].

Some aspects of the expressive behavior of a work group may therefore be perceived from a traditional management perspective as "deviant" or dysfunctional. However, apparently dysfunctional behavior is translated through expressive forms to become functional for the work group and/or the organization as a whole in a number of ways. In the discussion which follows, I shall describe and exemplify various types of expressive forms and characterize their explicit and implicit functions.

WORK LIFE AND EXPRESSIVE BEHAVIOR

All groups of people are, to some extent, sensitive about their traditions and to the potential for misunderstanding or misuse by an outsider, and this is no less true of organizational networks. In work situations where a structural dichotomy of "workers" and "managers" exists, and their relationship may be perceived as adversarial by either or both groups, the expressive behavior of the workers may deal explicitly with the fear of suppression or manipulation of their traditions by administrators.

In the late 1960s, I began working during the summers as a camp counselor at a Girl Scout camp located on an island off the coast of

Southern California. As a part of the initiation process, new staff members and counselors-in-training were told a ghost story known as "Red Eyes." The narrative took the form of a local legend and involved the haunting of the camp site by the restless spirit of a drowned Indian ("Red Eyes") who was searching for his lost love. Skilled narrators played upon the isolation of the site and the audiences' natural fears of indigenous creatures and phenomena.

The "Red Eyes" legend was deemed to be so frightening and to have caused such wholesale panic and hysteria that the Girl Scout Council which operates the camp was reputed to have forbidden its narration. The prohibition of "Red Eyes" was really another narrative device, serving as a prologue to the actual storytelling in order to stimulate interest and predispose audience response. What is interesting to me about this particular camp tradition is that the behavior which is *believed* to have been banned by the organization—the narration of "Red Eyes"—was an integral part of the work culture and the enculturation process.

I returned to the camp to conduct research in the early 1980s and found that a fragmentary version of "Red Eyes" was still being told, and that the element of banning by the organization remained an important aspect of the narration. Individuals who had not actually heard a narration of the legend *had* heard of "Red Eyes" and that its telling had been forbidden. The work group apparently found the existence of organizational policies which prohibited aspects of the work culture fully credible, and the belief in such policies seemed to have been perpetuated beyond the active survival of the tradition in question.

In any organization, conflict may exist between the work inclinations and values of an individual and the organizational premises. Aspects of the organizational policy may at times be irrelevant or seem absurd for a given work situation or environment (as the saying goes, "When you're up to your ass in alligators, it's hard to remember that the original objective was draining the swamp!"). There may be great disparity between the ideal codes of behavior espoused by organizational literature and inculcated in the training of organizational participants, and what becomes appropriate or necessary for individuals to survive and do their jobs.

When I was growing up and involved in Scouting (in the late 1950s and early 1960s), fledgling Scouts were required to memorize a credo composed of a promise and 12 laws that dictated values, attitudes, and desirable behavior. While the text of this credo has been altered and abbreviated in accordance with cultural and social changes in America over the last 15 years, the original values, attitudes, and codes of behavior are still pervasive within the organization, and the "Girl Scout image" remains relatively unchanged. To many, both within and outside the organization, the image is asexual, capable, polite, and straight to the point of being "goody-goody." We are reminded that a "A Girl Scout is clean in thought, word, and deed; a Girl Scout is a friend to all and a sister to every other Girl Scout; a Girl Scout is kind to animals," and so on.

As I learned while working as a counselor at Girl Scout camp, living up to this kind of image is difficult at the best of times and becomes even more so in a work environment that is isolated, stressful, and often hostile, and in which there is intense confinement and enforced communalism. Behavior and impulses were restricted both implicitly by Scouting codes and explicitly through organizational policies forbidding profanity, liquor, drugs, and sexual activities on camp property. Camp staff were required to wear a uniform consisting of a white blouse with badges and insignia, green shorts, and green knee socks—all Girl Scout issue. The uniform conformed neither to prevalent styles nor the contours of the average female body. Nor was it particularly well-suited to the physical nature of the work or work environment. The occasions on which it was to be worn, and the extent to which deviation from Girl Scout issue was tolerated, were dictated by an on-site administrator. Staff generally worked three to six weeks of *de facto* 24-hour-a-day duty with little or no opportunity to leave the work site. After a three-day break in midsummer, when they could leave the island, the staff returned for another four to six weeks. In the staff of this camp, we have a group that exhibits the features that Jansen cited as being particularly subject to the esoteric-exoteric factor in folklore: isolation, customary wearing of a uniform, danger of occupation, knowledge or training that is or seems to be peculiar, and being considered by others to be particularly admirable (Jansen, 1965: 49-50)

Many of the workers coped with these relatively long periods of isolation, stress, and frustration through jokes and joking relationships, eccentric behavior, and/or ridicule or rejection of the Girl Scout image. One summer a group of staff members spoke to each other with lisps; during another season, spurious Southern accents were popular. Individuals or cliques adopted bizarre modes of dress, such as wearing men's boxer shorts or 1950s-style housedresses. The camp uniform itself was sometimes defaced (or "personalized," depending on one's point of view) through complete recutting of the shorts, addition of decorative braid or ribbon, or the wearing of jewelry, badges, or buttons stating or implying the philosophical and/or political beliefs of their wearer. Parodies of camp songs—obscene, scatological, or merely silly—were passed on or recomposed regularly. For example, "Girl Scouts together, happy are we" became "Girl Scouts together, *sappy* are we." In a song in which each letter in the words "Girl Scout" stands for a different virtue or attribute, "She wears a G for Generosity" became "She wears a G for Gonorrhea."

Particular sayings or catchphrases that seemed to describe or epitomize shared attitudes toward their work or a tone that was set for the season appeared with marked frequency in both the speech and graffiti of staff members. Such phrases were often borrowed from popular media. For example, "Just when you thought it was safe to go back in the water...."—the advertising slogan for the film *Jaws II*—was adopted readily as a humorous way to deal with the very real hazards of operating an oceanfront camp, sharks being only *one* of many potential problems. "As the surge turns"—from the daytime television serial "As the World Turns"—was the phrase for a season full of mishaps, petty squabbles, and personality conflicts. By regarding each new incident as an episode in a soap opera, staff members were able to use humor as a distancing device. "Another day, another dime" commented on the unrelenting sameness of daily tasks and the remuneration for same. "It's Miller Time"—a beer slogan—denoted both pride in the completion of arduous labor and the need for a well-earned break. Giant killer sharks, soap operas, and beer may seem strange icons for an organization whose pantheon includes God, country, and its national and international founders.

Camp-owned sailing craft have carried such names as "Daiquiri," "Margarita," "Harvey W." (for "Wallbanger"), and "Shirley Temple"— renamed and repainted by the waterfront staff. Graffiti in the staff house (off-limits to campers) have included slogans such as "Hire the morally handicapped," the GSUSA logo retouched to look like Mr. Zig-Zag (of cigarette paper fame), and an elaborate painting of a Coors can.

Status boundaries, power, and interpersonal relations assume looming importance in this kind of enforced community life. Pranks aimed at undermining or ridiculing authority or the organizationally sanctioned hierarchy were common. A large bell was sounded for wake-up call and mealtimes, thereby regulating daily activities. This bell was frequently stolen and hidden—no mean feat, as it stood four feet tall and weighed over 100 pounds. The underwear of the administrative staff often found its way to the top of the flagpole, and unless noticed and retrieved early, had to be publicly reclaimed during the formal flag-raising ceremony. High-ranking individuals sat apart from the *hoi polloi* during meals at a "staff table." It was not unknown for this staff table to appear— completely set—on the dining hall roof. One particularly imposing and feared program director opened her cabin door one morning to find herself completely papered in by a solid wall of her own requisition forms. "T.P.ing"—the practice of enshrouding a symbolic object or building with toilet paper—was commonplace and on occasion rose to such epidemic proportions that all supplies were kept under lock and key.

Much of the behavior that I have discussed would seem to the management of the organization to be dysfunctional, because it is not in accordance with organizational image and policy; nor does it seem to help further particular organizational objectives. Such behavior does, however, function for members of the work group as survival tools, aesthetic outlets, and expressions of group identity, community, and solidarity. All of this makes it possible for human beings to do their work. And it may help in achieving *other* organizational objectives—a paradox of "functional dysfunction." For example, the flaunting of codes of dress and behavior—while violating the image of the organiza- tion—may actually promote both immediate group solidarity and individualism, values encouraged by and integral to the organization. The placing of the staff table on the dining hall roof may be a gesture of defiance against the organizational hierarchy, but the task itself requires imagination, initiative, planning, problem-solving, and teamwork—the very skills and techniques that the staff are charged with teaching to the campers. In the example with which I opened this section (the legend of "Red Eyes"), the assumption of organizational dysfunction has become an integral part of the tradition for members of the work culture.

It is important to note that the behavior that I have described, and that could be characterized as being dysfunctional, was confined to the work site. The most serious violations of the Girl Scout code and/or image occurred only within the context of the work group, never in the presence of campers or outsiders. In fact, there seems to have been a conscious effort on the part of staff members to preserve the public image of Girl Scouting and to regard the initiation of campers into the traditions and values of Scouting as a sacred trust.

The code "A Girl Scout is clean in thought, word, and deed," while no longer articulated in those terms, was still a strong regulator of staff behavior in the presence of campers and in public. One summer, several staff members generated an "unofficial staff song." The words "Shit, fuck, hell, damn, son-of-a-bitch, I don't give a flying crap" were set to a familiar tune, which could be hummed with impunity in any company, yet communicated a message in no uncertain terms to other group members. On the occasion of a particularly boisterous night out in the island's single town, a group of staff members found themselves being questioned by police and asked to leave town for disturbing the peace. All publicly disassociated themselves from the Girl Scouts and the camp, claiming to work for a different organization at another (rival) camp on the island.

While privately violating the Girl Scout image through ridicule, obscene and/or scatological materials, bizarre modes of dress or behavior and pranks, there seems to have been an awareness of and a conscientious effort toward the preservation of public image. The work group presented a united front for the organization in public life.

IMPLICATIONS

The nature of particular aspects of the expressive behavior found in the workplace may relate directly to personnel policies, general organizational climate, and the quality of work life. The isolated, stressful, and often hostile environment of the Girl Scout camp, in which behavior and impulses were restricted both implicitly and explicitly, gave rise to a wide variety of creative, eccentric, and sometimes adolescent behaviors, some of which have been characterized in this article. There are three implications that I wish to examine by way of conclusion.

(1) Aspects of the expressive behavior of a work group that are perceived from a traditional management perspective as "deviant" or dysfunctional may actually strengthen the organization's "culture." Such behavior does not constitute rejection of the organization and its myths, symbols, and rituals. Rather, the essence of parody—in the case of the uniform and traditional songs and symbols of Girl Scouting—is that it is an *esoteric* phenomenon. If the members of the work group did not also conceive themselves to be participants in the larger organization, their symbolic violation of organizational taboos would be meaningless.

For this group, the particular behaviors that I have described or characterized are more than responses to stress or methods of stress reduction. Such behaviors illustrate the multilevel interplay of organization symbolism/myth/ritual and individual or group expression. The parodies of the Girl Scout songs cited earlier in this paper are both an acknowledgement of organizational myth and symbol (the ideal Girl Scout) and a recognition of reality—that being human we fail to meet the ideal. In an organization in which mottos and slogans abound, it is not surprising to find expressions of subgroup identity and solidarity taking similar forms. The aphoristic graffiti found in the staff house testify, in form if not in content, to the strength of organizational patterns of expression.

(2) In any organization, the existence of multiple groups—each with the potential for its own subculture—not only is not harmful to the organization, it is the normal state of affairs. The recent emphasis in management studies on corporate or organizational culture seems to stem from a desire to provide a blueprint for success. The nature of particular cultures is correlated to their degree of "excellence." There has been a tendency to equate the strength of an organization culture with its degree of homogeneity. The notion that an organization must be homgeneous for that organization to succeed predisposes managers to view as necessarily negative any behavior that deviates from codes or rules established for organizational participants. However, as we have seen in the examples from organizational life in the previous section, apparently dysfunctional behavior may actually further organizational aims and strengthen organization cultures.

(3) The perspective and methods of folklore studies can be particularly useful to the student of organization culture. Whether their primary interests lie in discovering similarities or differences, continuity or change, folklorists tend to look at the specific (an individual person, expression, or product), the general (the immediate group or classification to which the aforementioned person/thing belongs), and the universal in order to discern patterns in human behavior. This peculiar micro/macro perspective yields a clearer understanding of the culture of the workplace, the structural and interactional aspects of organization life as they are patterned by the particular work group.

The study of folklore (or traditional expressive behavior) in the workplace may be used as a diagnostic tool in determining the health of the organization. For example, narratives (such as the "Red Eyes" legend) may provide insight into worker management relations.

Folklore study may also be used prescriptively, showing how cultural mechanisms may be used as a strategy for achieving particular goals. For example, incorporating both workers and managers in rituals may be used as a method of engaging group participation in a particular project or endeavor. In the Girl Scout camp setting, the camp director symbolically joins the staff together as a group through a ritual known as the "Staff Tie Ceremony." This ceremony, which usually incorporates music and inspirational readings, takes place at the end of the precamp training period. There are two parts to the ritual: the presentation of the ties (strips of colored cloth approximately 42" long by 2" wide) by the director, and the tying of the ties in a special "friendship knot" by some other staff member that the individual holds in high regard. The work group is symbolically bound together as a tribe or a family, and subsequent wearing of the tie is a badge of identity and solidarity. Similar rituals of incorporation are used with success in many organizations.

6

LETTING OFF STEAM?

Redefining a Restaurant's Work Environment

Gary Alan Fine

University of Minnesota

In much sociocultural analysis the concept of play has been posed in opposition to that of work (see Hans, 1981). Play is conceived as being that which work is not. Perhaps the critical distinction in the definitions is that, whereas work is seen as motivated by external rewards (often in the form of monetary payment), play is defined as activity that is intrinsically motivated (Berlyne, 1969: 814). Work is seen as being explicitly goal- or task-directed, whereas play is emergent and hence has no necessary direction. Further, work is often depicted as forced, whereas play is considered purely voluntary. I argue that it is unnecessary to establish this rigid dichotomy between these two categories of human activity.

The world of work is also a world of play and expressive behavior. As a long series of ethnographies of work environments have shown, there are few, if any, occupations that can be characterized by continuous grimness (Roy, 1959-1960; Bradney, 1957; Ditton, 1979). In most occupational settings—factories, coal mines, hospitals, or bakeries—the opportunities for play are abundant. Fun is part of the successful completion of tasks and is necessary for the creation and maintenance of a sense of satisfaction. The now classic time-and-motion studies that suggested that a work organization should be based on efficiency of motion do not, in fact, produce maximal efficiency *in human terms*. The social demands of workers take precedence over considerations of logic.

Most writers on organization theory now dismiss time-motion studies, at least in their classic form, in part because they don't allow for the display of expressive behavior; in its place they have postulated a view that expressive behavior is necessary to "let off steam" (see Bales,

1950). This view suggests that play in itself doesn't directly accomplish the doing of tasks; rather, its role is to permit work by providing a safety valve or outlet for energy that otherwise would negatively affect production. This is essentially a hydraulic model of behavior, which suggests the successful worker will be the worker who lacks hostility toward what he is doing (since hostility is drained by the play).

An alternate approach I shall emphasize is that the work culture may directly contribute to productivity by supporting values that, in turn, support the conditions of work. The first approach sees play as essentially opposed to work, while the second sees work and play as expressing the same value system and as promoting the adjustment of the worker to his or her environment. Work and play are mutually reinforcing. Although joking or other play time formally represents time away from work, in practice it contributes to increased satisfaction and productivity by changing the definition of the work environment from an institution of coercive control to an arena in which the workers have some measure of control over the conditions of their own employment.

In this essay I focus my discussion of the world of work on one particular industry—restaurants (sometimes known generically as "the hospitality industry"). I have conducted intensive ethnographic observation and in-depth interviews in the kitchens and with the staffs of three restaurants in the Twin Cities metropolitan area. The first, La Pomme de Terre, is an haute cuisine French restaurant, by all accounts one of the best and most creative restaurants in the Upper Midwest. The second restaurant, The Owl's Nest, a multi-year Holiday Award winner, is a continental-style restaurant, best known for its fresh fish. Its primary clientele are wealthy businessmen. The third restaurant is Stan's Steakhouse. Stan's is family-owned and operated. It is particularly well known in its part of the Twin Cities, an area that is not acclaimed for the quality of its restaurants. Stan's has received metropolitan awards for the quality of its beef.

In terms of organizational structure these three restaurants are quite similar. In all three the owner and/or his children manage the restaurant and are on the premises virtually every day. Each restaurant has a head chef, two or three other cooks working every evening, and a crew of waiters (in the case of La Pomme de Terre), waitresses (Stan's) or both (The Owl's Nest). All can be classified as small restaurants in terms of the size of their staff, although they differ in their customer turnover. On an average Saturday night Stan's serves 500 customers, the Owl's Nest 150, and La Pomme de Terre 75.

Every occupation must deal with particular problems that derive from the specific conditions of work, and each develops its own solutions. For cooks, one of the major strains they must face is working under intense pressure for a relatively short part of the day, and having relatively little pressure for the rest of the time. Typically the period 6:30 until 8:30 in the evening will be hectic in the kitchen, and the rest of the time from 3:00 until 11:00 will be much more leisurely. This provides the opportunity for cooks to prepare for their "real work," and time for them to relax after the pressure. This temporal organization of the workday structures the location of play for the workers. Up until the rush, work is leisurely, mostly consisting of preparing everything for the busy period so that work can proceed smoothly and efficiently. Unless there is a large party coming in that night, or a huge number of reservations, or a shortage of cooks, the cooks know they can complete their tasks with time to spare, and so can joke with each other, take breaks, or talk about personal matters while they work. During the rush the focus is much more task oriented; cooks rarely take breaks or leave the kitchen, and most talk is oriented to the work at hand. By the time the rush has ended (either with all the customers seated or with few more reservations on the books), joking can resume. It is particularly in this period after the rush that joking and playing will occur and cooks will take lengthy breaks. Clean-up need not end at a particular time, so cooks don't feel they are on a schedule after the rush.

PLAY REINFORCES WORK

I suggest that play in the kitchen reinforces kitchen work in four ways. First, kitchen play fits into the workday in such a way as to diminish the likelihood of boredom. Second, play, like work, builds collective cooperation. Third, the existence of expressive behavior at work serves to maintain the worker's allegiance to the workplace and prevents turnover. Fourth, one may play at work, and add "joy" to one's occupational requirements.

The Fit Between Play and Work

Play in the workplace doesn't just happen; rather, it is socially situated. Much play occurs when there is a lull in work. Most cooks agree that they prefer busy nights to slow nights, because slow nights are boring. The hardest part of cooking for many cooks is just standing around doing nothing, waiting for something to happen. It is at this time that cooks will trade jokes or will play pranks on each other. For example, on slow evenings at Stan's, when one of the cooks takes a break and leaves the kitchen, the other cooks will quickly put up a large number of old tickets so it will appear to the returning cook that they were suddenly flooded with orders. At such times, too, cooks play catch with items of food or spike each other's soda with Tabasco sauce. Cooks try a wide variety of entertaining devices to maintain their interest throughout the evening. At busy times such playful activity is not necessary, because the work provides a sufficient challenge for the cook.

From this perspective work and play have a reciprocal relationship, but not a contradictory relationship. Play doesn't let off steam from work, but provides for a continuation of interest.

Play is also found after a long period of intensive work, and here play is used to contrast with the strain that occurred over the evening. The play provides a counterpoint to the hectic activity of work by slowing down the activity—as in jocular discussions about one's female friends, recreational drug or alcohol use, or entertainment preferences. Play can be seen here as a way of providing an alternative to the demanding requirements of cooking.

Several things should be apparent in this discussion of the social and temporal locus of play. First, not all play is identical. Play takes different forms and consequently has different positions in kitchen work. Some play fills slots in which cooks need to be motivated. Other play fills slots in which cooks need to regain their cognitive and affective equilibrium after a long period of rushed activity. However, play always is fitted into one's schedule; that is, play is responsive to the requirements of the work situation. In all three of the work sites examined, work took priority over play, and play did not interfere with work but supported it.

Play Builds Cooperation

Any efficient work organization relies on the cooperation of its members. Workers are expected to aid each other in the completion of their duties. In each restaurant cooks were willing to help coworkers in the performance of their work roles, and it was common for one cook to ask another to help him do something when that other cook was not busy on a project. In some cases cooks asked their colleagues to take over for them when they wanted a break. In all three restaurants cooks defined themselves as members of a team. However, to think of oneself as a member of a team one must not only have similar work tasks or a similar physical location, but one must also recognize a sense of community.

It is in the construction of a sense of community that play at work is important. In many occupations rituals of initiation occur. In some cases this is a formal initiation, although perhaps more often (as is true in these restaurants) the initiation simply consists of establishing the recognition that one's fellow cook is "a good guy," can "take a joke," and can be trusted (Haas, 1972). In the early days on the job cooks send new workers on mock errands. One cook commented:

> Sometimes when we have a new busboy we tell him to go down and get a can of prunes and we don't have any prunes at all. [Prunes don't come in cans.] We had a busboy and a bartender down there for half an hour looking for them.

It is even better if one can convince a new worker to look for something ridiculous like a left-handed knife or a can of steam. The social importance of these tricks emerges in the reaction of the novice. If he shows that he is a good sport about it, he is accepted. This play serves as a signal that all are willing to give up something of their "self-image" for the enjoyment of their fellow workers: They have given part of themselves to the organization. They, therefore, can be trusted.

This initiation to the group also ties them to the *goals* of the group. One now can hardly refuse the request of a coworker. If the workers were alienated strangers, any request for aid could be met by a refusal— it is not the job of the other person to help. But if informal friendly relations have been established, the aid flows naturally through the social network. Thus the cooperation that is cemented in the playful activities of the cooks can be duplicated in their task-orientation to the benefit of organizational efficiency.

Expressive Behavior and Allegiance

Every organization needs the members of its workforce to be loyal to it and to its goals. When the work is not intrinsically interesting and the pay is not high, there exists the potential for alienation from one's employer with detrimental effects on productivity and quality. How can organizations help to increase the likelihood of organizational loyalty? In the last decade, students of organization have discovered the motivating power of corporate culture (Fine, 1984; Ouchi and Wilkins, 1985). Much of the discussion of corporate culture has focused on the imposition of this culture "from the top down." In this article I wish to discuss the creation of corporate culture (or "expressive culture") from "across."

I have previously suggested that every small group develops a small-group culture—what I term an "idioculture." This is "a system of knowledge, beliefs, behaviors, and customs shared by members of an interacting group to which members can refer and employ as the basis of further interaction" (Fine, 1979: 734). This cultural creation was found in each of the restaurants examined. Each restaurant had customs and traditions of its own—after-hours activities, nicknames, rituals, or simply ways of doing things that were functionally irrelevant to the task at hand. This culture ties the workers into the organization. In the words of Robert Freed Bales (1970: 153-154): "Most small groups develop a subculture that is protective for their members, and is allergic, in some respects, to the culture as a whole . . . They [the members] draw a boundary around themselves and resist intrusion."

These symbols of the idioculture serve as badges of belonging, and even though some forms of expressive behavior may take time away from the formal requirements of the job, the consequences are sufficient to produce benefits for the organization. One of the important conditions of work is how a person feels about his fellow employees, and expressive culture not only ties one to the organization, but also connects one to one's coworkers. Rarely is cooking a high-paid occupation and the work is often boring and routine, particularly for short-order cooks who do not have much opportunity for creative cookery; yet cooks report that they remain on the job primarily because of their affection for their coworkers. They find the work environment to be pleasant, primarily because of their interpersonal relations and the expressive behaviors that go along with them. The relatively low rate of turnover helps employers profit, because they do not have to advertise for, or train, new workers, and so the existence of an expressive culture among the workers directly contributes to corporate efficiency.

At two of the restaurants, cooks would occasionally sing together as they prepared the meals. Perhaps this off-key vocalizing was distracting, but it also lightened the mood in the kitchen, and had attendant psychological benefits for the performers. The tradition at two of the restaurants for the staff to form sports teams (outside of work) also contributed to the *esprit de corps* that small organizations need in order to survive. It is my contention that expressive behavior is not only a means of letting off steam (in a psychological hydraulic model), but that it very directly contributes to the doing of work in the kitchen; hence, playing is not subsidiary to the process of working.

Joy in Work

Mihalyi Csikszentmihalyi (1975) speaks of the phenomenon of "flow" that he finds in several intense leisure-time activities. In a state of flow the actor immerses himself fully in the activity without a sense of self-consciousness. One is totally engaged in the action. Such a concept of flow applies most directly to what we call our "peak experiences"— those components of ourselves that could be considered self-actualizing.

Such a state of flow is not normally considered part of the work experience. However, there were some occasions in restaurant kitchens when something very much like flow seemed to characterize the cooks' activities. This was especially evident in the busiest periods in the restaurants. On those occasions when things go smoothly, cooks may transcend their work roles, feeling that a sense of joy or a "high" characterizes their actions. As one cook commented, "I just love the activity . . . I concentrate totally, so I don't know how I feel . . . It's like another sense takes over." Mundane experiences are transformed into something resembling joy. The cooks are working very hard and are in constant motion, but while this is occurring they are not conscious of their mounting exhaustion. When everything goes well, the cooks are totally immersed in the requirements of their roles without being aware of them. The restaurant operates like a well-oiled machine. As one cook commented when I asked what constitutes a "good" day:

> When everyone's working together and you have an awful lot to do. Your time is spent real constructively. You organize it so that everything gets done and everything works smoothly like that. When the restaurant opens, you're ready. You're set up and everyone feels good and everything's done and the restaurant is busy. . . . That doesn't happen often.

As this cook implies, the joy or flow in one's work is a rather fragile phenomenon. Many things can break the mood. A dish that burns, a customer who sends his food back to the kitchen, or a mistake such as switching around orders can change a "good" night to one that is disappointing. Yet, there are times in the experience of most cooks during which everything works right, and they feel happy in doing something that would otherwise be tiresome. Of course, after the "rush" is over, cooks typically find themselves exhausted, and it is at this point that the more overt aspects of play manifest themselves.

This sense of "joy" or "flow" in one's work clearly contributes to the smooth working of the kitchen and, as a result, to the efficient operation of the restaurant. Once again we see that expressive activity need not be seen in contradiction to the doing of work requirements but as part of them.

CONCLUSION

In this article I have attempted to erase part of the boundary that separates work from play. I have suggested that the perspective claiming that play is necessary because it allows the worker to release feelings unconducive to the workplace is not an adequate picture of what occurs in at least one work setting—that of the restaurant kitchen. Work and play are intertwined. Both task-oriented behavior and expressive behavior emerge from the immediate situational requirements, and one serves to reinforce the other. Further, the two cannot be separated. As I indicated in talking about the concept of "flow," there may be some situations in which workers "play at their work"; that is, their work serves as an expression of collective identity and as an expression of individual self. Similarly the traditions that emerge within the workplace tie the workers to their organization and to their coworkers; these ties increase the likelihood the organization will survive.

We should not make the mistake of assuming that all expressive behavior in the workplace is constructive and supportive of the organization. As Marxists would quickly and correctly inform us, some expressive culture is profoundly subversive of the aims of the organization. Some play has negative consequences—such as those fast-food workers who urinate on the grill or those who take breaks from work that are excessively long or excessively intrusive. Most workers practice some form of output restriction, but in efficient organizations this is balanced against a desire to do one's job well.

The point is that the effects of play and expressive behavior must be understood within their own immediate situational context, and should not be analyzed *in general*. What works in some places with some employees with some organizational problems may not have a positive effect elsewhere. This reminds us that the social theorist or the management consultant can only hope to understand an organization by watching, describing, or acting upon the workers' behavior as it emerges *in situ*. If qualitative sociology and folklore studies can teach nothing else, they at least remind us that meaning resides in performance and the active manipulation of symbols. Meanings have effects in the real world of organizational efficiency.

7

"DEVIANT BEHAVIOR"

Achieving Autonomy in a Machine-Paced Environment

John F. Runcie

Organization Re-creation Associates

In any social situation, certain behaviors will be defined as outside the range of acceptable behavior. These "deviant" behaviors will in turn fall into two categories: behaviors that bring negative sanctions and those that do not.

Acceptable deviance tends to occur in those areas not considered threatening to workers or company, such as games or horseplay. Although many organizations explicitly forbid these behaviors, they occur, and often with company acquiescence. In fact, it is often the "deviant" behaviors that aid the workers' adaptation to assembly line work. The camaraderie of extra-legal pastimes makes assembly line work considerably less boring and dehumanizing. In the plants to be described, workers often yelled obscenities, threw objects about, played games, insulted tourists, and did numerous other things that made the day go by more easily and that helped their adaptation to the assembly line.[1]

There were, of course, behaviors seen as threatening—drugs, absenteeism, stealing, and even violence. Even in these more extreme cases, however, ambivalent definitions of the behavior meant that individual acts were not *necessarily* condemned as deviant. What came to be defined as deviant was generally deviant in context, rather than absolutely deviant. A violation of the norms, if it fits into the cultural context of the workplace, will probably not be considered deviant behavior. On the other hand, behavior that fails to fit into the cultural context may well be deviant (even if it might not be so defined "on the outside"). In this article I will examine "deviant behavior" and the context in which that behavior occurs from the point of view of the worker. Rather than assuming (as management tends to do) that violations of rules require punishment, I will attempt to understand rule violations and try to fit them into a theoretical framework. Malicious and destructive behaviors, while important to management in the plant, are not considered in this discussion.

BACKGROUND

Deviance can be defined simply as behavior at variance with a norm. However, not all deviance is necessarily dysfunctional, either from the point of view of the deviant, the organization, or one's peers. Bensman and Gerver (1963) point out that deviance may be positively functional for an organization, being used to further the cause of the organization, not to defeat it. For Bensman and Gerver, norms simply measure some desired end points that may be internal or external for an organization.[2] Deviance for Bensman and Gerver, then, becomes deviance from norms that are external to the organization. Of interest is the fact that Bensman and Gerver find that some deviance is looked at by employees (both management and hourly workers) as something that benefits the company. The behavior, while "against the rules," is functional to the extent that it aids the organization's adaptation to its environment. It is precisely the notion of adaptation, but at the individual worker level, that is of concern here.

Morgan (1975) examines the concepts of autonomy and negotiation in industrial arenas as they apply to workers' adaptations.[3] He suggests that most workers will seek to increase the degree of autonomy they have. According to Morgan (1975: 224), autonomy is looked upon as something that is

> constantly open to change, modification, rediscovery, use and denial. It is not something which is "just there" or even "given," but something which is used, bargained about, enjoyed in private or flouted in public, taken and accepted.

A worker can increase or decrease his or her autonomy through negotiation with others. A worker can unilaterally increase autonomy to some extent—by doing a predesigned job in an idiosyncratic way—but to retain the autonomy requires negotiation. An implicit bargain is struck between worker and supervisor: I let you do the job your way and in return you will (1) send no repairs (i.e., make errors), (2) work overtime when I ask, (3) support my decisions, and so on. Thus the

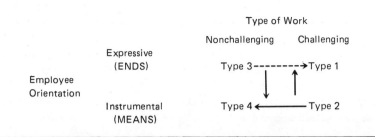

Figure 7.1

degree to which an employee has autonomy is negotiated (overtly and covertly) with management.

Strauss (1974b) also looks at autonomy and attempts to understand how workers adapt to jobs. Strauss posits a two-dimensional property space to describe workers' adaptations.

For Strauss, the Type 1 employees are the lucky ones; they are the employees who look for self-fulfillment, challenge, and autonomy on the job, and they get it. Types 2 and 3 are inherently unstable; employees who find themselves in these situations either move to Type 1 or Type 4 or become increasingly dissatisfied (with all the inherent problems). The Type 4 person is one who works for something other than challenge. These Type 4 employees are apathetic and unmotivated, although they are probably not dissatisfied.

Strauss sees legitimate adjustment to lack of challenge coming in three ways: improving social life *on* the job, union participation, and recreation off the job. Other adjustments, such as movement from Type 3 to Type 1, are available through "sabotage, fantasy, or empire building" (1974b: 30).[4] For Strauss, then, adjustment to autonomy and challenge comes about through looking beyond the job or nonlegitimate behaviors.

Combining the approaches of Strauss and Morgan, one might ask: Are some forms of employee "deviance" really techniques by which a worker makes nonchallenging work into challenging work through covertly negotiated job redesign? In other words, what I as a worker do may be looked at from the firm's perspective as unacceptable, but I look at it as a means for increasing the challenge and/or autonomy in my job.[5] Further, I look to increase the challenge/autonomy through overt or covert negotiation with supervisors. Such negotiation may well be part of the unspoken (or implicit) understandings of the plant's culture. Some of what employees do may be deviant in the truest sense of the word (sabotage, theft,[6] and so on) but much may not be.

In the pages that follow, I will examine some "deviant" behaviors and see the extent to which they are harmful—to employees, to the firm, and to the quality of the product produced. The last measure is included primarily because firms often assert deteriorating quality as a reason for banning certain behaviors.

"DEVIANT" BEHAVIOR

Job Enlargement

In almost any machine-paced production environment, workers are expected to do their own jobs without assistance except in certain specified instances. However, in many assembly situations, workers have begun to "trade jobs," "double up," or even "triple up" (or redesign their jobs in other ways) in clear violation of the rules. When workers "double up," it simply means that for some period of time I (as a worker) do both my job and the job of the person next to me. The person next to me can rest, sit down, or whatever during the period. At the end of the time, the other person does both jobs and I sit. Companies argue that this behavior increases error and lowers quality. Workers argue in return that "doubling up" increases challenge, allows them more participation, and does nothing to affect quality adversely (but perhaps improves it, because of their increased interest).

Kreman (1974) interviewed assembly line workers at the General Motors plant in Lordstown, Ohio, and one of the topics covered was "doubling up." One worker, in response to a question about quality, said:

> I'm working, working, working. If something else should happen, if I fell in the hole and missed a job, I call my sidekick again. He catches it, repairs it . . . you get 100 percent perfect. Because we don't want no problems, you know what I mean? We're doing a good job, and I defy you to find somebody who's doubling up disciplined for bad work. (1974: 140)

In another assembly plant (in which I worked) a similar approach was taken. In this plant "doubling up" could also mean two workers agreeing to do both jobs, but on every other car. Thus I do both jobs on cars 1, 3, 5, 7, and so on, and you do both on cars 2, 4, 6, 8. . . . One night while we were "doubling up" the foreman walked by, noted what we were doing, and said something to the effect that as long as we were not "sending repairs" then he "did not see" what we were doing.

In many cases, workers negotiated with each other to "trade" jobs for some period of time. In my case, the employee to my left and I often traded jobs for an hour or so as a means of reducing the boredom and monotony. The supervisor on that part of the automobile assembly line indicated that as long as we were sending no repairs and were not causing *him* problems, job trading (although against shop rules) was acceptable.

Job Enrichment

One of the more interesting forms of covert (and overt) negotiation to increase autonomy involves employees selling merchandise or services to other employees. The behaviors are interesting, because shop rules (the rules promulgated by the company) normally forbid selling items in a plant without permission (and permission is rarely granted). In the automobile plant in which I was employed, some of the "concession stands" were very elaborate, while others were run almost as an afterthought.[7] One coffee-and-doughnut concession, for example, had two large coffee urns operating continually throughout the shift, and the owner (entrepreneur) could be seen well before the start of his shift, arriving at the plant gate with numerous boxes of doughnuts and other pastries. How this man was also able to do his job (that is, the job for which he was paid by the automobile company) while also tending to his concession is hard to say. It appeared that other workers would act as counter help when the owner had to refill the urns or return to his "other" job. A slightly different situation confronted an employee in another production environment whose official job was to push a wheelbarrow around the plant collecting refuse, and whose unofficial job was to take bets. At least he did not have a truly machine-paced job to which he had to return.

What is so interesting about all the concession and sales gimmicks is not simply that they are declared to be illegal by the shop rules. It is first that the company knows they are there and yet ignores their existence. It often happened that supervisory personnel (even including plant superintendents) were observed standing in line for coffee or were seen sitting around the concession stand drinking coffee, eating a doughnut, and chatting with the hourly employees. The second point that makes the concession stands so interesting is that the company was (unknowingly) subsidizing the entrepreneurs in these concessions. The company was providing free electricity, free water, free space, and a large mass of captive customers. In addition, it would appear that none of the concession-stand operators bothered to pay taxes on purchases, even though the state demanded a certain amount of sales tax to be paid.

The workers who ran the concessions had added to the standard behaviors they were paid by the company to do. They had, on their own, taken on a second job while working at the first. They were moonlighting *on* the job, and yet they got away with it. They had created autonomous and challenging work situations for themselves through the creation of a second (and nonlegitimate) job within the boundaries of the first (legitimate) job.

Absenteeism

Absenteeism is often used as the classic example of worker deviance in the mass-production industry. As Aronowitz (1973: 26) indicates, automobile companies acknowledge that

> absenteeism, particularly on Mondays and Fridays, constitutes its most distressing discipline problem. Workers report line shutdowns "for as much as half hour" on Mondays because there are simply not enough people to perform the operations. But many young people are prepared to sacrifice higher earnings for a respite from the hassles of assembly line work, even for one day.

On this particular subject we can relate, in passing, a story that many workers have claimed to have heard (I heard about it "secondhand" from a number of persons with whom I worked). According to Norman (1972: 250):

> There is one story, often repeated and possibly apocryphal, about a worker who constantly showed up four days a week. His absence the remaining day was virtually certain. After this had gone on for a number of weeks, his foreman approached him:
>
> "Look, I've been noticing that you only show up four days out of the week. Do you want to tell me why you're only working the four days?"

"Because, man, I can't make enough money in three."

Absenteeism has become so prevalent that the workers in one plant who do not take days off often refer to those who do as "part timers."

It was true that there were many times when the plant in which I worked was late starting in the morning as the supervisors rushed around to find enough "heads" to man the line.[8] However, the majority of the workers who were interviewed indicated that they did not like the excessive absenteeism and that the company ought to do something about it.[9] The workers seemed to feel that taking time off occasionally was an acceptable form of job redesign, but abusing the privilege was not. Some time off to deal with one's feelings about the plant was an acceptable solution, but too much time off caused other workers to be penalized and therefore was wrong.

Rather than being a somewhat random phenomenon, absenteeism seems rationally considered by workers. Thus workers absent themselves on Mondays and Fridays to take advantage of longer weekends. Workers also choose other times to take their absences. One utility person said that he felt that

> people take time off because they're bored. They get tired of them same old routines. Maybe they don't like to work. Most generally now, it's been taking quite a few penalties [time off from work without pay] to get the problem straightened out. We've been having a lot of people off, which is strange when we're only working 40 hours. I could understand it when we were working all that overtime.[10]

It would appear that the utility person fails to understand the absenteeism problem—people take time off from work when they are working a "normal" shift and do not take time off when they are working large amounts of overtime. It seems, in other words, that workers who choose to take time off do so when the time away from work will cost them less. It is cheaper to take time off when pay is at straight time than when it is at time and one-half.

When questioning assembly line workers, some differences were noted in attitudes among various categories of workers in terms of their feelings about absenteeism. Those workers in the more repetitive (and consequently less interesting) jobs were more likely to say that they must take time off occasionally.[11] In addition, it is the people with the lower job satisfaction and the higher degrees of alienation who also felt they must occasionally take unauthorized time off. Finally, and somewhat contrary to what we might have expected, females also felt they needed to take days off more than did males. This latter finding may be owing to the fact that it is the women who tend to be in the lower status and consequently, less interesting, jobs.

Drug Use

Another area of great concern to companies and the unions is the use of drugs (including alcohol) among workers. According to O'Toole (1974: 85-86):

> Our interviews with blue-collar workers in heavy industry revealed a number who found it necessary to drink large quantities of alcohol during their lunch to enable them to withstand the pressure of overwhelming boredom of their tasks. Our interviews with younger workers on similar jobs uncovered a surprising amount of drug use on the job, particularly among assembly line workers and long haul truck drivers.[12]

Widick (1976: 14-15) also discussed the problems of substance abuse among automobile assembly line workers. Widick suggests that while drug abuse is becoming extremely prevalent, management and union officials continue to focus on alcohol as the substance most abused. My own observations suggest that both are used extensively—drugs among the young and alcohol among the older workers. The question for us is "What relevance does drug use have to the matter of increasing autonomy and challenge?"

How bad the problem of drug abuse on the line is depends to a great extent on whom one talks to. Workers tend *not* to see what they are doing as "abusing" various substances. A large number of workers see their drug use as positively functional—it helps them adapt to the boredom of their jobs. As one young male assembly line worker indicated, "if I smoke [marijuana] I can stare at a spot on the floor all day long and not get bored." The drug alters the perception of what one is doing as well as the time required in which to do it. On the assembly line, it is the passage of time (and not alone the boredom of the job) that is being adapted to through the use of drugs.[13] Or, as a popular country and western song entitled "Detroit City" (Bare: 1963) puts it: "By days I make the cars, by night I make the bars."

Drinking did seem to be relatively widespread in the plant on lunch breaks *and* on the job but it did not seem to affect the quality of the work as much as some people might think. I have seen Friday evening shifts when a number of bottles were being passed around, and yet the workers seemed able to keep up with the speed of the line and with no obvious decrease in quality.[14] It was not unknown for a worker to bring a plastic gallon milk bottle into the plant filled with orange juice and vodka or gin. How it was brought into the plant past the security guards is not clear. One worker who did bring in liquor with some regularity claimed to be sufficiently well-connected in the plant that he was easily able to get away with it.

The use of other drugs in the plant was also widespread. While the drug of choice (after alcohol) tended to be marijuana, I have seen workers using a variety of other drugs (often in combination). One worker bragged, for instance, that he was a user of heroin, had an illegal prescription for a codeine-morphine cough syrup, usually drank a few beers at lunch time, and smoked marijuana while on the job. He also had to be sent to the company hospital one evening because he appeared overdosed on his various "medications." On another occasion a worker was unable to finish his shift either because of drugs or alcohol, or both. The other workers "hid him" so he would not be disciplined, and then they did his work for him so that he would not be missed.

The repetitive nature of the job and the degree that the worker is alienated either from self or from the job, as well as a low level of job satisfaction, all led to a greater probability that he or she will have gotten high while working on the line. While in many other areas there was a noticeable difference between males and females, there was none here.

When asked about smoking marijuana, workers seemed to be divided on its positive and negative effects. One worker, a male assembler, said the following:

> I know a few guys that gets completely messed up and they can run their job just as good as when they're straight. There's a lot who couldn't. On second shift, I've seen them take a guy and hide him 'cause he was so messed up. I don't like to get stoned when I'm working, 'cause I don't know if I've done the whole car or not. On Christmas I was drunk in there. I was drunk before we even got started. I smoked a bit too. We went in that day and I didn't like the feeling, I was scared I'd get caught.

At Christmas time, this worker was not the only one who was drunk. A large number of the workers appeared at work that morning at the 6:00 a.m. starting time, and they were, like this young man, already drunk. One worker wanted me to share a marijuana cigarette with him so that we would be better able to get through the day—this at shortly after 6:00 a.m. I refused.

The alternative view of the use of drugs can be summarized in the words of a male extraman, when asked if he thought there was a drug problem in the plant:

> I don't think so, any more than alcohol is. Maybe less of a problem. From my point of view, I can work better when I'm stoned. I'm more in control of my hand-eye coordination than I would be drinking. Drinkin' is harder to shake the effects of than pot. That's about all I can relate it to, 'cause I don't do chemicals. Maybe I'll take a "cross-roads" [amphetamine pill marked with a cross] now and then.

The opinion of this worker, as well as many others I spoke to, is that the use of drugs actually improves a person's performance on the assembly line. The improvement occurs through an increasing ability to tolerate the relatively high levels of boredom and monotony in the jobs.[15] As with absenteeism, negative reactions by other workers occur only when a person's behavior causes others hardship. Management, on the other hand, generally deals more harshly with this problem (unless, of course, the worker is well-connected).

Workers use drugs (including alcohol) to change the nature of the jobs. This change involves adjusting the challenge and autonomy through (1) raising the risk of termination if caught, (2) decreasing boredom through anesthetization, and (3) increasing conviviality of the social group that centers around the sanctioned behavior.

SUMMARY AND CONCLUSIONS

Workers know that certain behaviors go against society's standards, but see these behaviors as adaptations to life on the assembly line. Only when the behavior goes beyond the limits defined by the informal rules is it considered "bad." I know my behavior is dysfunctional, the group may know my behavior is dysfunctional, the management may know my behavior is dysfunctional, but until what I do goes beyond acceptable limits nothing will be said or done. Nothing will be said or done even if my behavior violates formal rules promulgated by the company or society. Everyone knows that violating federal safety rules is wrong unless there are extenuating circumstances that are defined as such by those involved—management, other workers, or the union. In a sense, all behavior is filtered through the informal rule structures and it is at the filtration point that the modifier "good" or "bad" is attached (Lupton, 1976; Meissner, 1976).

In the plants, for behavior to be "bad" deviance it must violate commonly accepted definitions of the proper way for an employee to act—and these definitions may or may not be part of the official rules of the company. What has come to be defined as deviant is that which affects other workers in a negative manner. Violence, drug use, absenteeism: All are defined as deviant by workers when that behavior affects them. Absenteeism is not acceptable (and thus is deviant) when too few workers are on hand to start the line. Drugs are acceptable as long as they are used in moderation; they are not acceptable when the worker becomes dangerous to himself or others.

The deviant behavior noted, while serious, may be the kind of behavior that arises in situations where workers have to use only a small portion of their minds.[16] Workers expand their jobs and thus their autonomy through behavior that management often calls deviant. This is not to say that the company ought not to be concerned about deviance nor that the company ought to do nothing about it. Rather, it would appear that the company might look on the deviance as being a reaction to boredom and not necessarily as a means for "getting back" at the company. In order to "cure" the deviant behavior, the company would do best to "cure" the boredom and monotony that accompany the job of assembly line workers. Thus companies might well ask for volunteers who want to learn more than one job at a time. One approach might involve constituting these workers in groups of five, which would mean that employees could rotate to a different job on each day of the week. Clearly, other approaches might also be feasible if worked out with the concurrence of the local union.

NOTES

1. Data for this article were gathered through participant-observation during employment as well as through interviews of selected employees. The plants on which these observations are based are engaged in coking and automobile manufacturing.

2. Note also Ritzer (1972: 300), who suggests in his discussion that there is both legal and illegal deviance. Bryant (1974a and b), discusses violations of social norms, about which we could also ask, violation from whose point of view?

3. See also Hackman and Oldham (1980: Chapter 4).

4. Empire building is a term used by Strauss to describe the development of elaborate social networks in the plant.

5. I may also be attempting to overcome the nonchallenging nature of the job rather than trying to create challenge.

6. For a popular treatment of theft, see Johnny Cash's 1976 song, "One piece at a time."

7. Items for sale included numbers (i.e., illegal betting), cutlery, macrame, peanut brittle, popcorn and numerous chemical substances. The latter were sold much more covertly than the rest.

8. Calling the workers "heads" has nothing to do with the worker's propensity to use dope, but is symptomatic of the majority of the supervisors' attitudes toward the workers—they are not people, they are "heads." This attitude was manifested throughout the ranks of the managers I was in contact with, and was true for both staff and line managers. When confronted by such attitudes, it should not surprise us to find workers searching for ways to increase autonomy.

9. For a company look at absenteeism, see Oldsmobile Division, 1971. See also Runcie (1980b).

10. This same comment could probably be used to explain much of the deviance in the plant.

11. Walker and Guest (1952: 120) found basically the same relationship, albeit thirty years earlier.

12. On the subject of drug use among truck drivers, see a contradictory statement in Runcie (1971: 242-246).

13. There were numerous times on the line when I was sure that at least two hours had passed and when I checked my watch I found that less than one-half hour had gone by. Time on the line can drag and when it does, workers find ways to occupy their minds— either through games or through some form of anesthetic.

14. I have also seen foremen engaging in drinking with the workers in such situations. While the foremen's drinking is not done flagrantly, when workers see this it cannot have a positive effect on their feelings toward official company statements against drinking on the job.

15. A suggestion that some form of controlled test of this folk wisdom be undertaken by the company was not met with great enthusiasm.

16. Deviance of the type mentioned here occurs in environments that are not machine paced as well (e.g., universities, offices, and so on). The degree to which this deviance is used to further autonomy can only be assumed at this point.

8

THE COMMUNICATION OF POWER RELATIONS IN ORGANIZATIONS THROUGH CULTURAL RITES

Janice M. Beyer

New York University

Harrison M. Trice

Cornell University

Scholars in organizational communication, like those in other fields of organizational studies, have recently begun to examine cultural aspects of organizations as a way of furthering their understanding (e.g., Pacanowsky and O'Donnell-Trujillo, 1982; Putnam and Pacanowsky, 1983). Taking a cultural perspective helps to sensitize researchers to the complexities inherent in the social processes of communication. Communicative acts—like other acts—do not have single consequences. They have multiple consequences. Each can have, at one and the same time, both intended and unintended, manifest and latent, practical and expressive, and functional and dysfunctional consequences (Trice and Beyer, 1984b). Also, from a cultural perspective all actions, whether intentionally communicative or not, have the potential of expressing meanings—that is, of communicating.

Understanding organizational communication processes is central to understanding organizational cultures because cultures are based on shared understandings and meanings (Trice and Beyer, 1984b; Pettigrew, 1979; Schein, 1983a, 1983b). The central question for those studying organizational cultures is how understandings and meanings come to be shared by members of the culture. One obvious answer is through communication. Thus, researchers in organizational culture inevitably face the more specific question of how the understandings and meanings of a culture are communicated among members. Various approaches have been taken to begin to answer this question. Among the most prominent are those that focus on the symbolic aspects of organizational life (Putnam and Pacanowsky, 1983; Pfeffer, 1981), on myths, stories, and sagas (Martin et al., 1983; Clark, 1972; Wilkins, 1983b), on language (Meissner, 1976; Roy, 1959, 1960; Pondy, 1978), and on socialization (Van Maanen, 1973; Schein, 1978; Louis, 1980). This paper extends the latter approach, which incorporates rites of passage, to identify and analyze a wider variety of rites that are present in modern organizational life.

In an earlier paper (Trice and Beyer, 1984b), we defined rites as relatively elaborate, dramatic, planned sets of activities that consolidate various forms of cultural expression into organized events, which are carried out through social interaction, usually for the benefit of an audience. Six types of rites that occur in both modern organizations and in the accounts of tribal life written by anthropologists were identified. Table 8.1 lists and gives organizational examples of these rites.

Because they involve a dramatic presentation of multiple forms of culture—each of which conveys messages about the underlying meanings of the culture—rites are important vehicles for communicating and affirming the shared meanings that constitute the substance of a culture to its members (Beyer and Trice, 1987). As Rohlen has pointed out, rites can be very potent communicators of the culture because "fragments of the ideology presented on each occasion are sufficient to suggest the entire arrangement [to members of that culture]" (Rohlen, 1973: 43).

Rites also provide important communications about a culture to outsiders, including researchers. Geertz commented that "the culture of a people is an ensemble of texts, themselves ensembles . . . which the anthropologist strains to read over the shoulders of those to whom they properly belong" (1973: 29). Thus those who want to discover the meanings of a culture must look at the many different ways in which that culture is communicated to its members. Rites provide especially rich occasions in which to read a culture because they typically consolidate several culturally expressive forms—e.g., myths, stories, legends, sagas, rituals, symbols, language, gestures, settings, and artifacts—into an event or a coordinated series of events. Furthermore, because they are preplanned, public, and held for the benefit of an audience in which the researcher may be minimally reactive, rites are more convenient, practical, and accessible for researchers to study than some of the other expressions of culture (Trice, 1985b).

Schein (1983b) suggested that cultural meanings and understandings operate at several levels of awareness. In his schema, assumptions are

TABLE 8.1 Examples of Six Rites Occurring in Modern Organizations

Type of Rite	Examples
Rites of passage	managerial and occupational training programs
Rites of enhancement	performance awards, tenure conferral in academia
Rites of degradation	congressional censure, firing of corporate chief executive officers
Rites of conflict reduction	collective bargaining, ombudsmen
Rites of integration	company Thanksgiving dinner, festivals
Rites of renewal	quality-of-work-life programs, employee assistance programs

the meanings and understandings that form the most basic, taken-for-granted, unconscious level. From Kluckhohn and Stodtbeck (1961), he identified five sets of issues that cultural assumptions are concerned with: relationships with the environment; the nature of reality, time, and space; human nature; the nature of human activity; and the nature of human relationships. Building on Clegg's ideas (1975), Conrad (1983) argued that power is important for organizational communication because it affects the structures of interpretation that connect surface dimensions of meanings with deeper structures like assumptions.

Other researchers have pointed out that the issues surrounding power itself are important and central in the meanings and understandings that form the substance of a given culture. Weisz et al. (1984) recently contrasted Japanese and U.S. cultures in terms of their relative emphasis on what they called primary and secondary control. They defined primary control as the way in which "individuals enhance their rewards by influencing existing realities" and secondary control as the way in which "individuals enhance their rewards by accommodating to existing realities and maximizing satisfaction or goodness of fit with things as they are" (1984: 955). According to their analysis of childhood socialization practices, religion and philosophy, work values, and the practice of psychotherapy in the two countries, U.S. culture emphasizes primary control, while Japanese culture emphasizes secondary control. In U.S. culture, the self is all-important, and enhancing power for self is the preoccupation; in Japanese culture, harmony is all-important and the power of the collectivity and maintaining social order are the preoccupations.

Such cultural understandings about power concern two of Schein's five basic assumptions: the relationship with the environment and the nature of human relationships. From the Weisz et al. (1984) analysis, the U.S. culture shapes its members to want to dominate and control both their environment and other persons; the Japanese culture, on the other hand, shapes its members to be more willing to surrender some personal control so that they can better harmonize with their environment and with other persons.

In this article we will focus upon primary and secondary control as two sets of rather different meanings and understandings associated with power and will consider how each is communicated through organizational rites that we and others have observed in U.S. organizations. Examples of each of the six specific rites identified in Table 8.1 will be discussed and analyzed in terms of typical messages that each is likely to convey about power relations in organizations, and about primary and secondary control. The analyses that follow are based on our interpretation and on those of other scholars. They are intended to be illustrative; their applicability to particular rites in particular organizational settings is, of course, a matter for further study.

COMMUNICATING POWER RELATIONS THROUGH RITES

Rites of Passage

As Van Gennep (1960) observed, all societies use rites of passage to facilitate the transition of persons into roles and statuses that are new to them. Such rites as marriages, funerals, initiations, commencements, and retirement dinners are used in modern societies when persons pass from one distinct social status to another. Because all statuses carry with them certain powers and privileges, rites of passage give those who are the focus of the rites certain new powers; they also relieve them of certain old constraints, but are likely to subject them to new ones.

Rites of passage ideally incorporate three distinct stages. The first is the *rite of separation*, during which the focal person is symbolically, and often physically, removed from his or her current status. For example, in a management training program we observed, the recruits selected from rank and file employees were physically removed from their normal work settings into assessment centers, where they were tested and evaluated for two weeks. This first phase communicated both to the participants and to the audience (other members of the organization) that the recruits had been identified as candidates to receive additional powers and that they were going to be carefully screened and tested to be sure they were worthy to actually assume these new powers. Meanwhile, they were separated from their old statuses as a sign and indication that they would no longer have these statuses in the future, if they were selected for the new status. In this particular rite, the scientific trappings of extended testing symbolized the rationality that is valued in managerial cultures, in general (Trice et al., 1969; Feldman and March, 1981). Testing helped to provide a "rational" basis on which candidates could be certified as worthy to exercise additional powers. Such certification was bound to reassure the new candidates themselves and thus relieve some of their tensions about having and exercising new powers (Conrad, 1983: 190); it was also likely to reassure those not selected or those who would be subject to the new powers assumed by these candidates that they would exercise these new powers appropriately.

The second stage is the *rite of transition*, during which the focal person(s) is instructed with new information and lore about the status to be assumed and put through various ordeals that represent, in concentrated form, the new problems, difficulties, and responsibilities associated with that new status. In the managerial training program observed, this stage included a three-day sensitivity training program, in which the trainees experienced the ordeals of ritualized small-group processes during which others in their groups fed back to them their impressions of their behaviors in the group, how well they communicated, and in general how they, as group members, reacted to them. Other examples of elaborate rites of transition are commonly found in the training of recruits into dangerous and anxiety-producing occupations, such as the military (Bourne, 1967), police (Van Maanen, 1973), firefighters (McCarl, 1976), doctors (Becker et al., 1961), and even missionaries (Wilson, 1981).

The ordeals undergone by novice smoke jumpers, whose jobs entail parachuting into forest fires in locations difficult to reach by other means, illustrate how rites of transition both communicate new information, and also symbolically and practically prepare recruits for the rigors of their new status. The first month rookies spend on the job is "one of almost total submission to a strict regimen of physical conditioning, parachute handling, landing techniques, power jumps, equipment construction and repair, mental conditioning, and physical harassment from experienced jumpers, squad leaders, and pilots" (McCarl, 1976: 49-50). Clearly, in such rites the experienced members of the occupation are demonstrating their expert power by instructing the rookies in how to technically perform the various tasks associated with that occupation. The message is clear: We have lots of expertise (and power) and you have next to none.

Also, by their harassing activities the present members of the occupation are signalling to the initiates that this occupation has distinct boundaries, that not everyone will necessarily be accepted within these boundaries, that conformity and some degree of submission to the existing group are necessary to win this acceptance, and in general, that the initiates should not try to assume power—either interpersonal or expert—too quickly. The initiates are also being told that they are in a liminal state—that they do not yet belong to the new status to which they aspire; they are still only in transition toward that status and its powers. In many ways, the experienced members of the occupation let the rookies know that they are not yet ready to assume the powers that they, as experienced members, have.

The third phase of rites of passage is the *rite of incorporation*, during which the focal person(s) actually assumes the new status. In the management training we observed, during the incorporation rites the trainees were brought back to the plant, where a brief induction rite was held during a shut-down of the production processes. The production superintendent gave a short speech emphasizing the rigors of the training that the recruits had just received. He then read the names and new positions of each of the new managers, thus formally assigning them their new statuses and powers as "bosses." A cocktail party in honor of the new managers took place in a nearby management club that evening; wives and other managers were invited. This final event clearly was intended to communicate that the new members were now part of the management group, and so were their wives.

Rites of passage also communicate messages about the issues surrounding both primary and secondary control (Weisz et al., 1984). By according people new statuses and their accompanying powers, it is obvious that rites of passage may increase the feelings of primary control of those who pass from one status to another. However, some rites can actually decrease feelings of primary control because they remove whatever powers the former status conferred. For example, a retirement dinner serves notice to all that the person(s) retiring will no longer have the powers of the old status. Probably, most rites of passage involve both increments and decrements in primary control. For example, through a marriage ceremony, the persons married may gain some powers and privileges, but they also lose some of the powers and privileges they formally had as dependent children. Rites of passage are also likely to increase feelings of secondary control in areas that could be sources of uncertainty for the focal person(s). In particular, the ordeals undergone foreshadow and tend to prepare the initiate, at both a practical and emotional level, to accept the additional responsibilities and constraints of the new role, which might decrease the individual's feelings of primary control and thus require some compensating increase in feelings of secondary control.

Rites of Enhancement

As defined in our earlier work (Trice and Beyer, 1984b), rites of enhancement are used to mark a distinct improvement in a person's social identity and personal power. They differ from rites of passage in that the enhanced persons are already in well-defined roles, and the rites provide occasions to applaud their performance in that role. In the recent rediscovery of culture, management and organizational researchers have uncovered many examples of these rites of modern corporations. Deal and Kennedy (1982a: 61) described "attaboy" plaques presented with much flourish and ceremony during regular working hours to recognize exceptional work dedication; similar awards in other companies include special jackets for those who have accumulated 100 points for above-average performance, attendance, and few errors (*Time*, 1983: 46); and the "you want it when" award, in which scrolls are presented to persons who exhibited exceptional efforts, like working overtime and late at night (*Harvard Business Review*, 1980: 111).

The tenure conferral rite in academic organizations provides an excellent example of how rites of enhancement communicate multiple messages about power. In general, rites of enhancement reinforce the power of those who have formal authority by showing that they have the power to evaluate and reward others. The series of meetings and decisions by various faculty groups—the department, an ad hoc committee, the school-wide faculty—involved in most tenure conferral rites reinforces a crucial component of collegial authority, namely, the collective power of faculty to evaluate and judge one another, and to make all decisions concerning academic matters. Even the advice used by the faculty reinforces collegial power; only other high-status and tenured members of the professoriate are normally called upon to provide outside assessments of the qualifications of the candidate. Whether or not the recommendations of the faculty in tenure decisions are usually followed by the deans, president, and members of the board of trustees carries important messages about who has ultimate control in that university or college. If the faculty recommendations are usually followed, the faculty have collegial control. If they are often overturned, the administration has the balance of power and the university or college cannot be considered collegial in its governance. Also, of course, all of the effort expended to reach a decision carries the message that this is an important role and status, and thus serves to increase the prestige and power of the focal professor and of the professorial status, in general, in that organization.

At a more immediate level, rites of enhancement also give power to those who decide who will be enhanced by providing them with the opportunity to reinforce some behaviors and not others. Through conferring tenure on some persons and not others, and through the criteria that are inferred by onlookers from the decisions made, senior faculty can shape the behaviors of junior faculty to perpetuate their own values—particularly their research interests—in succeeding generations. The faculty member who gains tenure has been reinforced for certain behaviors; other junior faculty, who are usually watching very closely for signals, are provided with vicarious learning and sanctioned role models worthy of emulation. Those faculty who exhibit unapproved patterns of behavior are not rewarded, and indeed, may fail to obtain tenure, in which case, they are usually forced to leave that department.

By enhancing certain individuals on a selective basis, rites of enhancement probably increase their feelings of primary control. Even when individuals are rewarded for service to the collectivity, they gain in individual stature and power. For example, an unmistakable message received by those who achieve tenure is that they now have more primary control. Less obvious is that, as already discussed, these rites also increase feelings of primary control among those who make the evaluation and decision about tenure. Rites of enhancement are also likely to affect feelings of secondary control among members of the audience—in the case of a tenure decision, those junior faculty who are watching and learning vicariously what they can expect to happen in their cases. Where the rite is most effectively practiced, junior faculty members who observe the tenure rites of others may thereby recognize that they are unlikely to be awarded tenure by their senior faculty; they can then accommodate to that reality by leaving for another position before they come up for tenure, rationalizing that they did not fit with the standards of that particular department or school.

Rites of Degradation

Rites of degradation signal the destruction of a powerful social identity and its replacement by a downgraded one. These rites are not precise opposites to rites of enhancement because they are usually reserved for relatively powerful members of the collectivity, whereas any member of the collectivity is eligible for enhancement. Like rites of passage, rites of degradation ideally have three stages: rites of separation, discrediting rites, and rites of removal.

In the first stage, focal persons are *separated* from other members of the organization or other collectivity by focusing attention on them in such a way as to associate them with problems and failures. This stage serves to question the basis and legitimacy of their power. The second stage involves *discrediting* the focal persons with data or other evidence substantiating the accusations implicit in the first stage. This stage serves to justify the next stage. The third stage involves the actual *removal* of some of the valued statuses and powers of the focal person.

The attempted impeachment of Richard Nixon is an example of a truncated rite of degradation because, although the separation and discrediting rites clearly occurred during the long investigation of the House Judiciary Committee, he resigned rather than face the full degradation of actual removal from office. The censure in 1983 of two U.S. congressmen for sexual involvements with congressional pages was carried to its denouement, but did not involve actual removal of the two men from office. However, they certainly suffered decrements in power, since they were stripped of their committee posts; they also suffered loss of esteem and personal influence as they were publicly rebuked in front of a national television audience and their assembled colleagues. The high level of emotionality at the censure ceremony was evidenced by the fact that one of the two congressmen broke down and cried during it. The other gave an equally emotional defensive statement, denying any wrongdoing. Other classic and complete rites of degradation involving the firing of chief executive officers of the Northrop and Gulf Corporations were described by Pfeffer (1981).

Like rites of enhancement, rites of degradation proclaim the power of those who are judging and changing the status of the focal person(s). Often, these ceremonies serve to reinforce the power of the collectivity itself rather than the power of particular members within it. Ultimately it was not the power of Congress that was proclaimed in the impeachment and censures just discussed, but the power of the U.S. citizenry. All societies must make some provisions to deal with instances when persons must have power taken away from them in order to avoid severe strains on the social order. Degradation ceremonies thus are often enacted on behalf of the entire collectivity by designated representatives of that collectivity.

Somewhat paler versions of rites of degradation have been called *rites of intimidation* (O'Day, 1974). Such rites are used to deal with persons—such as whistleblowers—who are seen by those in authority as presenting threats to their legitimacy or to the social order of the collectivity they control. The process and steps are the same as for rites of degradation. However, rites of intimidation appear to affirm, reinforce, and protect the power of the officials involved, rather than that of the society or collectivity as a whole. Lee Iacocca (1984) recently described the rites of intimidation that Henry Ford used against him when Iacocca was president of Ford Motor Company. First, Ford called in consultants who decided that the company should be run by a troika, thus substantially diluting Iacocca's power as president. Ford subsequently added a third member to the top management team. Next, Ford discredited him by questioning and investigating whether Iacocca was connected to the Mafia through a business associate and friend. Moving to the third stage, Ford next began to threaten to fire Iacocca in talks with members of the board of directors, finally threatening to resign if Iacocca was not fired. According to his account, Iacocca tried to ignore and overcome Ford's attempts to intimidate and degrade him, but in the end, Iacocca resigned. This is often what happens with whistleblowers; they are not actually fired, but are intimidated into resignations.

Clearly, the focal person's feelings of primary control are drastically reduced through rites of degradation. The larger system of power that rests in the general social consensus is powerfully reaffirmed, and thus, in a sense, all members of the collectivity involved may experience feelings of increased primary control. The main messages of rites of degradation for secondary control concern the necessity that all persons accommodate themselves to existing realities, including whatever constraints may limit their primary control. The main messages of rites of intimidation regarding secondary control are that members of the collectivity must accommodate themselves to those persons who presently have more formal power and authority than they do.

Rites of Conflict Reduction

Unlike the previous rites, the next three rites operate at the collective level. Rites of conflict reduction, for example, have the manifest and intended purpose of reducing conflict and aggression among mutually hostile factions. They moderate the disruptive and aggressive impulses that arise within groups or among groups in a larger system. The same factors that tend to produce subcultures or countercultures are the target of rites of conflict reduction, which seek to reduce hostilities arising from perceived differences. Such rites, however, do not resolve these differences; they merely manage them by reducing their disruptive consequences.

Modern organizations use various mechanisms to enact rites of conflict reduction. Some observers (Pfeffer, 1981; Edelman, 1964) see committees, task forces, and other such groups as pervasive rites of conflict reduction. Often these entities do not need to make substantive changes to reduce conflict. Their existence and holding meetings are sufficient to dissipate endemic conflicts for a while. Other common mechanisms are ombudsmen, ethics committees, consumer complaints departments, and various other roles and groups whose task it is to negotiate some kind of peaceable solution to problems involving adversaries.

The most prominent such rite in modern work organizations is collective bargaining. In the early stages, management and labor each present long and extravagant lists of proposals—far more than either expects to obtain. As ritualized bargaining proceeds, informal cooperation tends to emerge via norms of reciprocity with each side responding to the other's proposal with "alternating moves" in which "each side is expected to step toward the other's position—most simply demonstrated in percentage point moves of wage negotiations, each side offering a point in turn" (Glick, 1983: 8). In the process of negotiations, "false fights" often occur in which "tough stands" are taken; midnight sessions are held to dramatize the conflict, even though both sides are much aware that these behaviors cloak the realistic outcomes expected by both sides (Blum, 1961).

In terms of power, rites of conflict reduction are efforts sanctioned by collectivities to try to minimize power differences that are causing or have the potential of causing overt conflict. The interests of the collectivity are in sufficiently resolving the conflicts so that the social order will not be so severely disrupted that the system cannot continue to operate. Basically these rites convey the message that both sides are powerful, and if they do not resolve their differences peaceably, the whole system could be threatened. Through the rite, the larger system is telling the combatants that they must reduce their conflicts to avoid damage to the larger system. The combatants are also reminded that to proceed to overt conflict is to risk losing some of their power—either because they could suffer deleterious consequences from hostile acts, or because, if they are perceived as intransigent, they will lose the acceptance and legitimacy conferred by the larger system.

Negotiation is a conflict reduction mechanism that is suited to cultures that emphasize primary control. If the parties are concerned with risks of losing primary control, the very act of negotiation is an acknowledgement by the other side that they have some power. Negotiation is clearly one way to avoid losing all primary control or power. In societies where secondary control is more important, rites of conflict reduction may focus more directly on inducing participants to surrender or give up primary control. For example, the Andaman Islanders use a rite of conflict reduction in which members of hostile factions are randomly assigned to two different roles in a dance. During the dance, one set of dancers shakes the other set; those who are shaken are expected to respond with acceptance and even humor (Radcliffe-Brown, 1964). In terms of increasing their feelings of secondary control, they are being encouraged by the collectivity to dramatically accommodate themselves to a difficult reality—namely, that others can have sufficient power over them to cause them discomfort. The randomness of the way in which the participants are assigned their roles also appears to carry the message that being in a favored position can be a chance event; next time, the powerful (the shakers) could be on the other side, and be the ones who are powerless (are shaken).

Rites of Integration

Although relatively frequent in modern organizations, rites of integration—which encourage and revive common feelings that bind members together and commit them to a social system—are not nearly so potent in these collectivities as they are in tribal societies. These rites are quite inclusive, usually public, and secular in the sense that they flourish in rather complicated systems where subcultures inevitably form. Divergent subcultures increase their interactions with one another through their common participation in these rites. One function of many modern holidays and festivals "seems to be to give occasion for men to rejoice together—to interact in an ambience of acceptance and conviviality—thus the festival is a prime device for promoting social cohesion, for integrating individuals and groups into a society" (Smith, 1972: 167).

Dandridge (1983) observed an interesting rite of integration in a manufacturing company. In this company, an annual layoff of production workers usually occurred just before Christmas. The layoff was announced, however, in late November. The announcement was followed by a management-financed and employee-prepared Thanksgiving dinner held in the production areas of the plant. In one way or another, almost all employees played some role in the preparation of the dinner. Members of management, in turn, served the employees as they filed by the food-laden tables. Both participated in cleaning up and generally returning the production area to its former condition.

This rite, like other rites of integration, attempted to minimize power differences. It communicated to all involved that status differences were not very important when all got together, and that interaction across statuses was both possible and desirable. All gained in primary power because all were included as belonging to the group, and thus had the power that membership conveys. The rite thus encouraged feelings of reflected power coming from identification with the company and its power. It also served to remind the relatively powerful that they should not be too distant from those they govern, and that they were not really so different from them. It thus encouraged them to curb somewhat their impulses toward primary control by reminding them that their power rested on the good will and cooperation of the workers. Also, the role reversal involved in management serving food to the workers in this particular rite conveyed to both workers and management that this company was governed according to an egalitarian ethos, and that management felt workers were important and "as good" as they were.

However, rites of integration do not always achieve their intended purposes. If members of subcultures and countercultures are not persuaded that they want to belong, these rites can further aggravate feelings of differences and accompanying tensions. Those who feel different may rebel and resist the rite in one way or another, even using the rite to express openly their grievances with the larger system. During the 1960s and 1970s, student rebels in universities frequently used commencement ceremonials as occasions to stage demonstrations or to wear silly costumes that ridiculed the meaning of the commencement rite, and by implication, the meaning of higher education.

Rites of Renewal

These rites rejuvenate and reinforce existing social arrangements and help to legitimate the current social order. In effect, they refurbish the status quo and make it more palatable. In modern societies where rationality is an overriding value, research is frequently used as a rite of renewal. Edelman (1977), for example, pointed out that the findings of social science research may reinforce the power of decision makers and detract from their opponents' powers. Weiss (1981: 200) observed that "merely sponsoring research and analysis can be a ritual protection by giving the organization and its authorities the coloration of rationality and responsiveness." To Feldman and March (1981: 410), the overconsumption of research information in work organizations indicated "that information use symbolizes a commitment to rational choice. Displaying the symbol reaffirms the importance of this social value and signals personal and organizational competence."

Other common rites of renewal in modern organizations include the many programs ostensibly intended to change and improve organizations; they include such efforts as organizational development activities, MBO programs, job redesign efforts, and quality-of-work-life programs. Although many of these programs are advertised as and proclaimed to be change efforts, there is a dearth of evidence that they have lasting practical consequences. The persistence of such energy and effort devoted to activities without evident practical consequences is a likely sign that the activities involved are preserved for their expressive rather than their practical consequences. In addition, such programs rarely propose changes that are likely to disturb the existing social order. Rather, they are efforts that result in "fine tuning the system" (Burke, 1980: 431).

A less well-known variant of an ostensible change program that is really a rite of renewal is the Employee Assistance Program, or EAP. Like many of the other programs already mentioned, these programs are ostensibly designed to remove possible impediments to employees' productivity—in this case, by assisting them with any personal problems that may be interfering with their productivity. To the degree that EAPs succeed in their aims, they certainly qualify as rites of renewal, because they help to refurbish and strengthen existing work arrangements (Trice, 1985a). They also tend to minimize disruptions to ongoing arrangements from employees' personal problems. In a recent field study of several of these programs in a large corporation (Trice and Beyer, 1984a), we found that they had several other expressive consequences consistent with rites of renewal. Interviews with top level managers revealed that they felt that major benefits of these programs included the support and protection they afforded to lower levels of supervision in dealing with disruptive employees, and the renewal of confidence in the company the program engendered among rank-and-file employees. Management was concerned that the company had suffered a loss in confidence among employees as a result of unprecedented layoffs that had occurred during the economic recession of the early 1970s.

By refurbishing and strengthening existing social structures, rites of renewal clearly reinforce existing distributions of power. They communicate that the status quo is basically right and proper and only requires minor adjustments to work even better than before. To the degree that these rites succeed in making the existing arrangements more effective and increase their legitimacy among those subject to them, they tend to increase managerial power and control (Warner, 1981: 172). Although some of these rites are advertised as ways to achieve power equalization, none gives workers power to decide anything of consequence for the system as a whole (Perrow, 1972). It is conceivable, however, that they may sometimes increase workers' feelings of primary control. They also acknowledge that power differences exist to the degree that they deal explicitly with issues of power equalization.

What is most interesting about these rites is that they are likely to strongly reinforce the dominant tendencies in U.S. culture toward valuing primary over secondary control. Consistent with dominant cultural values, those who design such rites assume that U.S. workers desire and therefore should have increased primary control over their work environments and relationships. Although the programs usually fail to deliver this increased primary control to workers, tending instead to increase the primary control of management, the ideologies they proclaim may contribute to undermining workers' beliefs and values supporting secondary control. A likely result is that those who are inclined to accommodate to existing realities are encouraged to believe that they can have more primary control—which is, unfortunately, usually not very realistic.

IMPLICATIONS

Whether or not organizational cultures can be deliberately created, changed, and managed is currently a matter of controversy. Some writers on culture express grave doubts that managers can create, change, or control organizational cultures (Uttal, 1983; Schwartz and Davis, 1981). Others are comforted by the notion that culture is basically a spontaneous creation of ordinary people, and thus cannot be imposed from above (Dorson, 1972). Some feel that the diversity of subcultures within organizations militates against their homogenization into a single, dominant culture (Barley and Louis, 1983). Still others argue that cultures can probably only be changed in minor ways— deflected slightly into new trajectories—by the efforts of management (Martin and Siehl, 1983). Although we do not believe cultures are easy to change, we agree with Jones (1985a) that, like other social phenomena, cultures inevitably change, and that it is natural for managers and others who seek power to attempt to initiate and manage such changes. Our analysis of cultural rites and power in organizations suggests to us that those who control organizational rites control a form of communication that can help to reinforce or change existing distributions of power.

Although our interpretations of the cultural meaning of various rites are only suggestive at this stage, it is striking how easy it was to read somewhat different messages about power into each of these six rites. From even this brief analysis it seems clear to us that many rites probably convey important messages about the distribution of power in organizations, and about primary and secondary control. Furthermore, it seems highly likely that multiple messages, focusing on different members of the culture, are involved. In sum, our interpretative analysis of just a few examples of these rites strongly suggests that they could be rich sources of data on the communication of culture.

A combination of research methods would clearly be desirable to learn more about how rites communicate culture. Systematic observation combined with unstructured interviews of sponsors, participants, and members of the audience would be a good place to start.

Finally, if we want to consider all of the ramifications of culture and power, we must address the difficult issue of what effects we, as social scientists, are likely to have when we investigate and explain how cultures work in modern organizations. Thus far, research on organizational cultures has proceeded in the same spirit as most past research on organizations—which was typically designed and carried out without much concern for the possible effects of implementing its findings. In particular, the focus on cultures seems a logical extension of the recent emphasis on cognitive processes in organizations (Weick, 1969; Staw, 1980). What makes both cognitive and cultural research different from past research is that it seeks to tap forces that are less conscious and thus potentially more insidious than those tapped by most previous research. Presumably, the less obvious the phenomena being manipulated, the less the opportunity for those who are targets to be aware of or able to resist the manipulation. Some researchers studying cultures are at least aware of the dangers; Smircich (1983b: 239) recently stated that she hoped new knowledge gained by research in the cultural tradition will be used to create nonoppressive power systems. This is a laudable hope. But with popular treatments of how to manage cultures selling like hotcakes, and U.S. managers playing "catch up"—just how realistic is it?

PART III

THE ARTS OF ORGANIZING

"A well turned investigation is something like a well turned piece of furniture," remarked Sandra Sutherland, a private investigator in San Francisco. "There are cases where everything fits together beautifully," she said; "facts and procedures flow into logical conclusions." The result is "the elegant solution," as her husband, also a detective, phrases it, "meaning a solution that cuts through chaos to utter simplicity." Such a case he calls "the perfect job," she added. For, she explained, "We're after . . . not so much the truth, but coherence."

When asked what the perfect job would be from her point of view, Sutherland replied, "the chance to do a case where the only limitations would be the reach of your own creative abilities: no time or money considerations." Under such conditions, she implied, the ideal form of investigation, culminating in an elegant solution, might be attained more often. "The reality," however, she explained, "is you do the best you can with what you're allowed" (Lewis, 1979: 74).

Words and concepts essential to a study of art appear in the statements above: beauty, elegance, perfection, and the like. Rarely, however, are detectives, managers, secretaries, executives, accountants, or others whose livelihood does not entail sculpting or producing easel paintings thought of as artists, or their activities considered aesthetic phenomena.

Nevertheless, as Franz Boas writes in *Primitive Art*, "All human activities may assume forms that give them esthetic values" (Boas, 1955: 9). What is required is the manipulation of qualities appealing to the senses and imagination in a rhythmical and structured way so as to create a form ultimately serving as a standard by which the form's perfection (or beauty) is measured. Throughout his book, Boas speaks of "the perfection of form." He writes that "we cannot reduce this world-wide tendency" to perfect form "to any other cause than to a feeling for form" (p. 58). In other words, people have as an aspect of being human the impulse to emphasize the form of objects they make and the activities they engage in. They also have a compelling need to take pleasure in the achievement of formal excellence (Jones, 1987).

Sometimes the forms produced elevate the mind above the indifferent emotional states of daily life because of meanings conveyed or past experiences associated with them, but they need not do so to be appreciated. Perfection of form is enough to satisfy; if the forms convey meaning, that adds to their enjoyment, but it is not essential (Boas, 1955: 9-10).

In the course of our daily activities we may have an aesthetic response to a form. As dictionaries indicate, "aesthete" is from the Greek "aîsthētē," one who perceives form (through feelings and sensations). The word does not mean one who perceives good or pleasing form only, or one who necessarily likes the form that is perceived. When positive, an aesthetic experience consists of a unique configuration of intellectual state and physiological condition: physical sensations of muscular contraction and release, a heightened awareness of form, a reduction in importance of other stimuli, and the suspension of time. Taken together, this produces a feeling of well being, sometimes even a sense of "oneness" with the object of attention or with others in the event. Hence, not only is a positive aesthetic experience enjoyed when it occurs, but also the conditions precipitating it often are cultivated so as to trigger the response.

But an aesthetic experience may be negative. Such a reaction, like the positive response, is a unique configuration of intellectual state and physiological condition; the two are of a difference nature and result, however. The tension created in a negative aesthetic response goes unrelieved. The intellectual state is one that welcomes, indeed cries out for, other stimuli to distract attention, and time is drawn out rather than suspended. The result is not a feeling of well-being at all, but of doubt, loathing, or even disgust (Jones, 1987).

This section treats managing, organizing, and participating in organizations as aesthetic phenomena. The thesis is that whatever else may be said about their interests, intentions, and activities, *organizational participants are craftspersons and aesthetes*. They seek positive experiences while avoiding the negative. They develop skills, and put them to use to do something or make something. They take pleasure in the excellence of form. They develop criteria to measure the quality of their performance as an aesthetic, as well as technical, phenomenon.

Some might object that creating form or perceiving form is not a primary concern or condition, if it is manifested at all, within organizations. Many individuals, they would contend, are preoccupied with the "bottom line," enjoying a warm glow when profits exceed expenses and suffering a sinking feeling in the pit of the stomach when the books don't balance (and thus measuring the quality of the company's "performance" simply by hardnosed economic criteria). Some managers seem to juggle figures, materials, and people as if they were all just raw materials, or perhaps pieces of a puzzle, to be shaped or fitted by strong will and dint of personality into some sort of gestalt. A number of supervisors appear to want their units to run "like a well-oiled machine"; they don't use orchestra or ballet as metaphors (although it has been said of Polaroid's Edwin Land that his leadership was like that of a conductor directing a symphony). Where is the art, the craftsmanship, the aesthetic?

The absence of artistry or its appreciation, and of a pleasant ambience, in no way negates the need or desire for them. Not everyone dwells on their activities as aesthetic, either; the exigencies of organizational life often preclude rhapsodizing. Most participants would agree, however, that skills and expertise are required in their endeavors, and, like sculptors or easel painters, they expect their work to be well received. They would admit that when things go well there are moments of pleasure; memories are later relished, rather as a thespian or musician mentally relives an especially good performance or a woodworker admires a well-turned piece of furniture.

Uncertainty and doubt would be disturbing. Often a source of confusion, frustration and unrelieved tension, doubt generates a *negative* aesthetic experience. Coherence, and making sense of a situation (see Louis, 1983) would please and satisfy, providing one with an assumptive framework and set of beliefs. This would enhance one's sense of self-esteem and well-being, necessary to function in meeting the demands and solving the problems that have to be confronted daily.

Whether consciously considered or not, the perceptual and the sensory inhere in organizational life, as they do in other activities (Fine, 1985; Jones, 1987). The essays that follow are informed implicitly by elements of an art model, examining attempts of individuals as craftspersons and aesthetes to perfect form and to seek coherence when organizations are created, changed, or challenged.

STUDIES ON AESTHETICS, MANAGING, AND ORGANIZING

The essay by McDonald concerns the Los Angeles Olympic Organizing Committee, which was intended to endure only 1,051

days. In less than three years of existence, its 20,000 employees and
50,000 volunteers were to plan and implement a complex program of
three weeks' duration to be viewed by more people than any other
event in human history. How was a sense of mission communicated?
What promoted dedication to the cause? Why were the subcultures,
despite stress within them and tensions between or among them, able
to transcend individual differences? Through McDonald's reportage
as an insider we experience the impact of symbols and symbolic
communication on members, thus understanding firsthand how
organizational culture was generated in a short period in the context
of great urgency to carry out a project of enormous proportions
requiring an all consuming commitment.

The circumstances examined by Arora in the second article involve
the creation of one committee within a larger organization—that of
the university. Over a two-year period, Arora documented 159
examples of proverbs, proverbial comparisons, and other forms of
traditional speech. Such forms function to instruct, influence, and
persuade. Moreover, they are associated with contexts of close
relations; their use by strangers may create the impression of such
contexts. One chairman employed figurative language five times as
frequently when in a leadership role as when simply a committee
member. This and other facts led Arora to hypothesize that leaders
used expressive forms to generate an ambience in which working
relations developed (and produced results) in a relatively short period
of time.

The third report, by Snyder, concerns organizational participants'
frame of reference for making sense of a situation. In this instance, a
new Vice President of Manufacturing in an aircraft plant seeks to
institute a new philosophy of respect, participation, productivity, and
integrity. Other organizational participants, inured to a previous
attitude of coercion and intimidation, are incredulous. To convince
them of his sincerity and commitment, he uses homey slogans and
expressions describing and memorializing the new philosophy and
desire to change; employs humor to promote frank discussions and
open communication; and builds a team spirit by becoming a symbol
of the new order through his actions and through sayings that
become traditional. The executive crafted a new form—the
managerial philosophy of the factory and its application in daily
practices. He also contributed to a change in ambience, which
produced a positive response in participants.

The circumstances described by Martin in the fourth essay differ in that the organization, which manufactures computer software, was from its inception dedicated to human welfare. Then came the crisis when suddenly everyone realized that the company was faltering, the victim of unexpected competition.

After a ritual of budget trimming, a decision was made (albeit reluctantly) to reduce the workforce. As Martin's report indicates, the stories, slogans, and rumors following Black Tuesday—the day of the layoffs—were generated by the turbulence of the situation. This turbulence included the challenge to longstanding assumptions and cherished beliefs, the sudden uncertainty and need to eradicate doubt, and the urge to protect the organization and restore its form as a viable and functioning entity. Several expressive forms arose, their origins owing much to the need for coherence and belief, both of which are necessary for self preservation and survival.

In the fifth essay, Evanchuk turns attention to those who once were members of an organization but now have retired. Many who now are apart from the organization find the organization a part of themselves and want to be part of it again. They tend to see their role as that of preserving and perpetuating the unique character and ethos of the organization as they came to understand it, and as they shaped it, through their involvement in years past. In reporting on research among members and retirees of a folk dance ensemble, Evanchuk presents insights into the aesthetic and expressive requirements of current and former organizational participants, the need for certainty, and the urge to find meaningfulness and to convey meanings.

As a whole, the articles in this section illustrate that however prosaic our activities are, and however practical, expeditious or instrumental, they are also informed by aesthetic imperatives. Organizational participants seek meaning and strive for coherence, perceiving form and analyzing it for guidance and direction. As the articles show, there is more to organizing than simply designing work, and more to working than merely carrying out a task.

9

THE LOS ANGELES OLYMPIC ORGANIZING COMMITTEE

Developing Organizational Culture in the Short Run

Peggy McDonald

UCLA-Graduate School of Management

The Los Angeles Olympic Organizing Committee was an unusual organization with an unusual task. Its purpose was to organize and operate the Games of the XXIIIrd Olympiad from July 28 to August 12, 1984 in Los Angeles, California. Shortly after that date the organization virtually ceased to exist.

The organizing effort began 1,051 days prior to the opening of the Games on March 26, 1979. Starting at that time with only a handful of employees, the organization grew immensely and rapidly, from 200 employees one year to 2,500 by early 1984. By the time the Games began, the Los Angeles Olympic Organizing Committee (LAOOC) had some 20,000 employees and 50,000 volunteers at its service.

One of the largest challenges the organizers faced was hiring and training this huge, short-term work force. It was understandably difficult to lure highly skilled and personable people from permanent jobs to join the Olympics effort. The glamour and excitement of working for an event with high visibility and historical implications could catch the attention of the target group of employees, but it took more to enlist and retain their services. Elaborate plans were laid, therefore, to make each employee feel a personal stake in the Olympic movement, encouraging him or her to "Play a Part in History."

Formal orientation at the Olympic committee was done relatively well, given the brief time and the huge numbers of new recruits. A permanent organization has considerably more time to train and enculturate its new members than did the LAOOC. Given this situation, the staff's organizational learning came primarily from informal means, drawing heavily upon the stories and behavior of coworkers. Myths and rituals sprang up surprisingly fast for such a young organization, though many were rooted in the history of the modern and ancient Olympic Games.

I experienced the orientation and training process of the LAOOC firsthand. I was hired April 1, 1984, at the height of the hiring upswing, to work in the Design Department. It is difficult to separate my viewpoints from those of the organization or the department, but many notes and interviews initiated in my first contacts with the organization and continued until the Games have allowed me a measure of objectivity.

In much of what follows, I adopt an anthropological convention of speaking in the present—even though the Games have been played, the event is history, and I no longer work for the organization (which has been dismantled). I follow this convention both because I wrote this report before the Games occurred and because the present tense conveys more of the feeling of being "inside."

ORIENTATION

At the initial orientation meeting, I was introduced to the LAOOC headquarters building in Marina del Rey. The building is a former helicopter factory and retains the high ceilings and wide open floor plan of an industrial manufacturing site. The drab, sterile interior is fortunately relieved by the fabulous colors and shapes that are suspended from the ceiling in the form of banners and huge sculptural mobiles. The bullpen-like setting of many of the offices is brightened by the addition of large, colorful pillars and scaffolding that will be used to decorate the actual competition sites during the Games. These elements add a necessary interior decor to the physical space, while serving as a constant, vibrant reminder to the employees of their role in the spectacle to come.

The process of entering the Olympic headquarters to see the workspace is not simple. Each visitor is subjected to approximately four waves of security, from simple oral identification to elaborate frisking and x-ray procedures. The exterior of the building is completely unmarked as belonging to the Los Angeles Olympic Organizing Committee. Rather, the uniformly dull building has only a large sign stating the street address. This certainly makes insiders feel secure, but also serves as a constant reminder of the horror of the Munich Games, which were marred by political violence.

The formal orientation session introduced me to the format of LAOOC meetings. A large number of highly-placed managers spoke to the group of 70, all speaking briefly and casually. They spoke of the organization's philosophy and purpose. Several key points that have been constantly reiterated are:

The athlete comes first.
Private sector financing will be used exclusively to avoid burdening the taxpayers. These are, then, the "Spartan" games.
New building will be strictly limited.
The committee structure will be highly decentralized, with many services contracted to private vendors and organizations.
The community will gain long-term benefits from the committee's efforts.

Several of these goals are befitting of any short-term organization, while others are specific to this peculiar event. All have been evident in decisions made by the committee.

The orientation session continued with self-introductions of all those joining the staff. Besides name and duty, we were told to mention any previous Olympics we had attended (only a small proportion had done so). We were told for the first of many times that we were now playing a part in history. The scheduled "inspirational films" were deleted for time considerations. On the whole, the group left the small, bare room confused, overwhelmed with policies and procedures, and not particularly inspired or confident of the organization's ability to carry out its task.

All new staff members had their photos taken for a permanent identification badge, promised in two weeks. We did not yet sense the importance of the permanent blue badges, compared to the temporary red one we wore. In an organization with a history as brief as the LAOOC's, even those with a week's seniority have a measurable difference in status, at least until the permanent identification badge arrives. For the unfortunate members of my entering group, our badges were delayed six weeks. This did little for our rapid adoption into the organization and did even less for our confidence in its ability to make things happen on time. Even among the holders of permanent blue badges, the numbers are sequentially ordered, so one can hear, "Wow! 131! What was it like back then?"

As a whole, the staff is extremely young, bright, and attractive. The manager of age 42 can seem like an old timer. While this may well be a function of the availability of workers and flexibility of careers among younger people, it does give the organization a different character. One can notice a lot of flirtation and socializing, and sex seems to be a frequent topic of conversation. The interest of the vast majority of the staff in athletics and other healthful, vigorous behavior is also a distinguishing feature.

ORGANIZATIONAL POLICY AND CULTURES

At Orientation, new staff members are given a policies and procedures manual and are reminded of the most important rules. It is only after we went to work in our departments that we began to learn which ones really count and which are considered ridiculous. The most frequently discussed policies are the dress code, the need for numerous signatures on every transaction, the "Peter" test (named after Ueberroth), and parking restrictions.

The dress code stipulates that women should wear dresses and always must wear stockings and "proper undergarments." Men must wear neckties at all times and should not have beards. Many people take great offense at these restrictions, though to the knowledge of those I interviewed, no one has ever been fired for violating them. Many, though, have been warned or reprimanded. One woman, who was wearing long shorts one day in preparation for moving heavy boxes to the warehouse, was told by an older woman in a "gross polyester floral muu-muu" that she was attired inappropriately. For the two weeks' duration of the actual Olympic Games, the entire staff will be working at the competition sites. The polyester uniforms that will be assigned are causing reactions ranging from apprehension to horror.

The pursuit of signatures on paper is the most obvious activity of staff members. Tight fiscal constraint is the motivation behind this, and "Spartan games" philosophy prevails. Nevertheless, the staff appears to be quite action-oriented and is frustrated by the endless rounds of paperwork. Most staff members are acutely aware of the dwindling time (53 days as I write this report) and rail against the bureaucracy.

Coercion is used to force new staff members to become active participants in the international spirit of the Games. At the time of hire, each person, no matter how comparably important or insignificant her or his position appears, is randomly assigned a country. People are told that at any time Peter Ueberroth, the President of the Los Angeles Olympic Organizing Committee, could call someone into his office and ask the person to tell him everything about Somalia or Mozambique or whatever his or her assigned country is. The alleged purpose of this exercise is to have a ready source of current information should a delegation show up unexpectedly, but it clearly forces the new recruit to do homework and feel potentially pivotal to the organization. It also establishes an awareness of the chief executive in everyone's mind. I was told that several months before I started, a delegation from Finland arrived. Peter called all four people in the organization who had been assigned Finland. Only one was prepared. The consequences were never clearly stated, but the impression was given that lack of preparation is grounds for immediate dismissal. When I received my assignment, I was relieved to see that I, too, had Finland. Presumably, someone was a Finnish expert by now.

Another sort of "Peter test" was announced at Orientation, striking fear into the hearts of most present, especially those many years removed from school and tests. All new staff members are required to take a test administered by the President himself. The material to be tested includes "everything" about the history of the Olympic Games, current international and local news, and infinite details about the LAOOC. Horror stories abound about unexpectedly being required to name the countries in Africa, the city council members in Los Angeles, and the sports commissioners for 23 events at the 1984 Games. Those being tested are given 24 hours' warning. The test is as treacherous as promised, but studying for it does help quickly acquaint the newcomer to the organization and its environment. No one has been fired for not performing well on the "Peter test," but it is widely reported that Peter came down to personally congratulate the only person ever to have received a perfect score.

The fourth frequently discussed policy is the newly instituted parking permit system. The huge increase in staff has finally filled the extremely large outdoor parking lot. Additional parking was arranged at a sponsor's headquarters some 20 minutes away (though advertised as 10 minutes). Each department head was assigned enough parking permits for approximately two-thirds of his or her staff. Others must park in the distant lot and be shuttled to and from the LAOOC headquarters according to a fixed and inconvenient schedule. Department heads divided the passes in a variety of ways—randomly, by favoritism, by seniority, or by rank within the department. The discussion about who has passes, who doesn't, and how to beat the system is an absorbing subject of hallway discussions.

Other organizational policies, some tacit, govern a great deal of the mood at the LAOOC. One of the first stories I heard was about the person who was fired for not walking fast enough. With so much to do in such a short period of time, the staff is frenzied, and people sprinting down the hallways are a frequent sight. By contrast, those moving calmly can appear sluggish. Through this recurrent story, the organization seems to be applauding expeditiousness and, perhaps inadvertently, hyperactivity.

The staff is encouraged to eat "on campus" at the "Cafe du Coubertin," named for Baron Pierre de Coubertin, founder of the modern Olympic Games. It has standard cafeteria fare, varied by the day and thoroughly unexciting. The staff, though, is offered a $2.00 per day subsidy to eat at the Cafe, which makes for a cheap, or sometimes free, lunch. Keeping the staff in the same location for lunch presumably reduces downtime caused by lengthy drives or too many errands. It does increase camaraderie among staff, with common food to complain about. Additionally, the Cafe is used as a site for information dispersal. It sports a "Days to Go" calendar; a route map of the Torch Relay's progress, which is updated daily; and a screening room, which shows inspirational Olympic newsreels at lunch. Uniforms for the Games are modeled at lunch, and sports demonstrations occur weekly. It is impossible to eat regularly in the cafeteria without being genuinely excited about the Olympic Games and, by transference, the LAOOC.

The only three sources of revenue for the 1984 Games are television rights, ticket sales, and sponsors' fees. Of these, sponsors have the highest profile. The current jokes about "Official Toilet Paper of the 1984 Olympics" are even more frequent within the committee, where sponsors seem to run rampant. As staff members, we are required to use the official Brother typewriters, IBM computers, Xerox copy machines, and even official printers and pin manufacturers. We receive free M & M's, Snickers candy bars, and Perrier water. Free Coca-Cola and coffee machines line the halls. It can get unnerving. I noticed a delivery man with a handcart full of boxes wearing his t-shirt inside out. I joked with him about it, and he replied that the loading dock required all delivery people to turn their company shirts inside out if they were not from a sponsoring firm. Investigating this, I found that a sponsor had complained to Peter Ueberroth, saying, "How much did Joe's Printing pay to be a sponsor?" Official sponsors paid an average of $11 million dollars for the right to be Official.

The colorful look of the Games is called "festive federalism." A conscious effort was made to select a color scheme for use in buildings, uniforms, pageantry, and all printed material that will not reflect political themes. The predominant magentas, aquas, vermilions, purples, and periwinkle blues of the palette are not found in any country's flag. They fill the building and the publications, and will soon fill the streets and venues of competition. Though most employees were expecting red, white and blue as the colors, the festive federal look of colorful bars, stars, and confetti has caught on and is even evident in crudely made employee notices for parties. Indeed, one large staff party not officially related to the LAOOC called itself "Venuization Sensation" (for the process of sending employees permanently out to the competition venues for the duration of the Games) and required all people attending to wear a minimum of three festive federal colors. In attendance at the party was Sam the Eagle, the Disney-created official mascot of the Olympics. Party-goers, out of the work environment, took special pains to continue the mood and look of the Olympics. The organizational culture has become quickly powerful.

Also in an effort to use the staff to spread Olympic awareness throughout the community, the LAOOC has a company store. The store has a variety of Olympic paraphernalia available at terrific discounts. Many sponsors such as Converse shoes, Vuarnet sunglasses, and Sony consumer electronics have made their products available to Olympics staff and volunteers at dealer cost. While these bigger-ticket items are reserved for staff only, employees are encouraged to purchase the Olympic trinkets to give away. The major item in this category is Olympic pins, which have spawned an intense trading process that accompanies every Olympics. For the 1984 Olympics, approximately 400 approved pins have been developed, and many staff members have become serious collectors. Pin trading can become quite vicious, with incidents of hoarding and swindling. The *Los Angeles Times* actually devoted a lengthy article to "pin fever."

There is a strictly enforced security policy that prohibits cameras in the building. Many staff members have expressed a desire to photograph the sprawling and colorful offices for their own mementos, but have been unable to do so. The first photograph of the interior I was able to show anyone was in an article in *Time* magazine. Similarly, the offices are constantly full of television cameras shooting documentary footage, interviews, and reports. It seems ironic, then, to disallow camera use by staff, and complaints are frequent.

As the end of the organization's tenure draws near, and with it the staff's jobs, one of the most common topics of conversation is future plans. People are understandably distressed. Severance pay is being offered to employees of six months' duration or more, but that does not ease the tension. When Peter Ueberroth announced that he would be accepting the job of Commissioner of Baseball after the Games, the administration hoped it would be an inspiration to employees looking for ways to combine their Olympics responsibilities with previous job experience. Instead, animosity developed to the point that the administration instituted a job placement service. The service collected resumes from all who were interested, and convinced a number of sponsors to hold open currently available jobs until after the Olympics so staff members could fill them. Predictably, the only jobs currently being offered by the Job Opportunity Office are for data processors, secretaries and security guards, leaving the vast majority of employees, who were told they were the "cream of the crop," on their own.

DEPARTMENTAL CULTURE AND INTERACTION

In joining a large organization like the LAOOC, the anchor and key socializing unit seems to be the department. With so many new employees constantly coming on board, few people can keep track of many names beyond their own department. I joined the Design Department, and without the overt activities planned by the administration to stimulate organizational unity and common purpose, I would have become completely loyal to the Design Department alone.

Projects move along at a brisk pace at the Olympic committee, but deadlines seem to move faster. The Design Department, as a service provider, is at the tail end of the project production process, and therefore suffers from the delays of others to an acute degree. The department consists of 11 people, who are completely responsible for maintaining a consistent visual image in all printed material for the Olympic Games. There is no doubt that people are overworked, but so are the majority of Olympic staff. The department interacts with virtually every department in the organization, sometimes on an adversarial level, dealing with design, budgets, deadlines, purchasing, and constant changes and delays. The people in Design are on the whole more creative and potentially more volatile than other department staffs. Conflicts are inevitable, and all parties are constantly reminding each other that we are all on the same side—that is, a spectacular event is the bottom line.

The most common method of dealing with the overwhelmingly tense and stressful environment is through humor. The whole department laughs a lot at stories, situations, and silly practical jokes that reflect the organization. While showing reams of files to client departments, you will run across a huge plastic cockroach or a particularly trashy *Singles Register* porno magazine. The momentary shock and embarrassment are relieved by the hysterical laughter of coworkers watching your expression. When Olympic staff rings looking much like high school rings were offered, the plastic ring-sizer for fingers ended up being circulated through interoffice mail with an official-looking memo asking the recipient to measure another appendage and report immediately to Thelma in Health Services. For people balancing an average of 30 immediately pending projects per day, this level of humor is a catharsis.

The design staff tends to sit together at lunch causing a scene with loud laughter and reveling in its position as the only group engaging in raucous behavior. Every small department within the LAOOC must have a sense that it is the sole possessor of reason, commitment, and integrity. The Design Department is no exception. It is also the sole possessor of a camera within the building, a Polaroid, presumably for design documentation but used more frequently for ridiculous staff portraits (for instance, with push pins seemingly stuck into foreheads) or photos imitating our boss, the Design Director.

As in many organizations, complaining about the boss is a frequent pastime. The Design Director has a distinctive voice that is eminently imitable. At least once an hour, someone will loudly imitate a "Huh?" The current Design Director is the third in that position since the LAOOC was formed. To its credit, the committee hired him after he had written a lengthy, scathing, but very accurate expose in a major national design magazine of the failings of the LAOOC in handling the look of the Games correctly. The former Design Director had quit in frustration after complaining that by submitting design work to top management for review, "major design decisions are being made by two lawyers and a color-blind travel agent!" It is apparently true that Peter Ueberroth is color blind and, as the former president of a travel agency, has no professional design expertise. With the new Design Director, the policy was changed to keep artistic and creative decisions within the department trained to deal with them.

The vaunted precision of the Design Department is a problem when dealing with other departments. While publicly defending the Olympics and the LAOOC at every turn, the design staff does seem to derive a quiet pleasure in seeing evidence of the incompetence of other departments. When a "trial-run" shooting tournament was held a month ago, the news that someone had forgotten to bring ammunition, forcing the competitors and spectators to wait around for several hours, was met by ill-concealed glee from those in the Design Department who had dealt with the shooting department's neglect of deadlines. Similarly, the recent failure of the ticketing machines at the grand opening of ticketing centers was met with "I told you so's" from design staff.

The department functions efficiently from an organizational standpoint, since all staff members will work together diligently most of the time. Certain rituals of language and action keep everyone working on an even keel. Just when tensions are running highest, someone will slide in a wheeled typing chair across the department, imitating a luge in the Winter Olympics. Alternatively, someone will loudly say, "No budget? No problem," reacting to our most common dilemma. On mornings when the fever pitch begins immediately after people walk in the door, someone will inevitably say at 9:00 a.m., "Is it lunch yet?" And lastly, when a particularly nasty project is assigned, a coordinator will sarcastically intone, "Make my day."

ORGANIZATIONAL EFFORTS
TO CREATE A CULTURE

The Los Angeles Olympic Organizing Committee has no problem finding appropriate ways to inspire the staff. Celebrities and the media pay a great deal of attention to the dealings of the committee, and every staff member can share the feeling of being in the center of attention. It is certainly an unusual job that presents its employees the opportunity to read about their staff meetings as front-page news.

The symbols exist. The problem is in communicating them to the staff in a manner that involves everyone and generates a shared purpose. The most effective method the LAOOC has used is without a doubt the "staff meeting," which includes every employee and volunteer. Every two to three weeks, loudspeakers are turned up throughout the building to announce an important guest who will address the staff. The result is sometimes pandemonium, as when it was announced the morning after the California presidential primary that Jesse Jackson would be addressing the staff in five minutes behind the building. Evacuation officers were used to get the crowd calmly out the back doors. Other recent speakers have included Howard Cosell and Tom Bradley. Most of these meetings are casual, but the largest, most formal gatherings are real production masterpieces.

My first experience in a large staff meeting was a hastily prepared effort to let the staff know the latest news on the Olympic boycott by the Soviets. Many people heard radio reports on their way to work, and the news spread like wildfire throughout the staff. Many people's projects were directly affected by the pullout. A memo went around in the morning telling staff not to discuss the incident by phone. At noon, the executive vice president called everyone to the central bullpen area, where the entire staff stood around people's desks watching a small stage. The executive vice president read aloud the exact wording of the Soviet news release and expressed a great deal of hope that they would reconsider. He then quickly changed the subject to the morning's launch of the torch relay and gave an inspiring talk about teamwork and the increased importance of the work we were all doing. The staff stumbled back to their desks, tentatively hopeful.

I attended an orientation meeting at the USC McDonald's Swim Stadium for all people who would be staffing the pool and the USC Olympic Village during the Games. There were approximately 5,000 people in attendance. Fifteen different people gave two-minute speeches, standing on the pool deck surrounded by the flags of every competing nation. Their talks were informational, but the crowd really came alive when they were treated to a demonstration by the world champion synchronized swimming team. The performance was so glorious, the participants suddenly realized what their Olympic role meant. As I looked around, many people were crying, clapping and screaming for more. It was a stirring sight.

The Jesse Jackson staff meeting was not exciting for political reasons. Most of the staff are probably staunch Republicans, but their enthusiasm was generated by his "star" status. As the staff waited in the hot sun for his helicopter to land on the roof, they eyed the stage set up next to the cafeteria. Many comments were heard like, "He's probably going to announce the luncheon special." "No, he's going to tell us to eat before 11:30 or after 1:00 to avoid the rush." The poised television cameras added to the excitement.

When the Reverend Jackson arrived, the crowd went wild. It was not an ordinary staff meeting. Peter Ueberroth talked about Jackson's role in negotiating with the Russians. Jackson spoke at length about the symbolic role the Olympics play in world peace and harmony. He spoke of the importance of athletics in increasing the self-esteem of minorities. He was given a torch from the torch relay by the granddaughter of the legendary Jesse Owens. He ran in place with it, smiling for the television cameras. The crowd shrieked. They happily stampeded back into the building. While Jesse Jackson had nothing to do with any of the staff's projects, the affirmation of the purpose and importance of our task was well-timed.

The most inspirational and largest staff meeting by far was orchestrated to coincide with the anniversary of the date the Games were awarded to Los Angeles. The boosterism behind the meeting was transparent, but the meeting was terribly effective by doing exactly what it set out to do—make the staff feel part of the organization, and a part of history.

The staff was herded into the normally forbidding and drab warehouse. It had been transformed. Banners, bunting, and festive federal columns disguised the walls. A huge stage with grand piano and movie screen had been constructed at one end and the entire room was covered in white wooden chairs. As each staff member entered, he or she was handed a specially designed, festive federal commemorative mug half full of champagne. Heroic music was playing that turned out to be the first presentation of the music that will be used for opening and closing ceremonies. The Director of Human Resources led us in a toast to the anniversary and to the fact that this was the first time alcohol had ever been served at a staff function.

A fellow staff member sang several songs she had written, accompanied on the piano by a man dressed like a combination of Michael Jackson and Liberace. The crowd groaned at the signs of a homespun talent show, but the woman's songs were surprisingly funny, singing about the L.A. "Oh Oh" C., being "venuized," and making nasty innuendoes about top management personalities. We saw the brand new orientation film that is a tear-jerker, heard from former Olympic medal winners, and were introduced to a lovely old woman who had been an organizer of the 1932 Los Angeles Olympics and is now volunteering five days a week for the current Games. The staff could see the commitment that the Olympics experience would inspire and gave the woman a five-minute standing ovation. Many were crying by this time.

The executive vice president spoke in very human terms about the Games and the staff's role and told funny and endearing stories about the LAOOC's beginnings.

Finally, a vice president who had been on the road for several days with the torch relay as it ran through small towns throughout the East and Midwest shared a few of his favorite moments. As he told about the runner going over a winding road in the hills of West Virginia and encountering a man standing alone on the top of a hill with a trumpet playing "America the Beautiful" as the torch passed, there was not a dry eye in the house. The speaker himself broke down, overcome by emotion, and could not continue for several minutes. The staff filed out to the strains of ceremonial music, clutching their ceremonial mugs and pins reading "Team '84"—that were handed to them at the exit.

CONCLUSION

The fleeting nature of the Los Angeles Olympic Organizing Committee compressed the time available for the natural development of an organizational culture. The management made the conscious decision that it would use all available historical and ceremonial resources to provide its employees with a common sense of identity as rapidly as possible. This intense environment proved to be a fertile field for symbolic interaction and expressive behavior.

The focus appeared to be on inspiring the individual to strive for a common goal, rather than encouraging group interaction for the same purpose. This was sensible, since beyond the Games there would be no need for these people to interact, and long-range behavior modification was unnecessary. As long as each individual was motivated to perform at his or her peak for the duration of the Olympics, and retained pleasant memories of having "played a part in history," the human resources role of the Olympics was successful.

The LAOOC is not necessarily a model of how to organize and generate traditions, loyalty, and dedication. But it is certainly an example of the creation of organizational culture in the short run—of how beliefs, stories, jokes, rituals, and ceremonies arose out of an unusual combination of circumstances, both orchestrated and spontaneous.

10

"NO TICKEE, NO SHIRTEE"

Proverbial Speech and Leadership in Academe

Shirley L. Arora

University of California, Los Angeles

A little over 50 years ago sociologist William Albig wrote in an article in a professional journal that "the proverb is a language form that has largely passed from usage in contemporary American culture"—except, perhaps, among "first-generation foreign language groups of peasant origin" (Albig, 1931: 527). Based on subsequent studies over the years we can say at this point that reports of the death of the proverb have been greatly exaggerated; but it continues to be true, as Roger Abrahams has pointed out in a well-known overview of the proverb genre, that "we still know little of why and how people use proverbs, or anything of the range of social uses and cultural situations in which they are encountered" (Abrahams, 1972: 119). Later Abrahams notes in passing that sophisticated cultures may tend to be somewhat antagonistic to the use of proverbs, it being "strongly felt in many groups today that those who use proverbs do so because of an inability to converse effectively in any other way" (Abrahams, 1972: 123).

One might think, given statements such as these, that the weekly meetings of a university committee—made up, one assumes, of "sophisticated" academics who are competent, even fluent, conversationalists—would be a poor place to study contemporary proverb use. I hope to show that, on the contrary, American proverbial speech is alive and well, even in the halls—or committee rooms—of Academe.

The members of the committee, whose meetings I was able to observe over a period of two years, represented—in keeping with university policy—a carefully apportioned cross-section of the campus community in terms of fields of professional expertise. All were senior members of the academic community, at the rank of full professor and in some instances in the uppermost reaches of that rank. For all but one, English was a native language; and so far as I was able to ascertain all but two were born in the United States, although there was a fairly broad regional representation—somewhat dominated by New York. With two exceptions, the committee membership was entirely male. The workings of the committee demanded that these individuals of diverse personal and professional backgrounds come together for several hours a week to carry out a thorough and presumably lucid discussion and analysis of various matters of concern to the university community, and reach decisions or recommendations on the basis of that discussion and analysis. Based on my observations, I would say that the committee functioned with considerable success, and I am inclined to believe that the various kinds of proverbial language used in the course of the meetings operated on a variety of levels to contribute to that success.

"TRUE PROVERBS,"<br>"PROVERBIAL PHRASES," AND
"CONVENTIONAL INTENSIFIERS"

When I use the term "proverbial language," I have in mind several kinds of traditional expressions. First and foremost are the "true proverbs," which are complete, independent statements (complete from the standpoint of meaning, not necessarily of syntax): "A rolling stone gathers no moss," "Nothing ventured, nothing gained" (to cite examples used by committee members). When we use the term "proverb," it is to this group that we normally refer. A proverb may be uttered unchanged and in isolation, if the speaker so wishes, or it may be modified in some way to suit the particular circumstances of its use; but the definitive quality of the proverb is its ability to convey in and of itself a complete idea. "Proverbial phrases," on the other hand, have no life of their own, so to speak; they *require* grammatical modification or syntactical incorporation into a surrounding verbal context. Thus "not to touch [something] with a ten-foot pole" must become "I wouldn't touch it with a ten-foot pole," or "they wouldn't touch...," etc.; and "to buy a pig in a poke" becomes "they bought a pig in a poke" or "we're buying a pig in a poke," and so on. Similarly, a phrase such as "when push comes to shove" is not used alone, but typically introduces a statement as to what occurs, or will occur, under force of circumstances ("When push comes to shove, he'll agree to do it"), although it may also be otherwise modified ("That's where push will come to shove").

The term "conventional intensifiers" (Abrahams, 1972: 123) has been applied to certain proverbial phrases that have an adjectival or adverbial function; these include proverbial comparisons and similes ("smooth as an egg," "tough as nails") as well as exaggerations ("a hole [in an argument] big enough to drive a truck through," "a list [so big] that [it] would choke a horse"). Because of the special function that intensifiers share, it is often useful to consider them as a category or subcategory apart, and I shall do so here.

For purposes of this study, therefore, the items recorded are divided into three groups: proverbs (i.e., "true proverbs"), proverbial comparisons (including exaggerations), and miscellaneous proverbial phrases. I shall be concerned here particularly with proverbs, and shall comment only briefly on the use of other kinds of proverbial expressions.

USES, FUNCTIONS, AND EFFECTS OF PROVERBIAL EXPRESSIONS

The committee I observed is a fairly large one, with a membership that changes partially each year so that over the two-year period 16 individuals were involved. From these 16 persons I noted down, during the period in question, 36 proverbs plus 4 more-or-less familiar quotations; 39 proverbial comparisons; and 80 miscellaneous proverbial expressions—159 items in all. The number of items per person ranged from 2 to 46, with one individual being responsible for no fewer than 12 proverbs, 29 phrases, and 5 comparisons. The visitors who occasionally appeared before the committee in one capacity or another contributed to the list an additional 4 proverbs, 9 phrases, and 2 comparisons, for a grand total of 174.

The numbers themselves are significant chiefly as a statistical reassurance that Albig's assertions as to the demise of the proverb were indeed premature. What is of greater interest, however, is the variety of ways in which these elements of proverbial language were employed, and it is on this aspect that I shall focus here.

Instruction and Persuasion

We are generally accustomed to thinking of proverbs as bits of "traditional wisdom," and on the basis of this assumption to conceive of their primary, and proper, role as one of instructing, or at least persuading and influencing, those to whom they are directed. Indeed, the didactic or persuasive function is so often considered an attribute of proverbs as a category that one might term the function itself "traditional," taking care, however, not to confuse "traditional" with "normal" and thus to imply that other uses of proverbs constitute departures from some accepted norm. Unquestionably this "traditional" role of proverbs is an important one, although it is far from being their only function and may not even be statistically the most frequent. (Abrahams' comment concerning our lack of information on the actual use of proverbs is relevant here.)

The use of proverbs for "instruction" assumes a certain disparity in status—whether social or chronological or of some other order— between proverb user and proverb hearer that is not applicable to the situation being described in this study. Among peers, where the role of proverb-sayer or community spokesman alternates with that of proverb-hearer or audience, it is more appropriate to think in terms of persuasion, either toward a certain action or toward a certain attitude (depending upon whether the proverb applies to something yet to happen or to something that has already occurred). Although it is often difficult to separate this function entirely from others, I would say that roughly one-third of the proverbs (true proverbs, not phrases) that I noted down during committee meetings were employed in this manner.

The proverb used in the title of this paper was a case in point—and had, incidentally, the distinction of being the only one used on three separate occasions, several months apart, by two different individuals. As employed here, "No tickee, no shirtee" is a kind of proverbial synonym—one might even say euphemism—for the notorious "Publish or perish," which may itself be considered an academic proverb. The intent of the speaker in each instance was clearly to remind other committee members of a recognized facet of academic life, the prescribed relationship between performance and advancement. Why do so in proverbial terms, or with this particular proverb? The answer to the first part of the question reflects the nature of the proverb as a recognized statement of accepted principle—the "traditional authority" that all proverbs supposedly enjoy and of which all proverb sayers take advantage. So why this proverb instead of the harsher but perhaps even better-known "Publish or perish?" One of the noticeable characteristics of "No tickee, no shirtee" as a proverb is, I suggest, its conspicuously nonacademic nature, residing both in its implicit attribution to a nonacademic personage—the stereotypic Chinese laundryman—and in its reproduction of what is assumed to be the kind of "pidgin English" that such an individual would employ. This nonacademic nature makes the proverb stand out in stark contrast both to the subject context—academic achievement—and to the situational context—the academic discourse in which it is embedded. The contrast attracts attention and therefore gives extra emphasis to the statement, and the language itself—together with the proverbial form—serves to imply that the principle enunciated by the proverb is a general truth, applicable not just to the academic world but to the "real" world as well—a principle that even the "man on the street" or the laundryman in the next block would recognize and approve of. I have no way of knowing how many committee members had actually heard the proverb before; it was known to me from my own childhood as "No tickee, no washee," and I had always associated it vaguely with the California gold rush and the influx of Chinese immigrants that took place at that period. But the structure and language of the saying clearly labeled it as proverbial, and I would be willing to wager that even those who had not heard it before identified it as a proverb and reacted to it in those terms. The same would, of course, be true of "Publish or perish"—but this phrasing of what is essentially the same principle has more negative overtones and so far as I am aware is used primarily in a critical sense, as an indictment of the existing system rather than a defense of it. "No tickee, no shirtee" softens the statement; it suggests, in effect, not that one may or should perish, but perhaps—by association with another well-known phrase—that under certain circumstances one could lose one's shirt.

I have gone into some detail on the use of this particular proverb partly because of its repeated occurrence and partly as an indication of the many dimensions of proverb use that may and should be considered. Space here is too limited to do so with each item from the list of those employed, but I will mention a few other examples that were applied in "traditional" fashion. Most, though not all of them, are well-known, "standard" sayings:

"Half a loaf is better than none" (said in reference to a part-time appointment).

"You can't look a gift horse in the mouth" (referring to a researcher willing to work on a project without salary).

"Lightning wouldn't strike twice in the same place" (said of an event that presumably could not occur again).

"Let sleeping dogs lie" (a warning against bringing up a certain matter).

Finally, a characterization of the desirable rate of progress up the academic ladder:

"Not too fast, not too slow, sort of half-fast."

Commentary on Events

Apart from, or sometimes along with, their persuasive functions, proverbs may serve as comments on events that have already occurred or a situation that already exists. To the extent that they imply that the listener should adopt or at least accept as valid a certain attitude toward those events or that situation, this usage too may be considered "persuasive" or "traditional." Used in this fashion, the proverb serves to "label" a particular situation, assigning it to a class of similar situations toward which there is, the proverb implies, a socially accepted or "authorized" attitude. A sizable group of proverbs used by members of the committee fell into this category:

"Honesty really *is* the best policy" (said after a visitor had made an exceptionally candid, "warts and all" presentation of a proposal, which the committee subsequently approved).

"Their loss is our gain" (on the imminent departure of a certain individual to take a position at another institution).

"We live by the sword, we die by the sword" (a visitor's response when asked his reaction to criticisms of his policies).

"With a friend like that, X doesn't need enemies" (when a "friend" wrote an unfavorable letter of reference).

"With enemies like that, who needs friends?" (when opposition from an unpopular individual apparently brought about departmental approval of a proposal).

"Behind every silver lining there's a dark cloud" (an expression of pessimism that may or may not have been intentional).

Humor

Apart from—or even simultaneously with—their use for persuasion or comment, proverbs may be employed for a variety of purposes difficult to classify except under the general heading of "humor."

Humor itself can have many uses—some of them very serious indeed—and the term, while conveniently broad, is far from satisfactory. Yet to describe these uses simply as "nontraditional" is to imply that they depart somehow from the established roles of proverbs, and I am not persuaded that this is so. Perhaps a better way to characterize these other uses of proverbial language is to say that they involve instances in which performance, or certain aspects of performance, becomes the principal focus, rather than the proverb as such.

One might contend that the humorous use of proverbs signals a kind of degeneration in the proverbial tradition—that people no longer take proverbs seriously and therefore resort to mocking them through "nontraditional" usage. I think this judgment would be a mistake—first of all, because it ignores the fact that some of the serious purposes of humor—instruction, persuasion, influence—are the same ones that we find in "traditional" proverb use. Secondly, a judgment of this sort involves precisely the sort of "deviationist perspective" criticized by Bauman and others in regard to language in general (Bauman, 1977: 17). For proverbial language, as well as for language as a whole, we should adopt a multifunctional point of view, one that does not entail a norm and a set of deviations from that norm, but merely a range of options—registers or varieties of speaking. Moreover, the humorous use of proverbs does not reflect the disappearance of a proverbial tradition but its preservation; it assumes knowledge of that tradition on the part of the listener, otherwise the performance—the attempt at humor—will fail.

In his essay "Verbal Art as Performance," Bauman provides a list of communicative means that may serve to "key" performance, that is, to identify what follows as performance and not some other kind of communicative frame (Bauman, 1977: 16-18). The list can be applied virtually item by item to the use of proverbs, but I would like to concentrate on one particular portion: the use of figurative language, and the three different aspects of that use, which may be stated concisely as reproduction, originality, and application. All use of proverbial language involves reproduction—the repetition of a phrase or sentence invented (presumably) by someone else. Accuracy of reproduction can be an important facet of proverb performance, humorous or otherwise; the more accurately the proverb is quoted, the greater the likelihood that it will be recognized as such. Indeed, from the point of view of the listener a completely "original" proverb—if perceived as such—is ipso facto not a proverb at all.

Originality in proverb performance consists instead of variation—

deliberate changes in wording that will be recognized by the hearer who knows the proverb itself. Thus "The mountain labored and brought forth a mouse" became, as used by one committee member, "The committee labored and brought forth a mouse" (in reference, I should add, to another committee, not the one dealt with here), and a visitor to the committee provided an original variation of his own: "A bad tooth in time saves nine," based on the familiar "A stitch in time saves nine." This latter example, incidentally, illustrates the fact that not all performances are particularly successful; while the source of the variation was quite clear—the subject under discussion was dentistry—and the basic proverb was probably known to most if not all of those present, the general reaction of the listeners suggested that the meaning, within its context, was far from clear; nor was there any visible response to the (presumably) intended humor. Still, the speaker's decision to use—to *perform*—a proverb in this particular situation is significant, suggesting an attempt to establish with the committee a kind of common ground based on mutual familiarity with a particular saying, while at the same time inviting agreement with the general principle expressed. By definition, performance entails "the assumption of responsibility to an audience for a display of communicative competence" and is in turn "subject to evaluation . . . for the relative skill and effectiveness of the performer's display of competence" (Bauman, 1977: 11). Judging by my observations of audience reaction in this instance, the evaluation was not especially positive.

Appropriate application is an important component of proverb competence, but the application may also be a novel one, that is, it may depart in some way from the usual or expected context of a particular saying, while still remaining "appropriate." A simple example would be the literal application of a saying that is normally figurative, as in "That's putting your money where your mouth is," applied to the purchase of expensive banquet tickets. A proverb may be quoted purely for the sake of achieving a pun, as in "When the cat's away, the mice will play" (a colleague name Katz, whom the committee wanted to consult, was away on leave) and "A rolling stone gathers no moss" (suggested simply by the surname Moss).

Impression of Familiarity

The humorous use of proverbs approaches, in purpose and effect, the use of other kinds of proverbial expressions, such as comparisons, exaggerations and metaphorical phrases, that also serve to liven conversation and to "informalize" speech and, by extension, the interactional situation in which speech takes place. Thus although these performances involving humor often seemed tangential to the business at hand—that is, the use of the proverbial expression had no effect, and did not seek to have any, on the matter under consideration—there was an overall effect, and an important one, on the functioning of the committee as a whole.

In this connection I will refer back to my earlier description of the committee as a bringing together of individuals of very different backgrounds, academic and otherwise. Effective functioning of the committee demanded that these individuals reach, in a relatively short time, a degree of familiarity, of easy give-and-take, that would encourage a free exchange of opinions and ideas. The use—the performance—of proverbial language implied certain assumptions about what these individuals shared in terms of a common way of speaking and a common way of looking at things, deemphasizing differences and offering reassurance that even representatives of such diverse fields as the humanities and the "hard" sciences did, after all—literally and figuratively—"speak the same language."

Furthermore, because proverbial language is frequently associated with contexts of close relationships—informal conversations among family, friends, members of one's own community—it helps to create the impression of such a context, even when the context itself does not exist. A committee such as the one I observed, in which persons of diverse backgrounds must come together and function on fairly close terms, is an artificial construct, a relatively modern phenomenon that is, to be sure, not limited to academic environments, but exists wherever traditional community or group boundaries have been disrupted and new kinds of interactional relationships established. Roger Abrahams has pointed to the role of certain "conversational genres"—jargon, colloquialisms, slang, special languages—in defining the membership of a group (Abrahams, 1976: 201), although he reserves for proverbs (also a conversational genre) a more "traditional" function of conveying "social wisdom." In the case of the committee observed here, proverbs as well as other kinds of proverbial expressions helped to *form* the group, to define it not so much in relation to "outsiders" as to itself, and to foster the kind of group interaction essential to effective functioning of the committee.

Over the period of observation it was quite apparent that certain members of the committee were more inclined to use proverbial language than were others. The uneven distribution was borne out in the final tallying of the expressions recorded: In addition to the leading user of proverbs or proverbial phrases (with 46) there were four others who made up a "top five," one with 20 individual items and three more with 15 each. Thereafter the frequency dropped dramatically. What was particularly striking, however, was the fact that the "top five" included the two members who served as chair of the committee during this period; one who served as vice-chair; one who became chair the following year; and one who served as the committee's representative to its university-wide equivalent at the principal campus.

A further look revealed another interesting statistic: The leading proverb user had employed a total of 12 proverbs (true proverbs, not phrases) during the two-year period of observation—ten while he was chair and only two subsequently—and his use of proverbial expressions of other types was likewise concentrated in his period of chairmanship, so that overall he employed twice as many elements of proverbial speech during that period than when he was merely a member of the committee. The other chair had a grand total of 15 proverbial expressions—two before he became chair and 13 thereafter. His successor—the one who was selected to assume the chairmanship the following year—looked very promising indeed as a user of proverbial language, with seven examples of proverbs and eight phrases during his first year of service on the committee, but unfortunately the period of observation ended before his term as chair began.

I believe that these data may be seen as a corroboration of the role I have postulated for these proverbial expressions, not only in communication but in the evolution of an environment in which communication—proverbial or not—could take place. Bauman (1977: 29) refers to certain performance roles that "constitute a major dimension of the patterning of performance within communities," and notes that performance may be either a definitive criterion of such roles or an optional attribute. I would suggest that skill in manipulating proverbial language was an "optional attribute" for those who were accorded places of leadership in this group composed of their peers and who carried out that leadership successfully. I would not go so far as to attribute that success to their use of proverbs and proverbial language, but I do believe that the *performance* of proverbial language was a component of that success, as well as of the successful functioning of the committee as a whole. Going back to Bauman's definition, we are reminded that performance entails a responsibility to the audience (the committee) for a display of communicative competence, which in turn "rests on the knowledge and ability to speak in socially appropriate ways" (Bauman, 1977: 11). Communicative competence is clearly a prerequisite for effective committee leadership; the appropriate use of proverbs and other proverbial expressions is only one aspect of communicative competence, and not an indispensable one, but it can be a significant adjunct to other skills of interpersonal communication.

CONCLUSION

The implications of these observations for understanding organizations are several. When people of diverse backgrounds come together to accomplish a common purpose, they require an ambience conducive to effective interaction, an ambience characterized by cordial relations and, if possible, good humor as well. Skillful use of proverbial language can help to provide such an ambience. Pithy sayings that encapsulate "traditional wisdom" in dramatic, highly "visual" form have an impact often missing from ordinary discourse. They call attention to themselves, they emphasize, they persuade. Or—when used "nontraditionally"— they amuse, they add verbal "color," they relieve tedium, they underscore common bonds that may not have been otherwise apparent and so further the interaction of the group.

This is not to suggest that a committee chairman, an administrator, or a manager can lead effectively by uttering proverbs every once in a while. The observations made here in this paper must be viewed as *descriptive*, not *prescriptive*. Competence in the use of proverbial language is not lightly or quickly achieved; and as in any other performance, competence is the key to the approval of, and acceptance by, the "audience" and therefore to the effectiveness of that use. On the other hand, the effects of incompetent performance can be most unfortunate. Most of us can recall without difficulty instances in which public figures have made use of proverbial language, only to find themselves permanently linked, in the media and elsewhere, to the use—or misuse—of a particular expression. It is when traditional expressions are employed skillfully, naturally, and spontaneously that they are most effective, and as has been suggested here, their overall effect may be very significant indeed.

11

NEW FRAMES FOR OLD

Changing the Managerial Culture of an Aircraft Factory

Richard C. Snyder

University of California, Berkeley

> Sir James Frazer, when asked if he had ever seen one
> of the primitive people about whose customs he had
> written so many volumes, tersely replied "God forbid!"
> —Beattie, *Other Cultures*

In some regards, the study of organizational culture change is reminiscent of the study of anthropology and folklore in Frazer's days. Although much has been written about organizational culture and organizational change, there is still little in print to document the actual practices of managers who have successfully changed some aspect(s) of an organization's culture.

The present study, a historical analysis of the process of implementing a new managerial philosophy and making other changes in managerial practices in parts of the Lockheed-California Company, addresses that issue. The particular change studied was the "turnaround" of the L-1011 wide-body jet manufacturing program, a program that had caused the company severe problems for many years.[1]

WHY ORGANIZATIONAL CHANGE IS IMPORTANT

Managers are often called upon to make changes in their organizations. Such changes include improvements in innovation, productivity, ethical behavior, customer service, and other attributes desired by various stakeholders.[2]

Many of these changes are driven by the competitive demands of the marketplace. AT&T, for example—after years with a virtual monopoly on telephone service and equipment sales—has recently found itself competing with MCI, SPRINT, and other common carriers for the sale of long-distance services. It also competes with ROLM for the sale of switchboards, Northern Telecom in sophisticated gear for telephone operating companies, and IBM in personal computers. Given such changes in its business environment, it recognizes the need to compete more effectively, and is now attempting to become much more marketing-driven (O'Reilly, 1984).

Some companies' desires for change are motivated by the ethical values and social concerns of high-level executives. For example, after the burning of the Isla Vista branch of the Bank of America in 1970, Chairman Louis Lundborg traveled around the country talking with students and other critics of the bank, and developed greater awareness of the social issues his company faced. Lundborg subsequently denounced U.S. involvement in the Vietnam war, and in 1971, B of A's President A. W. Clausen emphasized the bank's "determination to aid minorities, preserve the environment . . . and be a catalyst for change in the 1970s" (Moskowitz et al., 1980: 451). This new orientation of top management led to many internal changes, including the development of a social policy group and more active philanthropic efforts through the bank's foundation. B of A is not alone in this regard; managers at companies such as Levi Strauss, Control Data, ARCO, and Olga have also made many such changes for reasons based on fundamental values (O'Toole, 1985).

Many other organizational change efforts—ranging from executive health programs to quality of working life programs, to alcohol and drug abuse programs—originate in a concern for the well-being of employees. It is generally expected that such programs will also offer paybacks to employers in the form of greater employee longevity, reduced absenteeism, lowered medical bills, and the like.

However, as Ackerman (1973) has noted with regard to issues of social concern, top management efforts to make changes often die in the corporate midlevel—the "heart of the beast," so to speak. In failed change efforts, it often appears that existing organizational routines (Graham, 1971) and norms (Allen, 1980; Schwartz and Davis, 1981) block the implementation of top management intentions, resulting in what will be referred to in this study as an "implementation gap." (This problem is also common in competitively oriented change efforts.

Kiechel [1979] claimed that as many as 90% of corporate strategies fail in implementation.)

Recent works aimed at managers, such as *In Search of Excellence* (Peters and Waterman, 1982) and *Vanguard Management* (O'Toole, 1985), suggest that one of the ways to make such changes—and by implication, to overcome the implementation gap—is to change the culture of the corporation.

Culture, as Schein (1985) defines it, includes the artifacts and creations, values, and assumptions of an organization. With few exceptions (such as Allen, 1980), most authors agree that culture change comes rarely and is not easy to manage.

What can be done in such circumstances? How can the manager become a successful culture change agent within his or her own organization? Only a few authors have offered specific advice on the matter (see, for example: Baker, 1980; Sathe, 1983; Davis, 1984; Snyder, 1985; Peters and Austin, 1985). And none of these works offers extensive documentation of the role of the manager or management team in a culture change process.

To shed light on these questions, I studied the experience of the management team in charge of the Lockheed-California Company's Plant 10—a group that recently changed some aspects of its managerial culture in order to improve manufacturing effectiveness, managerial treatment of employees, and the quality and accuracy of information within one of its large manufacturing facilities. (The types of culture changes I will refer to in this article are primarily those in managerial practices or norms. No claim is made that fundamental assumptions changed.)

HOW THE STUDY BEGAN

I originally met Robert Batchelder and Dale Daniels of the Lockheed-California Company in December 1982, at a USC conference on Ethics and the Culture of the Corporation, where I had made a presentation on how to study corporate culture. At the time I was a doctoral student and lecturer at the USC business school. Dr. Batchelder, a minister by training, served the Lockheed-California Company as a management trainer and ethicist, and Mr. Daniels was the company's vice-president of manufacturing. Both had strong interest in ethical issues, and both were interested in the impact of the company's culture on ethical decisions.

Batchelder and Daniels subsequently invited me to Lockheed to discuss the possibility of conducting a study of the company's culture. I asked Professor Larry Greiner of the USC faculty to join me on the project because of his long experience with consulting and organization studies projects. As our discussions proceeded, the focus of the study changed from a total company study to a study of the turnaround of a plant where the L-1011 jumbo jet was assembled and flight-tested.

We were funded by the company to conduct the smaller study—with the understanding that we would prepare a case for research and teaching purposes, and would be free to use the material in the cases for other purposes. The company had the right to review the material for factual accuracy and matters of business sensitivity, but the project was otherwise conducted at our discretion.[3]

METHODOLOGY

The methodological approach was essentially that of the historian, seeking to find relevant facts from various sources of information, and to confirm or disconfirm them with other sources (Barzun and Graff, 1977). Most data were gathered through intensive interviewing and analysis of historical documents and photos. I also had an office at company headquarters and had free access to headquarters staff and the plant where the turnaround occurred. This provided the opportunity for various types of observation, including some participant observation. Interviews were conducted in various locations.

Research took place over a fifteen-month period. Following Louis' (1983) advice to focus on a particular level of the organization, attention was paid to the top- and mid-management culture in the plant. Initial interviews were aimed primarily at answering the following questions:

(1) What did the interviewee do at Lockheed; how long had he or she been there, and what types of jobs had he or she held?

(2) What had been the most significant events in the company's history while the interviewee had been there?

(3) Had they noticed any changes in the style of management of the plant over the years? If so, what had changed?

(4) If there were changes, how had they been brought about?

(5) What was the philosophy that underlay the changes?

Subsequent interviews generally pursued specific points of fact (or interpretation) needed in order to prepare a written history of the changes. Several dozen key managers were interviewed formally, and dozens of informal interview were also conducted. The average formal interview ranged from one to two hours, and some managers were interviewed multiple times. Over 50 hours of interviews were tape recorded. We also examined thousands of pages of company memos, technical materials, press clippings, books on company history, and other documents, and had access to company photo archives.

The people we worked with were extremely cooperative and went to great efforts to help us obtain the information we sought. As we examined documents and gained more data, we went back to reconduct interviews both to fill in holes in our data and to clarify apparent discrepancies in various participants' recollections of the changes in the plant. This required a great deal of time (and no doubt, patience) from many of our interviewees. During this time, however, we were never denied access to anyone with whom we requested an interview.

A summary of the turnaround story follows, followed by an analysis of some of the techniques used to bring about the changes. Although the actions of many people brought about the changes in the plant, this condensed version of the story will focus primarily on the actions of the company's vice president of Manufacturing, Dale Daniels. (More extensive documentation of this turnaround is provided in three research cases: Jansen, 1983; Snyder, 1986a and 1986b.)

THE LOCKHEED CORPORATION

The L-1011 program. In 1966, the Lockheed-California Company (CALAC), a Lockheed subsidiary, decided to enter the market for a wide-bodied medium-range jet, the L-1011 TriStar. The plane was beautifully engineered, equipped with extra-quiet Rolls Royce RB.211 engines, and reputed to be one of the best flying airplanes of all time. A later model of the plane—the Dash 500—was additionally equipped with superior avionics that allowed it to land in conditions of near-zero visibility.

The L-1011 program's first major crisis was the bankruptcy of its sole supplier of engines, Rolls Royce, in February, 1971. This exacerbated a financial crisis in the company that led it to the edge of bankruptcy. Later that year federal loan guarantees were passed in the Senate by a vote of 49 to 48, saving the company from financial death. The Rolls-Royce failure also led to massive layoffs at the Lockheed plant in Palmdale and cast considerable doubt on the future of the L-1011 program.

In 1975, Lockheed was involved in an international "questionable payments" scandal, which eventually toppled the prime minister of Japan. Shortly thereafter Lockheed's top management signed a consent decree, which—while not specifically admitting any wrongdoing—promised that such events would not happen in the future.

All told, the program was a financial disaster for the company. It led it into a bloody competitive war with McDonnell Douglas, in which both companies lost immensely. Lockheed's total losses on the program exceeded $2 billion. Within Lockheed it is said that "Mac Dac" lost $1 billion on its end of the battle.

Plant 10. Looming out of the desert in California's Antelope Valley, Plant 10 was the major-assembly, final-assembly, and flight-testing facility for the L-1011 program. Throughout its history the plant had been plagued by problems. These included trouble keeping production on schedule and within budget, quality problems, and a long series of changes in the management of the plant.

One Lockheed manager later commented that, over the years, the plant had become "an albatross" for Lockheed's top management. It was particularly well known for the autocratic and demeaning style of many of its managers. As he described it,

> [CALAC's President] had been receiving 3 or 4 letters a day from hourly workers, supervisors, and, I heard, even the wives of some members of management. They were complaining about overworking people, a dictatorial style of management that was just unnerving to some people, public humiliation, etc.

Management changes. On February 13, 1976, in the wake of the foreign payments scandal, Chairman Dan Haughton and President Carl Kotchian resigned, "in the best interests of Lockheed." Lockheed's board responded by appointing a new chairman, Robert Haack, who helped restore the company's credibility in the financial community. Haack was succeeded by Roy Anderson, the company's vice-chairman.

In 1979 a new president of the California Company was appointed—

Dr. Edgar Cortright, described by Lockheed Corporation's President Larry Kitchen as "an internationally recognized scientist and administrator." Dave Watson, who later became the manager of Plant 10, described Dr. Cortright as

> one of the most humanistic managers in the aircraft industry. He wanted to be successful not only in terms of producing products, but also in terms of producing people. He lived and conveyed that message wherever he went, and made it believable. More than just talking it, he conducted himself very personally. He was willing to talk with people, to meet with people, to be one of the people.

As CALAC's new president, Dr. Cortright wanted to change the situation in the plant. One of the first steps he took was appointing Dale Daniels as vice president of manufacturing, a position that gave Daniels direct responsibility for the Palmdale plant.

DALE DANIELS' BACKGROUND AND MANAGERIAL PHILOSOPHY

Daniels began his career at Lockheed in 1943, working as a drill-press operator while still a student at Van Nuys High School. After going to college, serving in the Navy, and working at GE for four years, Daniels returned to Lockheed. His background included work as an engineer and manager in aircraft design, safety inspection, and shipbuilding. He also spent time overseas (both in engineering and marketing) and had been well received in Japan, where he represented the company during and following the "corrupt payments" incident.

Over the years he had developed a managerial philosophy that, as he later said, "had been tested and proven to work." This philosophy differed markedly from that of many of his peers in manufacturing, and included a number of beliefs that he frequently stated to others:

"Don't sell your integrity—it's the only thing that can't be bought."

"You may be *better at* something than someone else, but you are not *better than* they are."

When facing persistent difficulties, "attack the problem, not the person."

There are many different ways to accomplish a given end. "You don't have to make people do things your way to get performance."

If you want people to tell you the truth, then when they do—and something is going wrong—"don't shoot the messenger."

During interviews, Daniels said that he had made it a practice to find people he could trust and then delegate "total authority and total responsibility" to them. He told us that he believed in letting them do their job, and not breathing down their backs, but he also told them "if something is going wrong, you'd better tell me about it."

SUMMARY OF THE SITUATION DANIELS FACED

When Daniels was appointed, he faced the following problems in Plant 10:

- Aircraft production was behind schedule. Delivery dates to several customers had been missed.
- Parts were arriving late in the assembly cycle, which slowed production and added to the number of hours it took to do a given job. Some purchased parts were arriving as much as 30 days late.
- Production costs were significantly over budget. On a project of this magnitude, this could run into millions of dollars.
- The ships were suffering from quality problems, that—although they were caught before the planes were certified for flight—were costly to repair.
- It was very difficult to ascertain the true status of production costs, quality problems, and behind-schedule conditions in the plant. Previous managers (and some still there), it seemed, had so scared the people in the plant that they were afraid to tell the truth, fearing that they would be punished or humiliated in front of their peers.
- There was open hostility between departments of the organization (e.g., between Production and Quality Assurance).
- A number of managers in the plant persisted in publicly humiliating their employees in front of other people.
- Beyond this, lingering resentment over previous treatment of the company's employees was felt throughout the organization, and morale was low, owing to years of having been viewed as losers by other organizations within the company.

MAKING HIS PHILOSOPHY KNOWN

Within his first week on the job, Daniels sent out a memo describing his philosophy to all of the people in the organization. He also spent much time walking around and getting to know the people in the plant. As he described it, when he first started, some of them were so afraid of the firm's managers that when they saw him coming they walked the other way. In some cases, he said, he would follow them around until they could go no farther, and then introduce himself to them.

As Daniels walked around the plant he promoted his philosophy. Initially many managers were skeptical of the new philosophy. Some didn't believe it would work, or—as one put it—"thought it was BS." Others underestimated Daniels and thought that he would be soft-headed and not make tough changes in the organization. They soon discovered otherwise.

THE ROOTS OF THE PROBLEM

As Daniels talked to employees and got to know them, he was constantly reminded of the management style previously in operation there. A prior high-level corporate executive, Archie Folden, had left an unforgettable stamp on the plant. Stories that circulate at Lockheed describe Folden as a man who was "a master builder," but also a highly feared manager. In an effort to cause people to think positively, he had forbidden the use of expressions such as "I hope," "I think," and "I can't," insisting that people state exactly when a job would be done, how many hours it would take to accomplish, and so on.

Folden had a reputation for technological brilliance—he had helped turn around one of the company's major suppliers (Rolls Royce) in times of crisis, and under his leadership, the people of Plant 10 had produced aircraft for the least hours reported. But during the Folden era, we were told, many people came to be afraid to speak the truth, and some developed the practice of covering up problems lest they be chewed out—or perhaps fired—by Folden or a "Foldenized" manager.

As Daniels came face-to-face with the residue of this style of management, he realized that he would have to send a very clear message that life was going to change in the plant. How, he wondered, could he do this in a fashion that was clear, convincing, and motivating? Daniels had at one time worked for Folden, and knew many of his "tricks." Perhaps unwittingly, he decided to use variations of Folden's approach to send a new message that would signal the exodus of the old style and the genesis of a new one.

Daniels believed that people "judge what you do, not what you say." Folden had prowled the plant, chewing out people and filling them with fear. Daniels would prowl the plant and get to know the people, encouraging them to level with him. Folden had gotten there early, determined the status of the ships, and used that information to put people on the spot. Daniels would get there early, determine what needed to be done to solve the problems, and work with people to get their sections up to speed without attacking their dignity. Folden promoted men who got results, but often at the cost of publicly embarrassing employees. Daniels would promote people who could plan, treat their subordinates decently, and get results.

PUTTING THE PHILOSOPHY INTO ACTION

Daniels realized that in order to change the perception of management in the shipyards, he and all the people who worked with him would have to act consistently with this new philosophy. Without that consistency, he had learned through previous experience, people would assume that the new philosophy was not for real, and would not give it the backing it needed.

Daniels emphasized certain points over and over again. "You must get out of the office and walk the shop floor," he told the people who worked for him. He religiously practiced this approach himself, often arriving at four in the morning to check on aircraft status and meet with key people in the plant. He would stay around for the second shift, then go out for dinner, and come back later to meet with people on the graveyard shift.

"Attack the problem, not the person," Daniels reminded people when they tried to focus blame on someone else. If a production manager sitting in a ship status meeting said, "We woulda had that segment of the hull finished on time, but the guys in fabrication didn't get us the parts we needed on time," Daniels would reply, "Did you give them a list of the parts you needed?" If the person replied no, he would ask, "Well, then, how would they have known what parts you needed?"

If the production manager said something like, "Well, he's supposed to know," and Daniels was convinced that the man was just trying to shift the blame, he would continue, "Do you mean to say that you came here to this meeting prepared to embarrass these guys rather than go and see them before the meeting and let them know what you needed so that you could work together to solve the problem?"

In time, Daniels later said, people got the message that it could be dangerous to "try to get smart on someone else," and they would come to meetings saying things like, "I've met with people in the fab shops, and they got a list of what we need. They say that we'll have the parts by Friday. Given normal assembly times, we should have the job done by midday Wednesday."

When he met with people and as he walked through the shipyards, Daniels focused his attention, and the attention of those around him, on the things he believed would really make the difference in turning the operation around. Every meeting was a chance to ask questions such as:

— What do you need to get this job done?
— What is the true status of the ships?
— How can we get these reports shaped up to the point where they tell your story in a way you believe is really accurate?

BUILDING A TEAM

In order to have his philosophy spread throughout the plant, Daniels had to build a team of people who would align themselves with the new philosophy. Without the active support of the plant's management, the change would never occur—because Daniels' philosophy statements would be discredited unless the whole team acted them out.

One of his first challenges was a high-level manager, Bob Baskin (a pseudonym). Baskin would call people into his office and chew them up one side and down the other in front of their peers. There was much bad feeling against him and several of his subordinates among the ranks of the workers and supervisors. Commented one employee about Baskin's style: "He was a hell of an airplane producer, but he wasn't much of a people producer."

Daniels realized that Baskin's actions were discrediting the new policies he was promoting. People were becoming cynical when he said one thing and Baskin did another. He explained the situation to Baskin and worked closely with him to get him out of his office walking the shop floor, practicing the personal contact that Daniels found essential.

However, Baskin continued to chew people out in front of others, attack them when they told him unpleasant truths, and use a style that could be described as "management by fear." Daniels later reported that he walked around the shipyards for months, trying to get him to change his style. In time however, he was convinced that Baskin would not—or, most likely, could not—change his style, and he decided to replace him.

When Daniels replaced Baskin, he went around and explained his actions to all of the key people of the plant. He said that he wanted them to know that he had replaced him, not in retaliation, but because he "had not been able to change the perception of the management of the plant" as long as Baskin treated people the way he did. When he replaced him, Daniels later said, many people started to think "maybe he really means it."

A subsequent high-level manager was also not able to get the plant on schedule and, according to Daniels, was not providing accurate information on the status of the plant. He too was replaced. All told, it took about two years and over a dozen changes in key management personnel before Daniels felt that he had a team that would give him accurate information, treat people humanely, and at the same time, meet tough standards of performance. Eventually he found a young manager, Dave Watson, who had worked his way up from the shop floor and was widely respected in the plant. Watson was known as a humanistic manager, a first-rate planner, and a very hard worker. He had already been working as an assembly manager, and was later promoted to head production operation in the plant. Eventually he became plant manager.

To build team spirit, managers were issued with special blue flight jackets to wear while working in the plant. They had bright L-1011 patches on them, and Daniels wore his to status meetings. In time the managers became proud to be part of the team and wore their jackets as a symbol of pride. (While being interviewed for this study, many of the managers from the L-1011 program, even those who had been reassigned elsewhere, appeared for interviews in their blue jackets.)

The top management ranks of the company were also strengthened. Paul Frech was appointed as executive vice-president of CALAC. Frech was a corporate vice president who had been brought back from a job in Georgia to lend his expertise in manufacturing to the operation. Daniels reported to Frech, and Frech gave him tremendous backing with corporate senior management. With the new management team in place, the problems fell into line more quickly.

With improved top management backing, they were able to try riskier things in the plant. For example, at one point they were so short on parts that they decided to stop the production line for 15 days in order to catch up. This was a bold move, because they were already behind schedule and were concerned about possible reactions from customers and the financial community. But after they did it they were almost completely caught up on parts, and the number of hours needed to produce a ship dropped dramatically.

RESULTS

By December 1981, the situation in the plant was greatly improved. Managers we interviewed agreed that most of the major problems in the plant had changed for the better by this time. These included the following:

- the practice of mutual attack between various departments in the plant
- public harassment of employees by members of management
- the difficulty of obtaining accurate information on the status of aircraft

In addition, as Watson described it:

The entire plant was on schedule and under budget. This was the first time in five or six years . . . that this was true.

The number of manufacturing hours had also dropped dramatically and were continuing to fall. Costs came down along with hours, and the schedule improved at the same time. The parts problem was also greatly improved. One manager said the following:

Wing-mate was ahead of schedule. Structures and Fuselage Complete were also ahead. All three together were about 55,000 to 60,000 hours under budget. At about $32 per hour, that's a lot of money.

As teamwork increased and long-standing problems disappeared, morale also improved. Watson later commented on this change:

You need to understand that for years when somebody asked you where you worked you [sort of covered your mouth, looked away and] said "I work at Palmdale." You just didn't want them to know where you worked. It was that embarrassing. But now, people became very, very proud to work at Palmdale, because they were becoming winners. It's contagious. People like to win. They got that first taste of success and all of a sudden they were winners instead of being losers. And they felt great about it. They said: "Hey, this is nice. We like it. We're going to keep winning."

ENDING THE PROGRAM

On December 7, 1981, Lockheed's Board of Directors announced their decision to end the L-1011 program. The decision was met with disbelief from many of the plant's employees. The plane, they said, was too fine; the results of the program too good.

The reaction in the financial community was quite different. As one Lockheed manager recalled, financial analysts "had been saying all year the company should get out of the commercial airplane business" and thought the decision "was the neatest thing since peanut butter." The company's stock price shot up immediately. It closed December 8 at 49¼ (up 7⅞ points from the day before).

The program was phased out over a two-year period, and many of the managers associated with the turnaround moved on to other jobs in the company. (Daniels ultimately would become the Corporate VP of Operations, and Watson would again report to him as vice president of operations at Lockheed Aircraft Services, another Lockheed subsidiary.)

A new program, the C-5B, eventually moved into the plant, but it was to offer only a fraction of the jobs provided by the L-1011 program. For workers and managers who could not find jobs in other parts of the company or who wished to stay in Palmdale, CALAC sponsored COPE, the CALAC Outplacement Program for Employees. COPE included a resume typing service, banks of telephones with company paid long-distance privileges, career counseling, and cooperative efforts with Rockwell International, which was bringing a new program into a nearby plant in Palmdale.

THE ROLLOUT CEREMONY

On August 19, 1983, the company held a celebration at Plant 10 to recognize completion of the last L-1011. Hundreds of people were at the plant, including production workers, company officials, newspaper reporters, and television crews from Los Angeles.

Standing under a banner that said "THE END OF AN ERA—THE BEGINNING OF A LEGEND," CALAC's new President Graham Whipple (appointed just a few months before) announced that additional work would be moved to Plant 10, ultimately providing some 700 jobs. Daniels followed him, speaking of the accomplishments of the people in the plant. Nearby stood a stand-in for the final L-1011 ship, 1250.[4]

Following the speeches, the sound track from "Rocky" started playing, and the plant's immense doors slowly opened. Emotions rose as the theme song came on. The air filled with electricity, and Dave Watson announced "Ladies and Gentlemen—the final L-1011." Tears filled the eyes of many of the people who had been associated with the program.

The symbolic final ship (number 1250) was pulled outside the hangar into the sun, nose to nose with ship 1001, the first L-1011 ever built. When it pulled into position we were able to see a sign on the port side that said "THE END." Suddenly, it flipped down and revealed another sign that said "AND THE BEGINNING, C-5B."

On the heels of the departing TriStar, a large white truck pulled into the plant to take its place. Sporting a sign that said "THIS IS C-5 GALAXY COUNTRY," it carried tooling for the new program.

Afterward, lunch was served.

TECHNIQUES USED IN THE
PLANT 10 TURNAROUND

What can we learn about culture change from the story of the turnaround of Plant 10? This analysis will focus on the techniques that the plant's managers used to signal their intention to change many of the organization's practices, and to encourage others to support their efforts. A number of such techniques were mentioned repeatedly in our interviews; eight of them are listed below:

(1) clear articulation of the desired vision and associated practices
(2) translation of that vision into simple, memorable language
(3) top management modeling of the desired practices
(4) building a team that embodied the desired practices
(5) working close to the shop floor and monitoring perceptions in the "deep structure" of the ranks
(6) engaging in other symbolic acts
(7) removing technical barriers to performance
(8) practicing the golden rule

A brief discussion of these techniques follows:

(1) *Clear articulation of the desired vision.* Bennis and Nanus (1985) emphasize the importance of managerial vision in the creation of social reality in organizations. Initially, through the use of a memo, Daniels stated the essence of this vision, which included his managerial philosophy and goals for the plant. This memo articulated what Davis (1984) calls the "guiding beliefs" of the new culture. These guiding beliefs were subsequently supported with specific guidelines for practice ("daily beliefs"). Both types of beliefs were subsequently conveyed in

meetings, personal contact on the shop floor, and in detailed procedures.

(2) *Translation of that vision into memorable language.* Many of Daniels' phrases use the type of construction that Watzlawick (1978) refers to as "right-hemispheric language patterns." According to Watzlawick, such constructions—often colorful and imagistic—tend to bypass the usual logical filters of the mind. They also have aesthetic qualities that make them attractive and memorable.[5] Phrases such as "don't shoot the messenger"; "attack the problem, not the person"; and "you may be *better at* something than someone, but you are not *better than* they are" exemplify this type of speech.

(3) *Top management modeling of the desired practices.* Daniels wanted his managers to work closely with people on the shop floor, to tolerate honesty in their direct reports, and to chastise people for attacking others. By modeling these practices himself, and thus demonstrating specifically how they could be carried out, he provided a basis for what Bandura (1969) has called "vicarious learning."

(4) *Building a team that embodied the desired practices.* It turned out that it was not enough for Daniels, alone, to embody the desired practices. When the actions of managers such as Bob Baskin ran contrary to Daniels' stated policies, people in the ranks found it difficult to accept the policies as credible. (In the literature of family therapy, such incongruence is referred to as "transactional disqualification" of a message.) Through the use of techniques such as changing the composition of the team, working with team members on a daily basis to get them to try out the new practices, and publicly questioning undesirable practices, the team gradually came to embody the new philosophy, and thus act it out congruently.

(5) *Working the shop floor and monitoring perceptions in the "deep structure" of the ranks.* By staying close to supervisors and workers, the plant's key managers were able to monitor the "deep structure" (Greiner and Snyder, 1983) of beliefs and feelings among the people who worked there. Thus, when a policy or act was questioned or misunderstood, managers were able to "reframe" (Watzlawick et al., 1974; Bandler and Grinder, 1982) perceptions that they considered inaccurate.

(6) *Engaging in other symbolic acts.* When managers such as Bob Baskin failed to support the new policies, this raised serious questions in the ranks about whether the policies were "for real" or not. When noncomplying managers were replaced, that signaled top management's commitment to the new managerial philosophy. Other examples of symbolic acts include the provision of blue jackets to signal that the

managers were a team, and the final ceremony, which signified the end of one of the most remarked-on eras in corporate history.

(7) *Removing technical barriers to performance.* The literature on organizational culture and symbolic leadership (see Pfeffer, 1981; Bolman and Deal, 1984) tends to emphasize the purely social aspects of management. However, in this case, at least, technical solutions were an extremely important part of the change process. Technical solutions included improvements in the planning process, providing needed tools and other resources, stopping the line to catch up on parts, etc. According to Daniels, the efforts of a team who straightened out the parts problems "were 50% responsible for the success of the turnaround."

As indicated above, technical solutions—such as stopping the production line temporarily—also serve a symbolic function when they signal commitment to a change.

(8) *Practicing the golden rule.* According to Daniels, one of the guidelines used for managerial decision-making during the turnaround was "How would you like to be treated if you were in that person's shoes?" This question is similar in structure to both the Christian version of the Golden Rule ("Do unto others as you would have them do unto you") and the version expressed by the Jewish Rabbi and philosopher Hillel ("Don't do unto others what you would not have them do unto you"). Functionally, such practices appear to invoke the essentially universal norm of reciprocity.

CONCLUSION

Because of the amount of turnover experienced when the L-1011 program ended, the transfer of many of its key managers, and the subsequent low numbers of people working in the Palmdale plant, it is difficult to predict whether the new philosophy will be carried on in the plant.

Although the facts of this case do not prove that a permanent culture change was obtained, the experience at Plant 10 does illustrate the use of a number of techniques often mentioned in the literature of management and organization (managerial vision, team building, modeling of desired behavior, etc.). It also illustrates the use of several techniques associated with the literature of organizational culture and symbolic leadership (language, symbolic action, and ceremony). Furthermore, it demonstrates the utility of communicational models (such as congruence, reframing, "right-hemispheric language patterns," and transactional disqualification) in the analysis of organizational change. Could these techniques be applied elsewhere, to similar effect? This, too, is difficult to predict, for the turnaround was based on a number of unique factors. These included the tremendous amount of power that Daniels was able to bring to bear, the support of top management, the backing of managers such as Dave Watson and colleagues, and the willingness of the people in the plant to rally to solve the company's problems. Without such factors, we would not expect to see replication.

However, as Schein (1985) has noted, a turnaround is one of the most extreme forms of culture change. While it might not be possible to replicate the full extent of this success, it does seem likely that many of the techniques used in Plant 10 would be applicable elsewhere, especially in less-demanding situations. Other articles in this volume suggest that a number of these techniques have been used in building organizational cultures, and it would not be surprising to find them in use in other culture change efforts. However, further studies will be necessary in order to test their utility, and to offer guidelines for application.

NOTES

1. Turnaround efforts are discussed in Schein, 1985.

2. Rowe et al., (1982: 62) define a stakeholder of an organization as "any internal or external entity upon whose actions the organization depends or who in turn depends on the organization for the realization of some of its goals." A university's stakeholders, for example, would include its teachers, students, suppliers, regulators, football fans, and so on.

3. Subsequently, I invited Erik Jansen, a fellow doctoral student at USC, to join us on the project. Professor Greiner, Jansen, and I worked on the project for over a year together, eventually producing three case studies of the turnaround. Since then, I have continued research and analysis on my own.

4. The real ship 1250 had not yet had its engines installed, as they were costly and had not yet been ordered. Without its engines, the plane looked incomplete and tilted backwards. Rather than install the engines from another ship (at significant expense) for the ceremony, ship 1248 was renumbered and used as a substitute.

5. Patterns mentioned by Watzlawick (1978: 48-90) include the use of concrete imagery, aphorisms, ambiguities, puns, allusions, and the like.

12

SYMBOLIC RESPONSES TO LAYOFFS IN A SOFTWARE MANUFACTURING FIRM

Managing the Meaning of an Event

Jodi Martin

University of California, Los Angeles

It is becoming increasingly common to consider management a symbolic activity. For example, Morgan et al., (1983: 5) state that in the process of vesting elements of an organization with a pattern of meaning and significance, a manager creates symbols. Pfeffer treats managing itself as a symbolic action providing "explanations, rationalizations and legitimation for the activities undertaken in the organization" (Pfeffer, 1981: 7). If one were to focus on a manager during a time of crisis requiring a work force reduction, one would likely ask how he consciously tended to the task of explaining the need for the layoff, what moral considerations guided him, and what symbolic impact his actions and policies had on the remaining work force.

Some of these questions are not easy to answer, or the answers are necessarily ambiguous, since the attitudes of people are ambivalent. Moreover, a preoccupation with the notion of a "symbolic manager" assumes that the manager is highly conscious of his or her actions and their effects, which is not always or necessarily the case. In addition, it ignores how other people manage the meaning of an event.

In this article I examine not only how the vice president managed his division of more than 400 marketing, technical, and administrative personnel through a time of crisis, but also the way in which certain expressive forms evolved in the behavior of other members of the company. I conducted 29 interviews in the four weeks following the layoff; 5 at the vice-presidential level, 4 at the department manager level, 10 at the supervisorial level, and 10 at the worker level. I had been interviewing people for two months before the layoff as part of a field study for a course on corporate culture and organizational folklore; I made my observations and took notes whenever time permitted, within the division of the company where I had been employed for four years as a clerical worker. As a part-time, albeit permanent, employee, I was one of those at the company whose position was terminated. With the vice president's approval I continued to carry out my research after the layoff.

THE COMPANY: ITS CHARACTER AND VALUES

The mission of Data Management Corporation (a pseudonym), as expressed over 20 years ago in a company prospectus, is to be a leading computer services company. In five years the company's work force grew from its three founders who had set up office in a house in suburbia to 349 employees. Nowadays, according to the 1983 annual report, the company "relies on the talents of more than 2,800 people to develop, market, and support its offerings."

From the start, people were considered the company's key resource, for the quality of a software product is directly related to the quality of the programmers who design it. The company courted and recruited the best programmers; it initiated policies encouraging all employees to develop and expand professionally, to innovate in their jobs, and to consider themselves members of a select fraternity. The pervasive assumption that Data Management Corporation (DMC) cares about its people is communicated and reinforced in various ways. Being hired at even the lowest clerical position requires multiple interviews with at least two people, followed by an offer in writing requiring signed acceptance. A personal tour of the facilities on the first day of hire, a welcome-aboard luncheon with the new hire's immediate supervisor within the week, and a group lunch orientation meeting with the appropriate vice-president within the first two months of work are standard. As suggested by Trice et al. (1969), such apparent rigor in the selection process communicates to entering and continuing employees alike their specialness and selectivity.

Those wishing to move up to a technical job or into management positions at DMC are provided tuition reimbursement for college courses and in-house training programs. Those wanting to improve in or enlarge their own job are guided through a biannual, goal-setting review ritual. Individuals are treated "like adults," said a junior programmer. "An adult and a person," added another person; "not just some kind of number." Other evidence of caring includes flowers from the corporate offices whenever an employee or one of his or her family members is in the hospital, a gift certificate to dinner at a nearby restaurant on an employee's birthday, a personal note of appreciation from the vice-president on the anniversary of the date of hire, and unexpected bonuses awarded at the discretion of individual managers that may equal as much as two weeks' pay.

The crisis that occurred in May 1984 must be viewed against this background of attitudes and feelings. A company division that is people oriented, that is believed by employees at all levels to care sincerely about them, suddenly lays off 27 of its 240 employees. While the number of layoffs constitutes a mere 1% of the larger corporation's work force, the 27 people comprise a more startling 7% of this division's work force of 400 and an emotionally unnerving 11% of the population at the headquarters office where the people worked. How was the layoff conducted and rationalized, and what impact did it have on people's attitudes, beliefs, and behavior?

THE CRISIS, THE MAN, AND THE DECISION

As the 1980s dawned, so did the realization that Data Management Corporation was being beset by competitors, that its star software product from the sixties was no longer viable, and that it was necessary to shift from a technology-driven, inventor's organization to a market-driven company. DMC hired Matthew Lewis as vice president of marketing in the Software Products Division. A man with years of marketing experience, Matthew set a tone of accountability by establishing quarterly goals for the sales force and instituting hiring standards that demanded IBM sales experience and knowledge. The division had been running in the red; it made a profit after Matthew's first year with the company, earning him a promotion to vice president of the division.

Having been listed on the New York Stock Exchange in 1983, DMC became more concerned about profit margins. With $200 million in sales and only 5% pretax profit margin, the company began 1984 by selling its least profitable unit, Data Services Division. This led to rumors and conjecture at Software Products that this division, which had the next lowest profit margins, might become a target.

"Corporate said 'You're expected to return a certain level of profit,'" explained Matthew. The division "has been profitable, but it's not at the level of profitability the industry expects. We had built up over the last maybe 18 months to a level much higher than previously, in terms of manpower. We also significantly increased our investment in the future, which comes from new products and distribution channels." He continued, justifying these actions: "It is very important that we do those things because it affects all the careers of the people here. It affects our ability to give raises, to give career advancements to challenge people. We must make that investment." But the investment "has to be returned through revenues. That wasn't happening."

Sensing that the division's expenditures were outstripping income, Matthew began examining the figures more closely. "I finally determined that at our present spending rate and our projected spending rate, we would be in severe trouble at the end of the year." One solution to the financial problem, arrived at reluctantly, seemed to be to reduce the work force in the division. Attracted to the company because it was one that "wanted to do good things," that met its obligations to the business world, that cared for its employees, Matthew was concerned about "doing the right thing" for all parties and interests. As he put it, "It was my responsibility to do the best thing for the business, which includes all the employees and the stockholders."

Acted out in ritualistic, progressive rounds of financial cuts that started at the vice-presidential level and proceeded in the stages through the three levels of management, Matthew's first clear message was that the work-force reduction was the very last option, and one to be avoided unless and until absolutely necessary.

The two weeks or so of budget trimming and cost cutting had two effects, one instrumental and the other symbolic. "We got a significant amount off the forecast," said Matthew, meaning that the difference between expenses and revenues was less extreme than previously and than predicted; "but it wasn't enough," he said. By the time he found it necessary to declare a 10% work force reduction, all the managers were intimately familiar with the figures. Even those who did not agree with the decision understood, in concrete dollars and cents, the basis on which it was made; hence the symbolic impact of the preoccupation with budget review and eliminating expenses. Word of the decision to lay off employees was passed down the line of managers from Matthew to the vice presidents under him to the department managers to the supervisors. Not everyone agreed with the decision at the time, or later. The vice president of group operations, for example, said after the layoff that he still thought targeted attrition might have been used just as effectively to achieve the desired reduction. Nevertheless, he issued Matthew's directive to his subordinates.

"It really took me as a very big surprise," said Helen, manager of quality assurance, about the orders from the vice president of group operations.

> He called me at 4:35 and said, "It looks like you're going to have to lay one off." I said, "No, I'm not, I'm not going to have to. I have two people quitting." Oh, I was miffed, tiffed. I was bewildered, absolutely bewildered. And I paced and I paced and I paced and then I decided that there must have been a misunderstanding on someone's part—not mine! I went over to talk to him that night, and went in on Friday morning again, bewildered over the whole thing. He explained it to me again. Financially. He wanted to know who it was [to be laid off], and I told him.

In some instances, the decision of whom to lay off was uncomplicated. Two departments had people on probation who were let go. Another department laid off an employee who had already been urged to look for work elsewhere. International Marketing, requiring a bilingual secretary, let go the secretary who spoke only English. Finance and Administration, however, did not have such obvious choices; it was decided to first terminate all part-time positions and then to cut those connected with revenues, which were down. The choice was based variously on seniority, skill level, or the ease with which a particular position's workload could be divided.

MANAGING THE EVENT:
RITUALS, STORIES, AND SCRIPTS

The midmanagers faced the people who would be losing their jobs on "Black Tuesday," as one department manager referred to the twenty-second of May, 1984. The level of anxiety was high. Committed to, but not enthusiastic about, the task of announcing the layoffs, the managers went home the Friday before and suffered separately with their shared burden. "I had a shitty weekend, if you want to know the truth," said one; "I was in tears by the time I got out of the parking lot on Friday." Another department manager who had to fire five people suffered ulcers. Troubled sleep was common.

Meet with employees to be laid off on Tuesday at 2:00 p.m.

(1) Inform employee that he/she is being laid off effective May 22. Verbally review reasons for layoff.

(2) Ask employee to read letter from Matthew Lewis.

(3) Review the layoff benefits with the employee.

(4) Complete the Termination Checklist and collect Data Management's property.

(5) Ask the employee to call Sylvia Greene for an appointment for out-placement counseling. (Meeting will be held off-site.) Out-placement counseling will consist of:

- career counseling/planning workshop to be held on 31 May 1984

- reimbursement of actual expenses for resume writing and printing. $100 for full-time employees and $50 for part-time and temporary employees

- contacting other employers and circulating mini-resumes

- resume writing and interviewing tips

(6) Inform the employee that he/she will need to clear out his/her desk and leave that day.

Meet with employees not laid off on Tuesday at 3:00 p.m.

Figure 12.1   Reduction in Force: Procedures for Managers

On Monday, top management gave the midmanagers scripts and schedules, as well as forms requiring signatures. These materials outlined the actions and utterances that in the end defined the event for the shaken managers and unsuspecting workers.

Their anxiety evident in the way they avoided eye contact with others in the halls, the midmanagers met behind closed doors to commiserate and support one another emotionally. At 2:00 p.m. on Tuesday, as scheduled, the managers called those who were to be laid off into their offices. Individually the terminated employees were told that they were a part of the work force reduction and would have to leave the premises that day. They were shown a copy of a letter from Matthew expressing his regret and emphasizing that it was *the position, not the person*, that was being terminated. Each individual was informed of the layoff benefits and told to call for an appointment for out-placement counseling and assistance. At 3:00 p.m., a meeting was held with the remaining employees—to tell them of the layoff, to explain the rationale, and to review future prospects of company success.

At 2:00 this afternoon DMC had a reduction in force. In addition to many cost-cutting programs, it has become necessary to reduce our work force head count. These cost-cutting steps are an attempt to bring our expense base in line with our current revenue projections.

- We believe these are the only reductions needed.
- We are not being sold.
- We *are* profitable. We produced a $750,000 profit before taxes in 1983.
- Our plan for 1984 is to produce a profit in excess of $1,400,000.
- System development is not affected. We must continue to enhance, modify and develop new and better products.
- We are actively pursuing the acquisition of a company and/or a product to complement our existing product set.
- We are continuing to develop joint venture efforts with micro vendors.

In summary, the *future* of DMC continues to be positive. We must all work to achieve both our Group and our personal goals.

Figure 12.2 Remaining Employees: Key Points for Remaining Employees

Few people ever accepted the sterile, euphemistic term "work-force reduction." Insistently they called it a "layoff." But most seemed to accept the concept that was beginning to emerge, namely, that the action was not directed at particular people, and was neither malicious nor personal. "They were good people. We were terminating the positions, not the people," is an expression that was used over and over, almost as a chant. Said one of the department managers who laid off an employee on probation: "If there's an issue that's hard to differentiate in people's minds, it's that we were laying off good people, not poor performers. We were laying off people who could do the job, but we just couldn't afford to have them do the job." In his own situation, however, the manager was dealing with someone on probation who in fact was not performing especially well at the assigned tasks. "It was a weird circumstance for me," he said, "because I had someone who was in trouble. So I had to pull these two issues apart, because otherwise I would defend to the end that she could get better and we should keep her."

Little work got done the Tuesday afternoon of the layoff. Most people were sent home; those remaining were not really expected to work and were too stunned to accomplish much anyway. Some walked the halls to see who had been "axed." Others, including many managers, purposely avoided investigating details of the layoff outside their individual department. Most people I interviewed said it was at least a week before any semblance of normalcy returned. "It was a black week," contended the secretary in International Marketing. "That whole week was just like the plug was pulled out." Said Sarah, the new manager in Quality Assurance: "The hardest part was dealing with the reaction of the other people who were not laid off. Some people didn't handle it at all," she continued; "I mean very, very badly. To the point that I was glad somebody went home the next day. And stayed there. It was almost a week before that person was fit to be dealt with." A supervisor in Development explained how she finally came to grips with the situation: "I realized that I have to present a certain face. It's not the end of the world. It's not exactly business as usual, but still, things have to go on." As a recent entry to the ranks of management, she seemed to feel that a "professional," stoic countenance was expected, and she worked hard to comply. In the weeks that followed many worked in earnest, even if grumbling about the extra load or the defensibility of the decision, to bring in those all-important revenues. Said a clerk in Accounting: "Every day I ask, Is there any big money coming in? There isn't, and I'm having to call people a lot. To collect."

WEATHERING THE CRISIS: THE USE OF EXPRESSIVE FORMS

When I began my field study, I realized that during the four years I had worked in this organization I had heard many stories. None of them, however, were division-wide. Rather, they were about this person or that event in a particular unit, an easy or difficult sale, or some personal experience. And during my two months of systematic research before the layoff, I was unable to find a single story that was universal among members of the Software Products Group, although some values and beliefs pervaded the division, particularly the emphasis on the company's concern about people and the selectivity (professionalism, quality) of employees.

After the layoff, however, a number of stories and other expressive forms emerged that were division wide. Below, I describe four of these expressive forms which originated and were perpetuated during the weeks following the layoff. The first is a story about unprofessional behavior; the second a slogan that rationalized the layoff, perhaps alleviating some feelings of guilt; the third a rumor among management about a rumor among employees (which never existed); and the fourth a principle of business serving as conventional wisdom and perhaps worldview that gave meaning and coherence to what was happening in the company.

Dena's Story

Although 27 people lost their jobs, the story of one person's layoff was told most consistently and was known most widely in the division. According to various accounts, Dena reacted more emotionally than any of the other terminated employees. One junior programmer told me, "I don't know what she said. I know she cried a lot. And she threw some things around. It took her like until five o'clock to get her out. She just held on."

Dena started in the company as a secretary and then moved up to programmer. She had just transferred into Product Communications, where she was to begin training as a technical writer. Unwittingly transferring at the moment when the department was being asked to cut staff, Dena became vulnerable in her new position.

Some people who heard or told the story about Dena's being terminated seemed to identify with her as one of the "troopers" who was working her way up. Her unfortunate request for transfer provided an especially poignant commentary about the layoff. Many of the accounts pointed to precariousness of professional prosperity; in a company like DMC in which career progress is encouraged, guided, and supported in a way that makes it difficult to fail or even consider failure, a false sense of security can set in. Four managers and two other employees remarked that the layoff had reminded them that stability is at best a comforting illusion. Dena had seized an opportunity promoted by the company, and lost. Her tears, anger, and sense of betrayal evoked sympathy among those who told her story, as if the account encapsulated and expressed their own feelings of doubt, uncertainty, or betrayal.

But no matter how sympathetic the tellers and listeners were, and whatever the extent to which they identified with Dena's anger and frustration, Dena's behavior, as described in the story, *was not condoned*. She was, well, *unprofessional*! An ubiquitous value in the company, "professionalism" means being in control, rational, pragmatic, dispassionate. Dena, as characterized in accounts of her behavior, was out of control, irrational, highly emotional. There seemed to be a sense of puzzlement or disbelief in descriptions of her reaction: "Can you *believe* she did that?"

Fortunately for Dena, her story had a happy ending. A month after the layoff, about the time I was concluding this study, she was called back to work to replace one of two technical writers who had quit the department. Aptly summing up the strong bias for "professionalism," however, one supervisor remarked angrily, "After the way she acted, they shouldn't hire her back. What does that say to the people?"

The Slogan: "They Were Good People"

As gracefully and graciously as possible under the circumstances, the people who were laid off were shuffled out the door. The remaining employees watched numbly as locks were changed, then traded in their old keys for new ones and chose new computer passwords. In their own words, they felt "guilty," "tense," "upset," "shocked," "shaken," "sad," "fearful," "depressed," "worried." Following the schedule and script provided by top management, they were gathered together by midmanagers at 3:00 and given an explanation of the financial reasons for the layoff, assured that this would be the only layoff and that the company had a bright future, and informed of the generous benefits given the terminated employees.

Although many seemed to believe that there would be no more layoffs, were relieved to hear of the benefits provided the terminated employees, and were glad they still had their own jobs, they were at a loss to explain why they were selected to remain while others were chosen to be laid off. And some felt guilty. "I was disappointed; it should have been me," said a young applications programmer with the least seniority in his group; he was retained while a part-timer with a reputation for handling a full-time work load was laid off. "I think they just picked some people for shock value," remarked a bewildered secretary when referring to the termination of a six-year veteran, a senior secretary in International Marketing considered to be a better worker than the secretary who was retained because she was bilingual.

Matthew, in the field at the time, left a letter to be read by midmanagers to the workers to be laid off, expressing his regret and emphasizing that it was the position, not the person, being terminated. Returning from the field on Friday, he held a stand-up meeting. Poised on two orange crates and drawing his remaining division in around him,

Matthew said about those who had been laid off: "They were good people." He once again emphasized that it was the positions, rather than the people, that were terminated.

In interview after interview, whether with clerks or vice presidents, I heard this same sentiment echoed: "They were good people. We were terminating the positions, not the people. It had nothing to do with the people. They were all good guys. It was just business necessity."

As it evolved, developed, and achieved concrete expression in the form of "they were good people," the concept that it was positions rather than people that were terminated undoubtedly reduced some of the confusion and uncertainty, and ameliorated some of the feelings of guilt. "It was the jobs, not the people, terminated" removed the issue from the personal realm to some extent. It had never been a choice between a so-called good worker and an allegedly undesirable one; that was not the issue. Everyone was a good guy, everyone could do the job; those who remained were not beholden. It was simply that some jobs could be phased out without affecting the production level of the division, and it was wise for the continued vigor of the company to terminate these jobs at this time.

Simultaneously, however, the notion that everyone is a good guy might also have been interpreted—as was Dena's story—as evidence of the uncertainty and randomness of life. If everyone is a good guy and the terminations had nothing to do with an individual's meeting or not meeting performance standards, then what security is there, after all?

A Rumor About a Rumor About a Second Wave of Layoffs

According to a junior programmer, at the Friday stand-up meeting following the layoff Matthew "kept emphasizing that it was not going to happen in a second phase. This is a one-shot deal." The same message was scripted into the midmanagers' remarks to the remaining workers on that "Black Tuesday."

Yet within two weeks after the layoff, a rumor was spreading among managers that workers in the company believed a second wave of layoffs was planned. In actuality, the people I interviewed empathized with their managers. They felt that no more layoffs were planned, and that management was dealing with them as honestly and openly as they always had. "We know they can't give you a written guarantee that it's not going to happen again, because it could; I don't think that they are planning on the next layoff or anything like that," said an accounting clerk. "But I know it could be. The revenues, you know. It all depends on how the company does the next six or eight months."

If the workers believed their managers, why was there a pervasive rumor among managers that the workers suspected a second wave of layoffs was being planned? Of all the organization's members, the managers and supervisors were the most shaken by the events surrounding the layoffs. After all, they had to determine which positions would be terminated, they had to inform the employees who were to be laid off, and they were the first to face the shocked workers who remained. After years of prosperity, promotions, and seeming security in an organization that strives to be the "best, most professionally-managed software company," with a supportive management style encouraging trust and mutual respect—working with people cherished and cared about—there are layoffs. Were the managers still trusted? Should they be trusted? Could they in turn believe what they had been told and had repeated so insistently: that there would be no more layoffs? Absolutely convinced that the workers believed there would be a second wave of layoffs, half the midmanagers I interviewed repeated the rumor about the rumor of a second wave of layoffs—a form of projection, because of guilt, anxiety, and self-doubt.

The "Three-Year Rule": Conventional Wisdom and Worldview

It was Dov, the young, forceful vice president of Development, who first articulated the "Three-Year Rule," a business principle (read "worldview") that seemed to make sense to many people, offering them an explanation of what had led to recent events, helping to diminish some of the sense of "crisis" being experienced by those in the division.

After the layoff, Dov spoke to each of the groups under his supervision—60 people in all—to explain the financial strategy involved, to deal with "what is the spirit, how we operate, what is the rationale," he later told me. "And I talked with them about the Three-Year Rule in an organization like this: When you want to make a change—that the first year you essentially learn about the problem. The second year is the year we implement solutions. And the third year is the year you see the results."

"After this summer we start the third [year]," he said. "And I told them that I expect to see that we are on the rise. We're all on the rise. It used to be very hard the first year of the change. Very hard."

The changes referred to involve having begun the development of several new products a couple of years before that would hopefully give DMC the competitive edge. "When you go through a change, you have to try a lot of things. I know that we have to try ten projects to select seven that are successful," Dov explained. In fact, Dov's people had made more than one expensive mistake. Most visible to the work force was a project to create word processing software for a piece of acquired hardware that, it turned out, nobody wanted. Another notable failure was the development of a product linking to mainframe a piece of micro-accounting software that the public had effectively rejected by the time the linking software was completed. These mistakes had drawn criticism from people in other departments who, moreover, felt unsettled by recent changes they encountered in their daily contact with Development. According to Dov's Three-Year Rule, the difficult first year was over. Occurring at the end of the second year's struggle, the layoff merely represented a financial regrouping. The third year, scheduled for just beyond summer in the fourth quarter of 1984, would be one of prosperity. According to Dov, it would be a year in which "we are going to exceed twenty deliveries [of completed software products]. That's a *lot*. In the past we'd had only three or four a year, but already [we've had] eleven for the first five months."

I do not know the extent to which Dov's conventional wisdom encapsulated in the Three-Year Rule concept was satisfying to those outside Development; the precept must have been meaningful within the department, however. Members of this unit had been criticized for visible failures and perhaps, to some extent, blamed for the crisis. Moreover, Development was resented for having emerged relatively unscathed from the work force reduction, having lost only one staff assistant. Throughout all of this, the developers had been under tremendous pressure to produce: to create viable, income-generating products in a fast-moving, highly competitive market. Evidence of the pressure—and the developers' awareness of it and attempts to deal with it through projection—appeared as a form of "Xeroxlore'" posted on the Development bulletin board a month before the layoffs. Entitled "New Sick Leave Policy," it begins with the statement "Sickness: No excuse. We will no longer accept your doctor's statement as proof, as we believe that if you are able to go to the doctor, you are able to come to work" (for other examples, see Dundes and Pagter, 1978).

The Three-Year Rule provided a logic for understanding the current events, and perhaps for legitimizing or rationalizing the layoffs. It may also have helped channel the energy of some of the developers toward future goals and away from the emotional morass of the division's financial problems and the recent work-force reduction. Furthermore, implicit in the Three-Year Rule is the expectation that the developers would emerge as heroes, creating an unprecedented number of products that would be eagerly sought in the marketplace. In fact, morale in Development continued to be high. The degree to which the Three-Year Rule can be attributed with generating this condition is difficult to determine, but surely the frame of mind that the concept created had something to do with the high level of morale in a situation that could have been frustrating, disappointing, and deleterious to self-esteem and self-image within the Department.

AFTER THE LAYOFFS

As mentioned before, no work was done on "Black Tuesday"; in fact, the appearance of normalcy was not restored for at least a week, and then only because some people absolved themselves of guilt through symbolic forms, outwardly restored their professional demeanor, assumed a stoic countenance, rationalized the event and set about their tasks with a renewed vigor as a ritual both to preoccupy their thoughts and to try to bring in the needed revenues. Said Sophie, a member of the marketing team: "I find I get more cooperation now than I did before, from everyone, from managers to workers, from people in Development to people in the field. I think it's because the company is so revenue-oriented now. Everybody feels the tension, knows that every sale really counts. The layoff probably raised in people's minds the feeling that revenues are very important now."

The weeks following the layoff were a time of reflection. Some people criticized Matthew, who had been in the field attending to company business during the layoff. Some thought he should have been present to speak on the day of the layoffs and thus serve as a more visible symbol of hope. Some felt he should not have held the Friday stand-up meeting on his return, as it only stirred up painful emotions that had begun to settle. Some managers were concerned that he was unable to stop the numerous rumors and leaks about the layoff prior to its occurrence. A number of employees contended that he should have given all people terminated at least two weeks' notice rather than having them ushered out the door on the day of the announcement. Many felt Matthew should have cut management, which lost only one member as a result of the work-force reduction. The upshot of the debates was the widespread feeling at *all* levels in the company—at least among the people I interviewed—that the layoff probably was necessary, even a good idea: "A good move for the company, trimming."

As expected, a few people left following the layoff; most of these were not replaced, thus reducing the work force further. But most stayed, perhaps in part because the basic character and the principal values of the company remained largely intact, owing to how the layoffs were managed and to the expressive forms like stories and sayings that people generated during the crisis. People I talked with seemed to feel the way a clerk in Accounting did, who said, "Out of every company I've ever worked for, this is the only company that thinks of their employees first. It keeps me from quitting at times when I'm really upset: I'd rather stay here and hope for the best. I want to get my five-year pin," she said. "You know, it's the kind of thing you work for. And if it [the company] folds, then we'll all go together and they'll help us with jobs."

Initially (and understandably), managers were distraught about having to select positions to be eliminated and informing employees that they were being laid off; some questioned, and perhaps still do, the wisdom of work-force reduction or of accomplishing it in this way. Nevertheless, the general feeling several weeks after the layoff seemed to be that it had been executed the best way that these things can be. One manager commented, "In retrospect, it went very well. I think we did it in a clear, quick, painless-as-possible, humane way." Despite the fact that the layoff occurred, employees seemed to feel that management really cared. Dolores, the switchboard operator who has been with the company for ten years, best expressed this feeling. "Basically, hard shells are what gets around people when they have to do this," she said. "But this company didn't have that hard heart, hard shell, sarcastic 'No, I ain't gonna answer nothing, don't look at me cross-eyed.' They go into a shell, management. These people did not; they stayed out in the open. And that was really a neat thing, to see them still walking around like human beings. And feeling the hurt."

CONCLUSION

In my interview with him, Matthew doggedly insisted that "there is nothing positive to be gotten from a layoff." Since the layoff, however, many employees and managers have contended that, in hindsight, the layoff had its virtues—in reducing expenditures, making people more cost and revenue conscious, and reminding everyone of the dangers of complacency. Perhaps, too, it generated an increased sense of commitment or community among the people who, having confronted a crisis and survived, came to have more clearly defined goals and a greater awareness about themselves. The implementation of the layoff had a pronounced symbolic dimension: removing the terminated employees quickly, changing locks and computer passwords, offering benefits and counseling, giving a "pep talk" to those remaining about the bright future of the company, having a stand-up meeting later with Matthew atop orange crates and seeming to draw the division into his protective arms, and so on. The decision itself—to reduce the work force—was an economic one, yet in a way symbolic. "You can accuse me of rationalizing," said Matthew in my last interview with him, "but it's the reason we did it. We didn't want to wake up January 1 [1985] and look at each other and say, 'Wow! We're gonna have to knock off half this company.' That would have been irresponsible on my part," he said, alluding to the symbolic aspect of leadership: "And that would have been a terrible failure."

Some may question whether Matthew did the "right thing" in deciding to terminate positions, and whether the other managers were right to carry out his decisions; whether the way in which the layoffs were announced or executed was the best procedure to use; whether more or less conscious attention should have been given to the possible impact of words and actions. The layoff took its toll on those who were terminated and on those who remained. Yet some might just as defensibly contend that the human misery was minimized through genuine expressions of grief by management, through the procedures used to inform all concerned, and by the benefits extended to those laid off.

It seems that there are no easy answers to these questions. What is unquestionable, however, is that statements and deeds often carry meanings transcending their ostensible intent, and are reacted to as symbols. Moreover, there are fundamental processes that take over in a crisis such as this. Expressive forms are generated and evolve, their shape and substance deriving from the sequence of events as people manage meanings for themselves.

In this instance, some long-cherished beliefs and assumptions were challenged. Confusion and uncertainty reigned. Some people panicked.

The story of Dena developed as an exemplum illustrating how *not* to behave. The slogan "they were good people" and the chant that it was "the position, not the person, terminated," assuaged guilt about the work-force reduction. The rumor about the workers believing that there would be a second wave of layoffs projected the managers' own doubts about what they had been led to believe and their feeling that they had betrayed those whom they supervised. The "Three-Year Rule" made sense of the circumstances that allegedly precipitated the layoff, explained away some of the product failures of Development, and even held out hope that division members soon would be heroes turning the company around by creating eagerly sought after products. In sum, a naturally occurring process was at work, one that was set in motion by the need for personal and organizational survival.

There are some important implications for management and especially the growing concern over wellness in organizations. While more attention is being given to developing instruments and ways to appraise health risk and wellness, little has been done to identify and analyze expressive or symbolic behavior of the type described above. More ethnography of how people symbolically manage the meaning of an event would assist counselors and consultants whose responsibilities require understanding what is happening and why, as well as what to do about it.

In addition, a number of organizations are considered people oriented, caring, and humanistic just as is Data Management Corporation. It might be argued, ironically, that the relatively small work-force reduction at DMC was perceived as a "crisis," and had the impact it did, because it was unanticipated and seemed (until it was rationalized) to fly in the face of basic values. A false sense of security had set in—"false"in that everything about company policy and procedure augured for a bright future: There were no doubts, and hence no contingency plans. While most members of the organization seemed to think the layoff was handled well and might even have been beneficial (financially, as well as reminding people of the vicissitudes of our time), it was, nevertheless, wholly unexpected (and unwelcomed by Matthew Lewis himself). The moral appears to be that "people organizations" need to consider "what-if" scenarios. Concern about immediate welfare is only the beginning. Moreover, if managers create symbols, and if managing itself is symbolic action, then anticipating the patterns of meaning and significance suggested by actions seems to be required even, or perhaps especially, in the company that cares for its people.

13

CREATING, PRESERVING, AND COMMUNICATING TRADITIONS

A Role for Retirees of a Dance Company

Roberta J. Evanchuk

University of California, Los Angeles

In the popular press, articles about retirees usually concern one or another of three topics: company benefits, what former employees are doing with their leisure time, and how to manage diseases of old age. The possible reinvolvement of retirees with their former organizations has been little explored. One exception is Joel Dreyfuss's essay (1983) "Handing Down the Old Hands' Wisdom." The author reports on the experiments of Ed Uhl, Chairman of Fairchild Industries. Uhl mounted a project designed to involve retirees in helping train current executives. By having them tell stories, he hoped that retirees "would transmit wisdom from one generation of executives to the next," sharing their own personal experiences and giving direction on how to avoid errors of the past.

Taking Uhl's experiments a step further, we may envision retirees being requested by organizations to participate in operations in an even greater capacity. The other side of the coin is that many former employees may still identify with the organization and want to play a role.

In what follows, I report the results of a study requested by the director of the Aman Folk Ensemble in which it was determined that it would be beneficial for former members to reenter the dance troupe in a significant ex-officio way. The director of the dance company, and others, had for some time been aware that a valuable resource, the former members (or "alumni," as they are called), had been left untapped. Though there was a list of more than 1,000 people who at one time or another were among Aman's singers, dancers or musicians, current members of the organization had not been able to reach all of them, and few ex-members made an effort to keep in touch.

Much of my research focused on the image, goals, and leaders' philosophy of the dance company as perceived by the retirees. But I also elicited information about why the individuals left the organization and suggestions about how alumni might play a role in current activities of the dance troupe. In virtually every interview people told me stories illustrating their experiences in Aman, expressing their feelings and beliefs, and implying what it is about organizational life that they as participants had found satisfying. Hence my research uses folklore in the form of narrating and narratives as a data base. In addition, the general theme of symbolic needs and expression dominated interviews. That is, the activities and events remembered warmly were those of socializing, celebrating, and taking part in festive occasions; the roles proposed for alumni today tended to be those that would communicate this aspect of the organization's past or recreate it.

There are other traditions, too, that alumni would preserve and transmit for the benefit of both the individual participants and the organization as a whole. Suffice it to say by way of introduction that the organization is still a part of the identity of many Aman alumni (as it is for retirees of other organizations), and many retirees want to be part of the organization, especially as perpetuators of traditions giving the organization its unique ethos.

PROCEDURES, TOPICS, AND THEMES

Nine ex-members of Aman were interviewed at considerable length. They were selected as examples from the early, middle, and recent years that Aman has been in operation. Former members 1, 6, and 7 joined the company almost at its inception in 1964, and were involved during its early years. Subjects 2, 3, 4, and 5 joined the group in the middle of its 20-year history at a time when the group membership was at its largest, with over 70 performing members. Subjects 8 and 9 joined much later and stayed for only about three years.

Six of the interviews were conducted in person and three were carried out by phone. Questions to the interviewees varied slightly in wording and sequence, but all were intended to elicit information about the values, goals, philosophy, and basic culture of Aman as seen by the alumni and articulated by them or suggested through expressive behavior.

The first questions asked during each interview covered the history of the group. Most of the Aman alumni were consistent in relating Aman's early history in the beginning and middle phases of the 20-year period that the group has been in existence. Subjects 1 through 6 were also apprehensive about knowledge of the history being lost. The lack of knowledge of subjects 8 and 9 in regard to Aman history seemed to support the fears of earlier members; these two subjects, who joined Aman at a much later period (between 1975 and 1980), were vague about what happened during the early years of the company. But all were clear about things that were happening at the time of their entrance into Aman and were specific about their reasons for joining.

Joining and Leaving the Company

Reasons for joining Aman included quality of performances, self-fulfillment, and self-esteem. "I saw an Aman show, and that was it. I knew I wanted to be part of a group that had such quality," remarked one person, whose sentiments were echoed by others. All nine interviewed also mentioned the impact of the social life within the group. "People were close. They had a common bond." Several illustrated this by telling stories of their touring adventures (unique ways in which they aided others or others came to their aid during performances and rehearsals). In addition, ongoing jokes and teasing seemed to be a typical way of bonding.

Reasons for leaving the company were more varied or vague. "I left for personal reasons. That's all," said one person. Growing older is a frequent reason for leaving a dance company and always is difficult for the dancer: "Leaving was for me a monumental and shocking decision. I was 27, I was getting older, and the end was in sight. It was time to move on." People sometimes leave because of injury: "At the end it was bad because I couldn't dance at the level I wanted to. I used to be so good. I was at the top."

In 1977, owing to differences of opinion one of the founders of the company left to form a new performing troupe. This change in leadership prompted some others to depart: "I left, but I wasn't ready to leave. It was total emotional politics. I could no longer support the company as it was. On the one side I wanted to stay, on the other I wanted to leave. I regretted it at times. I missed it. I missed it, but I wouldn't regret my decision."

Finally, leaving can be a transition to a new phase of life: "I had a new job, a new career. I knew leaving would be best for economics. It was hard." Said another: "The majority of people in Aman leave to better themselves. They grow and change. The group takes more of your time. You have little left for family, home, job, children. But if you get involved in a group like Aman you get involved emotionally. You can never really leave it. You can't go back, but your memories are good."

These responses seem to suggest that whatever the reasons for leaving an organization, whether aging, injury, change of lifestyle, family commitments, or "politics," many retirees find the decision extremely difficult and continue to wonder if the decision was the right one.

Reactions to Leadership

From the years 1964 to 1977 Aman had a dual leadership. A leader of an organization may be "symbolic," for his or her views are influenced by others or influence those of other participants, and thus may come to stand for a set of feelings, assumptions, and associations. Interviewees said little about one leader who continues to the present, but commented extensively about the other leader, who left in 1977; it seemed they were clearer about his goals and aspirations, whether they agreed with them or not, and whether his philosophy necessarily was best for the company throughout its history or is most appropriate now. "The only catalyst in Aman was Tony [Shay]. The groups around him do a good job," said one person. Said another: "Tony's goal has always been to have a 100-person ensemble. Powerful. Big. This has always been his goal; to be the biggest and best in the U.S." A third person remarked, "When Tony left, I felt that legends were leaving." A fourth said, "With Tony we always felt that we rehearsed in order to perform," unlike with some company directors with whom one feels the "group performed in order to rehearse." Another commented, "Tony stood for quality. Tony was Aman."

In their book *Corporate Cultures*, Terrence E. Deal and Allan A. Kennedy speak of leaders of organizations who become "heroes." They write: "Perhaps most importantly, heroes provide a lasting influence within the organization" (p. 41). Among some of Aman's former membership this seems to be the case. All but informants 8 and 9 still shared Tony Shay's aims, especially his goals regarding company size. Informants 1 through 7 were most emphatic in their support of a large company. "At its peak Aman was a large group. We had 80 dancers and musicians. That was the best time," said one person. "Aman was at its best before the small group was formed," reported a second. "We used to have so many people," said a third, implying by tone that this was valued; "that many people wouldn't be feasible today. The professionalism loses, because there is no crowd of Aman people on stage." Another said, "You can't do the kinds of things now that you could do with an 80-person company. You cannot do Podravina [a Yugoslavian wedding scene]. In Podravina without the large group, the singing, the dance, the stage movement—well, the impact is down the drain."

As shown by the increased number of dance companies in the 1980s of every conceivable size (and their growing popularity among American audiences), however, "impact" seems to have very little to do with the numbers of dancers on stage. Despite their insistence on the value and "rightness" of larger size, the Aman alumni justified the existence of a smaller company in the present in terms of "feasibility" and "practicality." "I understand the reasons [for a smaller company]. They are mainly financial," said one person. "Aman had to go this way," remarked another interviewee; "the way it's going is correct." The implications are that the alumni, though unhappy about the decrease in size, are willing to accept the change as "sensible."

Values and Goals, Fellowship and Rewards

All but one of the alumni I interviewed felt it appropriate that some aspects of the company culture have changed and should change with time. There was simultaneously a concern among ex-members that Aman would lose its original values and goals (as perceived by each of those interviewed). This concern was brought out in response to questions designed to encourage the alumni to discuss their feelings and attitudes about the Aman of today compared with the Aman of their own time. Remarks on performances and leadership, descriptions of celebrations and rituals, the telling of stories, and the revelation of beliefs suggested what individuals' ideas of Aman's culture were, are, and should be.

Though it was not severe, a mistrust of the organization surfaced at the beginning of this study. I had assumed that the people questioned would give their names, mention when they entered the group, and describe their place in the organization, with perhaps only the omission of their reasons for leaving. Also, tape recording the interview seemed the best way to make sure that the responses were accurately documented. At the time of the first interviews it became obvious that this procedure was unworkable, owing in part to a persistent rumor that "at one meeting of Aman a hidden tape recorder was used without anyone's knowledge." Although nearly all said that there probably was no truth to the rumor, and even though my tape recorder was in plain sight, it was decided that the interviews would be done in the old-fashioned way: They would be written down as the person spoke, and each interviewee would have a chance to look over my notes at the end of the session and change or clarify anything he or she wanted. None of those interviewed ever expressed a desire to go over my notes, and none did. The only two ex-members who had not heard the rumor were interviewees 8 and 9, the two newest members. This suggests that the rumor started before the year 1979. It also seems to show that the mistrust expressed through the rumor has more to do with an earlier period of Aman than now.

All nine participants in the study agreed that the present company possesses and strives for technical and artistic excellence; this, they maintain, has always been a primary goal of Aman. All but three believe that the excellence sought was achieved more often during the time they were in the group than it is now. "I feel the so-called golden age was from the year 1972 to 1977. This was when we had the largest repertoire, the most flexibility, good performers, and we had been together long enough to be a real ensemble," contended one person. "I go by [number of] the performances and there was a steady upsurge beginning in 1972 to 1977." The difference between past and present performances as perceived by alumni became especially apparent when I asked them if they had attended recent shows. "Now, watching the company is like looking at Blue Boy done in pink. The old painting is there, but the coloration is wrong," said one person; "things seem not in focus." Insisted a second: "I don't go to Aman performances. The reason is that I see things that need to be fixed. I'm sorry I'm not close enough to be involved, sorry I can't fix it."

Not all of the alumni were critical of Aman. Many had great difficulty watching shows because of strong emotional ties with the group: "I don't go to shows. Absolutely not. I have never seen one since I left. I am too nervous. I know too much."

Only one of the former members was able to articulate in any way the basic philosophy of Aman: "The philosophy of Aman is the acceptance that music and dance that is termed 'folklore' has merit on its own terms and can stand on its own terms, not a stereotypical reduction to some lowest common denominator." Whether or not this agrees with the current philosophy of Aman will have to be determined by those now in the group, and those who have seen its performances.

Ritual and celebration can do much to establish beliefs and goals within an organization, and Aman is no exception. The goal of artistic and technical excellence was brought up when referring to one ritual that none of the members liked while in the group, but in retrospect consider valuable. This particular ritual began when a new member first entered Aman. Rather than being permitted to sing or dance in rehearsal right away, he or she was left to sit on the sidelines (sometimes for weeks) without ever being put into a suite. "In the beginning I was not a part of things. Not in the dances. I had to sit a lot and watch what was going on." Most alumni now feel that this procedure was a much more valuable one than they had first realized. The value the alumni saw in this ritual was the subtle demand that it made for excellence. "When a new member finally did get to dance they really tried!" The possibility also exists that the time spent on the sidelines was useful as a delicate orientation device teaching and acclimating the new member to "the way we do things around here."

Celebration and the social aspects of the company were seen by alumni to be one of the most important things Aman had to offer. One function for some of them was to unify the group offstage (which may have continued to their performance on stage). "The tours were the best. Being with the performers on the bus. Those were the greatest times." Another person said, "The best time was the great party atmosphere while touring." This social dimension of the organization attended to a fundamental need in at least one person. Two days after my interview with subject 5, I was surprised to get a phone call from this person, who said, "I felt I was not taking your questions seriously enough. I have done some soul searching after the interview, and I feel I wasn't completely honest with you. I have my career, but I have a feeling of dissatisfaction now. My transition out of Aman was successful in one way, but in another it was a total failure. Career-wise it was a very smart move, but my social life didn't fare as well. When I left [Aman] it [my social life] left. The social aspect, I realize now, is terribly important. Looking for my social place now is a problem, and it wouldn't have been if I were in Aman. Not at all. . . . Knowing what I know now, if I had to make the career decision I made again, I'm not sure I would make the same one. I'm not sure that the career is that important."

The significance of the orchestra in the social activity was also mentioned. "I always felt that the true catalysts were the directors and musicians. They were the socio-emotional leaders of the group. The fun element in the people [was] definitely from those that were in with the musicians." Said another interviewee: "The orchestra was a pivot point. It was independent from the organizational structure. Tony used to say, 'Dancers are a dime a dozen, but we must keep the orchestra.' We had autonomy." This person added, "The orchestra was a catalyst on bus rides and at rehearsals. The reason I think is because their constant stationary position can give them time to make fun. All it takes is a few crazy personalities, and our orchestra had a number of them."

To summarize, elements that alumni valued are as follows: (1) Quality of performance and material performed, (2) Aman as both a people-oriented and product-oriented group, (3) large size, (4) cost effectiveness when necessary, and (5) socializing and celebrations, which gave a sense of fellowship and personal satisfaction.

Celebrations and festive events were frequently mentioned by the alumni and were regarded by them as being very important. This final point led to valuable suggestions for the nature and purposes of an alumni association.

PRESERVING THE HISTORY, CULTURE, AND WELL-BEING OF THE ORGANIZATION: AN ALUMNI SERVICE

Participants in this study were supportive of Aman, but in regard to the matter of preserving Aman's history and culture they gave its present members a very low rating. By doing so, they also suggest a crucial way in which alumni might participate in the current activities of the company. Their recommendations may have fundamental applications for other organizations.

I would like to see the alumni give Aman its history. I had a chance to go to the Aman costume storage area. You have to look up the code numbers to get to the costumes. The person helping me said, "Oh yes, this is S.U.M. 95." He really didn't know any more that "S.U.M." means SUMADJIA. "K.A.T." to him could have been a shoe size or a direction to take. "K.A.T." is for KATANKA. Everyone should know that!

While to some referring to items in the Aman costume depository by letter, number or color was simply expedient, to others there are meaningful referents to the cryptic code; these referents are enhanced by many associations fondly recalled by informant 3, who feels others would appreciate the items more from knowing what the codes mean.

"I have no idea what Aman is doing. There is no basis. It's like you called your doctor and got TRW instead," said another individual. After being questioned further, this same person said, "I feel that the traditions are not thought to be worthwhile. The newer members are really more experienced than the older ones in many ways, but they don't have the same interest in their culture that they used to." Another stated, "The purpose of alumni should be to spend time in the history of the ensemble, sharing memories. When the alumni meet they will want to talk. That's really where it's at." When they were asked to describe the Aman rehearsal hall, alumni implied another possible contribution by an alumni association: "The office is simply a series of rooms in a suite of offices in a downtown office building. Aman has seen many offices. They have gone from a house to [a place on] Gower Street to their present location. Actually the office has had more stable working conditions than the performers do." After complaining about the bathroom facilities in the current rehearsal hall, another interviewee stated, "The rehearsal hall is inadequate. They have always had these problems. The best thing that the alumni could do would be to try and raise funds for a building that would be Aman's own. That would be the most meaningful thing that an alumni association could do."

Perhaps the idea of a new building indicates a desire on the part of ex-members to have a place to socialize with other members both active and retired, but it appears that initially they would like to interact with each other. "I would like an opportunity to socialize in a social atmosphere with song, dance, drink, and food," said one. "No performance. Just old times and old numbers."

Their interest in historical events and telling stories of old Aman performances could be extremely valuable later, especially in socializing new Aman members. These story-telling sessions, held in an informal atmosphere, not only would provide continuity to the organization but also many of the stories would serve as exemplars. Stories can be subtle reminders of what to do and what not to do during Aman rehearsals and performances, and can serve as an important addition to written rules and regulations.

INSTITUTING AN ALUMNI ASSOCIATION

One person contended, "When you're in Aman, you're in; when you're out, you're definitely out. I would just like it to be acknowledged that I exist." Stating that an alumni association "might be important," this individual elaborated as follows: "It could be important to Aman because of contacts and networking. I have knowledge that I would really like to share. They wouldn't have to do much. They could do it all by phone. They could have, like, a consultant service with a list of knowledgeable people." Remarking on the present, this person declared, "Now, it's like we are over the hill, we have nothing to say. We care about the product. We care about Aman. This is the alumni message!"

In June 1984, I submitted a report of my findings to Aman members, who then began to organize an alumni association. Three events involving ex-members have occurred or are planned: An invitation was extended to alumni to participate in the 1984 Olympics opening ceremonies; a former alumnus returned to active status; and an "Aman Gala" was scheduled to take place in the Los Angeles Music Center in early 1986.

For the opening ceremonies of the Olympic Games in Los Angeles in 1984, Aman brought together 200 members, friends, and ex-members to wear Aman costumes from several countries and participate in the "Parade of Nations" in the Coliseum. Alumni participation in this celebration focused on the Olympics and not the Aman organization. Alumni not only joined with old and new company members to do something other than give or see an Aman performance, but also were able to team with participants of other organizations such as new dance groups, Olympics volunteers of all sorts, and Olympic athletes. Soon after the opening ceremonies the dance company received notes and phone calls from ex-members expressing their enjoyment of the event and their pleasure in sharing the experience with Aman members. Building on the successful response, discussions were held to develop the next step for alumni involvement.

At the same time, prompted in part by participation in this study, subject number 5 rejoined the Aman group as an active member and regisseur of the company. In the months that followed, Aman members began to view their group through the eyes of this former member/active participant, giving them new perspectives on attitudes and ideas of ex-members. Through these discussions with their new regisseur a project was developed to involve alumni in the gala at the beginning of

1986. On the program for this evening will be "Podravina," the Yugoslavian wedding suite mentioned earlier with such fondness by former members. "Podravina" will be performed only by alumni. Preliminary response to the idea by alumni has been enthusiastic and positive. Aman hopes that performing in their own unit will give alumni a chance to participate and cooperate with active members in a single expressive endeavor representing Aman as well as alumni.

CONCLUSIONS

The results of Aman's gala event are not available as of this writing, but the project, though perhaps not a generic answer for all organizations, may indicate a possible new approach to working with retirees. In addition to bringing alumni of an organization back for discussions, meetings and lectures, returning these former participants for a set period to do a self-contained project may lead to innumerable benefits for the organization.

Former members who have left Aman because of advancing age or injury seem to feel the loss of the organization the most. They display feelings of having been cut off from the company before they were actually ready ("I left, but I wasn't ready to leave," was a frequent lament). They tend to identify closely with the historic and symbolic features of the company, and could be utilized as historians, consultants, and promoters of Aman traditions, a job for which active participants simply do not have time.

Those who have left because of a career transition or change of lifestyle—the majority of Aman alumni—place more emphasis on the social and celebratory aspects of Aman. "The social aspect I realize now is terribly important . . . if I had to make the career decision I made again, I'm not sure I would make the same one." The organization's continuing to encourage participation in these features after members retire might express the feeling to the alumni that there is still room for some of these occasions in their new style of living—a way of assuring that the ties with Aman do not have to be completely broken. The new directions the company is taking with its alumni should enhance Aman identification in both types of ex-members, but it is important to note that both types of alumni—those who grew older or were injured and those who changed careers—still retain a tremendous desire to express themselves and identify with the group through dance.

The Aman Alumni Organization will probably grow and thrive as long as alumni identify with Aman, participating in the organization as they once did by taking part in social, symbolic, and expressive forms in addition to creating, preserving, or communicating traditions giving Aman Folk Dance Ensemble its unique character.

As this report is studied by the present Aman staff and former members, further ideas for alumni activities will be considered, including the revival of the long defunct Women's Council, a group once composed of former women performers. It is to be hoped that this study will be the beginning of a strong, vigorous new Aman Alumni Association. In addition, perhaps from the experiences of this group will be found ways that retirees of other organizations who still identify with them can be a part of the organization again.

PART IV

CREATIVITY, COMMITMENT, AND COMMUNITY

"*We come at last to the deep seated belief in the incompatibility of people and production*" (emphasis in original), writes a former executive of IBM in the company publication *Think*. "At bottom, most of us feel uneasy about changing organizations in the direction of making work fun," observes Marvin R. Weisbord. "Playfulness, joy, excitement are what you work *toward* during the week, but experience only on weekends." An executive, while "wildly hedonistic on vacation," may be outraged by the sight of people engaged in horseplay at the office, for this is "a clear example of self-indulgence on company time."

"Can work be fun? Can it even be deeply and continually satisfying? The 'evidence' says no," reports Weisbord. "Most of our policies, practices, and job designs are such," he observes, that it is the rare person indeed in the rare company who "gets any fun out of organizational life" (Weisbord, 1972).

As Weisbord suggested a decade and a half ago, some long-standing assumptions about organizational life need to be reassessed. Principal among them is the notion of work. Often observation of people joking, socializing, and appearing to enjoy themselves leads to the impression that up to half the work day is spent "doing nothing" (Pope, 1979: 1). Much of this activity, recognized some years ago by one student of organizational behavior as the "seemingly trivial events" in a "humdrum context" from which individuals are able to "extract surprisingly rich meanings" (Strauss, 1974b: 31), is play and creativity, which are crucial to day-to-day existence, to generating commitment to an endeavor, and to producing a feeling of community.

Unfortunately, however, the words "work" and "play" are usually conceived of as antonyms (Jones, 1981: 265). Work is expected, demanded; it is productive in a tangible way; it is a serious endeavor in which joy plays no part; and it is necessary for survival in the real world. Play, on the other hand, is voluntary, nonproductive, enjoyable, and separated from reality. "Creativity" is vaguely distinguished from and yet also related to both work and play. To create is a serious business, requiring purposeful action; it is also somehow often amusing, playful, and intrinsically rewarding. Although usually isolated from one another, the three phenomena are in fact interrelated.

An illustration of how work, play, commitment to others, and a feeling of community are interrelated is offered by Donald Roy's well-known article "'Banana Time': Job Satisfaction and Informal Interaction," (1959-60: 158-168). Employed for several months in a factory, Roy worked a "clicking machine" which punched pieces of leather and plastic of various shapes and sizes.

The first few days on the job found him absorbed in improving his skill, increasing his rate of output, and trying to keep his left hand from being clicked. He developed a rhythm to the work, which was satisfying because of the resulting efficiency as well as what the mastery of techniques conveyed to him about his capabilities. In other words, he was striving to perfect form, bringing something into existence (both a product and a set of techniques) by manipulating raw materials (not only the plastic and leather, but also body movements) in a structured way that produced forms serving as standards by which these and other forms' perfection was measured. But soon the novelty wore off.

To combat fatigue, boredom, and thoughts of quitting, Roy began to vary the color of materials to be punched, the shapes of the dies, and the time to clean and smooth the block on which the material was placed. If the day's order required rectangular pieces in three colors, then Roy's game was to promise himself that after punching 1,000 green ones he would be enabled to celebrate by clicking some brown ones, after which he might punch white ones, or perhaps switch dies. Personal games such as these, which have parallels in the behavior of other workers, provided some intellectual stimulation for Roy—but not much. Increasingly he turned attention from a preoccupation with himself and his plight to a consideration of his colleagues and their activities.

His first impression was that conversation was just jabbering, that physical actions were childish horseplay, and that much of what took place was nonsensical. But as he became drawn into the interactions, he began to perceive structure, form, and meaning. His own behavior became more like that of the other men. And he realized he was actually savoring and appreciating the subtleties of their interactions, noting what had previously seemed unimportant.

There were recurrent "themes" in conversation, both kidding and serious. George, the lead man, who had emigrated from southeastern Europe, often remarked on the loss of his business in Chicago by fire. Ike, next in line, who was Jewish and from eastern Europe, complained of the problems created by his chronically ill wife and inept teenage son. Sammy was given to lamenting the loss of his small enterprise when he had fled his homeland invaded by Germans. In addition to such major misfortune narratives, there were topics of conversation such as "helping Danelly find a cheaper apartment" and "getting Danelly a better job" ("Danelly" was the broken English approximation of Donald Roy's name). Doggerel, snatches of song, repetition of pet phrases, taunts, and mutterings comprised "chatter themes."

Much of the verbalization occurred at certain junctures the men called "times," which periodically halted the work process. Breaks included coffee time, peach time, banana time, window time, lunch time, pickup time, fish time, coke time, and quitting time. Accompanied by banter and physical interplay, these interruptions marked the time of day but more importantly provided carryover of interest from one period to the next. Such recurrent forms of behavior at first were ignored by Roy, then regarded as silly intrusions on the work process, and finally conceived of as compelling, capturing his attention and holding his interest not only as an observer but also as fellow worker (see also Jones, 1982: 48-49).

"The antagonism of work and play leads ultimately to a deterioration of both," writes one researcher. "When we think of work as merely instrumental, and play as its reward, we demean the former as labor and trivialize the latter." He continues: "But they need not be enemies. Humanized work is really a form of playfulness; play when directed to worthy ends has all the features of workmanship" (Radest, 1974: 239-240).

Perhaps what is needed is the introduction of the concept "work-*ing*." A vital component of working—as a process—is playing. Limited attention span and the fatigue of intense concentration require relief, routine spawns monotony, continuation of tasks requires breaks with carryover of interest, cordiality among people compels joking and socializing, coping with stress demands

fantasizing and projection, success stimulates celebration, and
pleasant ambience encourages festive events.

A second concept is that of the *art of working* (Jones, 1984c).
Crucial to working, whether one is a machinist, secretary, engineer,
or manager, are positive aesthetic experiences and artistic production
or performance, that is, manipulating raw materials—objects, sounds,
or motions—in rhythmic and structured ways in order to produce a
satisfying form. The high quality or excellence of the effort and
output produces personal satisfaction in having done something well.

A third concept useful in characterizing and understanding work
life in organizations is that of *ambience*—the particular mood,
character, quality, or tone of a milieu. Superficially similar to the
notion of "climate" or "atmosphere," this concept differs in its
connotation that circumstances can be altered through one's
behavior, attitude, and influence on others (by contrast, the
meteorological model implies that the environment is a given, and,
like the weather, is not susceptible to human control).

A fourth concept is that of *community*. In its basic denotative
meaning, a community is simply an assemblage of people in a
particular place at one time. In this respect, the word differs little in
meaning from "group." To many, however, "community" connotes
mutuality of interests, sharing, and even unity. If and when such
qualities exist, they are transitory, fleeting. Most often these feelings
arise when people take part in an event in which individual preoccupations are momentarily subordinated in importance and
collective identity dominates. Such a state of being usually is
precipitated when people exercise their skills in cooperation with
others to achieve an agreed-upon objective, whether to make an
object, provide a service, solve a problem, tell a story, or celebrate an
event.

The expectation of meaningfulness, fellowship, and personal
satisfaction—essential elements in the feeling of community—is often
generated when people organize. These are the personal and
intangible outcomes of interactional, communicative, and experiential
networks, or ICENs (Blumenreich and Polanski, 1974). No wonder,
then, that a recent impetus in management theory and practice is to
seek alternatives to the bureaucratic model and to hierarchies, such as
the notion of "clan" (Ouchi and Price, 1978; Ouchi, 1980; Wilkins
and Ouchi, 1983), in order to stimulate in modern organizations the
character and conditions of community.

As the articles that follow suggest, a model cannot be imposed. A feeling of community and an attitude of commitment evolve only when there is participation and when the integration of playing and working that results in a particular ambience encourages respect for the capabilities and accomplishments of others.

RESEARCH ON CREATIVITY, COMMITMENT, AND COMMUNITY

In the first essay, Dewhurst considers the behavior of "artist-workers" in foundries and factories in Michigan. While the urge to create characterizes all of us, some individuals in the workplace are accorded special status for their skills, imagination, and accomplishments. Through their artistry, suggests Dewhurst, these individuals enhance the intrinsic rewards of the work experience of others, serve as symbol makers for the occupational group, and increase the feeling of community by means of their presence and participation. Like creativity, with which it shares much in common, play can provide satisfying experiences and generate *communitas*, a spirit of unification with others. As Dandridge suggests in the second essay, celebrations and many ceremonies are playful, imaginative, and vital to work life. The lack of ceremony, especially with a festive element, leads to sterility of work and reduction in personal satisfaction. The combination of work and play, however, can result in people transcending the work role and experiencing personal satisfaction as well as a feeling of community. But the celebrations and ceremonies must be natural, spontaneous. An attempt to impose them strictly from a productivity perspective will fail. In the third article, Moore reports on his research concerning an unusual annual celebration in the Ozarks called Old People's Day. It originated decades earlier as a way of resolving factionalism and of creating a feeling of community. A week long event, it includes preaching, picnics, testimonials, and singing—all oriented toward recognizing and honoring the oldest residents of the area. Dramatic and participatory in nature, these expressive forms result naturally and spontaneously in feelings of fellowship and self-esteem.

According to Wilson, in the next essay, folklore not only reveals sore spots in an organization and helps people, but its study teaches us not to interfere with this interactional and psychological process.

These lessons are apparent in the ways in which young Mormon missionaries deal with stress generated by having to conform to a rigorous schedule of preaching their gospel away from home in another country where they must speak a foreign tongue and work with people who consider them intruders. That they survive is owing in large measure to their participating in pranks and practical jokes, and using expressions and telling stories that redirect some of their feelings of frustration, relieve tension, and even create a sense of community.

In the final article in this section, Stern examines the role of "emblem" at Garrett Corporation, a concept he employs to help understand why the approximately 100 individuals he interviewed spoke highly of Cliff Garrett and seemed to identify with the organization that he founded in 1936. There are many stories, ceremonies, plaques, buttons, pins, and slogans that communicate respect for the individual, recognize contributions to the organization and individual achievements, and communicate receptivity and reciprocity. A situation characterized by equality, flexibility, and an array of awards is responsible for generating and maintaining feelings of pride and loyalty, motivating individuals to see their identities entwined with the identity of the organization. Many people at Garrett Corporation created a reality through expressive forms and symbolic behavior. It was "mythic" in the best sense of the word, as suggested by the last essay.

All five essays have as a central focus the matter of community defined in terms of participation, common interests and concerns, and unity of spirit. The authors indicate that a feeling of oneness resulting from and leading to cooperation in organizations (if it obtains at all) depends largely on symbolic behavior and aesthetic expression. Ritualizing, celebrating, narrating, and the like project hopes and desires, enable people to transcend immediate circumstances, and transform situations in the evolution toward the realization of human potential. But the process is not without its dilemmas or paradoxes.

14

ART AT WORK
In Pursuit of Aesthetic Solutions

C. Kurt Dewhurst
Michigan State University

In his essay "Civilization and the Sense of Quality," the acerbic social critic Herbert Read writes the following:

> Art redeems our actions from monotony and our minds from boredom. We have to make things and to do things in order to live, but the routine of menial tasks would dull the senses and deaden the mind unless there was the possibility of doing things with a progressive sense of quality. That sense of quality is the aesthetic sense, and in the end, the aesthetic sense is the vital sense, the sense without which we die [Read, 1964: 176-177].

In this article I will explore the aesthetic sense of some workers in Michigan factories who have drawn upon their skills to gain control over the work experience and their lives beyond work.

The early literature in organizational psychology contended that individuals at higher occupational levels placed greater value on "intrinsic" job factors such as self-expression (a chance to use one's skills or talent), interest value of work, and a feeling of satisfaction from the work itself. Those at the lower levels were assumed to value "extrinsic" job values such as pay, security, and satisfying coworkers (Centers and Bugental, 1966). It was thus thought that levels of occupation were closely related to Maslow's need hierarchy (Lowry, 1973), and therefore little could be done to enhance the lower levels of work to provide self-actualizing experiences for workers who had basic extrinsic primary needs to fulfilled. Later the job enlargement and job redesign movement to "humanize the workplace" (Strauss, 1974a; Fairfield, 1974) seemed to challenge these assumptions to a degree, but not quite to overthrow them. Although ethnography focusing on the art of work was lacking, other research on alienation at work did imply a different set of assumptions about job (dis-) satisfaction. According to Walton (1972), the "roots of conflict" between the worker and the organization include the following:

(1) Employees want challenge and personal growth (reaction to simplified jobs requiring narrow skills).

(2) Employees want to be included in patterns of mutual influence and more egalitarian treatment.

(3) Employee commitment to an organization is increasingly influenced by the intrinsic interest of the work itself, the human dignity afforded by the management, and the social responsibility reflected in the organization's product.

(4) What employees want from careers is apt to be what they will no longer be willing to postpone their gratification for.

(5) Employees want more attention paid to the emotional aspects of organizational life, such as individual self-esteem, openness between people, and expressions of warmth. Yet organizations emphasize rationality and seldom legitimize the emotional part of the organizational experience.

(6) Employees are becoming less driven by competitive urges. They are less likely to identify competition as the "American way."

Ethnography of the pursuit of aesthetic solutions among workers in Michigan's foundries, factories, and small businesses reveals that individuals in the workplace cultivate behaviors providing opportunities for personal growth and enrichment. Through their artistic and expressive activities, workers certainly may develop a sense of self-esteem and a strong emotional bond to their work and peers. In addition, these "artists in the workplace" may be accorded special status and recognition. These individuals enhance the intrinsic rewards of their fellow workers' daily work experience through their interaction in the following ways: the actual *way* they work, their participation in the narrative traditions associated with work, and the creation of art that depicts the work experience or art in the workplace using materials from work. In sum, these workers serve as vital symbol-makers for their occupational group and may increase through their presence and actions the sense of community among workers.

ARTIST-WORKERS IN FACTORIES AND FOUNDARIES

Charles Julian was a "loose-work molder" who worked at a number of Detroit area foundries. He provides a fine example of the role of an artist-worker who enhances the sense of self-esteem and community feeling among his fellow workers. Julian took pride in his mastery of the techniques of "loose-work molding" and was recognized among his group of workers as especially creative and committed to his work. In addition to being a dedicated employee who cast the required pieces, he also experimented with bronze castings of anything that caught his fancy—to amuse his fellow employees and family members. His grandson, who has followed him to foundry work, described his grandfather and his work in this way (quoted from interviews with Chuck Juilian in 1982):

> He was the foreman—almost everywhere he worked he was the foreman. To a certain extent the foundries allowed people to make that sort of thing [art in the workplace]. . . . Competition existed [among the workers] to see who could make the most complicated [work of art]. . . . My grandfather was constantly battling to prove he was the best. . . . There was a competition, a fellow cast a cup and saucer together, which requires about a five-part mold; you have to pull the center out, then the bottom, and sides come out at an angle [very difficult]. [Then] my grandfather cast a cup and saucer—with a spoon in it *and* two lumps of sugar on the spoon. . . . They were always trying to best each other.

This account demonstrates a group of workers' attempt to find answers to the so-called "roots of conflict" between the worker and the organization by constructing activities that provide (1) "challenge and personal growth" in their work; (2) an expanded intrinsic interest in the process of the work itself; and (3) self-esteem and emotional connection to their fellow workers. The initiation of one worker's creative expression has played a substantial role in providing expanded meaning to work life through symbolic behavior.

The creative accomplishments of Julian have a direct connection with improving the quality of the foundry's product. David C. McClelland, in an article "That Urge to Achieve" identified a type of worker who habitually spends time thinking about doing things better—"the high need achievement man." Behavioral psychologists have described these individuals as

> not just born that way, [they have] special training at home, moderately high achievement goals but [they are] men who are from warm, encouraging and non-authoritarian homes. . . . They set moderately high goals but potentially achievable goals. They behave like this though only if they can influence the outcome by performing the work themselves [1972: 79].

The artist-worker with achievement needs does fulfill some of his needs informally among his occupational work group through creative expression. This usually results in a more effective work group with a strong personal investment in their daily work.

There are many examples of artist-workers in factory settings in Michigan. The practice of using the raw materials of work and the related technical processes has led to a wide array of creative efforts (sometimes referred to as "government work") by factory workers. Like the "loose-work molder" in the foundry, one artist-worker in a factory can ignite a work group to explore the same idea. One such example began with the creation of a belt buckle from the trunk lock ornament in a Fisher Body assembly plant. Before long, workers in this assembly area were welding belt clips on the back of the ornament and then taking them home to friends and relatives. Naturally, this presented a potential parts-supply shortage, but the practice grew out of creative exploration of the potential of the ornament form and the workers' desire to be identified with the company emblem. In fact, workers wore their belts with pride (outside the work setting), and some men even went so far as to put pictures of their wives or girlfriends inside the buckle, below the rotating keyhole cover. Management seemed to recognize the emerging pattern of loss of ornaments and countered by commissioning a cast Fisher Body emblem belt buckle as a gift for workers on Family Day. However, the response of the workers to the "company belt buckles" never approached the satisfaction they gained from the trunk-ornament belt buckles that they crafted themselves.

Another example of the presence of artist-workers in factory settings may be helpful here. In a number of paint rooms in Michigan auto plants (and no doubt similar production plants), workers fashion jewelry, keychains, and belt buckles from the excess drippings of car paints and finishes that collect on random pieces of metal. These are later refashioned into jewelry for wives, daughters, and female friends. Earrings, necklaces, and pendants are often made with the assistance of local jewelers, who apply the clasps, chains, or pins.

This activity has been common in many of the paint rooms of the auto plants that have been investigated. The participants represent a worker group that is often actively involved in expressing their personal connection to their work every time they create a new piece of jewelry. Julie Turner, a worker in an Oldsmobile paint room in Lansing, Michigan, described the practice of creating art from the dried excess painting dripping in this way (quoted from interviews in 1984):

> The paint takes a long time to build up on the chassis of the assembly line—but it would build up so thick though, you could kick it off. Workers

made belt buckles (inlaid in wood), rings, pendants, necklaces, and even decorated fish tanks with pieces of dried paint drippings. There were no prohibitions about making things from paint as far as I could tell. The dried paint was just considered scrap.

When asked why workers made these items, Turner responded,

It was really exciting to do it. You could carve it, sand it, break it—then varnish it. There were just so many ways you could create with it. The workers wore their jewelry and belt buckles to work. It gave them something to talk about, and the paint-room workers were proud of the things they made from scrap.

This artistic activity provides valuable insights into workers' lives and individual artists' desire to improve continually upon their mastery of the artistic expressions.

CONCLUSIONS

While this article has focused on the artist-workers in factory situations, the manager or supervisor also can approach his or her work as an aesthetic performance. The human concerns of these individuals are indeed very similar to those of the artist-workers studied here, as they too seek to master techniques and shape an intrinsically rewarding work life. In an essay entitled, "Making Art Work," Michael J. Bell describes this potential for virtually everyone who works:

To say that work has the potential to become art or that art requires work for its making is to say nothing extraordinary about either work or art. . . . We recognize art by the conscious intentions of its creators to make what they do into aesthetic performances, by the technical skill with which they accomplish these intentions, and by the aesthetic pleasure this process gives to those who do it and for whom it is done [Bell, 1984: 211].

Perhaps the most difficult hurdle is to accept the premise that art and work life can be constructively linked. Along with this belief comes the awareness that virtually everyone has a creative potential and already pursues aesthetic solutions in the spirit that Herbert Read suggests— even though many of those engaged in this art do not conceive of themselves as "artists" or "worker artists." Again, Michael J. Bell provides further insight:

Art is anything—process or event—that calls attention to its own artifice, that displays the skillful construction which makes that artifice possible, and is interpreted by its creator and audience within a recognizable aesthetic. Clearly, work has the potential to display all these features [Bell, 1984: 211].

I would suggest that the artist-worker and his or her role in the occupational work group should be studied as a way of understanding the relationship between job performance and job satisfaction. These workers seem to be individuals with substantial need for achievement who have mastered the technical skills associated with their particular job assignment; they are actively participating in work that brings them a strong sense of self-esteem; they nourish their personal affiliation with their company or organization and the performance of their work; and they maintain a strong emotional bond to the work group.

Fieldwork with workers such as those considered in this article supports the premise that workers frequently use their mastery of occupational technique to alter their individual consciousness. Alienation as a condition of employment in industrial settings, while apparent, need not be thought of as an absolute barrier to individual expression. Herbert Read's cautions regarding the effects of boredom and monotony as resulting in "the dulling of the senses and the deadening of the mind" are appropriate, but not necessarily accurate. In reality, people—whether at home or at work—act out of human needs and desires, including the individual desire to gain greater control over the place of work and one's life. The aesthetic sense can be thought of as a formalized solution to the boredom, repetition, and limitation of many tasks of work. By researching the occupational experiences of artists and their fellow workers, we will come to better understand the use of aesthetic solutions to human needs.

15

WORK CEREMONIES
Why Integrate Work and Play?

Thomas C. Dandridge
State University of New York, Albany

In a major U.S. bank, election as an officer is seen as the key to one's success. A complex of rituals surrounds this transition, including the method of notification, the older officers taking the new one to the Officers' Dining Room for the first time, and the new officer's buying drinks for all members of his office on the Friday after his notification. Another instance of ritual and ceremony is found in a Boston investment firm at the height of an interdepartmental power struggle. One director's employees took him to dinner and presented to him a silver dish inscribed with their signatures and a pledge; supposedly only those present know its contents.

Obviously, in these cases and uncounted other examples throughout organizational life, members join in activities which seem to be beyond the rational work content and are performed for their symbolic value. Until recently, however, little attention was paid to the existence of symbolic behavior in modern organizations.

Many of the examples presented below are drawn from my earlier fieldwork at the Mattel Toy Company and the Hyatt Regency Hotel in Los Angeles (Dandridge, 1976). My research of organizational symbolism ten years ago was not intended to diminish the importance of accepted concepts in organizational theory or to challenge how organizational behavior was studied. Rather, my research sought to look through a different lens at the rich inner coherence of organizational life. By focusing on symbols at work, it tried to point to the way in which we outsiders can experience the feelings that energize or control life within the organization.

The present article indicates the ways in which we integrate our lives into one organization/living *gestalt*. For it will be seen that we use certain activities to bring work and play together into one experience (rather than keeping them separate, as so often assumed in the research literature). I draw attention to the ceremonies or celebrations in which we engage in relation to work. In addressing the questions of what constitutes work and what characterizes play, I suggest that the work ceremony or ritual lies on the dividing line between the two.

I do not distinguish sharply among ceremony, celebration and ritual, for it is their similarities and overlap, rather than differences, that interest me. Ceremony is often thought of as solemn yet it may contain clowning behavior or buffoonery. While celebration seems to connote a festive or joyous occasion, it may have a sacred or serious basis. Ritual is common to both ceremony and celebration; and it may be found in seemingly trivial or routine daily activities as well as in large-scale, preplanned events. My intention is to suggest what these symbolic behaviors have in common as a group with the play act. A few examples will illustrate these expressive forms and also provide a basis for discussing the concepts of work and play and their relationship to one another.

EXAMPLES OF CEREMONY AND PLAY AT WORK

The coffee break provides an event on which many specific examples can be based. The break's characteristics and importance vary both between and within organizations. At the Hyatt Regency in the mid-1970s, a coffee break was a random event—often a continuation of a conversation with someone, or a pause if alone. At Mattel, however, coffee was brought to some departments at company expense, while in other departments the members went together to the cafeteria at an appointed time. In other companies the coffee break may begin at the invitation of members who have somehow acquired that role. A visitor to a company such as Mattel is often offered coffee as a gesture of hospitality, a ritual that is different from the regular break. The break and the customs that surround it incorporate the event into the workday, while often separating it as a bounded event. Its importance and the messages the event can carry are indicated in the dilemma posed by a female manager who said she didn't know whether she should have coffee with her friends, some of whom were female secretaries, or with her peers, who were all males. If the event was totally "nonwork" the question wouldn't occur.

Birthdays are times for celebration and usually thought of as play times, but ceremonies at work, and the ritual patterns for celebration, are other examples of the integration of work and play. A birthday might go unnoticed, it might be recognized with a perfunctory announcement in a very routine way, it could be celebrated with a departmental lunch, or it might be the call for a truly extravagant event. At the research and development department of Mattel a practice developed of making outlandish and highly creative gifts for the office directors. One was a "bomb." It was a device "like a tape recorder with a button on it," said a respondent who told the story of the event. The button read "Do Not Push." "So of course he does and it lights up a screen which says 'Release To Detonate,' so he walked around for 20 minutes before he had the nerve to release the button." Another gift was a slot machine that paid off in beer.

> We were going to buy [one of the directors] some beer for his birthday, so I said "What the hell, let's make him earn it." So we made up this slot machine out of cardboard on the wall, and it had a tube that went up over the top into the next room. There was a guy on a stepladder and two guys standing down below. [The director was in the room, surrounded by all the department members.] We said, "We bought you a one-armed bandit for your birthday," and gave him a quarter. He put it in the slot and pulled the arm. There's a silence, and then all of a sudden a BANG! BANG! CLANK! and a flap opens and a can of beer comes out, which he catches. So we give him another quarter and the same thing happens, but as soon as the first drops we send another one, which he had trouble catching, and then we just poured these cans one after another and they'd jump out into the room about six feet and in the end they had *all the directors* with trash cans trying to catch beer cans. I've never seen people laugh so hysterically. These cans were coming into the room—sometimes they'd rip the tops off and by the time it came out it was spewing foam all over. Another time they would just pour the beer down the chute. The whole room was saturated with beer. Other guys piled beer cans up in the middle of the room until there was a mound about six feet. Four hundred cans of beer is a lot!

These birthdays were obviously play events, but remember where they occurred—in the creative heart of a major toy company.

A broader, company-wide event provides an example of a ceremony that was repeated in the work setting and was modified over time. For a number of years, Mattel held a "Thanksgiving dinner" in the production area; sometimes it took place as early as October, but generally it was associated with the first major plant layoff after a heavy production season (as toy purchases are highly seasonal and associated with Christmas, toy sales to the retailer and toy production are also as seasonal).

There was a tradition at Thanksgiving that the company would buy turkeys and would ask employees to prepare them, on a voluntary basis. Then the management group did the slicing of the turkeys and served as people went by. This was an informal kind of serving, not sitting at tables. This was in the factory, with perhaps 500 people then. It was an informal, disorderly kind of thing. People would file by and say whether they wanted white or dark meat, and you might have your controller, your general manager, whatever officials doing the slicing and the serving and having a chance to say hello to everybody. That tradition persisted for many years. When we became multiplant it became difficult [but continued]. When we became multinational of course you had other cultural problems, but chiefly the problem was size.

This tradition was replaced by giving a free turkey to each employee, then by a gift certificate on an IBM card to exchange for a turkey or other food in a market; finally, however, even this gesture was eliminated. Some of the responses of employees reveal the value of the ceremony, and the turkey that later represented it, to these people:

Mattel's way of repaying us for all the nice things we do this year was take our turkey away.

"No turkey, no workee," that's what somebody said, but nobody minds. What are we giving up—six or seven dollars . . . people joked about "I'll donate my turkey" [with the sound of sacrifice] but that's all.

The last token of warmth and friendship got wiped out this year. They used to give out a turkey every year at Christmas time. Five bucks worth on an IBM card. Putting up a memo saying, "We are trying to close all economic loopholes," left them open for the crack, "we're not going to get the turkey this year, we're going to get the bird."

They used to have a Thanksgiving potluck and then they gave away free turkeys at Thanksgiving, and last year we cut out the free turkeys. We eliminated it because of the economics; it was too expensive. I don't know if it was a big economy—it was $20,000 or $25,000. We may have wasted that much time with everyone bitching about it.

The dinner was not self-consciously planned to serve some function, but it appears to have had strong impact on the employees, out of proportion to its cost. One manager believed that it and similar play events at work contributed to a remarkably high return rate of laid-off employees when production resumed in the spring. In the bounded "play" period of the event, people related in new ways, outside their normal roles. For older employees the free turkey became a representative of the event. Using the concept of Victor Turner (1974), a feeling of "communitas" or a sense of a common bonding emerged from the event.

Mattel may be unique in its relation to play. In fact, the personnel manager noted that for a long time people looking for a production job expected that the factory would be like Santa's workshop, and the orientation had to modify this expectation somewhat. The point remains of people coming to work with an unusual expectation of a union of work and play, and being attracted by that union. Parties, ceremonies, or games in any work setting could well strike the same chord; they are only more visible in this setting.

The integration of work and play contrasts with the work ethic so prevalent in Western culture. In fact, not all participants in the above events had positive reactions or felt that the play served to integrate people in the work experience. One participant in the Mattel dinner said, "It's just totally disgusting to me. It's nothing but an excuse to have a free time, to go around sitting on everybody's lap and having an excuse to do it." Here we see a representation of the difference between work and play and the place of each.

THE DICHOTOMY OF WORK AND PLAY

The Protestant work ethic has been regarded as a foundation for the perception of work in Western society. Discussing this ethic, Greer (1975: 165) states, "We have been brainwashed into believing there is a split between work and play. Work is productive and good; fun accomplishes nothing and is often evil." As he describes characteristics of fun, Furling (1976: 80) concludes that Western society experiences a sharp division between "unpleasant work and joyful play." The more that work and play are seen as dichotomous, the more we are likely to separate mental states or types of satisfaction and associate them with one or the other activity.

If one considers ceremony as framed play within work, then the dichotomy of work and play is eliminated conceptually. Ceremony is valued when it is viewed as a merging of work and play that is natural or productive. Lack of ceremony may lead to the sterility of work and, in work's isolation from the rest of our activity, a reduction in personal satisfaction from carrying out the tasks per se. To understand this dichotomy better, we should look at the characteristics associated with work and with play separately.

A major review (Kabanoff, 1980) shows that clear and unambiguous definitions are not available to differentiate work from nonwork, yet the term "work" has a number of common connotations. Work is purposeful effort or activity for effect, such as material gain. We tend to associate the phrase "have to" with work, but rarely with nonwork. Work is productive; we focus on the outcome or goal as we work. Work occurs in "real time"—that is, in chronological time. The clock keeps running during the "breaks" for coffee or lunch, and events such as meetings are scheduled according to a constantly running clock. Time does not end when the five o'clock whistle blows. In work, as opposed to play, there is rarely a separate "game clock" under which workers operate independent of the chronological passage of time.

Play is contrasted to work, as it is a freely chosen activity. It is something we do because we *want to* rather than because we *have to*. A norm in our society until recently seems to have been that adults have to "earn" the right to play by first meeting standards of work accomplishment. "Pure" play lacks a productive goal other than personal enjoyment. (If it loses this purity we are likely to remind the other players that "it's only a game.") One writer (Stevens, 1980) describes the experiencing of play as a "flow" state that is rewarding in itself. Barnett (1976: 83) defines play as "the initiation of a response which is intrinsically rewarding for the individual, the process itself presenting enjoyment and resulting in feelings of satisfaction." Note that this definition does not support a separation of play and work. Its major distinction from our accepted view of work is that this definition emphasizes the *process* of play rather than the *product* of work.

In play we often substitute game time for chronological time. During a "time out" the game time stops. We are also likely to define boundaries around the playing field—that is, the area in which the play takes place. Both chronologically and physically we move in a separate reality. In play we may minimize the focus on the outcome or product, but also we often shape the play in such a way that the outcome is uncertain or is unknown to participants until the end. Generally we think of play as "affective"—related to emotions—but treat work as "effective"—related to product or outcome. There are certainly useful, desired or productive outcomes of play, such as providing a means of socializing, stimulating creativity and releasing tension, but these are intangible consequences rather than concrete products.

CEREMONY: THE INTEGRATION OF WORK AND PLAY

The justification for continuing to separate work and play conceptually and in daily life becomes less clear when we consider the characteristics of play in a work setting or the functions of play. Mergen (1978: 200), for example, discusses how play adds pleasure to the efforts of shipyard workers, and even seems to form "the 'flow' between the rhythms of work and the rhythms of family and individual life." Shiota (1982) reports that many Japanese workers integrate clear changes of pace by having ritualized coffee breaks away from the job. They are also likely to continue work in the evening together in a *sake* house, participating in ceremonial rounds of drinks. Among other authors, Rohlen (1973, 1974) also notes the functional importance of ceremony and work-group play in Japanese business. March (1976: 77) writes that "playfulness is the deliberate, temporary relaxation of rules in order to explore the possibilities of alternative rules. When we are playful, we challenge the necessity of consistency." It is useful, then, to integrate play and work. The creativity and release of play can be combined with the rationality of goal-oriented work. Ceremony can achieve this integration within the work setting or work period, but paradoxically it does so through activity that is separated in time or definition from other activities.

The designated space of a ceremony may be an area used for other activities at other times, but during the time of the ceremony the space is reserved for unique use. The Mattel "Thanksgiving dinner," served on the production lines, is an example, as is an office party held *in* the office. It is also possible that special space or a nonwork time may be set aside for the ceremony. For example, an office group may hold a Christmas party at a local restaurant after work hours, or have an annual picnic in a park on a day when work has been suspended. In the first instance the time and place are distinct from work; in the second, the time is the same as work time, but the place is distinct. In any of these examples of ceremony there is a planning of or preparation for activities and a transition to a new use of regular place or to a new, special place; and there are time boundaries stated or assumed around the period of activity. Participants are able to describe or acknowledge the difference from normal work activity.

An example from America's past of integrating work and play is found in the "bee," or country working party. One description (*Celebration*, 1982: 176) states that bees "combine work with fun and feasting. Often they ended with music and dancing. Bees broke the loneliness of rural life and helped to create a sense of cohesive community for scattered, isolated families," contends the author. "Sometimes they served as political and civic functions, and they always provided a time for people to exchange opinions."

As work and play combine through workplace celebrations, rituals or ceremonies, certain benefits accrue to the organization and to the individual. Within the event, separated from the rest of the work experience, any or all of the following can happen:

1. Participants may experience and build competence useful in the common practice of work; useful behavior can be "practiced" in the ceremony. This can include skills in temporary leadership, social skills, and so on.
2. Individuals can transcend their work role and experience a sense of cooperativeness or community. The unity of the organization can be seen, or the place of a department within that organization better understood.
3. In the face of separation, such as a retirement, group unity may be restated, or the continuity of the organization emphasized.
4. Certain kinds of ceremonies may direct attention to values, roles, or goals of the organization. Moberg (1981: 27) notes that "trainers should not disregard the importance of celebrations at the completion of training. Such rituals indicate the importance the organization places on the skills developed."
5. An inspirational ceremony may lead the participants to experience new vitality or renewed energy.
6. When a ceremony or ritual provides a haven from a problem it facilitates coping (Frost, 1982; Pfeffer, 1981).
7. New lines of communication may be created, or different lines not usually permitted within a hierarchy may be used, leading to better integration of work units or new information in vertical communication.
8. Power or importance may be invested in specific individuals or roles (Pfeffer, 1981).
9. New members can be incorporated into the organization or roles changed, with the ceremony serving as the rite of passage. Lessons are taught and status is changed, often in the context of fun, as in the transition of the bank officer described earlier.

A sudden burst of support for ceremony may be as dysfunctional as a continued lack of attention to it. Insensitive or inattentive efforts to impose ceremony may make it ludicrous or trivialize the activity, profaning the underlying feelings. If the ceremony is a sham it is likely to be greeted skeptically or it will make participants self-conscious. A ceremony can be consciously introduced, often based on a natural occurrence, as was the case with the Mattel "Thanksgiving dinner," but the success is more likely if the creation is a sincere reinforcement of roles, values, or goals that are already there.

CONCLUSIONS

A study of the experience of working in Sweden (Zetterberg and Frankel, 1981) may be representative of such experience in many industrial nations. The authors found that over the course of the decade of the 1970s many workers "have come to perceive work as an interlude between periods of leisure and as the source of the wherewithal to enjoy that leisure. . . . One of the chief rewards of work has become the privilege to stay away from work." The percentage of those finding work to be the activity that brings the greatest meaning to their lives dropped from 33% in 1955 to 14% in 1981. A significant component of organizational life, or source of satisfaction in work, appears to be missing: Is it play?

This article has presented ceremony, in its forms from routine ritual to celebration, as a potentially enriching component of organizational life. Ceremony combines attributes of play and of work for an integration that may be more natural than the perception of these as separate activities. Ceremony's bounded time and place gives it an important controllable dimension in a work setting. Reducing the long-standing dichotomy of work and play can enrich the quality of work life for the benefit of both members and the organization.

16

RESOLVING CONFLICT AND ESTABLISHING COMMUNITY

The Annual Festival "Old People's Day"

Michael Dane Moore

University of California, Los Angeles

Although most of the articles in this volume concern organizations of a corporate nature, certain principles of organizing seem to apply to a wide array of institutions. In this essay, I want to tell a story about a "naturally occurring" organization—a community; about an institution—the community church; about a problem which threatened the survival of both, and the unusual solution which the church and community leaders found. It's a true story, but it also serves as a parable with relevance for other types of organizations and institutions.

This community has an unusual name: 88. The 88 community extends across several miles of heavily forested hills in northwestern Arkansas. It takes its name from an old school district number, its geographical definition from the district's boundaries. 88 boasts no town or marketplace, and years ago it lost its one-room school. Since the 1890s, however, the Lone Elm Free Will Baptist Church has functioned as community center. Identification of the community with the church is so widespread that most people in the region simply refer to the church as 88.

88 appears to be a fairly typical hill community—except that it has its own unique annual festival: Old People's Day. In white North American cultures, one seldom encounters holidays devoted to the elderly. Old People's Day proves a rare exception. On the fourth Sunday of every June, 88's emigrants return home, and the entire community gathers at the church to express love and respect for their old people. They have done so since 1932. Old Folks' Day, as it is also called, always features the picnicking and play that often characterize large family reunions and

community celebrations, but it also involves a full day of preaching, hymn-singing, and testimonials, much as one finds in the revival meetings that sweep the South and Midwest each summer.

A committee of community members plans Old People's Day. Everyone who attends is encouraged to participate in one way or another—testifying, singing, or telling stories. All activities on Old People's Day, sacred and secular, are dedicated to honoring the elderly.

A CELEBRATION BORN OF CONFLICT

From the beginning, Old People's Day was intended to unite church and community behind a single goal—consoling the elderly in the face of their many problems. What is of interest in the context of this volume, however, is the fact that Old People's Day originated from a dispute between community members and their established leaders. The first Old People's Day was organized as a direct response not just to the traumas of old age, but to the broader trauma of dissension and alienation within the community.

For many years the area's only school and only church shared the same one-room building, and Reverend Ben Pixley essentially ran both. At one time Pixley also managed the community's only general store. For many years, Ben Pixley stood firm as the undisputed leader of 88.

Early in the 1930s, however, Pixley overextended his authority. As he recounted it, the church stood too far north in the community to suit him. Children from the southern end of the district had a long walk to school; perhaps their parents sometimes missed church services because of the distance. In an attempt to integrate the community more closely, showing favor to no geographic quarter, Pixley had the church moved south a mile or so to its present location. Pixley stated that he ordered the change out of a sense of fairness. However, certain families residing on the northern edge of the community took exception to the change, accusing Pixley of high-handedness. The Pixley family has become somewhat reticent to discuss the resultant feud in detail, but the northern opposition included Ben Pixley's brother, Plumber Pixley, and several well-known pillars of the church and community.

Seeing that his attempt to consolidate the community under his leadership had backfired drastically, Ben Pixley cast about for a strategy sufficient to the worsening situation. The solution, "an inspiration from

God," as he put it, came to him in 1932. He organized an "Old Folks' Day" to be held on the new church grounds. The idea was new to the community, but then so was the feud. Happily, the day functioned exactly as Pixley had planned.

A 92-year-old native of the region recounts: "As my Ma said, 'Why, we [elderly people] didn't have nothing,' she says, 'until Ben Pixley started Old Folks' Day.'" At that time there were no facilities designed to care for the elderly, let alone festivities in their honor; and those were hard times in the hills. In those Depression days, many community members were struggling for economic survival. Often the very old were shuffled back and forth among the grown children, fed and clothed by one child until the expense became too great, then sent to another who would share the economic burden. With its message that the elderly are a blessing, not a burden, Old People's Day offered the first public recognition of the community's indebtedness to its founders.

In organizing the first Old People's Day, Ben Pixley saw to it that everyone in the area felt welcome. He sent his children to escort the elderly to the church; he commissioned a special delegation to fetch his brother Plumber; he walked miles to the nearest towns to invite the local merchants. Pixley's skill as an organizer conspired with deeply felt needs in the community to ensure the success of the first Old Folks' Day. By all accounts, nearly every family in the community attended and the shouts of joyful participants "getting the Spirit" could be heard all through the hills and hollows. The Plumber Pixley family attended, symbolically bridging the chasm in family, church, and community. Word spread and the second Old Folks' Day saw an influx of people coming from the nearest towns on horse- and muleback, in buggies and cars. The feud was ended and harmony restored.

SOCIAL DRAMA AND CONFLICT RESOLUTION

That first Old People's Day provides a clear example of what anthropologist Victor Turner terms a "social drama" (Turner, 1974). As Turner defines these "dramas," they are "units of aharmonic or disharmonic social process, arising in conflict situations" among groups of people who then attempt to resolve the conflict through symbolic actions. Social dramas feature a four-part structure: breach, crisis, redressive action, and reintegration.

The breach phase of the process involves a "symbolic trigger of confrontation": an offense against community. In this case, Ben Pixley offended the families at the north end of 88 by having the church and school moved south. During the crisis phase, the breach extends "until it becomes coextensive with some dominant cleavage in the widest set of relevant social relations to which the conflicting or antagonistic parties belong." Here, the interconnected families of the community began to turn against one another, and in doing so, to break apart the community church. During the redressive action, the social leaders attempt to heal the breach by whatever means available, including "the performance of public ritual." Pixley instituted Old People's Day; he brought the feuding families back into the church to pay homage to their founding fathers, and thus to reaffirm their interconnectedness. The last phase, reintegration, needs no further explanation; the feud ended, the families were reconciled, the church survived and grew.

The first Old People's Day brought about no material change. The church and school continued to stand a mile or so further south than before. However, by meeting together as a group with a common cause—honoring their ancestors—the people of 88 symbolically closed the breach. Over fifty years later, Old People's Day continues to bring the members of the 88 community together to reaffirm their fellowship. The location of the church has long ceased to be problematic, of course, but other problems—such as large scale emigration to urban areas—always seem to arise.

The general format established for the first Old People's Day has been retained through the years. The day begins with socializing on the church grounds. Reunions, gossip, and children's games continue outside all day even while services are under way inside the church. Services begin with singing. Everyone joins in, and anyone is welcome to deliver a solo or organize a trio or quartet. Once the crowd has gathered and warmed up, two or more local preachers deliver sermons. Then there is picnicking—everyone samples everyone else's cooking—then more singing, preaching, and a testimony service. Anyone may stand up and testify concerning his or her struggles or triumphs.

Natives of 88 who have moved away often schedule their vacations so they can drive back for Old People's Day. Perhaps most important, many of the old people begin talking about the day long in advance, reminiscing about past Old People's Days and looking forward to the next one. They expect to encounter old friends, lots of food, spirited preaching and singing. To date, those expectations have never been thwarted. The event still generates a good deal of excitement and elicits some impressive testimonials.

One young church deacon claims "everyone always has a good time—it's the best there is." The most glowing praise comes from the elderly, though. A septuagenarian told me that he and his contemporaries have had "the greatest times there, greatest shouting times—some of the wonderfullest times you've ever seen in your life." For many of the old people, this is the only time during the year when they are able to come together with their peers.

Perhaps part of the reason that 88 still produces an annual Old People's Day is that the community still faces many of the same sorts of problems it faced in 1932. No feud currently rages, and the standard of living has risen considerably since the Depression. However, buying television and stereo sets has required shifting to semiurban commuter lifestyles, with all the characteristic erosion of traditional values, of extended families, and of community identity. Today's elderly receive better medical care, on the whole, but many remain poverty-stricken and lead lives of far greater isolation than their predecessors did. Some are consigned to urban rest homes and are left there, deprived of friends and family, for weeks at a time. "People used to visit each other all the time, but people don't have time anymore. Nobody comes to visit old people anymore." Many of the elderly experience this greater isolation as a loss of their traditional familial and social functions, as a loss of respect. Even the young community members express concern that growth and modernization may someday destroy the feeling of community (just as rapid growth and change have often destroyed the sense of belonging felt by organizational participants in corporate settings). Old People's Day continues to provide positive responses to many of these troubles and needs. The simple fact that the community gathers each year in the name of the elderly honors the old people and assures them that they have not been forgotten. The services' musical and oratorical performances are addressed to the elderly, and the oldest people present are involved in the proceedings in various ways.

Usually, the oldest man present is called upon to inaugurate services with a prayer. He or another elderly man will often be asked to act as master of ceremonies for the day. Singers dedicate their songs to old people present, or to those too ill to attend, or to those recently deceased. The oldest preachers in attendance are invited to preach. Testimonial services are led by an elderly man, and elderly people of both sexes are urged to rise from their pews and testify concerning their long lives. In the afternoon, gifts are awarded to the oldest man and woman present. Tributes to those who have died during the year are common, as are tributes to Old People's Day itself.

In practice, honoring the elderly becomes honoring the old ways, the community traditions. Reverence for the community's founders and its history in turn becomes an affirmation of the community itself. (Just as, in the same fashion, reverence for a company's founder and awareness of its history can contribute greatly to employees' allegiance.)

CREATING COMMUNITY

On Old People's Day, preachers tell stories about 88 and its people. Testimonials incorporate personal experience narratives—oral history. Singers tell similar stories to introduce their songs. Everyone narrates as part of the social interaction before and after services and during the picnic. One way and another, much of any Old People's Day is given over to telling stories about the church and community.

Since the event commemorates the community's reunification on the first Old People's Day, stories about that first great gathering are always repeated. There are other narratives about other Old People's Days, stories about the huge crowds in times gone by, and about the humorous or wonderful things that have happened in the past. Preachers and testifiers talk about the living patriarchs and matriarchs, emphasizing their importance to the community. People tell stories about elderly people now deceased, eulogizing them. According to many participants, Old People's Day is held partly in commemoration of Ben Pixley's contribution to the community; one always hears tales of Pixley's achievements. Finally, people simply narrate their own experiences with other community members.

For example, I recall an 88 native returned from another state talking about one of the day's elderly honorees—the woman who bought him his first ice cream cone many years past. As he put it, "You don't forget a woman like that."

Invoking memories of shared experiences and relating incidents from the lives of family members and neighbors, such narratives enhance the atmosphere of fellowship. Fellowship, after all, grows largely from shared experiences and a history of interaction. By telling stories about those experiences, one rehearses the origins of social bonds. In a sense, one symbolically reenacts the experiential bases of relationships. In other words, telling stories that illustrate warm relationships among community members helps establish and sustain warm relations among community members.

When neighbors meet to talk about their community, they may not only generate fellow-feeling, but they may also develop and refine their concepts about the nature of that community—the community image, as it were. By annually getting together to tell each other selected stories about the history of 88—and about the interpersonal relationships that define the community—the residents of 88 make a community, as opposed to a random assortment of individuals who happen to live in close proximity to one another.

Old People's Day provides occasion for people not only to express their senses of community, but also to generate them, to identify more closely with the community at large.

One nonagenarian told me that "there's power in us a' coming together" on Old People's Day. That power—the strength of belonging to a place, an institution, a community—is much in evidence. One feels it when everyone joins together in singing. It seems apparent on the smiling faces at the picnic. It is much on the minds of elderly people who look forward each year to their day of recognition. The powerful sense of unity that many Old People's Day participants sense—perhaps create—during the event may be the principal factor behind one elderly man's statement that Old People's Day "is the greatest thing that ever happened to this community." Another explained that 88 community has often seemed like "one big family" to him; and he attributes this closeness partly to Old People's Day. "That's what that day has done," he claims.

Why has it been so effective?

No doubt the widespread participation in Old People's Day activities plays an important role. The singing and testifying, as well as the picnicking and socializing, maximize individual involvement. On the Old People's Day stage, one is an actor among one's fellows, not a spectator watching strangers perform.

What is the nature of the action?

Natives of the 88 community assemble to honor the elderly, of course; but they also commemorate the origin of Old People's Day itself, and they relate stories about their community's past. They talk about their shared experiences. They publicly reaffirm their connectedness, and in doing so, they maintain those positive, productive connections.

In short, Old People's Day, established to reunite a divided community under a central leader, serves even today to promote a widespread sense of communal continuity and of belonging.

A PARABLE FOR CORPORATE COMMUNITIES

That's the true story of Old People's Day. I suggested earlier that the story could be seen as a parable. Let me review the story in that light: Faced with alienation, misunderstanding and mistrust of leadership, a creative leader, responding to the needs of his people, found a common interest—a common cause. That common ground was public recognition of certain individuals who sometimes were overlooked by others— recognition of their contributions and their general importance to the organization.

That leader understood fully the value and power of ceremony, and he knew also that efficacious ceremonies can only be developed around those events or values participants have a sincere desire to ritualize, commemorate, or celebrate.

Everyone was encouraged to take part in the ceremonies. Not just to attend, but to make his preferences known and to express himself actively—to help shape the ceremonies according to his true needs and desires. Full weight was given to establishing and then invoking an organizational history—a strong, human history of traditions and of relationships. And full recognition was accorded to the importance of the stories people tell about those traditions and relationships.

The ceremony—the symbolic, redressive action—not only cleared up the original misunderstanding, but also contributed to the general sense of organizational unity and continuity. What was instituted to ease tension became a celebration of shared identities and values, and a lasting symbol of those identities and values. The ceremony itself became an emblem of group mission and image.

To summarize—in a time of organizational crisis, leadership

saw the organization in human terms;
gave full value to the power of symbolic behavior such as narrative and ceremony both to express and to resolve points of crisis;
invited input and participation from all organizational members, including those temporarily at odds with official policy;
found common goals, values, and identities among organizational members, identifying a mission inherently worth working together for;

publicly proclaimed and celebrated that mission, taking special care to recognize those members who had hitherto been overlooked;

and thus successfully encouraged all organization members to renew their sense of commitment, thereby alleviating internecine tension and making the organization a better place for all concerned.

The principles working at 88 are operative in other social groups, and, as many of the field studies in this volume demonstrate, these same principles can be used to help resolve conflict in many types of organizations. Accordingly, we should not underestimate the power of narrative in shaping a common history and identity, and of ceremony in elevating them into a rewarding sense of community. When all members of an organization are invited to participate and benefit, celebration can become an extraordinary agent for organizational change.

17

DEALING WITH ORGANIZATIONAL STRESS

Lessons from the Folklore of Mormon Missionaries

William A. Wilson

Brigham Young University

A former Mormon missionary myself, I began research a decade ago on the folklore of Mormon missionaries (see Wilson, 1981) in a fairly typical folkloristic attempt to learn what the lore would tell me about the dominant values, attitudes, and anxieties of the missionaries and to discover how this lore functions in their lives. These are still my goals, but in achieving them, I have gained insights I had not expected.

As I remembered my own years as a missionary in the mid-1950s and as I attempted to make sense of thousands of pages of interview data, I began to realize that if those in charge of organizing missionary work and supervising missionary activity would take pains to become more familiar with the lore (or traditional behaviors) of the missionaries, they might be able to structure the work in a way that would achieve the same results with fewer emotional costs. I also realized that since the Mormon missionary system in many ways bears close resemblance to other organizations that put great pressure on their members to succeed, lessons learned from studying missionary lore might benefit organizations concerned with creating an environment designed to foster both

---

Author's Note: I have conducted this research in collaboration with my colleague John B. Harris from Brigham Young University. A summary of our results is in William A. Wilson, *On Being Human: The Folklore of Mormon Missionaries, 64th Utah State University Faculty Honor Lecture* (Logan: Utah State University Press, 1981). The present essay draws heavily on this material.

high productivity and emotional well being for members of the organization.

At present, some 30,000 Mormons (ages about 19-30) serve for two years in all parts of the world. Though they serve voluntarily, during the durations of their missions they give up much of their personal freedom. Their work is closely supervised and is highly programmed and routinized. They get up at 6:00 a.m, shower, eat breakfast, and study to 9:30. From 9:30 to 12:00 they proselyte—that is, they contact new people by going from door to door and they keep teaching appointments made with people contacted earlier. From 12:00 to 1:00 they eat lunch. From 1:00 to 5:00 they continue proselyting. They eat dinner from 5:00 to 6:00, and then proselyte again until 9:30. By 10:30 they are to be home and in bed. The next day the same routine begins again.

Occasionally, this routine will be interrupted by a zone or district conference that brings missionaries in adjacent areas together for a day or two of instruction, pep talks, and perhaps a little rest and relaxation. But in the main, the only break in the daily schedule comes on Saturday—which the missionaries call "Preparation Day." On that day, they get up the same time as usual, study until 9:30 and then from 9:30 to 5:00 are free—free, that is, to write letters home, wash their clothing, do their shopping, and, perhaps, even get in a game of racquetball. From 5:00 to 9:30 they proselyte again. Not only are missionaries expected to follow this rigorous schedule of preaching their gospel, they are also expected to *produce*: to win converts. And they must do all this away from the support systems of their home communities and frequently in a foreign land where they must speak a language not their own and work with people who consider them unwelcome intruders.

The result is an enormous emotional pressure that can easily destroy the missionaries. They survive, primarily, because they are highly committed young people who believe in what they are doing and are willing to sacrifice personal comfort for what they consider a greater good. But they also survive because they have learned to deal with this pressure through traditional patterns of behavior developed over time and passed on to each new generation of missionaries—through practical joking, which serves as an initiation rite; through the use of esoteric language, which contributes to social cohesion and serves as an outlet for frustrations; and through the telling of stories, especially hero stories, which give them a sense of victory over threatening forces.

When a brand new 19-year-old missionary, a "greenie," arrives in some distant mission field, frightened, feeling very much an outsider, and wondering if he should catch the next plane home, the first folklore he is likely to encounter will most likely be directed against him (although Mormon women are serving missions in ever increasing numbers, we have focused on males primarily because they still make up the bulk of the missionary force). In virtually every mission field newly arrived missionaries are subjected to pranks played on them by the older, more seasoned missionaries. Through these initiation pranks, they are abused, shocked, embarrassed, and humiliated. For example, in Norway, when a greenie arrived, seasoned missionaries

> sat him down in a chair; they fixed a light above him, and they interrogated him about his moral life. When he volunteered the information that he had kissed a girl before, they let him know that he was completely washed up as far as his career goes in the mission. He would always be junior companion, never be allowed to lead a discussion. And he believed the whole thing [This narrative and all other items of folklore cited in this paper are on file in the Brigham Young University Folklore Archive, Provo, Utah].

In London, England, new missionaries were told to save their bus-ticket stubs for a half-penny rebate per ticket. The greenies saved drawers full of these—some, following instructions, even ironed them—only to learn later that they were totally worthless. In Texas a senior companion instructed his new junior companion how prayers were to be offered in the mission:

> "Now, Elder [missionaries are called elders], out here we pray an awful lot. If we had to repeat these prayers all the time, we'd spend most of our time on our knees and never have time to do the Lord's work. Instead, we have all the prayers numbered." With that the two slid to their knees and the senior volunteered to say the prayer. "Number 73," he prayed and jumped into bed, leaving the new missionary in a crumpled mass on the floor.

In Norway, a senior companion, after going through essentially this same ritual, prayed, "Lord, number 10 for me and number 35 for the greenie."

Sometimes church members, posing as someone else, usually an investigator, have joined the senior missionaries in these pranks. In California, for example, a senior companion offered to demonstrate to his new greenie how he succeeded in placing Books of Mormon in people's houses. The two of them knocked on a door. A woman answered, and the senior companion threw a book past her into the house and then ran away, leaving the greenie to stammer out an explanation to the irate woman. The woman turned out later to be the wife of the local Mormon leader—the whole thing was a put-up job. Similarly, in Norway senior missionaries asked a greenie:

> "Do you have your first discussion?" And he said, "I have it. I've been studying it. I learned it when I was down in the mission home." And they said, "Okay, you've got to have it good, 'cause we're giving it tonight." So they went—four of them—over to this house to give it. And, of course, it wasn't really an investigator; it was a member. And they said, "This man is very musically inclined, and it gets a little bit mundane talking to him all the time. He likes us to sing him the discussions." And so they started out singing the first two lines of the first discussion, and then said, "Hit it!" And so the new elder proceeded to sing the rest of the first discussion in Norwegian.

What we have in these pranks, of course, is still another example of that old custom of "loading the greenhorn," of duping or playing a prank on the new, unsuspecting person on the job. Speaking of this practice on the American frontier, Mody Boatright wrote the following:

> Mountain men, scouts, cowboys, and Texas rangers felt that they had the right to know the temper of the men who were to be associated with them in such relationships that each man's survival often depended upon his fellows. They would not admit to their fraternity one who could not "take a joke".... Hoaxing of this sort was [thus] more than a form of adolescent horseplay. It was an economical means of establishing social relationships between men engaged in a common struggle, a struggle in which survival often depended more upon one's fellows than oneself [Boatright, 1961: 72].

But the pranks do more than just test the mettle of the newcomer; they also provide a means of incorporating him into the group, of developing esprit de corps and the sense of solidarity necessary to cope with stressful life. Through the prank—which is really just an initiation ceremony—the outsider is incorporated into the system. In scriptural terms, he puts off the old man, the greenie, and puts on the new man, the seasoned elder. He now belongs. He is first abused in some way; through the abuse he is humbled; as he recovers from the experience, usually through shared laughter, he becomes one with the group. "I felt kind of dumb at first," said one greenie, "but it was kind of fun after it was all over." Another commented, "It took me a while to cool down, but afterwards we laughed for days about the whole thing." Still another, who had been subjected to praying by numbers, said, "It took me a minute to figure it out, but after I did they all laughed and had a [real] prayer. We did it a few weeks later to some new elders." In this last instance the new missionary, only just initiated himself, soon began to initiate others and thereby was brought still more tightly into the system. Most missionaries participate in these pranks, then, as a means of establishing and maintaining a sense of community among their members.

Other folklore practices also contribute to this sense of community. Upon his arrival in the field, a greenie will often hear his companions speaking a language he does not understand. For example, a junior companion is not just a junior companion—he is "little brother," "the young one," "boy," "the slave." The senior companion, on the other hand, is "the boss," "the pope," "the chief," "sir." The mission home (or mission headquarters) is "the zoo," "the Kangaroo court." Investigators of the missionaries' message are "gators," "our people." Good investigators are "goldies," "dry Mormons." Investigators who are not interested in the message but like to talk to missionaries are "professionals," "gummers," "lunch," "the punch and cookie route." The Book of Mormon is a "bomb" (BOM). Baptisms are "tisms," "dunks," "splashes," "payday." Tracting (door to door contacting) is "bonking on doors," "self-torture." The tracting area is "the beat," "the jungle," "the war zone." Good missionaries are "spiritual giants," "rocks," "nails." Aspiring missionaries are "straight-arrow Sams," "cliff climbers," "pharisees." Bad missionaries are "screws," "hurters," "leaks," "liberals." The mission president is "the man," "Big Roy," "the head rhino." And so on.

No missionary, of course, will know all of these terms. But almost all will know some of them or others like them. They have been generated over time as missionaries have characterized the circumstances of their lives in specialized language—in missionary slang or argot. When we asked missionaries why they used this language (and they use it most when they are by themselves—never with investigators, and seldom with mission leaders), the most common response was that it creates a feeling of self-identification with other missionaries. It contributes, in other words, to that sense of community the initiation pranks help to establish. Once a greenie learns it he no longer is a greenie, an outsider. He is now a missionary. He belongs. He speaks the language.

But this is not the only use of traditional speech forms. The second most common response to our question was that the language was a means of letting off steam, a kind of "silent rebellion." One missionary replied, "It was about the only thing we could say that wasn't programmed." In this unprogrammed language, spoken in casual conversations, missionaries have found a means of dealing at least in part with pressures imposed by the system. A missionary who can laugh at his beat-up bicycle ("the meat grinder"), at his food ("green slop"), at his apartment ("the cave"), and even at chafing rules is likely to be much more effective than one who broods over these circumstances. If he can laughingly call his tracting area "the war zone," he is likely better to survive the battle.

Sometimes, however, the laughter makes nonmissionary Mormons uncomfortable. Many of them do not particularly enjoy hearing the Book of Mormon referred to as a "bomb" (How many bombs did you place today, Elder?). Nor do they like to hear baptisms called "splashings" or "dunkings"—after all, baptism is a scared ordinance. But these people do not have to see their names on a comparative list each month showing the number of books placed, and they do not have to struggle to meet mission baptismal goals. The missionaries are simply dealing with pressures in one of the ways open to them—by smiling through language at what might otherwise be their undoing. It is quite clear from the data that most missionaries admire the good elders, "the giants," and dislike the bad ones, "the screws." Yet for the missionary who never quite succeeds as well as he would like, who never leads the mission in baptisms, it is sometimes comforting to view those who do as "climbers" or "straight-arrow Sams." Similarly, when a small group of missionaries refer to the mission president as "Big Roy" instead of "President Jones," they are not setting out to overthrow the authoritarian structure of the mission; they are simply reminding themselves that the authority who presides over them—fearsome as he sometimes appears—is also a man.

Perhaps the most effective means missionaries employ to cope with pressures arising from proselyting or from the somewhat nagging rules imposed by mission authorities is not just using esoteric language, but rather telling stories in which the protagonists do for the missionaries what they are not allowed to do for themselves. Space will allow only two short examples.

Missionaries move constantly in a hostile world. Children tease and throw stones at them; adults curse and spit on them; dogs and cats lick and chew on them. Thus the beleaguered elders delight in telling stories like the following:

A missionary went to this discussion. The lady's cat was always bothering him. This cat just kept coming in and would attack everything on the flannel board [the board missionaries use for visual demonstrations]. He came up close to him and this elder just kinda reached down and flicked it on the bridge of his nose. Didn't mean to hurt the cat, but killed it. It dropped on the floor and the lady was out of the room at the time, so they [the missionaries] curled it around the leg of the chair. And he sat and petted it all through the rest of the discussion. The next time they went [there], the lady mentioned the cat was dead.

Without permission from the mission president, missionaries are not allowed to travel more than a few kilometers from the city to which they are assigned. Yet a widely known story tells of two enterprising elders who, deciding to take an unauthorized trip, fill out their weekly activity reports a couple of months in advance, leave them with their landlady with instructions to send one each week to the mission headquarters, and then leave on an unearned vacation. Shortly before their return, the landlady mixes up the reports, sends them out of sequence, and the missionaries are found out. The place of the unauthorized trip will vary—New York, the Riviera, Cairo, Moscow, the Easter Islands, the bush country of Australia—but in all other details, the story from mission to mission is the same.

Good missionaries, of course, do not do these things—they do not kill investigators' cats, no matter how bothersome, nor violate mission travel rules, no matter how chafing. Yet missionaries delight in telling stories about characters who do. Why? When I asked a recently returned missionary that question, he replied: "Those of us who were straight, who kept the rules, had to tell the stories like these to survive." Another missionary responded: "The elders told stories like this just to relieve the monotony, so you could just imagine what it would be like without getting in trouble for [doing] it." In other words, the missionaries relieve tensions by vicariously living the adventures of the miscreants in the stories without actually performing the acts.

The few examples of missionary folklore I have considered here do at least three things: They contribute to missionary esprit de corps; they incorporate new missionaries into the group; and they provide missionaries means of safely expressing frustrations and tensions imposed by the system, thus making easier the missionaries' remaining in the system. How does all this relate to organization and management? I can suggest three general lessons to be learned from the missionary material.

First, if nothing else, folklore will tell managers and leaders where the sore spots really are. The language people use, the jokes they play, and the tales they spin will tell the perceptive observer much about people's deepest feelings and concerns; they will help us locate the places where rules may need to be adjusted. If I were a Mormon mission president, or an organization leader, I would pay heed to the language used by people under my charge, to the stories they tell, and to the practices they engage in—not so I could manipulate them to my advantage, but so I could create a world in which we could all live in harmony.

Second, folklore will make us aware of the ways people are already coping with stress and, hopefully, will teach leaders not to interfere with processes that are already working quite well. A new and pious mission president who, however well-meaning, attempts to get rid of all the "childish" initiation pranks and who scolds missionaries for their use of language, may very well undermine the work he has been sent to accomplish. He may reap the wind and sow the whirlwind.

Third, to a sensitive observer folklore may suggest ways to remove the causes of the sore spots and in the process eliminate the need for coping mechanisms in the first place. Years ago, when I was half way through my mission in Finland, my wise mission president sent me and several other missionaries on a short but *authorized* rest and relaxation tour of Lapland, thus breaking the tension and alleviating the need for unauthorized-trip stories. In the Philippines, another wise mission president, aware of initiation pranks and their functions, conducted his own. When new missionaries arrived in his field and ate their first meal at mission headquarters, they were given green food, served on green plates, set on green linen—all reminding the missionaries of their own greenness. One of them said, "I felt like I had been baptized"—which, of course, is exactly what the president wanted the greenies to feel, baptized into a new life in which all, mission president and missionaries, would work together for their common good.

I want to conclude with mention of visual materials. Before missionaries enter the field, they spend two months in Provo, Utah, at the Missionary Training Center (formerly Language Training Mission), where they receive intense instruction in proselyting and language skills. Life there is even more rigorous and closely supervised than it is in the field. In 1977 the Center was moved from the old college dormitory where it had been housed for a decade to elaborate new quarters. When workmen began converting the dorm into an office building, they discovered elaborate drawings on the backsides of the removable ceiling tiles (see photos in Allen and Harris, 1981). Evidently, for the past ten years missionaries had been taking the tiles out in secret (probably at night); drawing, painting, and scribbling on them; and then replacing them before morning. On them, they put their personal pictures, comments on life in the Center, and long and short epistles and poems— my favorite is: "As I fly to Paris to begin my labor / I'm even gonna miss my town of Taber / Even with this all would be well / If only I was taking Lorrie Maxwell." They drew maps of exciting spots in Provo, and they depicted the countries where they would soon be working. The tiles give a fascinating glimpse into the *feelings* of the missionaries, some hostile, some frightened, some positive and enthusiastic, but all recorded clandestinely.

In the new center there are no removable tiles, so the missionaries have turned to another medium to record their messages—toilet paper. This time, however, there is a difference. A friend of mine, until recently a supervisor at the center, learned of the practice and decided to participate with the missionaries in their decorative endeavors. He became the "keeper of the roll." Each new group that came into the center under his direction painstakingly and lovingly rolled out the paper, made their own drawings, then just as lovingly rolled it back up and gave it to him to keep until the next group entered the center. My friend discovered that just as the mural paintings in Los Angeles give Mexican-Americans a chance to express their feelings in paint so too did the toilet-paper drawings help missionaries express their feelings and relieve some of the stress built up under the pressure of the necessary but taxing Mission Center rules and regulations. By cooperating with the missionaries, then, instead of scolding them for wasting valuable time in useless activity, he provided them a way of coping with tension and helped them develop an esprit de corps to carry them through the difficult days ahead.

I am not proposing that we all roll out the toilet paper. But I am suggesting that by looking carefully at the traditional working behaviors that have developed among us and by understanding how they operate we may discover how to make work more productive and lives happier.

18

SYMBOLIC REPRESENTATION OF ORGANIZATIONAL IDENTITY

The Role of Emblem at the Garrett Corporation

Stephen Stern

University of California, Los Angeles

While I was interviewing a division manager of the Garrett Corporation regarding the company's deceased founder, Clifford Garrett, the manager's secretary reminded him of a twelve o'clock meeting. He told me that he intended to inform employees of the company's progress. He invited me to attend. "Would you like to see Mr. Garrett in action?" he asked. I was taken aback, for the founder had died 22 years before. Sensing my confusion, the manager hastened to explain that Clifford Garrett had instituted the policy of regularly communicating to employees how well the company was doing. The manager was following suit, consciously modelling his behavior after the founder's. He seemed to be offering a tribute to Garrett, and in so doing demonstrating that his spirit still resides in the company and that his philosophies and policies are currently being practiced. The manager boasted that organizational participants continue to be devoted and loyal to the company and to Clifford Garrett's memory—a contention supported by information I obtained in interviews with many retirees and employees.

How is it possible for feelings of devotion and loyalty to persist in one company for over half a century? The answer is that Clifford Garrett founded a "symbolic organization," one in which individual attitudes toward the company are molded into a collective representation of the company's unity. I became aware of this unification process when I attempted to comprehend why I had not received any negative comments about the company from the 100 current employees and retired persons I interviewed between 1981 and 1984. I concluded that when participants praise the Garrett Corporation, they are not so much referring to specific activities, benefits, or personnel—about which they may, indeed, be critical—as to their overall positive association with the company and the role that the founder played in promoting employee identification.

How do employees transform their everyday opinions of the company to create an overall identification with it? In this article I argue that employees represent their collective identification symbolically by treating the Garrett name as the company's emblem. Mr. Garrett is esteemed by company employees very much as totems are by members of tribal societies. Consisting of the names, images, and figures of sacred beings drawn usually from the animal kingdom, totems serve to generate group identification, promote respect and admiration for the group and its representatives, and provide a source of explanation for the qualities associated with the company. During his lifetime, Garrett served as a constant reminder of the company's identity; after his death, his name and memory continue to be revered. The importance of the Garrett name is evident from the extent to which employees place it at the center of their devotional behavior. Garrett's name is featured whenever the history of the company is recounted. His name is likewise recalled in ceremonies that celebrate company successes and in rituals that reward outstanding individual achievements. Photographs of him discharging his duties are proudly displayed on company buildings and in newsletters, and a logo bearing his name is affixed to every company communique (see Figure 18.1). By focusing on these concrete manifestations of Garrett's role in the company, employees are able to keep alive company values, maintain unified goals, and derive meaning and purpose from their employment.

The name "Garrett" attained prominence as company emblem as a result of Garrett's contribution to developing an airplane accessory company that enjoys a worldwide reputation. Having founded the company in 1936 as a tool supplier for the then-fledgling aircraft industry, he expanded the company to include manufacturing, sales, and service of airplane accessories. From an initial handful of employees working out of a storefront office in Los Angeles, California, the company grew to 23,000 employees working in some 20 divisions and represented in several countries. The corporation is headquartered in a prestigious location adjacent to the Los Angeles International Airport and boasts annual sales of close to $3 billion. As is the case with royal seals, which base their legitimacy on members of a royal family, the Garrett Corporation's emblem refers to the man who is responsible for the success of the company.

Figure 18.1

But Garrett represents more than his role as founder of the company, and his memory extends beyond his tenure as chairman of the board. Recognition of the name "Garrett" is sufficient to elicit comments by employees and customers regarding those special features that make the Garrett Corporation unique and successful. Thus the Garrett emblem represents the very qualities with which the name "Garrett" is identified. In this sense, Garrett did not only originate the company; he gave it its character. In turn, employees working for the company do not merely recite Garrett's accomplishments; they absorb the qualities associated with the name Garrett and thus bind their identities with the identity of the company. The phrase "to Garrettize employees" is often used by those wishing to impart company values, implying thereby that participants can be infused with the "spirit" of Clifford Garrett. These qualities are admittedly more abstract and less tangible than are physical representations of Garrett and must be inferred from employee's comments and behavior. What appears on the surface, then, as the mere repetitious use of a name underlies a deeper orientation toward the company that serves as its primary source of strength and commitment.

The special organizational qualities attributable to Clifford Garrett and associated with his name are: (1) *reciprocity* between management and employee, (2) *responsibility* undertaken by employees for the success of their work, (3) *recognition* of employees' achievements, and (4) *reputation* of the company's products, services, and policies.

Although employees in other companies also promote these concepts as vital to their company's success, Garrett Corporation employees make them the *sine qua non* of the Garrett emblem.

In the following pages I explain how the Garrett Corporation emblem is created out of the relationship between organizational qualities and the character of Clifford Garrett. I conclude with a discussion of the processes leading to forming the Garrett Corporation emblem and the role it plays through its symbolic power in promoting organizational identification.

PERSONAL POLICIES AND ORGANIZATIONAL QUALITIES

Reciprocity

The loyalty that people had toward Cliff was absolutely unbelievable [Vice President of Product Support, August 6, 1982].

My father was loyal to people—to the corporation, to my mother, to his friends. If he gave his word, you could count on it [Clifford Garrett's daughter, April 15, 1983].

A fundamental condition for employment at the Garrett Corporation is that managers and employees be willing to offer each other maximum support. Formally, management is on record as adopting humanistically oriented industrial relations policies. The title of the Industrial Relations Department's manual, "Working Together," reflects this commitment. But the real basis of relationship between managers and employees at the Garrett Corporation is conveyed informally. Employees enter into what Alan L. Wilkins calls an "implicit social contract" (1983b: 29-33).

Although neither humanistic management nor reciprocity as a value need be based on "patronage," the informal contract at the Garrett Corporation specifies a relationship between a person who seems to have been a "benevolent patron" and his employees. As a patron, Clifford Garrett hired, protected, and guided his employees in exchange for receiving their uncompromising loyalty. He ruled autocratically and made decisions unilaterally. An example of his governing hand is his insistence that personnel be prepared to accept positions away from their home without their wholehearted approval. A divisional manager related to me (August 19, 1982) that a request to transfer to another city was tantamount to a command:

And there was never any question, did I want to move? You know, you're going to have to sell your house. You're going to have to take your kids out of school. He just said, "I want you to do this." And I guess it never occurred to Cliff that I would say no. And I guess it really never occurred to me, because Monday morning I was up there.

Clifford Garrett was, however, as generous to his supporters as he was authoritarian. He frequently initiated pay raises, offered bonuses, and extended company services to employees who needed medical or financial aid. For example, he provided extraordinary care to one employee who had been injured in an automobile accident by transferring her to a Garrett Corporation facility near her home town where she would be more comfortable. Throughout her convalescence, she lost no pay. Once, after visiting her in the hospital, he decided that her care was inadequate and summoned his personal physician to attend her.

A major feature of a benevolent form of patron/employee relationship is that neither employer nor employee perceives that he is behaving against his will. The exchange of support is accepted uncritically as if it were a sacred trust. Garrett believed that his employees would do what he requested; they in turn relied on him to provide their essential needs. The extent of such dependency is illustrated by the experience of the above-mentioned divisional manager who, after being sent by Garrett to sell off a losing company acquisition, realized that he had not been informed of his next assignment. He had, however, so much faith that his superiors would contact him that he was willing to wait to receive instructions rather than seek clarification.

To support this natural flow of assistance, managers and employees established a framework for treating themselves as equals. Garrett insisted on removing external trappings of rank and hierarchy. All offices had the same decor; no special decorations distinguished upper management. Managers were encouraged to eat in the same cafeteria as employees who, in turn, were discouraged from eating away from the plant. Garrett instituted an open-door policy by which employees could bypass their immediate supervisors to voice grievances. He believed that managers should read their own mail and answer their own telephone calls so that they would be more directly in touch with their employees and customers.

In demonstration that personal policy became organizational atttribute, employees frequently commented that the Garrett Corporation differed from other, more hierarchical, companies. As a section manager put it (February 1, 1985): "There's just a great deal of communication between people here. There is no caste system here. Anybody can talk to anybody they want to in Garrett."

Responsibility

Garrett has been peopled through the years by guys who just wouldn't give up. I can remember in the early days sitting next to a guy who came to work at eight o'clock in the morning, worked all the day, all that night, all the next day until 4:30 when he went home. Never got up from his desk. People do it because they want to, because they like what they are doing, and they want to see it get done. They just won't give up. They are going to see the job through and they are going to get it done [Section Manager, February 1, 1985].

At the Garrett Corporation, responsibility is measured by the degree of individual initiative taken in carrying out assignments. Employees are expected to accept challenges and solve problems creatively. Easily observable is the hard work put forth and long hours spent daily working on projects. Visible also are employees who participate in the decision-making process of the company. Employees express their reactions by filling out annual opinion surveys and by suggesting ways to improve the company.

There are, however, subtle obligations entailed in accepting responsibility at the Garrett Corporation. Employees are expected to follow through on assigned tasks, from their inception through their completion. Engineers who were originally involved in designing a project may find themselves asked to solve problems resulting from their design years after the product has been on the market. Engineers and sales and service personnel are requested to cooperate at every phase of the project. They are, furthermore, required to be knowledgeable about all aspects of a project falling under their jurisdiction. The section manager quoted above told me that he learned this lesson painfully. When he first joined the company, he offered to oversee a project for a friend who had gone on vacation. When questioned by Garrett regarding the project's progress, the manager could not provide a satisfactory answer. Garrett reprimanded him for not being adequately informed. Employees are encouraged to tackle new problems whenever and wherever asked, even though they may not have expertise. Managers who have spent years filling a position may suddenly be requested to accept another one totally unrelated to the previous. For example, a cafeteria manager was appointed to head an anchor division of the corporation while a vice-president of sales was asked to become director of Industrial Relations.

Responsibility also involves ensuring that standards of excellence established by Clifford Garrett are upheld. These standards include maintaining a high quality of workmanship and clean physical facilities. Employees strive to exceed the technical demands of the client. Garrett Corporation employees do not believe in cutting corners to produce a less than perfect product, even if they have to charge more for its superiority. Garrett's daughter illustrated (April 15, 1983) how her father's drive for perfection influenced every aspect of his life: "When he built a house, it always had to be out of the best material. Whenever he was planning anything for the corporation, it always had to be the best. Even though it cost more, you got the good stuff, the stuff that's going to hold up." Evidence of quality was demonstrated by the cleanliness and neatness of company quarters. "You can walk into any Garrett warehouse," stated a division manager, "and you'll always find them squeaky clean. You don't find any cigarette butts on the floor. You won't find any old coffee cups in the corner, or paper, or dirt, or anything else."

Employee initiative extends to social as well as technical aspects of company life. An Employee's Club was formed to offer a forum for socializing. It sponsored numerous recreational activities, including picnics, bowling leagues, and Christmas parties. One of the club's most significant functions was to act as a benevolent society. Charitable donations were made by club members to civic organizations. Funds were allocated to bereaved employees who required emergency assistance upon the death of a close relative.

Responsibility goes beyond internal company concerns to include consideration for the community at large. Employees seek to be recognized as "corporate citizens." Voluntary civic duties are vital to the organization's standing in the community. They include participation in cultural and civic affairs, in efforts to clean and beautify the environment, in programs to aid the disadvantaged and handicapped, and in activities to educate youth.

Allowed to accept ever greater responsibilities, many employees I interviewed felt that their careers had advanced considerably at Garrett. A manager described to me (February 1, 1985) a conversation he had had with his counterpart in another aerospace firm who lamented that he had been assigned to the same project for seven years. During that time, he had never personally met his Chief Executive Officer. He was astounded when he heard that employees at the Garrett Corporation are involved in a number of significant projects and that they have a direct line to executive officers. Especially appreciative were those employees without college degrees who, by their own hard work and initiative, were able to surpass their expected career objectives.

Recognition

On this, your second anniversary, I am most happy to express again my appreciation and thanks for your work and help during the past year. As I have stated before, it always gives me a great deal of pleasure to write these letters and tell you how much I have enjoyed working with you. . . . We must depend upon old timers like you to pass on our ideals and ways of working here at AiResearch.

> Sincerely,
> Clifford Garrett

The management at the Garrett Corporation assumes that every employee is productive and deserving of appreciation. As the retired chief executive officer wrote in an introduction to the industrial relations handbook, "Throughout our company we try to remember that each man and woman who works with us is an individual, intelligent, cooperative and productive person." The industrial relations department continuously monitors individual employees' needs and actively solicits feedback from employees regarding potential problems. Evidence of the company's concern with implementing industrial relations policies is the high esteem in which the director is held. The director is an executive vice-president of the company on a par with the executive vice-presidents of engineering and sales.

Further proof of a commitment to employees' well-being is the way newly hired employees are treated. Anniversary letters are sent to employees who have completed a minimum of one year of service. Although a year may not be sufficient time to prove one's worth, Clifford Garrett's letter praises what the employee has accomplished to date and sees in the employee's positive attitude the basis of accepting an "implicit social contract." Employees with one year of service are called "old timers" in the anniversary letter quoted above, indicating that even their limited training is considered invaluable to the company. Many employees regard Clifford Garrett's personal vote of confidence to be the most inspiring experience they have had at the company. Letters continue to be sent to employees every five years. One secretary neatly bound the anniversary letters she received during her thirty years of service and exhibited a great deal of pride in having been deemed worthy of so much recognition.

Other formal awards—such as pins and plaques—are also given to employees reaching milestones. Those completing 20 years of service are usually honored before an audience of their fellow workers and managers. Photographs of award recipients are published in newsletters. For those surpassing 25 years of service to the company, their photographs are framed and mounted on the interior walls of the respective buildings in which they work. Those select few who have worked for the company for 40 years are given special gifts during a ceremony in which laudatory remarks are made by company executives. A service recognition committee was formed especially to oversee rewards made to employees who had reached this milestone.

More important than formal acknowledgments was Clifford Garrett's informal praise of employees. His secretary remembers how, when he went into the shop, he would publicly thank employees for their company involvement. He lavishly praised employees at social gatherings, too, making them feel important by calling them by their first names and inquiring about the welfare of their families. Clifford Garrett believed that by rewarding employees he would be supporting their creative efforts and motivating them to be loyal to the company. He wanted employees to feel that working for the Garrett Corporation was its own reward. Employees interpreted receiving rewards as an indication of management's commitment to developing their careers rather than just as payment for the work they had done.

Reputation

You can tell a Garrett employee a mile away. There is something about the way a Garrett man dresses and talks that makes him known throughout the industry [Secretary, June 14, 1983].

The Garrett Corporation, and the employees who work for it, are regarded highly in the aerospace industry. The same standards—quality of workmanship and neatness—upheld by employees are recognized by customers and clients. Above all, Clifford Garrett stressed honesty and integrity in dealing with customers. His word was considered unbreakable. Garrett was known to have refunded money on products promised but not delivered.

The reputation of the Garrett Corporation is intimately bound up with a long list of aerospace accomplishments. Garrett has led the field in producing a line of small gas turbines, pneumatic starters, intercoolers and oil coolers, electrical motors and actuators, and turbofan engines. The innovative aspects of these products is reflected in employees' pride at having been the "first" to invent and produce them. The "firsts" are well known to employees and customers alike because they appear on numerous Garrett Corporation publications. Employees' assessments of what they have contributed to the company are tied to their own roles in producing, selling, or servicing outstanding Garrett Corporation products. These "firsts" were achieved, in part, because of the aggressive attitudes of the Garrett Corporation sales force—a fact well known in the industry. Garrett Corporation salesmen will go to extremes to make a sale. A vice president of sales related to me how his persistent efforts allowed him to win a contract away from a competitor to whom it had already been awarded. After being refused entry to see the purchasing agent who had bought the competitor's product, he informally invited the engineers of the company to witness a demonstration in a gas station parking lot. The superior functioning of the product convinced the engineers that their purchasing agent had bought an inferior product. The contract was then awarded to the Garrett Corporation.

The corporation's reputation for outstanding service is equal to its sales record. As early as World War II, Garrett Corporation employees were sent to air bases in India and the South Pacific to service planes that used Garrett Corporation products.

THE IMPORTANCE OF SYMBOLIC QUALITIES FOR PROMOTING EMPLOYEE IDENTIFICATION

Basing a symbolic organization on the qualities of reciprocity, responsibility, recognition, and reputation encourages employees to identify with the company. Each quality functions to emphasize a different but complementary facet of organizational affiliation.

The existence of *reciprocity* between management and employees results, for example, in employees seeing their careers and the fate of the corporation as interdependent. Employees rely on management to provide for their personal well-being, for meaningful social contacts, and for career development. Management, of course, depends on motivated employees for quality products and services. Participants become committed to the organization's values, which are compatible with their own. Allowing employees to take *responsibility* communicates to them that the fate of the corporation is dependent upon their careers. The message is also sent that every employee is making a unique contribution to the company's progress. As the division manager stated, "You are totally involved where you aren't just in some little niche. You work harder and take a better interest in the company."

Recognition of individual talent provides employees with perceptions of self-worth, of feelings of importance in the company. Employees thus take personal pride in their achievements. As a secretary stated, "This is the greatest company because everything you do is appreciated."

By earning a *reputation* for major accomplishments, employees feel that they are contributing to the betterment of the aerospace industry, and by implication, to society in general. Employees take pride in being associated with the corporation's major advances. As the secretary quoted above noted, "If everyone has a lot of pride in the company's standing, the organization works better as an organization. If you don't have any pride in what you are doing, then you are a loser right to begin with."

The Source of the Garrett
Corporate Emblem: Clifford Garrett

The organizational qualities prized at the Garrett Corporation stem from the character of its founder, Clifford Garrett. He personally believed in the virtues of a patron/employee relationship, in providing unlimited opportunities for employees, in recognizing the talents of others, and in creating an international reputation. Enormously compassionate to his employees, he established humanistic industrial relations policies before other aerospace firms. His benevolence arose not only from caring about the welfare of employees but also out of a desire to prevent unions from gaining a foothold; Garrett wanted to be in complete control of selecting the benefits to be distributed. Intense in action and speech, he strove for excellence in all that he undertook. He expected his employees to share his enthusiasm for creative research and so provided them with unlimited responsibility and challenges to manufacture, sell, and service products better than the competition could. He was able, however, to balance this intensity by finding outlets for relaxation, a state of mind he encouraged others to achieve. When the pressures became too great, he left Los Angeles to vacation in his favorite resort, Hawaii, to meditate at the Science of Mind headquarters in Los Angeles, or to participate in such hobbies as flying, ranching, and producing musical records. His belief in technical excellence was supported by a commitment to deal with others ethically. He refused to enter into shady deals and did not countenance unethical behavior among employees. He considered himself to be a spiritual person, believing his creative powers to emanate from God. His reputation for honesty and integrity extended to customers as well as to employees.

Because of his benevolence and honesty, he was a role model to employees. The tragic circumstances of his personal life also helped others to sympathize with his paternalistic style of management. His family was poor, and he had to spend his formative years working to help support his mother. His wife became an invalid after their only daughter was born. His brother was killed in an airplane accident. At the peak of his career in the late 1950s, he had a stroke which frustrated him as he attempted to discharge his duties as chairman of the board. Employees saw in his endurance of these hardships a man who epitomized the sacrifices that he demanded of them. Knowing of Garrett's personal sufferings made it easier for employees to agree to Garrett's demands when they ran counter to their personal inclinations. So, too, they were able to excuse his quick temper as resulting from unusual circumstances. Many employees stated that he was one of the finest men they had ever known. His secretary of many years describes his personal magnetism (January 24, 1982): "People liked him, and he had a way of presenting ideas and a way of treating people that seemed to make him very much loved and very much respected. And it made people want to do things for him."

His positive contribution to company growth was immortalized because he died before serious threats to his autonomy could possibly erode his popularity. The company had grown tremendously by the time of Garrett's death in 1963, and many executives speculate that his style of management might not have been suited to running a large corporation.

For all these reasons, employees equate the success of the man with the excellence of the company. Clifford Garrett's personal qualities became those organizational attributes admired by employees and customers. Garrett's desire to be a benevolent patron, to endow employees with responsibility for their tasks, to expand their capabilities; to insist on maintaining quality, integrity, and excellence in all dealings with clients; to behave ethically toward others, and to accomplish aerospace feats others thought impossible, became ideals that were reflected in company goals and philosophies. In short, Garrett epitomized what employees believed to be noble about organizational participation.

Formation and Function of the Garrett Emblem

I remember one year we produced a new catalog, and it had a bright yellow cover. Obviously, these are the catalogs that we hoped our customers will use. Some people said that Cliff is not going to like it because it is too bright. But I felt the customers would like it because they would be able to spot it from a distance. So I went in to see Cliff, and I had the catalog, and I had the binder with the front side, the binder side open. And I said, "Cliff, you see this name?" And he said, "Yes." He said, "That spells out Garrett." And I said, "Now you can see that all the way across the room, can't you?" And he says, "You betcha I can." And I said, "What do you think of our new catalog?" "Great. Great" [Division manager, August 19, 1982].

Although Clifford Garrett the person may be separated analytically from the qualities attributed to the company that bears his name, the Garrett Corporation emblem unites them. The unification process proceeds through three stages during which Clifford Garrett's personal qualities become those of the company. In the first, "contagion," stage, *Garrett* personally *imparts his mission* to loyal supporters. Each person touched by Garrett's charisma becomes a living representation of his ideals and an agent for their promulgation. In the second stage, *Garrett's character is transferred to* the *policies* he initiated. Even those not acting as his direct emissaries willingly espouse the virtues of his policies. Many personnel policies are accredited to Garrett when, in fact, they were originally suggested by others. During the third stage, *the qualities of the man and his policies are projected onto the products* the company manufactures. These products continually exemplify Garrett's character because they reflect his vision to advance air transportation.

Once the three-stage transference is complete, the concepts of founder, policy, and product are combined and linked. Each is contained in the other; the mention of one leads to the other by a chain of "natural associations." All three are symbolized by the Garrett emblem. The emblem may simultaneously refer to the founder, policy, and product. When the name "Garrett" is employed in everyday conversation it is often ambiguous as to whether it refers to the man or to the company. By using the emblem to refer simultaneously to the founder, his policies, and his products, employees are able to capitalize on various means to promote identification with the company. In one sense, use of the emblem serves as a herald, to announce the Garret name and to embellish it. In another sense, the Garrett name acts as a coat of arms for royalty serving as an insignia or badge. In yet a third sense, as a symbol, it serves to embody the qualities that brought the Garrett Corporation prominence in the aerospace world (Singer, 1984: 105-154).

In using a single name to connote these functions, the Garrett Corporation's emblem becomes a fixed and enduring reminder of the company's unity. The sociologist Emile Durkheim, who is credited with advancing the first systematic theory of totemism, states the importance of maintaining a single-minded dedication to the group's emblem: "It is by uttering the same cry, pronouncing the same word, or performing the same gesture in regard to some object that they become and feel themselves to be in unison" (Durkheim, 1915: 230). Focusing on a single object of attention curtails the natural propensity to reflect on negative aspects of company life and keeps employees' focus on the positive. In time, more loyalty may be expressed toward the emblem than to the company itself, allowing employees to espouse the virtues of Garrett and his representatives despite recognized company flaws. An analogy may be made to patriotic feelings evoked upon seeing the American flag that may be stronger than those produced by contemplating the merits of living in the United States. As Durkheim remarked regarding how belief in totems helps clarify values, "For we are unable to consider an abstract entity, which we can represent only laboriously and confusedly, the source of the strong sentiments which we feel. We cannot explain them to ourselves except by connecting them to some concrete object of whose reality we are vividly aware" (Durkheim, 1915: 220).

Through preoccupation with the Garrett emblem, an intimate bond, or "ritual relation," is formed between employee and emblem. "Ritual" in this context refers to an intense, continuous, and reverential response to an object of identification. According to the anthropologist A. R. Radcliffe-Brown, who first introduced the concept of "ritual attitude," any object or event and its representation may attract a ritualized attitude "which has important effects upon the well being (material or spiritual) of a society" (Radcliffe-Brown, 1952: 129). As I made clear earlier, Garrett certainly attained such status, having been considered by many employees to be directly responsible for enhancing their careers. He was praised and his name glorified at every possible celebratory occasion, actions that in turn helped reinforce the ritualized attitude.

CONCLUSION

Most organizations have logos and other visible signs of company identification. When do they achieve the status of "emblem"? In this article I argue that an emblem is formed when it is made an object of continuous focus, when it is promoted as representing the company's values, and when it evokes ritualized attitudes of reverence. An emblem does not attain the status of emblem automatically; it must be molded.

At the Garrett Corporation, the emblem is created when the qualities of the founder are transferred totemlike to individual participants and then to the organization. The accentuation and dramatization of four organizational attributes—reciprocity, responsibility, recognition, and reputation—serve as pivots to direct individual attitudes toward a radiant source of inspiration and to shape a concept of company unity.

At Garrett Corporation, it is apparent that the emblem's symbolic power lies in its ability to endure beyond the period in which it was introduced. Its longevity, however, depends on the attitudes of new employees, on whether the company can remain autonomous, and on the vicissitudes of the aerospace industry. It is always possible that the emblem's influence will wane. Certainly, when no one remains who knew Clifford Garrett personally, the emblem's perpetuation will be in doubt.

What will become of the emblem as the corporation's character changes? One possibility is that the emblem may lose its significance altogether. More than likely, however, as long as Clifford Garrett's name is associated with the company's achievements the emblem will reflect at least some of the qualities associated with Garrett. The main criterion for judging whether the emblem continues to be effective is the degree to which it invokes a *ritual attitude* for a segment of the Garrett Corporation work force. Were no such attitude to be expressed, the emblem would appear as a vague memory only, as a historical monument to the company's founder. However, evidence suggests that a ritual attitude toward the emblem is still held by the now third generation of Garrett Corporation employees. Clifford Garrett's two successors promoted the company's accomplishments as natural evolutions of Garrett's vision. Thus the Garrett Corporation emblem continues to be a powerful inducement for employees to maintain a positive organizational identity and for the company to hold a leading position in the aerospace industry.

PART V

PARADIGMS AND PARADOXES

A few years ago, Wiley published a "Fenton" cartoon strip centering on the youth, Oscar, who asks for assistance with his homework. "I need help in writing an essay on 'The Secret of Life,'" he explains to his grandfather. "Well, Oscar, I think that the secret of life is *goals* and *struggle*," replies the grandfather. "People should set *goals* and do their best to meet all of them!" The older man elaborates: "You see, without goals, there is no *purpose* to life. You merely exist!" The youth, of course, is taking notes. "So it's the *struggle* to meet your goals that makes life meaningful!" concludes his grandfather. Oscar looks up from his notes, and turns toward Murray, whose face is buried in a newspaper. "What do you think is the secret of life," Oscar asks him. "Breathing," replies Murray.

"Life" in the literal sense of existence is a matter as imminently practical as breathing, but "living," in a metaphorical sense, may be enhanced by having goals and a purpose, and the struggle to achieve these goals may itself be imbued with symbolic significance. Similarly, two seemingly paradoxical paradigms simultaneously apply in conceptualizing and developing organizations. One emphasizes instrumentality and the practical, while the other is committed to a view of people as social and symbolic beings; the former is pre-occupied with organization as an entity and the latter with organizing as a human endeavor and process of participation, interaction, and creation.

The extent to which the two views may be complementary rather than antagonistic, and the degree to which the humanistic perspective must be added to the older, more "scientific" approach, is illustrated by a report published in the *Harvard Business Review* (May/June, 1984). Titled "Of Boxes, Bubbles, and Effective Management," the essay by David K. Hurst reviews events following the 1979 acquisition of a Canadian steel company in which he was a general manager.

The acquisition could not have come at a worse time, given the recession that was looming, or have been handled more poorly. The

acquiring organization lacked managerial strength, had no compre-
hensive plan, and needed money. It became apparent to members of
the acquired company's corporate office that a turnaround was
necessary, and quickly. Principals included Hurst, an executive vice
president of Russelsteel Inc., a subsidiary of Federal Industries, Ltd.,
Canada; Wayne P. E. Mang, president and chief operation officer; Al
Shkut, executive vice president; and Michael J. Greene, vice president
and secretary treasurer.

Their job was to save the company. How to proceed was uncertain.
They found themselves describing what they had to do as "roles"
rather than as tasks. They realized that in order to gain cooperation
of bankers, suppliers, customers, and employees, they had to be open,
not secretive. Rather than resigning when informed of the financial
problems, members of task forces "tackled their projects with
passion. Warmth, a sense of belonging, and trust characterized the
groups; the more we let them know what was going on, the more we
received from them," a dramatic contrast to "our premerger
corporation" which "was a pretty cold place to work," for "people
didn't trust each other very much" (Hurst, 1984: 80).

Management by walking around, open communication, and
"sharing our views and incorporating others as appropriate had a
curious effect on the making and implementing of decisions," writes
Hurst (p. 82). In premerger days, management was decisive, acting on
hard facts. But few of the decisions ever got implemented, losing
impetus as they were handed down the organizational ladder "until
eventually it was unclear whether the decision was right in the first
place." Now decisions arise naturally out of a mass of shared
assumptions. "It's the assumptions that we spend our time working
on" (p. 82). When decisions are made, implementation is rapid, for
people have participated and are involved, and the goals are clear.

Management attitudes toward, and assumptions about, employees
changed, based on an implicit understanding of organizing and a
focus on the process rather than on organization as a machinelike
structure designed and imposed without concern for human nature.
"Now everyone knows that people are social as well as rational
animals," writes Hurst. "Indeed, we knew it back in the premerger
days, but somehow back then we never came to grips with the social
aspect, maybe," he writes, because a more aloof, mechanical
approach "has an appealing simplicity and clarity" (p. 82).

Hurst and others began to recognize people for their contributions and achievements, honoring them instead of simply trying to "condition" them with gratuitous incentives. They emphasized roles, open communication, and networks rather than rigidly defined job descriptions and a chain of command. "The immediate product is a high degree of mutual trust. This trust allows groups to develop a shared vision that in turn enhances a sense of common purpose," writes Hurst. "From this process people develop a feeling of having a mission of their own. The mission is spiritual in the sense of being an important effort much larger than oneself. This kind of involvement is highly motivating," he observes. "Mission is the soft counterpart of strategy" (p. 84). Once a sense of common purpose and mission is generated among people, they "act spontaneously without being "organized"" (p. 85). According to Hurst, the "hard" rational framework that managers had employed during the preacquisition days fell apart immediately in the situation of crisis. A new conceptual framework began to emerge, one that they characterized as a "soft," intuitive orientation: the bubble versus the box. In the new view, tasks are seen as "roles," "groups" take the place of structure, "networks" function instead of information systems, rewards are not just compensation packages but include "recognition" and celebration of people's achievements, and individuals are considered "social beings" rather than part of a machine.

One can infer that the effort entailed in saving the company caused a conceptual reframing: Executives who had perceived themselves as reflexively carrying out operations maintaining the structure of an entity began to see themselves as *organizers* actively participating with others in order to bring something into existence.

The executives have developed ways to prevent lapsing "back into boxes," writes Hurst. "If there isn't a crisis, we create one" (p. 86)— that is, they anticipate issues and then identify a "champion" who believes in the importance of the issue, putting that person in charge of a team to develop trust, build a shared vision, establish a strategy for dealing with the issue and then take it to larger groups for their participation.

In addition, they "infuse activities that some might think prosaic with real significance. The focus should be on people first, and always on caring rather than managing" (p. 87). They use figurative and graphic language, share information to create a common vision and promote trust, recognize performance and contribution through ceremonies, and in other ways encourage the generation and perpetuation of expressive forms and communicative processes. In the three-year period when we had to do things so differently, we created our own culture, with its own language, symbols, norms, and customs," writes Hurst (p. 87). "In contrast to our premerger culture, the new culture is much more sympathetic toward and supportive of the use of teams and consensus decision making." There continues to be concern about structure, facts, and "rational decisions," but this is balanced with respect for and attention to the expressive and symbolic. Writes Hurst: "The key to effective management of not only our crisis but also the routine is to know whether we are in a hard 'box' or a soft 'bubble' context," and to act accordingly (p. 79). Whichever way they act, one infers, they do not lose sight of the model of organizing as a fundamental human process originating in the urge to do something and carrying with it expectations of meaningfulness, fellowship, and personal fulfillment.

ESSAYS ON ORGANIZATIONAL
PARADIGMS AND PARADOXES

The studies in this section uncover the existence of varied conceptual frameworks inside organizations, and reveal numerous dilemmas or paradoxes in management, worklife, and organizational functioning. A case in point is the first essay by Mechling and Wilson.

Festivals, company picnics, open houses, product fairs, office parties, banquets, and company softball games—all are occasions, observe Mechling and Wilson, for public discourse about problems, ambiguities, and contradictions in the symbolic categories, norms, and values of an organization. An illustration is Picnic Day at the University of California at Davis, in which there is an unresolved tension in identity (between Davis as a general campus in its own right and as "The Farm'" to Berkeley). As the authors point out, any organization will have its root metaphors which are subject to either ritual or festive treatment. A key consideration, known only by members of the organization, is: What is *omitted* from the public event. And a central concept is that of the uses of ambiguity in the mediation of elements in opposition.

Oppositions are a focus of the second paper by Tommerup, who analyzes stories about the founder (Howard Hughes) and then the long-time general manager (Pat Highland) of an electronics firm. These stories are part of the oral history of the organization as constructed by participants who seek to make sense of the company. Contrary to what one might assume from some of the literature on corporate culture and the founder as hero, Hughes is characterized in narratives as a trickster figure, upsetting the natural order. Highland as his successor is not presented as a custodian of the world the founder created but rather as himself the creator of a meaningful structure. Ultimately the question of historical accuracy may be irrelevant, at least for understanding organizational participants' conceptions of the past. Individuals are inclined to construct and reinterpret organizational history as this makes the present understandable and the future possible. The resulting perspective might be considered a "world view"—that is, a set of assumptions or beliefs and values affecting people's behavior.

In the third essay, Rusted reports on research combining both qualitative and quantitative methods and concerned with "corporate culture." Trade shows, sales meetings, conventions, awards banquets, cocktail parties, and similar festive events abound in organizations. Most offer entertainment, sometimes very elaborate. The popular literature on corporate culture suggests that calendrical celebrations of organizations are occasions to exhibit collective values. If each organization really does have a distinctive culture, then studying the entertainment at large, organization-wide events should reveal differences in the form or content of public displays correlated with cultural differences.

Using quantitative methods, Rusted discovered that this is not in fact the case. Qualitative research of a production firm revealed why. Although producers vociferously contended, and greatly cherished the notion, that they catered to individual client taste, paradoxically they proffered to corporate clients only a few performers whom they trusted and on whom they could depend.

Having uncovered a rather significant contradiction in a service organization between company image and corporate action, Rusted presented his findings to members of the organization, beginning at the "grass roots," feeding back information to successive levels in the hierarchy after seeking emendations and approval from lower levels. When it reached top management, the ethnographic portrait was not well received. In his conclusions, Rusted suggests alternative ways of presenting findings that may be sensitive not only because they report themes of stories, rumor, and gossip but also because they reveal the reality of organizational life which may contradict long-standing assumptions about the "ideal."

In the final essay in this section, Wolfe describes a situation in a military hospital in West Germany in which people were neither talking nor listening to one another. Leadership was isolated and rendered ineffectual partly through the traditional expression "the command bunker." The author used a modification of the "fishbowl technique" to enable various groups to discover how they perceived each other, why they thought themselves powerless and how to resolve their conflicts. Outcomes of this intervention included much greater communication and cooperation, improved attitudes and increased satisfaction with daily interactions at work (and the term "command banker," pejoratively referring to the leaders, dropped from usage, no longer having any reason to exist).

Each essay, then, concerns one or more perspective, method, or organizational image. Sometimes these paradigms seem to be either ambiguous or contradictory. Paradoxes abound in organizations, and many dilemmas arise for both organizational participants and researchers. Perhaps this is not surprising, given organizations as the outcome of human endeavors, and of human beings as complex creatures whose actions sometimes defy the meanings of their words, whose words may either reveal or disguise deeply felt values, and whose values may be expressed, suppressed, or projected through a variety of symbolic forms and communicative processes the interpretation of which requires all the sensitivity and methodological variety and rigor that one can master.

19

ORGANIZATIONAL FESTIVALS AND THE USES OF AMBIGUITY

The Case of Picnic Day at Davis

Jay Mechling
David Scofield Wilson

University of California, Davis

How can complex organizations deal with ambiguity and contradiction in their symbolic representations? What we know about the force of rationalization in the dynamic process of modernization (e.g., Berger et al., 1973) would lead us to expect that organizational cultures would have little toleration for the sorts of ongoing ambiguity and contradiction we find in the symbolic cultures of some whole societies and folk groups. Yet, human actors and their social dramas often have ways of ignoring social theory, so it remains an open question whether or not there are some "uses of ambiguity" in the symbolic canopies of complex organizations.

We offer here a case study in one organization's use of ambiguity in its primary symbols, rituals, and ceremonies. The organization is large, a campus of the University of California, with 18,000 students and a full complement of faculty, administrators, and staff. Our focus is upon a single festival day in the calendar of the organization. A university is certainly a large organization. And a festival belongs to that larger genre of organizational performances (e.g., parties, open houses, picnics, product fairs) in which an organization "enacts" its identity, interpreting itself to itself and to outsiders (Stoeltje, 1983). We believe, therefore, that this particular case study might yield broader insight into the processes by which organizations make symbolic, ritual use of ambiguity to explore (or, in some cases, to ignore) potentially destructive contradictions within the organization's symbolic canopy or between its symbolic canopy and experienced reality.

BACKGROUND: HISTORY AND TEXT

From "the Farm" to a "General Campus"

Picnic Day at the Davis campus of the University of California dates from its early years as "The Farm" to Berkeley, a decade and a half (1906-1921) of agriculturally centered training and education, the spirit of which came to be symbolized for the public and participants both by a family-outing style of picnic and by dairy exhibits, livestock judging, and sheepdog trials. The next three decades, 1922-1952, saw the rise of a consciousness of the campus as "Cal Aggies." A four-year degree program gave the campus a separable identity, and the new name, "Mustangs," signalled the separate pride of the student body in its own, rather high-spirited and untamed liveliness, if not categorical wildness. A mustang is, after all, still a horse. Waldo Weeth and George Bath climbed up the water tower in 1926 and stencilled on it a large, block-letter "CA" for "Cal Aggies," displaying broadly a proud campus identity. The "Frosh-Soph Brawl," a tug-of-war in the mud, a "Labor Day" every February 29th (from 1924 to 1964), during which faculty and students turned out to plant trees and generally clean up the campus, displayed the still largely unselfconscious "Aggie" spirit of the place. Perhaps the last gasp of this older élan was the erection of a mock monument by the Sword and Sandals service and honorary fraternity in 1955. "'Ollie,' the Cal Aggie Mustang," was made from the hide of a cadaver horse, stretched over a wooden frame, attached with a hose to the fountain, and set up in a pool by the student union. A sign saying "Ollie passing over Chico" invoked student fervor for the upcoming game with the Aggie's chief rivals, and by dotting the *a* in *passing* achieved a scatological tenor still recollected by one of the pranksters as "pretty racy at the time."

With the post-war boom in building and enrollment and the expansion of the campus, the Aggies became "UCD," a general campus of the University of California. The campus established, successively, a College of Veterinary Medicine (1949), a College of Letters and Sciences (1951), a Graduate Division (1961), a School of Law (1964), and a School of Medicine (1965). In 1967 the College of Agriculture changed its name to the College of Agricultural and Environmental Sciences, signalling thereby the transition of the place's sense of itself from an "Ag school" to a "general campus" of the University.

Picnic Day as "Text"

Picnic Day as we know it enacts the consciousness of this latest campus community, on the one hand showing the wider public of 60,000 visitors to Picnic Day what the campus does and has to offer, and on the other hand feeding back to the campus population itself certain messages about what it means to be a Davis student. Picnic Day is an especially nice, public presentation of both official and "underground" versions of what UCD means, a "text" of considerable complexity and occasionally startling clarity.

The 1984 Picnic Day Committee's "call for floats," written by the students, leaves no doubt about the public relations function of the festival, which should exude an "'open-house' atmosphere" as well as display "the diversity of the University of California at Davis." Floats must be described beforehand to be accepted or not by a committee with "the exclusive right to choose which entries will be allowed to participate in the parade." Floats must enact the theme somehow, be of good quality, and entertain. They may *not* feature alcoholic beverages, sell anything, solicit or collect funds or donations, preach, philosophize, politicize, advertise, throw things, or distribute printed matter. "We cannot allow"—says the committee in good bureaucratese, hiding behind "cannot"—"we cannot allow political, philosophical, or religious themes." There had been a Peace Float in the 1983 parade, a few years before that a float protesting the University's research funding connections with California's agri-business community, and in the 1970s the Native Americans sneaked in at the end of the parade with floats of their own alternative sort. These events may be the origin of the present prohibitions.

While the intentions of the picnic planners and the rhetoric of their attempts to control the upcoming events would make a monograph all its own, authority is not our focus. Picnic Day seems to us like many public festivities—Fourth of July, Halloween, Christmas, New Year's Day—to be essentially "out of control" and, so, much more interesting than any one would-be planner would ever be able to design. The evidence that the planners and administration know this is their perennial calls for more control, their insistence on a theme, their rhetoric about what Picnic Day *is* and *is for*, and their appeals to history.

What the event does for the participants may very well be at odds with the supposed, even pronounced, purposes of the festival. It may even, as in dreamwork, be important to the work of the festival for its logic to remain subconscious. Which brings us back to our basic queries. What, really, is Picnic Day, this text we have taken to explicate? And are some of the subtexts more cogent than others in what they reveal about the spirit of the whole?

CONCEPTS: FESTIVITY, FRAMES, AND MEANING

Picnic Day as a Syndetic Work

We need to step aside from Picnic Day in particular now for a moment and take up some formal matters regarding festivity, frames, and meanings. We shall argue that the day as a whole, and most of its parts, amounts for one thing to a sort of text that we in the West are unprepared fully to appreciate intellectually, for it enacts a consciousness alternative to our dominant, artistic model of textual authorship and excellence. Picnic Day is seriously "syndetic," to apply Robert Plant Armstrong's (1981) superb invention; it is an accumulation of apposite instances rather than a synthetic achievement.

Picnic Day is no poem. It is not a "piece" as a sonnet is, or ballet. Parades are not poems, nor are potlucks and open houses, yet all are "made up" by people and make sense in a way hard to pin down. One way to get at the sense some of these seemingly empty enterprises make real is to look not at what they pretend to mean (and not at the flags and bands and women on floats and even rebel bands) but at what is not there, what would be out of place, an affront of some sort.

Imagine a parade in which every entry fit as finely into some artistic vision as each word fits into an Eliot poem, drawing on past associations and anticipating later turns. The fun of a parade is that high school bands follow tractors; tractors, Wells Fargo stagecoaches; the UC Berkeley straw hat band, a "serious" band from a local high school, and so on. No one entry leads to the next. It could be mixed up or run backward, and except for the color guard that signals the front of the parade, no one would be the wiser. This puts in a rather comic frame the "marshalls" who oversee the timing of the start and get each entry in place, who run up and down the line disciplining everybody as if it mattered at all. A parade is a fine folk instance of a temporal, linear syndetic work—an anciently legitimate kind of open-ended community work.

The geographical dispersal of displays here and there on campus amounts equally to a syndetic work. In this case, however, it is a "work" the visitor makes up ad hoc by wandering into this exhibit and on to another, different for each picnicker.

Festivities Versus Ritual

Another question: Is Picnic Day a spring "break" from everyday, taken-for-granted patterns of value and meaning, or is it a sort of ritual assertion of values and mending of patterns that have become frayed by daily use? Silly festivities seek to restore a kind of psychic economy by making fun of proprieties, by reversals of various sorts, as in Mardi Gras. The best evidence for such a reading of Picnic Day would seem to be the several mock drill teams, such as Alpha Falfa Oink, the Animal Science department's precision shovel drill team, or the Graduate School of Administration's Precision Briefcase Drill Team, or the Landscape Architects' Precision T-square Drill Team, all reminiscent of southern California's now-annual "Doo-Dah" parade that parodies the Rose Bowl Parade (Rubin, 1979). "Equestrian groups must be prepared," the rules regarding floats say, "to provide their own clean-up *during* the parade." Shovel teams exaggerate the clean-up and thereby tweak the nose of the committee. And the "Your Sewage is Our Bread and Butter" sign on the float by the civil engineers seems to follow in this nonsense tradition of making light of heavy matters.

But for all the scatology, there is little of the mockery of officials and mores we might suppose would go on with a spring "break," and certainly nothing as raunchy as Ollie's urinary comment on Chico in 1955. In fact, nothing is broken by this parade, except perhaps for some fancied decorum that has never been the tone of the parade as far back as we can discover. It looks more as if this Aggie school has chosen to act a bit bumpkinish, a bit rude as a kind of celebration and presentation of its own "aggieness" in the face of some fancied "taste" or college "Culture" with a capital "C." But the investment in the "rightness" of "the scientific" campus is too great—and simultaneously too fragile—to allow much silliness.

We begin to get at how the Picnic Day activities maintain and repair the "agricultural sciences" cosmos when we examine more closely the motifs running through a number of the exhibits and popular events. Since one of the themes enacted prominently in Picnic Day is the relationship between animals and humans, it is likely that we shall find something distinctively UCD Cal Aggie in the festival's dramatic displays of animals.

Animal-Human Relationship in the American Bestiary

Three or four sorts of animals appear regularly in the morning parade, but none is as prominent as the horse. Horses appear, of course, in the several "equestrian units," such as the "Mustang Precision Drill Team," "Block and Bridle," "Hoofbeats of Dixon (4H)," "Putah Creek Stables," and the national champion polo team. Horses in the parade also get to enact their uses as farm animals, pulling some of the antique farm machinery and, every year, the Wells Fargo stagecoach. Dogs appear much less frequently, usually in connection with the dog obedience classes conducted by the spouses of the Veterinary Medicine students. The parade seldom features cows and goats, and in those few instances the animal is subject to some sort of humorous treatment. The 1984 parade, for example, features no real cows but two representational ones—one a lavender, stuffed mascot of the Cal Aggie Square Dancers and the other a totally drunk, passed-out cow on the float of the Cal Aggie Marching Band. The 1984 Dairy Goat Research Facility group (a mixture of animal science and veterinary medicine graduate students) marched with a goat pulling a small, colorful wagon and with one of the students carrying a sign reading, "No Kidding." All of the animals provide the occasion for the scatological humor in the parade, with the human "pooper scoopers" often dressed as clowns, drawing attention to the "disorderly" nature of the manure (the "dirt") they are shovelling.

The on-campus displays bring into sharper focus the symbolic treatments of animals during picnic day. The 1983 Picnic Day program listed seven "Special Events." Putting aside the two that have nothing to do with animals (i.e., the Law School Moot Court and the academic minilectures), we are left with five events that, in the words of the *Aggie* cover story that day, represent Picnic Day "tradition":

> In keeping with the traditional agricultural theme of UCD, animals, too, play a big part in the participation of the day's events. Over the years, traditional events have been established, including the Picnic Day Rodeo, sheep-dog trials, and racing dachshunds. This year, in addition to the all-time favorites, a new dog frisbee contest is scheduled for 11 a.m. at the Rec Hall field (Walker, 1983).

Add to these four events the polo game between the current national champion team and the alumni of the UCD Polo Club. It is instructive to schematize the animal relationships in these five special events:

(1) The *rodeo* features *human/horse* cooperation to control *steers*.
(2) The *sheep dog trials* feature *human/dog* cooperation to control *sheep*.
(3) The *dachshund races* feature *dogs* in pursuit of a *rabbit* pelt.
(4) The *dog frisbee* contest features *human/dog* cooperation.
(5) The *polo* match features *human/horse* cooperation.

All five "Special Events," it turns out, involve *horses* or *dogs* as central characters working either in cooperation with *humans* or as the working extension of humans for control over less intelligent animals (see also Lawrence, 1982). We are reminded here of Sahlins's (1976) discovery of the special status of horses and dogs in the domesticated series *cattle-pigs-horses-dogs*. Evidence of the special status of the last two animals is the American food taboo on horses and dogs, strongest for dogs but also strong for horses, despite periodic attempts to get Americans to adopt horsemeat into their diet (but note the hierarchy implied by the fact that we feed horsemeat to dogs). As Sahlins says, "'everything happens as if' the food system is inflected throughout by a principle of metonymy such that taken as a whole it composes a sustained metaphor on cannibalism" (1976: 174). Moreover, notes Sahlins, dogs and horses "participate in American society in the capacity of subjects. They have proper personal names, and indeed we are in the habit of conversing with them as we do not talk to pigs and cattle" (1976: 174).

Leach's theory of taboo, demonstrated through his classic examination of animal categories and verbal abuse, helps us see even more clearly the crucial role of *horse* and *dog* as mediating animals in the American symbolic bestiary. In developing his notion that taboo operates to keep distinct and discontinuous the "named" things in our cultural universe, Leach focuses upon three sets of terms (1964: 33-37):

(a) self	— sister —	cousin	— neighbor —	stranger
(b) self	— house —	farm	— field	— far
(c) self	— pet	— livestock —	game	— wild animal

The most powerful, sacred, and dangerous terms in any such set are the tabooed terms that share characteristics of more than one category and, hence, pose an explicit threat to the neatly discontinuous "named" universe. "The thesis is," writes Leach, "that we make binary distinctions and then mediate the distinction by creating an ambiguous (and taboo-

TABLE 19.1

p	both p and ~p	~p
man	'man-animal'	not man
(not animal)	('pets')	(animal)

loaded) intermediate category," which relationship Leach sketches in Table 19.1.

ANALYSIS

Ritual Disguising of Cultural Ambiguity

Armed with insights from Sahlins and Leach about the ritual value of *horses* and *dogs,* we can return now to the Picnic Day animal displays and see how much these displays are aimed at universe maintenance of American animal categories and taboos. Of the animals "available" on an agricultural sciences campus for ritual treatment, the UCD Picnic Day displays confirm the sanctioned categories.

The animals in the "pet" category, those animals that are *ambivalent* in the sense that they share two normally distinct frames of reference, do appear in Picnic Day displays and performances, but they are not the subject of ridicule or symbolic inversions. The livestock animals are a different matter, ridiculed not only in the Picnic Day performances but in everyday student folklore, as well. When asked to collect UC Davis lore, for example, members of one folklore class provided the following joke texts:

Davis is the place where the men are men, the women are men, and the sheep are scared [male student, age 21].

Davis is where the men are men, the women are bored, and the sheep don't go out at night [male student, age 24].

Davis: the place where men run wild and the sheep run scared [male student, age 22].

UC Davis: Where Men are Men and Sheep are Nervous [male student, age 22].

UC Davis, where the men are men, the women are men, and the sheep are getting nervous [male student].

TABLE 19.2

p	both p and ⌐p	⌐p
human	pet	livestock
	dogs	cattle
	horses	pigs
		sheep
		goats (etc.)

> UC Davis—where the men are men, the women are too, and the sheep run scared [male student, age 20].
>
> Q: Why do fraternity men like sorority women?
> A: Because cows, sheep, hogs, and the other large farm animals don't know how to cook [female student, age early 20s].

There is much about student life at Davis packed into these jokes, but we want to keep our attention on the human/animal relationship. The basic joke formulae are well-known texts ridiculing farm boys or "aggies" (as students at several agricultural and mechanical sciences schools, like Texas A&M, are often called), so the Davis texts both see the campus as a farm and make bawdy fun of the "aggie." Moreover, the jokes are sexual, featuring bestiality, or "zoophily," as Legman (1968: 206-212) calls it.

There is other humor connecting beasts and sexuality during Picnic Day. The Friday noontime central campus quad event that has kicked off Picnic Day festivities for the past several years is a cow milking contest, won every year by the campus chancellor, a former professor of animal science. The sexual resonance of the event is not very subtle, especially when the campus newspaper one year ran a photograph and headline proclaiming, "Chancellor Puts Squeeze on Big Teats." In the same vein was a tee-shirt reading "Sigma Moo" and worn by a big-chested coed. Also available on a tee-shirt and on a bumper sticker is a cartoon cow, seen from the rear, with the slogan: "UC Davis...The Best Dairy-Air for 75 Years." And one of the students marching in the 1984 parade's Dairy Goat Research Facility ensemble carried a sign, "Feed Your Gal Goat Milk—It Makes Her Butt Better."

We also find something about humans and animals in the oral legends told by students, such as the following:

> My sister has a friend in law school who attended a fraternity party and showed interest in joining the fraternity. He was told by a member of the

fraternity that one of the initiation rites involved getting inebriated and sodomizing the pigs in the pig barn in Tercero [a dorm complex] [female student, age 23].

So there seems to be a free and humorous association between cows, goats, pigs, and human sexuality in a broad range of UC Davis folk and commercial culture expressions.

We also collected from students several independent versions of the same legendary practice, called "cow-tipping." When students get bored of studying, the story goes, they sometimes go out to the cow pen (near the dorms) and push over sleeping cows. Another common legendary prank is to strand a cow on an upper dorm floor.

This collection of UC Davis animal lore is as revealing in what it does not include as in what it does. It helps us see that cows, pigs, and sheep are "fair game" for irreverent humor about college life at an agriculture campus; but it shows us just as clearly that horses and dogs, those ambivalent pet-like animals in the Davis bestiary, are *not* the subject of play. The Picnic Day Parade and animal displays, in other words, serve as rituals affirming the truth, sanctity, and morality of the American hierarchy of animal/human relationships (Handelman, 1977). If Picnic Day were a festival, and thereby more like the play frame than the ritual one, then we would expect to find playful symbolic inversions mixing up these animal categories, drawing attention to their "made-up-ness." The lack of any such displays is testimony to the tameness of Picnic Day as a festival. Like many other secular rituals, Picnic Day "belongs to the structuring side of the cultural/historical process" (Moore and Myerhoff, 1977: 3); it stands on the side of order rather than disorder. Picnic Day is no safety valve to release tensions (Abrahams and Bauman 1978: 206). Given the alternative of either expressing some deep cultural ambiguity or disguising it, the ritual actors of Picnic Day choose the latter—choose in effect to discourage any thoughtful inquiry into the cultural ambiguities of life at UC Davis (Moore and Myerhoff, 1977: 16, 18; Babcock-Abrahams, 1975: 173-174).

But how are we to account for the conservative character of the animal displays during Picnic Day, for the lack of any activity even playfully disordering during Davis' festival time and space the official relationships between humans and animals?

Threats to Cultural Categories: Love and Cruelty

Our thesis is that everyday commonsense, taken-for-granted reality at an agricultural science campus like the University of California,

Davis, poses two distinct threats to the cultural categories. The first threat is the possibility of *inappropriate affection for nonpet animals.* Affection toward dogs and horses is quite acceptable, but affection toward cattle, pigs, sheep, goats, and other livestock at Davis is inappropriate *for animal scientists.* The threat first rears its head for school-age children who raise nonpet animals as 4-H or Future Farmers of America projects. Months of special relationship between a child and a nonpet animal end with the logical commercial conclusion wherein the animal is sold at auction. The child is likely during this time to have violated the "normal" relationship with the animal by naming it and by talking to it in ways usually reserved for pet animals. Part of learning to be a farmer, clearly, is learning to put aside these sentimental attachments to livestock. The problem is that the identical problem can follow the 4-H youngster into the agricultural college setting, so that animal scientists at UCD must fight the tendency to develop inappropriate affection toward research animals. Admission and scholarship application essays by UCD students testify that a great many of the undergraduates choose animal science or preveterinary medicine majors because they "love animals," especially horses. While this love of animals may have a place at a university still agricultural in orientation, faculty and students at Davis sense that theirs is more truly a science campus that may stress advanced animal science over, say, animal husbandry.

This threat of inappropriate affection for nonpet animals, incidentally, helps make sense of the bestiality motif in several of the UCD folklore items quoted earlier. Bestiality is, after all, "inappropriate" affection for an animal. Bestiality with dogs and horses appears far less in the lore than bestiality with sheep and pigs. Leach's three parallel sets of terms suggest that sex with a dog or a horse amounts to incest, just as eating a dog or horse would amount to cannibalism. Still, sex with livestock, while not exactly appropriate, can be the subject of aggie humor.

The second threat an agricultural science campus poses to the normal human/animal relationships in American culture is that of *inappropriate nonaffection (cruelty) toward pet animals.* Davis is a science campus beyond its agriculture functions, a transition signalled by the appearance in the late 1960s of the phrase, "major research university campus," in all of the campus' public relations releases. This means that Davis scientists conduct research with animals not normally considered livestock, the two noteworthy cases being primates at the Primate Center and dogs as part of an ongoing, federally funded project at The

Beagle Colony. The conjunction of graduate research programs in animal science, medicine, and veterinary medicine on campus also results in the sort of research with livestock, including horses, that one would not normally associate with an agricultural campus.

The disordering potential of research with pet animals—primates, dogs, cats, and horses—has always lurked beneath the orderly transition of the campus from an agriculture school to a scientific research facility. Occasionally there have been incidents disturbing the surface order, as in the 1978 discovery of a not-quite-dead black Labrador retriever in a dumpster serving an animal research laboratory. That unpleasant episode led to tighter procedural controls, but stories of cruelty to animals (e.g., at the Primate Center) continued to circulate on campus.

In the 1980s, animal protection groups took the offensive against University of California research with animals, particularly dogs, cats, and rabbits (man's pets), and primates (human beings' closest "relatives").

On April 23, 1984, a group called Mobilization for Animals staged a demonstration and vigil. In early September 1984, members of the Animal Liberation Front left bomblike packages on the door steps of the director and of the associate director of the California Primate Research Center, and spray painted "Killer" on the latter's cars. What was once a vague contradiction in UC Davis's research on pet animals has now become public drama.

If the Picnic Day festival displays have handled the first threat to order (that is, the danger of inappropriate affection for nonpet animals) by featuring dogs, horses, cattle, pigs, and sheep in their proper relation to humans, they have handled this second threat by *omitting* displays featuring research on dogs, horses, and primates. This was not always so. In the 1961 Picnic Day displays the Beagle Colony had been featured as an exhibit: "AEC Dog Project." Beagles were there irradiated in order to learn more about the effects of radiation. The dogs had their vocal chords altered to diminish the din for researchers, and the "barkless beagles" (as the program put it) were a common stop among visitors to campus. By 1963, however, the beagles were edited out of the festivities, though the facility appeared on the campus map.

Throughout the 1970s and into the 1980s, there have been no Picnic Day displays of research with petlike animals. It is significant that the only display of research that may be construed as "cruel" to animals is the famous "cow with a hole in its side," a fistulated research animal with a surgically-installed access to one of its stomachs for the study of the digestive process of ruminants. The cow never fails to draw large crowds, who are more often "grossed out" than morally offended. The animal is a cow, after all, and one Picnic Day account notes that the Holstein has a number, not a name. No threat to the natural order of cultural things, this cow. But there is not a beagle with a hole in its side.

CONCLUSIONS: ROOT METAPHORS AND THE USES OF AMBIGUITY

The University of California, Davis, has emerged as a "major research university campus" with an international reputation, but it is still the agriculture campus of the university. The name change in 1967 of one school from "The College of Agriculture" to "The College of Agricultural and Environmental Sciences" cannot erase the "aggie" residue that lives in older faculty members' attitudes and pops up at odd times in the symbolic culture of the campus.

Members of a society or organization usually adopt one or more cultural strategies for dealing with ambiguity, anomaly, or ambivalence (Babcock-Abrahams 1975: 173-174). The UC Davis community seems to have chosen a strategy that keeps the two realms separate and rigorously avoids public acknowledgement of the taboo-laden middle where science and agriculture overlap. Thus Picnic Day is awash with dual icons that stand for this unresolved dual nature of the campus. Early in the parade marches the neatly uniformed UCD Cal Aggie Marching Band, but later in the parade the same musicians appear as the rag-tag Cal Aggie Mav'rik Band. One bumper sticker celebrating the campus's 75th anniversary features a stylized mustang, long the official totem of the campus, while another bumper sticker sports the cartoon cow and "Dairy-Air" pun. The UCD mustang and the Cal Aggie cow coexist in campus iconography. Some Picnic Day revellers wear t-shirts with logos from science departments such as zoology, while others wear shirts with the "Dairy-Air" and similar jokes. The two white water towers on the main portion of the campus mirror the strategy—the tower nearer to the interstate highway has the letters "UCD" painted on it on the side facing the motorists, while the other tower looks away from the highway and toward campus with its "CA" Cal Aggie logo. Settling for the time being on neither the "UCD" nor the "Cal Aggie" identity, the campus community seems content to let the two images coexist, knowing that the Cal Aggie identity is becoming less real and more an identity constructed and "played" during the annual Picnic Day. Most emblematic of this inequality between the two identities is the Picnic Day fake facade put up every year on the entrance to the animal science building. The red barn facade is constructed like a flat on a theatrical set, assisting the audience's willing suspension of disbelief as it "pretends" along with the scientists that UCD is still "The Farm." But, like all pretenses, the constructed identity is a fragile one that must avoid unnerving reminders that, inside the building with the barn facade, there may be men and women in green lab coats walking the narrow line between inappropriate love and cruelty toward animals.

It seems likely to us that the uses of ambiguity we find in the Picnic Day festivities at the University of California, Davis, are to be found in the whole range of "definitional ceremonies" (Myerhoff, 1978: 21, 150) researchers come across in organizational symbolic cultures. To be sure, animals and their relations to humans will not be the "root metaphors" (Turner, 1974) in the symbolic canopies of most other organizations, but our point is that an organization *will* have its own root metaphors subject to either the ritual treatment that takes them seriously or to the playful treatment that calls into question their taken-for-grantedness. The general case, then, is one of symbols in tension. We must be alert to the "strategies of ambiguity" adopted consciously and unconsciously by the designers and participants in organizational ceremonies. Festivals, open houses, company picnics, product fairs, office parties, banquets, and company softball games become occasions for shared, public discourse (both verbal and nonverbal) "about" troubling ambiguities and contradictions in the organization's symbolic categories, norms, and values (Deal and Kennedy, 1982a: 59-84).

But, as we see in the Picnic Day example, organizations do not always use rituals and ceremonies to enrich and explore the participants' understanding of the meanings of organizational symbols. Sometimes, perhaps usually, the organizers of an institution's "definitional ceremonies" design the ritual in such a way as to "mask" the organization's conflicts, "to deny and disguise them and gloss the difficulties they present" (Moore and Myerhoff, 1977: 16). The participants who then must enact the ceremony or be its audience face the decision whether or not to "conspire" with the organizers and help repress inquiry into the organization's contradictions.

The danger of festivals, of course, is that they threaten to get "out of control," which may mean that the participants depart from the controlled, ceremonial "script" the organizers provide and embark on their own, anti-structural drama (Turner, 1969) that unearths, plays with, jokes about, and otherwise seeks to understand the meaning of the organization by confronting directly its most threatening puzzles. The symbolic drama we find in an organization, in short, may lie not only in its official rituals but more importantly in the struggle over who controls the interpretation of the place and whether that interpretation should acknowledge or ignore the organization's troubles.

20

FROM TRICKSTER TO FATHER FIGURE

Learning from the Mythologization of Top Management

Peter Tommerup

University of California, Los Angeles

Narratives are now being explored in the organizational literature in relation to a number of issues. Among the studies are those analyzing stories as "symbols which control the organization" (Wilkins, 1983b), channels for communicating either "truth or corporate propaganda" (Martin and Powers, 1983), diagnostic tools for "organizational problem solving" (Mitroff and Kilmann, 1975), and a means for articulating the "uniqueness" of organizations (Martin et al., 1983). One essay proposes myth making as an interventionist strategy (Boje et al., 1982). Simultaneously, more attention is being paid to founder's culture and to the influence of subsequent generations of managers (Martin et al., 1985; Siehl, 1985; Schein, 1985), although stories about founders and managers are not always examined.

Organizational history is largely oral history. Long time employees, who serve as the bearers of this heritage, are seldom more excited than when they are reminiscing about the people and events which they believe are responsible for their firm's past. Organizational history is also principally a "human" history. It is communicated through stories. Stories both reflect and create people's social realities. They focus primarily on the emotional associations among people in an organizational setting, as well as on the monumental events which help to make these associations more dramatic and memorable. By examining narratives concerning an organization's past, much can be learned about participants' collective reality—its values, attitudes and beliefs— thereby illuminating both the process and the fundamental role of "myth making."

What kinds of stories do participants in an organization tell about a founder or about managers? Is every generation of managers the subject of narrating? What sort of developmental "life cycle" of the organization do the stories as a whole depict? What are the implications for understanding "history," as well as the ramifications for appreciating participants' perceptions of the organization's past and their concerns in the present?

In this essay I present and discuss a sampling of the kinds of stories told by employees of Hughes Aircraft. The action revolves around the enigmatic founder, on the one hand, and a third generation leader, on the other. Oral accounts, strangely, are absent regarding the second and fourth (the current) generations of top executives. By emphasizing and exaggerating certain eras of corporate leadership, these narratives have not "documented" history, but rather have "mythologized" it according to some fundamental cognitive processes. In essence, these stories commemorate only the most salient and deeply felt aspects in the present of past events and their protagonists.

THE NARRATIVES

In many of the stories, Howard Hughes, the founder of the company, is the protagonist (in the stories below, all identities have been concealed except those of top management who are publicly recognized figures). In others, the central figure is Pat Hyland, a long time general manager. None of the stories concern the top managers immediately before or after Hyland. The time frame presented by the body of narratives resembles an hour glass (on its side), as in Figure 20.1. The distant and the recent past dominate.

The Hughes Stories

Howard Hughes, of course, is well-known outside the company. Once celebrated for his adventurous spirit, he attained more recent notoriety from an idiosyncratic way of conducting his personal life and business affairs. His penchant for secrecy, obsession with control, and manipulation of others are frequently dramatized in stories told by people including those who are not members of the organization.

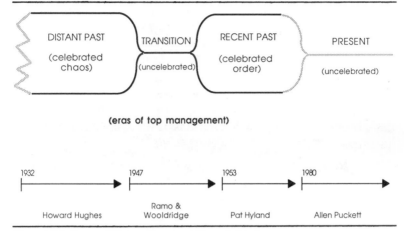

Figure 20.1 Sense of History Conveyed Through Stories

A characteristic often mentioned is his fabled quest for engineering perfection. According to one employee, he was a "genius. . . a man who didn't waste time recreating the wheel." Although his technical skill is admired, it is his inability to work with people that is most often memorialized. He is remembered as a strict taskmaster with time for tinkering but not for people.

An example emerges from the company's building of the giant Hercules flying boat, popularly referred to as the "Spruce Goose."

HH-1. As you know, everything was fashioned out of wood. . . . Eventually the workmen assigned to this project began to build tool boxes out of scraps of wood in their spare time. Of all the boxes being built, one was especially nice. When Hughes came in at night to inspect the progress, he noticed it and watched it develop. When it was nearly finished, he took an axe and chopped it up. Then he said, "That should take care of the tool boxes!"

A recurring theme in the stories about Hughes is that "the big boss is unpredictable and difficult to work with." Two subthemes also appear. One may be described as "he imposes order on the actions of others," while the other is "his own behavior appears to be random, unordered, and chaotic."

HH-2. Hughes flew in a couple of planes and left them at the Lockheed terminal at the Burbank airport. He flew one in, locked it and left. Later, he flew in a second one, locked it too, and left. He warned people to "leave them there!" As people had learned not to go against him, they left them alone and made sure nobody touched them. The planes remained there until after his death. The airport officials built an access road around the planes rather than move them.

Power and intimidation are additional themes in many of the narratives. Consider the following story, in which Hughes's influence at the company is extended mysteriously and unseen, but almost instantaneously.

HH-3. There were certain people here over the years who as long as they wanted a job could have one. A new VP one day was "cleaning house." He called people in one at a time and told them that they were laid off. Steve's reply to this was, "Well, I'm afraid you can't do that." To which the VP replied, "But I can, it's hard times!" Steve called a number at Romaine Street [the location of Hughes' headquarters for his many operations] that he had been given. When the VP returned from lunch, all of his personal articles were waiting for him outside of gate five.

Most of the stories involve relations between Hughes and employees. As the social drama unfolds, complications set in which undermine the individual's faith in his boss. Before the conclusion, Hughes has left the worker in an awkward predicament. Often this is because Hughes appears to be unaware of the social consequences of his individual actions.

HH-4. Hughes visited the plant site . . . in 1958 or 59. He flew to the site in his own plane. He was dressed in dungarees, tennis shoes, and a skipper's cap. He came to the guard gate and walked right through. . . . The guard didn't know who he was and drew his gun. Hughes's retort to the guard was, "If you shoot me, you're shooting the president of the company." Luckily someone who recognized Hughes and was known to the guard saw what was going on, ran to the scene, and settled the matter.

HH-5. Once Hughes wanted Chuck to fly him someplace. Hughes said that he would pick him up at three p.m. and did. While driving toward the airstrip where the plane was parked, Chuck noticed that Hughes was nearly out of gas. They found a service station and stopped. As it happened, Chuck had gotten $300 in travel expenses from the cashier before he left. Hughes had no money, and so he asked Chuck to give him some. Chuck pulled the entire wad out of his pocket and handed it to him. Hughes paid for the gas and put the rest in his pocket. Upon returning from the trip, Chuck inquired about how to account for the money. Everyone he asked said they didn't know what to do. Finally he asked

General Schoup. His reply was, "Just put down, 'Confiscated by Howard Hughes.'"

One of the stories told within the organization concerns Hughes's private life, but the theme of disregarding others is the same.

HH-6. He borrowed clothes from people but never bought clothes for himself. He wore the same suit day after day. Once, he borrowed a coat from his houseboy. After about six months, the houseboy asked Hughes if he'd like to have it cleaned. To which he replied, "No, I know it's yours, but wait a couple of weeks and I'll get it back to you." The houseboy answered, "Oh, no, Mr. Hughes, then people will think I'm wearing your old hand-me-downs."

The Hyland Stories

Pat Hyland came from Bendix. He was hired by Hughes at government insistence to provide professional management. His tenure lasted from 1953 to 1980, when he retired. His persona in stories is directly opposite Hughes's image. Whereas interactions with the founder left people feeling exploited or confused, those with Hyland were usually more satisfying and always less ambiguous. In fact an overall theme suggested by these tales is that the big boss is usually reasonable and pleasant to work with. Attention is also drawn to two facets of Hyland's character. These are the basis for two additional subthemes. They include "he is more flexible and thoughtful in his ordering of others' time and space," and "his own actions appear to reflect thought and planning." When dealing with employees, he takes their problems seriously.

PH-1. One of my earliest positions at Hughes Aircraft was driving a mail truck. One day, a Cadillac convertible swerved in front of me. I tried to avoid it, stopped short, but bumped it nevertheless. I swore at the driver and not just under my breath. As he got out of the car I realized who it was. "Oh no," I thought, "Now I've lost my job." It was Pat Hyland. He walked over to the truck and started to talk to me. He asked how I was and looked at the car and the truck. His Cadillac had a small dent, but nothing too bad. The truck wasn't damaged. He told me not to worry about it. He said that it was his fault and since there was no damage to the truck to just forget about it.

Arthur, who is blind, has had trouble getting and keeping a job in the mercurial aircraft industry. While the quality of his work is high, he is

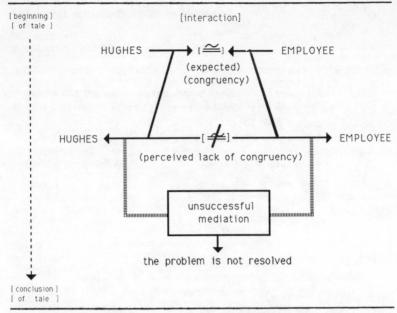

Figure 20.2   The Structure of Cognitive and Affective Dissonance

usually considered to be one of the more expendable people. After trying a number of jobs, he was hired by Hughes Aircraft Company.

> *PH-2.* When Hughes hired me, I was happy. I felt I'd finally gotten a job I could sink my teeth into. I felt it would be permanent, but there were layoffs on the B-17. I was out of work for two years. I wrote a letter to Pat Hyland. I prayed to the Holy Spirit to put the right words in the letter. I guess it had an effect on him—he must have passed it around from manager to manager—and within a month I was hired back. I pointed out that by staying at home I would make more with blind aid, but I wanted to work.

PARADIGMS AND POINTS OF VIEW

Interactional Paradigms

Clearly there are two different models of human interaction expressed through these narratives. Life under Hughes is marked by contradictions

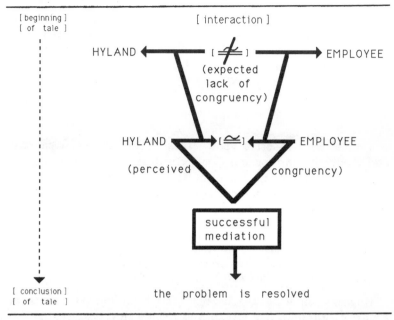

Figure 20.3 The Structure of Cognitive and Affective Assonance

and ambiguity. The behavior of the unpredictable big boss is juxtaposed with that of the loyal worker. Stories begin with the expectation of a shared understanding concerning the nature of organizational reality —one of reciprocity and mutual respect. This expectation disintegrates as the story unfolds, for Hughes acts with insensitivity. The very weak or nonexistent resolution properties of the story reflect the intensity of dissonance experienced on both a cognitive and affective level (see Figure 20.2).

The Hyland cycle is an entirely different matter. These tales present a paradigm of increased understanding between organizational members and top management. Stories PH-1 and PH-2, like others, present an emergent image of social and psychological unification. Hyland is portrayed as being able to avert such potential crises as those stemming from hitting the boss's car or wanting to work but not having a job. In contrast to Hughes, he is portrayed as fostering consensus rather than exacerbating discord. He is consistently shown resolving ambiguous and emotionally charged dilemmas. Characters in these anecdotes repeatedly evince surprise that the big boss (1) successfully negates ambiguity and (2) usually relates to people on a more humanistic basis. In fact, as narratives draw to an end, the previous tensions separating top management and other individuals are alleviated. Human interactions resolve in greater assonance and harmony (see Figure 20.3).

Point of View

The stories I collected about Howard Hughes were recounted exclusively in *the third person*. Coupled with a more distant time frame, this imbues them with the quality of "legend," which, according to one researcher, is rooted in the experience of unresolved tension and ambiguity.

> Crises or unusual events are ambiguous by nature; questions arise about the event which cannot be answered by ordinary means. . . . When a situation remains ambiguous the chances are greater that a traditional legend will survive [Mullen 1972: 105].

Hughes's untoward and unpredictable behavior was a constant source of frustration. It resulted in a continual state of disorientation for those who worked with him. His penchant for psychological manipulation left people feeling anxious, tense, and dissatisfied. Thus, these stories as "legends" memorialize what is perceived to be an unsolvable problem. They seem to bring an ongoing dilemma into closer proximity for inspection and sense-making (see Louis, 1980: 241), while simultaneously keeping it distant enough so as not to cripple interaction and daily routine altogether. Telling such stories may enable individuals to cope with a problem until it can be resolved.

Most of the stories about Hyland are presented in *the first person*. This rhetorical device tends to generate greater plausibility. "People believe their own senses in the first place . . . and then immediate testimonies" (Degh and Vazsonyi, 1974: 231). A typical consequence of "the first person point of view is a deeper involvement in the action of the story for the teller and listener" (Mullen, 1978: 143). It's the difference between personal experience "I" and hearsay "he." A story told in the first person is one of individual discovery and personal testimony, belief, and clarification and certainty (not ambiguity).

While the stories about Hyland do serve a didactic purpose, their main contribution appears to be imparting the message that his approach—which he labeled "management by principle"—is something with which people can identify in a positive way. Communicating this information via a first person point of view also reveals a newly discovered value in trusting one's perceptions. Under Hughes, intuitions proved to be unreliable indicators of how to proceed owing to his erratic behavior. Once a coherent paradigm is established under Hyland's leadership, the players become less defensive. The result, according to the anecdotes, is a greater sense of trust and fellowship permeating the workplace.

At this juncture, one might be tempted to ask, "Are the stories true?" Some of them might be, or at least aspects of them might be grounded in actuality. The truth or falsity of specific narratives is not as significant, perhaps, as the amount of belief invested in them, the larger organizational history that begins to emerge, and the issues that the body of stories present or grow out of.

A MYTHOLOGIZED SENSE OF HISTORY

While the interactional paradigms rooted in the Hughes and Hyland eras are juxtaposed in narrative, the second and fourth generations of management are not similarly depicted. What emerges is a mythologized picture of corporate history focusing on only two of four periods that have been significant for the company.

In the "native perspective," the founding of the company is shrouded in antiquity. The earliest period recollected is the chaotic distant past when Hughes was in charge. The second duration is vague and relatively unarticulated. It is remembered as a transition—a prelude to significant events rather than a noteworthy occurrence in itself. Although Simon Ramo and Dean Wooldridge have formally been credited with transforming Hughes Aircraft from Howard's private hobby shop into a professional outfit, their efforts are not memorialized in oral accounts. They have been largely forgotten and omitted from the mythological script. The third time frame is marked by Pat Hyland's rational approach to leadership. This is illustrated as a complete antithesis to that of the founder. Finally, the present appears to be largely unformulated in terms of dramatic and memorable stories (see Figure 20.4).

The sequence expressed through this sociohistorical model is not unlike a paradigm described by the French ethnographer Arnold Van

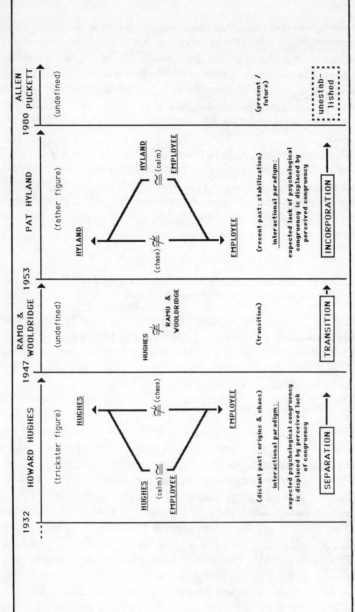

Figure 20.4 Mythologized Sense of History Conveyed Through Stories

Gennep with respect to individual "rites of passage." He noted that underlying a variety of rituals keyed to important passages or turning points in life (i.e., birth, marriage, and death) there always exists a syntagmatic configuration of *separation, transition,* and *incorporation.* "The underlying arrangement is always the same," he wrote. "Beneath a multiplicity of forms, either consciously expressed or implied, a typical pattern always recurs" (1960: 191).

This archetypal configuration of rites of passage seems to be projected onto the metaphoric "life cycle" of Hughes Aircraft through its oral history. The narratives which compose this history appear to serve the same fundamental need on a group level to symbolically acknowledge developmental life processes as do the more familiar rites of passage which are keyed to individual ontogeny. Stories from the Hughes period depict a growing feeling of psychological separation between the parties involved. This is demonstrated by the lack of resolution in these accounts as well as by the more distancing third-person point of view. Conversely, the Hyland era reveals a stronger sense of community. Incorporation is marked by such signs as strong resolution in plot and a more involving first-person perspective. The other historic time spans may remain uncelebrated in story because their role is transitional (Ramo and Woolridge) or as yet undecided (Alan Puckett). Their emphasis could mediate or dilute the ongoing oppositional nature of this corporate mythology.

That the organizational history is mythologized according to features of a process with which all human beings are familiar and engage in is further suggested by the semantic slots to which these dominant figures have been assigned. Hughes has been cast in the role of "trickster," the quintessential embodiment of unresolved appetites and contradictions. He unavoidably alternates between being calculating and merely out of control. In every instance, he reduces order to chaos. Unlike Hyland, who helps to put events into perspective, Hughes scrambles them and places them out of focus. In the words of one researcher, "the serious hero focuses events . . . [and] forces issues" (Babcock-Abrahams 1974: 154), whereas the trickster

> tends to confound the distinction between illusion and reality, if not deny it altogether. In fact, he casts doubt on all preconceived and expected systems of distinction between behaviors and the representation thereof [Babcock-Abrahams, 1974: 155].

While Hughes symbolizes antistructure and chaos, his successor epitomizes personal strength and order. This association of Hyland with the creation of a primal sense of order is significant. For one thing, it violates known fact. Hughes founded the company, and it was his duty to nurture a framework upon which the fledgling organization might thrive. That he is not thought to have accomplished this is related by the anecdotes. Although Hyland was not the progenitor, he has come to symbolize the coveted father figure of the company. Employees fondly refer to him as "Mr. Hughes Aircraft." One individual spoke of him as "the kindly old man steering the ship."

CONCLUSIONS

Greater understanding of and appreciation for the kinds of meaning that people seek to derive from their participation in organizations and whether or not these expectations have been fulfilled may be drawn from the stories they tell. Particularly revealing are tales that communicate a mythologized sense of history. The emphasis in these accounts is not simply on the accuracy of chronology of facts: "the ordering principle is . . . the emotional associations that people have with the events and the persons being described" (Allen and Montell, 1981: 29-30). Individual stories dramatize, through a process of selectivity, the memorable traits of protagonists. Historical "commentary" is also achieved through the narrative device of "point of view." The third-person point of view is adopted to express feelings of unresolved conflict originating in interactions with Hughes, whereas the first person appears to signal certainty and belief stemming from dealings with Hyland.

Overall what emerges is a relevant and deeply felt "human history"—a shared portrayal of a company's culture as it has been understood and *evaluated* by employees over an extended period of time. Within this corporate mythology is an ethical system that lays stress on the quality of human interaction between "the boss" and employees. Working relationships that are built on trust and lead to a sense of belonging (e.g., those encouraged by Hyland) are valued; those that diminish the human spirit are not (e.g., those engendered by Hughes).

Because Howard Hughes was unable to establish a meaningful relationship with people in his employ, they ignore in stories any positive human value his contributions might have made to the ethos of the enterprise. By contrast, Pat Hyland's apparently benevolent influence is celebrated with nostalgia. The dualities that these two figures represent have yet to be resolved. The polarization of issues (technical wizardry and innovation, on the one hand, and concern over human values on the other) continues to haunt the halls of Hughes Aircraft in the minds of today's workers. It is a duality that undoubtedly exists in other organizations as well, and in their mythology.

21

CORPORATE RHETORIC VERSUS SOCIAL ACTION

Identifying Contradictions in a Service Organization

Brian Rusted

University of Calgary

Cocktail parties, awards banquets, sales meetings, conventions, and trade shows are ubiquitous features of contemporary corporate life. Their symbolic value in the calendrical activities of corporations has frequently been commented upon but not so frequently investigated. Intuition might suggest that such ceremonies are exemplary occasions for the display of a corporation's cultural values. From the following examples it might also be assumed that the diversity of entertainers used might indicate a relationship between entertainment, taste, and different organization types.

The president of the United Consumers Club, a franchise, pyramid-style sales organization based in Indiana, underwrites a gathering of all franchisees every May. For the last ten years, between $5,000 and $10,000 has been budgeted for dinner and dancing entertainment on the first night of the session. In 1984, over $50,000 was spent to buy an evening's entertainment with the 1960s pop group "The Fifth Dimension."

In April 1985, the corporate officers of Motorola, Inc. were entertained by Johnny Cash and June Carter. They agreed to perform in exchange for a half-dozen cellular mobile phones.

The top management and district sales managers for Abbott Laboratories recently attended a barbecue in the desert outside a resort in Phoenix, Arizona. In the middle of the meal a band of outlaws rode up on horses, attacking the bartender. Just when it looked as if the evening's liquor supplies might be lost, strains of the William Tell overture were heard from a concealed public address system as Clayton Moore, the original

Lone Ranger, rode up on his white stallion, Silver, and chased the outlaws away.

To bring home a point for a produce manager in one of his Washington-based supermarkets, Giant president Izzy Cohen hired a band to play "Yes we have no bananas." Understocked bins do not receive commendation in his operations.

Corporate executives of farm equipment manufacturer J. I. Case host an annual trade show for distributors and the best customers. For more than a quarter of a million dollars, Bob Hope and the Osmonds were hired in the spring of 1984 to do five shows during the three-week duration of this event.

Every fall at the American Trucking Association convention, the officers of Cummins Engines offer an evening buffet gala for approximately two hours. In 1984, they spent close to $60,000 to decorate a ballroom with white velvet, white trees, and four white grand pianos.

Business organizations spend about $2 billion a year on ceremonies and events such as these. The figure would be much higher if trade associations and public sector service organizations were included (Shure, 1983). Entertainment is a major component of most ceremonies, and the processes underlying entertainment choice are occasions for enacting and communicating values that might distinguish organizational cultures. The research discussed here looks at this aspect of entertainment taste. Does taste reflect cultural differences among the organizations purchasing entertainment?

The scope of this question requires comparative data from a large sample of corporations. In order to keep the research feasible without sacrificing the diversity of the sample, my solution was to investigate the question in a company specializing in the production of ceremonies and entertainment for large corporations. Within this situation it was possible to gather information on the frequency and variety of entertainment events across the spectrum of their clients.

The producers' rhetorical strategies initially supported the research question: They described their job as catering to the particular values and choices of their corporate clients. However, the culmination of fieldwork within this firm suggested an answer to an entirely different question. The producers themselves were constraining entertainment taste, and their choices were a form of social action. Why this was so and what implications this held for their business will be considered after a brief discussion of methods.

METHODS

The data for this article were drawn from a year's fieldwork with a Chicago-based firm in the business of producing entertainment events for corporate clients. The structure of this business confounds a common sense view of the popular entertainment marketplace (Hirsch, 1969; Peterson and Berger, 1975; DiMaggio and Hirsch, 1976; Frith, 1981). In this business, communication is not a linear process from performer to audience because the intentions and meanings generated by the performers have been superseded by those purchasing and using their services. Rather than the entertainers seeking and establishing an audience, the corporate client looks for entertainers to match the ready-made audiences of employees, corporate officers or distributors. Eschewing a linear view of the communications process forces analytic emphasis on a much more interesting problem: accounting for entertainment taste, not in structural features of entertainers' skills or repertoire, but by locating taste within social contexts of enacted values.

After some pilot studies, it was clear that the most feasible site for this research was the midground between the corporations buying the entertainment and the entertainers themselves. Most research on the interface of corporations and entertainment/art worlds usually stresses the creative side because of accessibility or compatibility (Powdermaker, 1950; Gitlin, 1983). The midground is occupied by a specialized brand of middleman, the "producer," or what was at one time called a theatrical agent. It is his or her job to match the two ends of this marketplace.

The long-term nature of this research dictated the use of participant observation and ethnoscience ethnography (Werner and Fenton, 1973) for data collection. In exchange for learning about the business, I worked at everything from office duties and onsite production to research on meeting agenda. I kept a daily record (in a journal format) of conversations, stories, social activities, and informal responses to my questions. I sought to unpack the company's historical development and social factions within and without, as well as to describe tastemaking performed in the conduct of business. This nonstrategic or informal data was augmented by more strategic forms of communication: sales presentations to clients, training sessions for new producers, and the written documentation used to back up contracted work for particular clients. Analysis involved coding material from interview transcripts, journal notes, and so forth for recurrent terms, key concepts, relationships, and aesthetic criteria. Finally, statistical tests were employed on a sample of contract and account data from a 15-year period. This enabled me to extend the qualitative insights.

My observation and interviewing reached beyond the company, of course, and included entertainers, suppliers, and corporate clients. Survey methods and questionnaires were not used, primarily because collecting data in this manner would have altered the research roles and rapport I had established inside and outside the firm. More important, the goal of obtaining a native's perspective of this business meant that by the time enough knowledge was amassed to ask the right questions, the material would already contain the answers.

The goal of my research was to explore tastemaking as a form of cultural behavior in an organizational context. It was an attempt to move from the description of organizational ceremonies to the cultural constraints on the aesthetic choices shaping these occasions.

THE PRODUCTION COMPANY AND CORPORATE ENTERTAINMENT

Entertainment producers describe themselves as middlemen because their business takes place in a network composed of suppliers and clients. The production business has developed through the formation of particular social linkages and status discriminations that maintain viable markets and a distinct identity. All three groups—producers, suppliers, and clients (see Figure 21.1)—participate in this network of social relations. When suppliers were interviewed they were quick to point out that they had no direct involvement in corporate entertainment or the production firm in question. When corporate clients were interviewed, they were equally quick to indicate that the entertainment producers were simply one group among many other suppliers.

The production firm where I conducted my research is three generations old; it was founded in 1899 by the current president's grandfather. He was an orchestra leader and contracted his orchestra for weddings, community picnics, and the like. The contemporary character of the company can be identified with the innovations of the founder's son, a drummer and big-band leader during the transition in American entertainment from vaudeville to radio. In those days, an entrepreneurial band leader moved from playing vaudeville to dates on country-club circuits. Markets grew by tapping the networks of business executives who belonged to the country club. Eventually, the bands

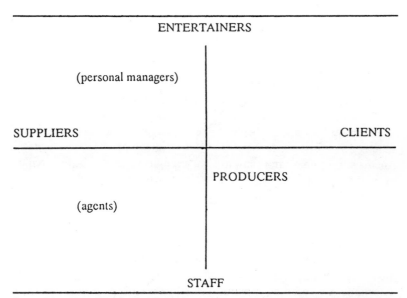

Figure 21.1   Key Groups in the Corporate Entertainment Business. The horizontal axis reflects distinctions among groups according to their relations as suppliers or clients to the central group, producers. The vertical axis illustrates how groups are ranked according to status distinctions. It also reflects the groups internal (staff) and external (agents) to the production firm.

began to provide background music at awards banquets and receptions for corporate personnel. When asked to add a singer or comedian to the bill, the band leader became an agent and booked the acts. As the business grew, more shows were booked than the leader might perform.

In discussions about this period, a concept of "loyalty" turned up frequently to explain relationships that made the business work. Entertainers who did a show for a producer's client could easily give out a business card, selling themselves cheaper yet making more money without the middleman. A stable of loyal entertainers became the real capital of the business. Those who could be trusted continued to be sent on jobs; those who could not were dressed down and not used again. According to the oldest producer of the production firm I researched—a woman in her 70's—agents went to great lengths to ensure this loyalty from their entertainers. One, she said,

> had a way of telling somebody that they had a date on January 27th at 8 o'clock. He did not tell them [the entertainer] where it was, who it was for. He never had a stenographer, he was scared to death of anybody taking his accounts. When it came time to take that person on January 27th, he

took them in his car to the job, and I don't think to this day they know who
they played for.

As members of this firm began to see the organization as a service
business, this network of loyalties shifted away from entertainers to the
clients themselves; if the producer could earn the loyalty of a client, then
the feudal control of entertainers was no longer crucial.

The term "producer" began to replace "agent." Today, producers
vehemently distinguish themselves from talent or theatrical agents.
Agents are suppliers and some are low enough in status to be referred to
as "worms" around the office. According to a producer now responsible
for training new producers, where an "agent's job ends, ours begins."
The distinction is drilled into the prospective producers: "We're not
agents," he remonstrates. "Don't ever call yourself an agent, don't be
known as an agent, you don't want to be known as an agent!"

To strengthen allegiance with the corporate client, the producers
must eschew any suggestion that they are representing particular
entertainers. According to the professed values of the producers, their
only intent is to cater to the individual client's taste. The goal is to
maintain a long-term loyalty with the client: such "loyalties are the
essence of our business."

This shift in external loyalties was paralleled by changes within the
production company I studied. The firm runs on a commission basis.
The producers, hired on a "draw" salary, expect to develop their own
client list and turn over about 40% of their profit to "the company." In
its early years, the company consisted of two or three producers, an
accountant, a receptionist, and a secretary. Since the son's takeover of
the firm in 1980, personnel has increased to 10 producers on commission
and 18 full-time salaried staff. With the elaboration and development of
a producer ethos, there has been a concomitant development of
subgroups within the company. There is a clear division between the
staff personnel on salary and the producers on commission. When I
observed them, staff met frequently outside the office over lunch,
dinner, or drinks or at parties to gossip and gripe. Much of the talk on
these occasions centered on unresolved communication problems
between the staff and the producers or criticism about the overall
management of the company. The office staff frequently had strong
social connections with local company suppliers and did not work as
earnestly as the producers to separate themselves from agents. For the
producers, if a set of clients was neither a recent account nor simply a
"yellow pages call," they were long time "friends" of the company. For
the staff these same friends were often referred to as "mutts" whose
needs they had to attend constantly.

My research within this production company led me to recognize the social actions that distinguished producers from clients and suppliers. The unique qualities of their relations and attitudes were more strongly evident when compared to those shared among the members of the production company's staff. By considering the aesthetic criteria used and shared among the producers, I began to see two distinct factions within the producers' group itself. From their strategies for enacting entertainment choice, I began to see an element of paradox in the rhetoric of their business.

THE PARADOX OF ENTERTAINMENT CHOICE

Although my research objective was to explore cultural differences in the entertainment tastes of this company's clients, the necessity of long-term participant research precluded getting "inside" the client organizations. The collection of longitudinal data—contracts and accounts—helped remedy this deficiency by indicating which clients had purchased which entertainers. It was also possible to look at pattern in the ceremonial occasions of different clients and, more importantly, to gauge the rate of innovation and variation in the types of entertainers used (that is, variation in type—when did chimpanzee acts begin to disappear? and differences in name—when was the Norm Krone Orchestra superseded by Dick Judson's Orchestra?).

The producers' rhetoric was that they "custom tailored" entertainment for their clients. Such an approach to business goes hand in glove with the realignment of loyalties and lends credence to the notion that entertainment taste will be related to cultural differences in the clients. It was a surprise, then, in correlating data on clients and their entertainment choices to find *no significant pattern* of similarity or dissimilarity *that might have reflected cultural distinctions.*

Within the raw frequency data, it was clear that recently deregulated industries or corporations increased their use of entertainment (during the span of my data, examples included banks, pharmaceutical companies, for-profit hospitals, and the recent AT&T offspring). Trade associations had more receptions (nonname entertainment) than concerts, and corporations in the business of matching suppliers and distributors tended to have a larger percentage of theme parties for informal socializing instead of dinner-dance combinations. There were no more specific correlations than these, however.

Producers had cultivated small, dependable networks of entertainers who were used again and again for similar jobs. *The custom tailoring of client to entertainer was a cultural fiction*, albeit one believed implicitly. The appropriateness of an entertainer for a given job was not an indicator of a client's culturally distinct tastes. In sum, longitudinal data indicated the social formation of taste within the production company.

This finding was confirmed by the frequency with which particular producers used particular entertainers. It was only necessary to determine whether the producer had entered the company before or after the change in presidency that occurred in 1980. The long-term producers used different entertainers than, or judged the skills of entertainers differently from, the other, younger producers. In fact, the subcultural tastes of either the younger faction of producers or those who had been with the firm prior to 1980 determined both the kind of entertainment provided and the type of client sought.

In this sense, the production company exemplifies the "garbage can" model of organizational decision making (Cohen et al., 1972). The firm "is a collection of choices looking for problems." Rather than maintaining a degree of flexibility in their tastemaking skills and responding to various differences in taste among their clients, the producers' tastes led them to seek compatible clients. Entertainment choice was constrained by the producers' standards alone. The actions of tastemaking were one further component the producers used to establish their identity and gain status among suppliers, competitors, and staff.

There is a coda to this work. Culture is not a thing or an artifact, but more like one of the traditional parts of rhetoric, *inventio*. The ethnographic depiction of a culture is an invention, a form of communication making an argument about culture plausible to both the researcher and the informant. When the culture is rooted in a particular company and the image portrayed derived from gossip, narrative, and observation, the result is potentially explosive for organizational members lacking the protection of power. In keeping with the rigors of data collection, the representations sketched here were returned to the company from the bottom up. The image was cleared and edited at each level on its way to the upper layers of management.

This project was not conducted with any diagnostic goals, and if its data had been collected with the avowed intention of changing the company, in all likelihood a very different image of it would have emerged. All the same, there were side effects from my work. The staff personnel generally admired my representation of the business and thought it valid. Producers were either indifferent or thought that the work might have some use in their own struggles for power inside and outside the company. Top management—the president and the vice-presidents—were shocked. The research findings contradicted their own ideals of what the company was about and what its goals and service objectives were. The fact that informal communication smudged their rhetorical image and internal harmony was unacceptable.

Rather than admit this image of the company, the president, in consultation with the vice presidents, did three things. They sought to formalize the communications channels within the company to reduce friction between staff and producers; they hired two new staff members to take on specific management duties; and they instituted routine company meetings in the hope of airing tensions before they became too submerged in the running of the business. Let me consider each briefly.

The company had been characterized by an ambiguity of roles and responsibilities among the staff members. This gave the company a high degree of flexibility in using internal resources on large-scale projects even though it meant a great deal of frustration for the staff members. In the attempt to combat internal communications problems, the president and producers devised an organizational chart to formalize links and channels of communication within the company and to specify the areas of responsibility for each staff member. Flexibility was sacrificed, and the previous integrity of the group was upset by the explicit emphasis on job classifications, titles, and hierarchy.

The communications problems and internal friction between producers and staff of the company resulted from the lack of a management tier within the company. The producers took care of themselves and appealed to the staff as best they could for their particular needs. The president and vice presidents all maintained their own accounts and were not reimbursed for taking on management duties. The hiring of two more staff members was an attempt to remedy this situation. One individual was hired to be in charge of personnel. In the limited amount of time I was able to witness this new role, its function seemed to be to deflect staff problems from the producers and vice presidents. An MBA was also hired to introduce a "management-by-objectives" strategy in the company; the business was expanding and staff were increasing in number, so someone had to take on the responsibility of guiding and directing the company. Ironically, both of these innovations were announced to the staff at the first in a series of meetings designed for staff and management to air grievances outside of normal roles.

The effects of this are fairly obvious: The producers and staff have been further polarized, and interaction across groups has diminished by the creation of a middle-management tier. Job descriptions, traditionally vague in order to maintain flexibility in handling a variety of tasks, have been formalized. The dissension among the staff cabals within the company is now more earnest, and turnover seems to be increasing.

CONCLUSION

There are several lessons to be gleaned from this research. It is apparent that the business of corporate entertainment is complex and embraces numerous groups and social networks, suppliers, clients, entertainers, and so on. The recent interest in using culture as a construct and research tool suggested that there might be a correlation between entertainment used in corporate ceremonies and the values of the corporations sponsoring the event. Yet in situations where subcontracted production companies are used, such a correlation was not apparent at this level of analysis. Rather than custom tailoring entertainment for clients, producers relied on their own aesthetic criteria based on socially derived networks of entertainers. Within the production company itself there were differing views on the nature and goals of the business. Among the producers themselves there were further subgroupings indicated by their entertainment choices.

In this case, the impact of my work did not alter the rhetorical image of the company. Management took steps to bring the wayward actions of staff more into line with how they felt the company should look. If there had been an opportunity to resubmit this research to the company, a preferable impact might have been achieved had the portrait of the internal working been presented as an unobserved strength rather than a suppressed paradox. Unless the researcher is prepared to stand by the data and suggest strategic alternatives and solutions to those who have power and those who lack it, the data may be suppressed or otherwise not used to resolve problems which the research has uncovered and clarified. As it stands, my version of the story is completed, but for those who told it to me, new versions continue.

22

THE "COMMAND BUNKER" IN A MILITARY HOSPITAL

Changing Power Perceptions Through a Modified Fishbowl Technique

Terance J. Wolfe

University of California, Los Angeles

The setting is an American military hospital in West Germany. At the last minute, the person scheduled to give a series of workshops to a midlevel group of doctors, nurses, and professional administrators had to cancel. The training officer called me to take over the series, aware that I had had the appropriate experience.

The first workshop was on participative decision making. I was struck by the irony, for participants had been ordered to be there. The second workshop, occurring about two months later, was again a two-day event oriented to midlevel managers across the three professional disciplines. The topic was team building and confronting conflict. It became painfully obvious that for all the talk of cooperation, there was conflict between or among the three groups. For example, nurses felt they were undervalued by doctors; in the team-building workshop, they were making a bid for more autonomy and more recognition of their professional competence. There was also conflict between doctors and administrators regarding whose priorities should influence hospital decisions.

A third workshop had been projected that would concern participative management. The three together were conceived to be an evolving structure of training that would help develop an effective, organization-wide communication and problem-solving structure. The third workshop was never held (at least not as it was originally designed).

What people needed was not training per se, but rather an opportunity to sit down and talk with each other about shared organizational problems and the fact that they brought different perspectives to the same issues. In the closing minutes of the second workshop I expressed my misgivings about holding another workshop, suggesting instead that someone else be sought for a consulting relationship—to work with top management and move through the hierarchy to help resolve the intergroup conflicts among the three professional units. At that moment, the commanding officer and his three immediate executive officers entered the room. Although I was not proposing to continue as a consultant, I was in fact asked to serve in that capacity.

In this article I summarize my discoveries about communication (or the lack of it) in the military hospital in West Germany, and describe an intervention technique that I employed to enable others to understand and get at the root of the problem. Looming large in all this is "the command bunker." What or who the term refers to will be considered after a brief review of some basic concepts.

THEORY AND CONCEPTS

Differentiation: Differentiation is a function of environmental uncertainty (Lawrence and Lorsch, 1967), the intent of which is to achieve a degree of efficiency and effectiveness through task or product specialization, chain of command, and an understanding of client and situational needs (Kast and Rosenzweig, 1970; Thompson, 1967). Because different departments and levels evolve to meet varying circumstances, they develop their own strategies, methods, and styles for interaction and task accomplishment. In essence, subcultures emerge within a larger organizational context.

Integration: To be successful, organizations must also be integrated as cohesive units. As an organization becomes increasingly differentiated, it is increasingly necessary for its integrative processes to be managed.

Boundary management: The processes of differentiation and integration are linked to the concept of boundary management. There must be control over the information and resources that flow into and out of groups, departments, and the organization itself. In this respect, organizations are "transaction systems." Transaction effectiveness will be influenced by the degree of boundary permeability, that is, "boundedness," of the organization.

Permeability: The ease with which information and resources can cross over and penetrate the boundary of the system is referred to as "permeability" (Oshry, 1976a; Rice, 1969). When information or resources flow freely across a boundary with little (if any) restraint, then the boundary can be regarded as highly permeable. Conversely, a boundary that imposes strict restraints on the passage of information and resources can be viewed as rigid. Permeability, then, can be measured by degrees, and this has implications for a system's integrity and ultimate survival. An "underbounded" system is one in which the boundary is highly permeable, while an "overbounded" system is very impermeable or rigid (Alderfer, 1980; Brown, 1980; Oshry, 1978).

The more differentiated an organization becomes, the more difficult it is to manage and control its internal and external boundaries. Hence there is a tendency for the organization's integrative processes to break down, for departments to create their own independent style and methods for goal accomplishment, for intraorganizational communication to become increasingly difficult, and for various subunits to become polarized in their attitudes and perspectives toward one another. As might be expected, the organizational consequences of such events are frequently a decline in cooperative working relationships, productivity, and morale. This is exactly what was happening in the Army hospital.

Meaning system: As people interact in organizational settings, they interpret the actions of others (Berger and Luckmann, 1966; Blumer, 1969). Attributions about actions are used to construct models—"realities"—of the situation (von Glasersfeld, 1984) that individuals use to promote their own welfare and advance personal interests (Culbert and McDonough, 1980, 1985; Goffman, 1959).

Each person is simultaneously a member of multiple interacting groups (Alderfer, 1977; Alderfer and Smith, 1982; Rice, 1969; Smith, 1977, 1982). Some are formal—supervisors, peers, subordinates, committees, task forces—and others are informal—church, civil, social. Each group places competing demands on one's skills, abilities, knowledge, emotions, and time. Dilemmas are created for organizational participants—those of group loyalty and identity. The making of either uncertain or overcommitments contributes to the fractionalization of an organization.

An individual or group's view of the organizational world, therefore, is to a large extent a function of position in the hierarchy: vertically, laterally, and diagonally. Each position in the organizational structure exists at a unique cross-section of individual, group, and organizational perspectives. Each perspective competes with others for attention and legitimacy, and also shapes individual and group perceptions and experiences of organizational events—an important point in view of the kinds of cultures that may develop, and that were in fact generated in the hospital setting. It is also significant in regard to how one perceives one's power.

Power: Irrespective of the existence of a rational organizing principle by which power is distributed within an organization, members of various groups or departments may perceive themselves as having less power than their position or organizational function warrants. A result is the "power paradox" (Lorenz, 1952). Members of one group see themselves as powerless relative to another, or to several others, who are viewed as powerful; members of the other group(s) see themselves as powerless relative to the reciprocal group(s) (Oshry, 1976b; Smith, 1975). The consequence is that of undermining one's own, one's group's, and the organization's effectiveness.

Change: In a situation like that described above concerning the paradox of power, there may be internal pressure to change an organization's functioning. Change has been conceptualized as a three-stage process (Lewin, 1947). "Unfreezing" refers to the breaking down of existing values, attitudes, and behaviors considered dysfunctional to an individual and to the organization's effectiveness and success. "Change" is the process by which new patterns are developed. "Refreezing" serves to reinforce these new patterns, increasing the probability that they will be internalized and sustained. By definition, change means a realignment of values. A central concept is that of boundary. The permeability of boundaries is instrumental to the efficacy of change efforts (which is why the fishbowl technique is often employed as an intervention strategy, as discussed later).

THE NEED FOR INTERVENTION

The Army hospital could be characterized as a differentiated professional service organization that failed to develop effective means of integration. Individual units or functions staked out their territory, increasing the difficulty of effective intergroup communication. Breakdowns in communication produced a paradoxical sense of powerlessness in which each group saw itself as the handmaiden of other, more powerful, groups. As a result, organizational participants from a cross-section of functional areas abdicated their personal and collective power. Through a set of unmanaged but implicit interactions, they imputed to the executive group a life and identity that was different from the nominal purpose of the group. This identity became more alive and real with each additional action taken that could somehow be construed as self-interested rather than in the best interests of the organization. How and why this was the case is explained below.

Communication Breakdowns

The senior hospital administrator—the Executive Officer (XO)— expressed concern about the behavior and deportment of those attending weekly Friday morning staff meetings. In particular he noticed that the department heads did not take notes. They doodled, talked with their neighbors, daydreamed, and otherwise failed to pay attention. The XO and other members of the command group meeting with these individuals felt that necessary and important information was not being disseminated by attendees to other members of their departments.

Hospital activities and events were announced and described at these meetings. Frequently these were the infamous military "work parties," but training classes, project reports, activity summaries, special events, and social activities were also discussed. In fact, the weekly Friday meeting was the primary vehicle for keeping the entire hospital aware and abreast of what was going on in the organization and the community. This was of particular concern to the command group, because scheduled work projects such as "police duty" and ice and snow safety details consistently yielded either "no-shows" or the same small group of "volunteers," who eventually felt they were being taken advantage of.

On one occasion as consultant, I had an opportunity to observe a long-scheduled and well-planned MASCAL (mass casualty) exercise, in which the hospital examined its responsiveness to an influx of casualties under simulated wartime conditions. In the "first wave" of the exercise, twenty-four "casualties" arrived at once, thereby testing the hospital's efficiency in initial screening and assessment and its ability to transport victims rapidly to various hospital activity centers, for example, emergency, X-ray, plasma. Enlisted personnel were needed as stretcher bearers. Two finally showed up after the exercise's scheduled beginning, having put the hospital's chief personnel officer through 25 minutes of hand-wringing anxiety. On their arrival, one inquired whether or not they were in the emergency room—the other had a broken arm! In short, it seemed the hospital was suffering from a genuine breakdown in communication.

Isolation

It also became clear that the hospital was composed of multiple cultures and professional identities. There were the doctors with their own pattern of intra- and extra-group relationships. They were defined by everyone within the organization, including themselves, as "prima donnas." They violated the dress code, wore their hair longer than regulation, and wore hospital "scrubs" in public places; they felt they were accountable to no one other than their profession. There were also the nurses, who viewed themselves as highly trained and qualified medical professionals, and who were constantly seeking to get the rest of the organization to agree. Finally, the administrators saw themselves as professionals, but couldn't for the life of them figure out how to get the command group to accept and utilize them as professional managerial resources.

There were also various intergroup combinations that produced their own cultural interfaces—for example, the doctor-nurse subculture and the doctor-enlisted subculture. The doctors sought to dominate the nurses and to maintain professional control over their work behavior, and the enlisted personnel sought to identify themselves with the doctors such that they would also wear "scrubs" in unauthorized (i.e., public) places, wear their hair longer, and appear for work unshaven. All of this took place within the context of a larger cultural milieu, that which the base commander sought to define as a "military hospital" (a concept that some saw as a contradiction in terms).

The "Command Bunker"

There is one additional group and subcultural identity that is of primary interest here—that of the command group: the base commander, chief of professional services (CPS), executive officer (XO), and chief nurse. This was the top management group of the organization. This group made decisions, requested and took action, and dramatically influenced the rest of the organization. They were a tight-knit group: if you saw one of them, you saw them all. They were, in fact, disparagingly referred to by most of the midmanagement group—be they doctors, nurses, or administrators—as the "command bunker."

The term "command bunker" was loaded with imagery. The connotations were authoritarian and directive. Organizational members perceived the people in the command bunker as insulated, sheltered, protected, and detached from the reality of the rest of the organization. In fact, those who held membership in the command bunker did not even know that they had been so grouped by their immediate subordinates, and were quite surprised when it was revealed to them. It took me a long time to catch on to the actual referent for the command bunker. Upon first hearing the expression, I was confused, and found myself wondering if it was the headquarters building, or perhaps a fortification in the basement. I imagined an actual physical structure—a bunker—camouflaged and nestled in the hillside in the distance. I even knew in which direction I thought it was. I was intrigued and wanted to search for it, yet was afraid of being stopped in an unauthorized area. The officers who referred to the bunker treated it as such a self-evident term that I found myself too embarassed to ask, "Where is it?"

As it turns out, there was no real bunker, no camouflage, nothing nestled in the distance—not even an unauthorized area. The headquarters building sat on a hillside—very exposed, very accessible. The reference was entirely symbolic. The professional staff—in particular the midlevel administrators—felt cut off, removed, and unused as information and decision-making resources. While they saw themselves as staff experts, they did not feel that the organization was effectively utilizing their professional expertise. They felt the command group was making organizational decisions on limited information. They were worried because they thought their own contributions were meaningless but that they would simultaneously be held accountable for providing justifications necessary for supporting command decisions. In short, they felt powerless. This, then, was the context within which the intervention occurred.

INTERVENTION

The intervention took place on the second day of a two-day workshop for upper- and top-level management. Participants included the "command bunker" and about 25 of those who direct reported to them. The theme of the workshop was power and organizational effectiveness.

The Paradox of Power

On the first day of the workshop the paradox of power, among other issues, was explored. To a person, the participants discovered that they saw their own subgroups—that is, doctors, nurses, administrators—as uniquely powerless relative to the other groups.

This perception was dramatized in the following way. I proposed three different power hierarchies, as represented in Figure 22.1, and asked participants to indicate which of them most accurately described the hospital's situation. That is, they were asked to choose which group had the greatest amount of influence in organizational decisions relative to the other groups (note that not all possible combinations are represented, insofar as no one really believed the nurses had significant influence).

The votes were unanimous. Administrators selected hierarchy I, doctors selected II, and nurses selected III. Regardless of the actual distribution of power and influence within the organization, members of each group saw themselves as powerless relative to the other groups. This awareness was itself important as a force for change within the organization; at the same time it set the stage for the second day of the workshop.

The workshop was the first in which the members of the "command bunker" had ever participated. Through their involvement in the workshop, it was clear they played a significant role in the life of the organization. On the first day the base commander and chief nurse were present throughout. While their participation styles were markedly different—the base commander was aloof but aware, the chief nurse was involved and engaged—it was clear that they exerted a positive influence on the day's activities and events.

By contrast, the CPS and XO repeatedly found pretexts for leaving the workshop situation. This exerted a negative influence on the doctors and administrators, respectively. The doctors felt abandoned and unrepresented—a sentiment that would emerge more strongly during the second day. For the administrators it confirmed what they already knew: The XO was unwilling to work with them as a professional group.

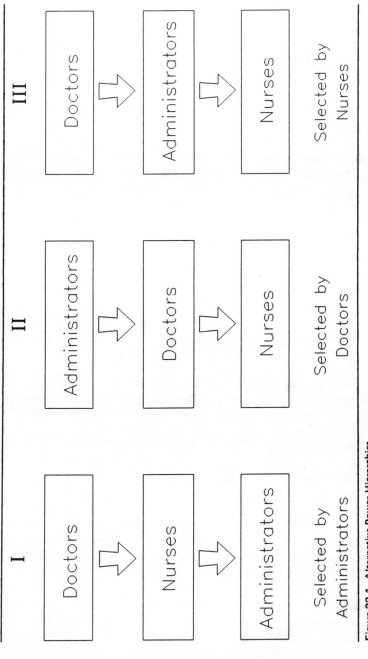

Figure 22.1 Alternative Power Hierarchies

I	II	III
Doctors	Administrators	Doctors
Nurses	Doctors	Administrators
Administrators	Nurses	Nurses
Selected by Administrators	Selected by Doctors	Selected by Nurses

Because of the obvious impact of the "command bunker" on the morale and attitudes of the professional staff, it became clear that this group had to be explicitly recognized in the life of the organization. This, then, was the agenda for day two.

The second day began with a brief review and discussion of the previous day: in particular, the paradox of power. A number of participants, the chief nurse among them, expressed genuine concern about the implications of the paradox for the organization's effectiveness. This led to a discussion of what could be done about it. I suggested that solution finding would be premature at this point and recommended that the workshop participants undertake a collective exploration of the "real" source of power within the organization—one that was largely overlooked in the previous day's analysis—that is, the "command bunker." I urged them to realize the role of this group in the functioning of the organization. I proposed that this group be explicitly constituted for the day's session and that the group, as an entity, be recognized and dealt with by the others.

The Fishbowl Technique

To achieve the objectives mentioned above, I constructed a modified fishbowl situation. The"fishbowl" is an organization development (OD) intervention (French and Bell, 1973; Fordyce and Weil, 1971) designed to give participants feedback on their individual styles of interpersonal communication, and group styles for problem-solving interaction. It is used to heighten people's awareness of their contributions to group decision making, and the impact of their style on others.

The fishbowl usually involves two groups arranged in concentric circles: an inner discussion and problem-solving group, and an outer observer/feedback group. The inner group is presented with a task and encouraged to use group interactions as the basis for discovering solutions. Each member of the outer group is assigned to observe a participant in the inner group and to be prepared to give feedback on the individual's and the group's interaction and problem-solving styles. Members of the outer group are asked to remain silent until a feedback session is formally designated. In this way, the decision-making group is allowed to develop, while simultaneously a structure is created that facilitates its learning and furthers its potential effectiveness (Argyris and Schoen, 1978).

I modified the basic structure of the fishbowl in three ways. First, the "command bunker" was made explicit. This served to put physical as well as psychological boundaries around the composition of the group and, thereby, dramatized its existence and life in the organization's culture and meaning system. Hence, the "command bunker" became distinct from the rest of the organization, and the workshop was then comprised of four, not three, groups: doctors, nurses, administrators, and the "command bunker."

Second, each of the participating groups was asked, in turn, to place itself in the center, with the three remaining groups assuming positions in the outer, feedback, circle. The outside groups were asked to cluster so that all of the doctors would be together, all of the nurses, and all of the administrators. This, too, was done to dramatize the unique identity of each of these groups, to contribute to the collective sense of "speaking with one voice," and to force the recognition of intergroup boundaries.

Third, the group in the middle was not assigned an initial task, but rather was asked to remain silent. The outside groups were asked to share their perceptions of either individual members of the inside group or of the group as a whole. I hoped that such feedback would provide the basis for "unfreezing" existing patterns of behavior. The objective was to provide feedback to each of the groups and their members on how they were being perceived both by the larger organization and by its subgroups.

After the outer groups had shared their perceptions the inner group was allowed to respond. Members were asked to refrain from reacting to the specifics. Rather, they were encouraged to reflect on how it felt to be described, either individually or as a member of their group, in the way in which they had been. This allowed them to identify both the points of congruence as well as incongruence with their own personal and organizational self-concepts. Further, they were asked to talk about what was important for them in their roles and how they would like to be perceived by others. In this way, they were providing the basis for "change" and a new definition of the organizational situation. This procedure was repeated for each of the four groups, and produced several important outcomes.

DISCUSSION

The focus of this intervention was the role and impact of the "command bunker" on the functioning of the rest of the organization.

By making this group explicit in the life of the organization, several opportunities for change and action presented themselves.

Results

The chief of professional services (CPS) was able to talk about his experience of being caught between the administrative responsibilities of the "command bunker" and his desire to be recognized by his medical peers as the chief clinician. This dilemma was succinctly captured by the phrase "wriggling sister" used by one doctor to describe his perceptions of the CPS. As a result, the CPS announced that he would provide greater representation for the doctors' concerns as expressed and revealed in the paradox of power.

The chief nurse committed himself to be more available and responsive to the expressed needs of the nursing staff. The XO, for his part, said he would work to overcome his tendency to second-guess his professional staff, and that he would actively seek their advice and opinions. Finally, the base commander said that he would make immediate provision for a civilian employee and a non-commissioned officer (NCO) to help reduce the work burden on the clinical services division. This would free the CPS to attend to the needs and interests of the clinical staff.

Taken together, these provided a set of specific action steps that workshop participants felt would aid their effectiveness. In addition, they provided the basis of commitment and support necessary for "refreezing" new behaviors. But what about the organization overall?

The primary objective of the consulting relationship was to develop an effective, organization-wide communication and problem-solving structure. As time passed, members of the organization reported improved attitudes and more effective communication. Individuals were more satisfied with their work interactions. More information was getting to lower levels of the organization, as borne out by increased attendance at, and more participation in, "work- parties." Finally, the "command bunker" phrase was dropped from people's vocabulary. These changes persisted long after the actual intervention.

Managing Boundary Permeability

In the Army hospital, there were three differentiated professional service groups each of which provided an integral, but interdependent, function to the organization. In addition, however, there was a fourth group—one that was not formally recognized, but was visible, salient, and powerful—that had assumed characteristics and a life within the organization independent of the interests or desires of the individuals who comprised it. This group—the "command bunker"—was the focus of the intervention.

By design or by default, the boundary separating the "command bunker" from functional management groups had become rigid and impermeable. Management groups across all three functional areas felt cut off and unused. They denied their own power, attributed greater power to other groups with which they engaged in conflict, held the "command bunker" accountable for their failure to be included in organizational decisions, and avoided recognizing and confronting their collective abdication of responsibility for changing an uncomfortable situation. Meanwhile, they saw the "command bunker" as insulated, sheltered, and out of touch with the organization's reality. Hence, a meaning system was created that organizational participants used to devalue and disparage the organization's top management.

The intervention sought to make the "command bunker's" existence explicit by imposing a set of physical and psychological boundaries on its group membership and forcing its public recognition. This created another intergroup constellation and group-identity problem in that the CPS, XO, and chief nurse were also functional leaders of the doctors, administrators, and nurses, respectively. Hence each of them was caught between administrative responsibilities of the "command bunker" and responsibilities as department head. Once the group was recognized as a significant organizational force, a strategy for managing boundary permeability had to be effected. Each group was able to receive feedback on how it was perceived by others. People were able to make individual and collective contributions to changing the situation both by defining how they would like to be viewed and have their work contributions valued, and through specific action steps taken by top managers as a result of the intervention.

CONCLUSIONS

The field of organizational development has long attempted to work with organizational systems to aid in the improvement of their efficiency and success. The focus has been on issues of motivation, job satisfaction, work re-design, interpersonal communication, and group problem solving (Burke, 1982; Huse, 1975) with more recent work occurring at the level of organization structure and design (Galbraith, 1973), and inter- (Alderfer, 1980; Brown, 1980) and transorganizational development (Cummings, 1984; Cummings and Motamedi, 1982). What has been less clear, though perhaps implicit in the literature, is attention to issues of organizational culture (see Deal and Kennedy, 1982a; Peters and Waterman, 1982), and intraorganizational language and meaning systems.

The present analysis has taken an organization's language and meaning system as the starting point. It has been argued that structural requirements for differentiation result in different methods of task accomplishment as well as different forms of communication. These differences may produce intraorganizational tensions that ultimately become dysfunctional. Hence it may become necessary for consultants to intervene into the meaning system.

Intervening into an organization's language and meaning system can be risky and itself dysfunctional and, therefore, dictates caution. In the case of the "command bunker" it was done in a constructive and useful way. Hazards are embedded in the situation, however, especially if the consultant does not have a full appreciation of the referent and of the role of language and meaning within the organization.

Much is yet to be learned about language, meaning, communication, and culture by those who intervene into organizational systems. Practitioners of organization development often take an organization's culture as deficient and, therefore, something to be changed. Folklorists, by contrast, take culture as something to be understood and appreciated, and as an important source of organizational meaning and information. Representatives of the two fields can benefit from sharing their respective expertise. Organizational consultants can bring a perspective on organizations and the theory and practice of applied organizational change, while folklorists can bring the methods of cultural discovery and a framework for interpretation. The challenge for both is not to create a unified culture within an organization, but rather to aid in the management of cultural differences facilitating integration in differentiated systems through active management of organizational boundaries.

Epilogue

We shall not cease from exploration
And the end of all our exploring
Will be to arrive where we started
And know the place for the first time.

—T.S. Eliot, "Little Gidding"

The setting is the offices of the Management Development Department of a major corporation in Southern California. Located in a building in Marina Del Rey, this department is physically separated from corporate headquarters in Beverly Hills where the group vice-president's office is located. A move to the corporate building is imminent, for the department (whose members now number more than two dozen) has rapidly outgrown the available space. Desks for several individuals have been squeezed into the reception area. Staff must share offices even though they may be carrying out quite different functions. The noisy computing and photocopy rooms are uncomfortably close to people who are trying to concentrate on developing training programs. A number of rooms have been given over to multiple uses, adding to the confusion and noise.

The production room often serves as a hallway between the front and back offices. Recently a sign was posted on the production room door: DO NOT USE THIS ROOM AS A HALLWAY. Obviously it was to no avail, for a second sign soon joined the first: THIS IS NOT A BARN. PLEASE CLOSE THE DOOR! Later someone crossed out the word "not" (Montepio, 1984).

Author's Note: The quotation is from " Little Gidding," in *FOUR QUARTETS* by T. S. Eliot, copyright 1943 by T. S. Eliot; renewed 1971 by Esme Valerie Eliot. Reprinted by permission of Harcourt Brace Jovanovich, Inc.

Demanding that the production room not be used as a hallway flies in the face of the human propensity to economize motion. Because attempts to dictate behavior often fail, especially when edicts go against human nature or deprive individuals of their autonomy, other means of influencing behavior are required. The second sign recognizes that people will use the room as a passageway; it requests that in doing so an individual extend a common courtesy to others. Before stating the injunction PLEASE CLOSE THE DOOR! the sign reminds one of the situation using metaphor from a familiar expression. THIS IS NOT A BARN gives an explanation, therefore, of the reason for keeping the door closed; the incongruity of offices and a barn being associated provokes a ludicrous image likely to produce a knowing nod and perhaps the beginning of a smile. Crossing out the word "not" is a metastatement: the room (read departmental offices as a whole) is not a barn—but might as well be for all the noise and confusion. The final act in the sequence of three precipitates a fundamental response in human beings: laughter (even if it is "gallows humor"). When someone does not close the door, others joke and banter with the transgressor, which leads to appropriate action while also producing a degree of fellowship and community rather than conflict (Montepio, 1984).

Whenever people organize, or participate in organizations, they must confront a fundamental dilemma of self versus collectivity. Each person has her or his own needs, objectives, concerns, beliefs, and ways of doing things. Organizing, however, requires cooperation and coordination of effort toward some common purpose, which in turn usually entails sensitivity to the needs of others, the subordination of individual identity at times, and even self-sacrifice.

This giving up of something is accompanied by an expectation of receiving something: trust in one's abilities to carry out tasks leading to the achievement of the goals of the enterprise, assistance from and cooperation by others, and recognition and respect. Individuals have joined together to do something that no one alone can accomplish, or can do as well; but in the process, constraints are imposed with which each member must cope. That they must face the tension between individual demands and the need for cooperation from others is suggested, even symbolized, by the signs just mentioned.

The process of coping in organizations is an ongoing one in which the balance is always delicate. Sometimes we need symbolic reminders that individual and organization are interdependent, as suggested by the example of the signs with which we began this section. The final act of crossing out the word "not"—THIS IS NOT A BARN—and communicating in an amicable way the intended message about closing the door, seems to characterize the ambience and style of the Management Development Department as remarked upon by members themselves. The first sign was not removed, however; its irksome injunction DO NOT USE THIS ROOM AS A HALLWAY remained juxtaposed to the (altered) second one. Whatever the reason for not removing the first sign, the effect is to provide the history of the process by which the message evolved.

The two signs and one alteration together poignantly remind us that all people in an organization are in fact "organizational participants" —human beings engaged in a common enterprise. Whether consciously intended or not, the signs take the reader through the steps required to achieve this understanding and appreciation. In this regard, their influence far exceeds that of causing someone to close the door on noise.

Essays in the present volume consider the basic dilemma of organizational life—that of self opposed to the collective—and ways in which it is expressed and coped with, if not always resolved, through symbolic forms and communicative processes essential to being human. In doing so, the authors contribute to the current reassessment of concepts and assumptions regarding organizations and of how to study management and work life (see Morgan et al., 1983: 3; Smircich, 1983a: 340; Louis, 1983: 39-40). Together these articles on the expressive and aesthetic aspects of organizing offer a new framework for appreciating the human element in enterprise and a theoretical perspective for helping make sense of changing attitudes toward work and expectations of organizations.

Three issues prevail:

(1) understanding participants' struggle to reconcile two very different conceptions of organization—one as a formally structured entity tending toward the impersonal, and the other as the outcome of a spontaneous process that is personal and symbolic;

(2) appreciating individuals' search for meaningfulness, fellowship, and personal satisfaction through organizing and in organizations; and

(3) developing organizations that are successful in achieving goals while simultaneously attending to the social, expressive, and aesthetic expectations of their members.

Although focusing on the above concerns for purposes of establishing a foundation of research and application, the articles in this volume suggest that the ramifications of organizational folklore study are many and varied. Some are mentioned below.

- Because different forms of folklore communicate people's aspirations, characterize their perceptions and transmit their interpretations, these forms can be documented and analyzed as *sources of information*— whether the purpose is to assess the quality of work life, improve performance and job satisfaction, or increase organizational effectiveness.
- Owing to the fact that folklore teaches and reinforces norms, and that it functions to persuade and even unite people, it may be *consciously utilized* by participants to manage change and continuity in human relations and organization development.
- Given the fact that they are social and participatory, expressive forms like customs, celebrations, and spontaneous organizations may *serve as models* for improving communication and cooperation and for building teamwork.
- Since traditions convey meanings, recall past experiences, and act as symbols, attention to them in orientation and training, management development, and community relations is crucial. The presence of organization-wide customs, folkways, and festive events that have evolved over time (and been maintained and guided—not imposed) *helps define* the organization's *uniqueness and demonstrates* its *vitality* as a human community.
- Some of the research tools and techniques of *ethnography* can be *utilized by organization members* at work *to improve understanding and to direct change.* For example, become familiar with categories of symbols and symbolic interaction and communication, including varied ways to interpret examples of these. Note especially stories, metaphors and aphorisms, rituals and routines (regarding one's own behavior as well as that of others), particularly as these shift subtly in content and tone. Learn to distinguish between symbolic expression and projection. Note inconsistencies in behavior or disparities between what is said and done. When change is appropriate, signal the changes through symbolic forms that by their very nature are dramatic, expressive and participatory.

There are numerous implications in the study of organizational folklore for management, human resources development, and leadership. A few are as follows.

- *Values, ways of doing things, issues and concerns*: One is that of painting a portrait of an organization as experienced by corporate natives themselves but with new insights from outside the culture. This will give the human story, revealing and communicating the heritage and character of the organization including the values and philosophy that underlie the customs and traditions. The community portrait may coincide with what was claimed to exist. Or it may contradict what was assumed or believed to obtain. It can bring to light discrepancies between the ideal and the real in what is professed and practiced, uncover problems or suggest solutions to issues and concerns.

- *Quality, performance, and productivity*: Enhancement of self-esteem and feelings of self-worth lead to improvement in performance and quality of production; attitudes of paid compliance yield to those of voluntary commitment. Cultivating the conditions of craftsmanship, in which individuals have a degree of personal autonomy and receive recognition for their achievements, increases the rapproachment between personal aspirations and group objectives (and the likelihood that individuals' needs are attended to while organizational goals are met).

- *Motivation and rewards*: Research on folklore in organizations demonstrates that individuals who are motivated to accomplish objectives anticipate tangible compensation but also intangible feelings like meaningfulness, fellowship, and satisfaction in personal achievement. Therefore, formal programs of motivation and rewards in organizations would be well advised to incorporate lessons from the model of spontaneous organizing—with recognition bestowed in the form of praise, public acknowledgement, and celebration (not only as preplanned ceremonies and rituals but also in terms of daily and spontaneous accolades, tributes, and public mentions).

- *Orientation, Training, and Development*: No matter what its nature or intended purpose is, an orientation or training program expresses a great deal to participants in regard to the values, assumptions, and beliefs of the organization. It behooves those who plan and implement such programs to ascertain the organization's traditions and to communicate them to others who both want and need to know the character of the organization—its goals, philosophy, and ways of doing things.

- *Leadership*: Virtually anything and everything that leaders say and do (or don't do) and how they speak and act is subject to inference and interpretation. Whether intended to be symbolic or not, appearance, demeanor, a turn of phrase, or other subtlety of behavior may be taken as a visible sign of a set of assumptions and values held by the individual (and even the organization). From the level of supervisors on up, those who lead need to know how their behavior is interpreted. In addition, they can generate narratives, rituals, and figurative language expressing their beliefs and concerns in order to reduce uncertainty and ambiguity (striving for consistency in the messages they transmit). Leaders, particularly, must be consciously aware of how traditions are formed, beliefs are formulated, values are transmitted, and feelings and concerns are expressed.

- *Decision making*: Regardless of the number of memos and reports in the "paperwork empire," most of the communication daily is oral (and nonverbal, as in demeanor, objects, etc.). Much of oral communication takes the form of stories, traditional wisdom and personal opinion, and metaphors and figurative language. Participatory, dramatic and symbolic, these forms crystalize attitudes, persuade, and influence actions for ill or for good. Before being acted upon, the basis of and ways in which crucial decisions were made need to be examined from an ethnological perspective with special attention to the process of belief formation and the impact of expressive forms.

- *Strategic planning, mergers and acquisitions, and organization change*: Affecting decisions and actions are not only expressive forms like stories and metaphors but also the customs and folkways of an organization (and even the traditions that are generated in the interactions of planners). An understanding of the character of the organization is essential, lest plans be inappropriate or opposed. Organizational expansion might be better guided, with less human misery and financial loss, through ethnography (documentation and analysis of customs and ethos of the organizations involved). The preservation and perpetuation of traditions may prove to be either preferable or crucial to change efforts.

We conclude this volume by referring to a statement that Chester I. Barnard made at the beginning of *The Functions of the Executive* (1938) in which he lamented being unable to "convey the *sense* of organization, the dramatic and aesthetic feeling. . . ." He contended that many lack an interest in the scientific study of organization "because they are oblivious to the arts of organizing, not perceiving the significant elements. They miss the structure of the symphony, the art of its composition, and the skill of its execution, because they cannot hear the tones" (Barnard, 1938: xiv).

Regardless of particular ramifications and implications, the overall import of organization ethnography is that it directs attention to the arts of organizing by focusing on the expressive and the aesthetic aspects of individuals' communication and interactions. Research of folklore in organizational settings reveals, perhaps uniquely, what makes us human.

References

Abrahams, Roger (1972) "Proverbs and proverbial expressions," pp. 118-127 in Richard M. Dorson (ed.) Folklore and Folklife: An Introduction. Chicago: University of Chicago Press.

Abrahams, Roger (1976) "The complex relations of simple forms," pp. 194-214 in Dan Ben Amos (ed.) Folklore Genres. Austin: University of Texas Press.

Abrahams, Roger and Richard Bauman (1978) "Ranges of festive behavior," pp. 193-203 in B. A. Babcock (ed.) The Reversible World: Symbolic Inversion in Art and Society. Ithaca, NY: Cornell University Press.

Ackerman, Robert (1973) "How companies respond to social demands." Harvard Business Review 51 (July/August): 88-98.

Agar, Michael H. (1980) The Professional Stranger: An Informal Introduction to Ethnography. New York: Academic Press.

Albig, William (1931) "Proverbs and social control." Sociology and Social Research 15: 527-535.

Alderfer, Clayton P. (1977) "Group and intergroup relations," pp. 227-297 in J. R. Hackman and L. Suttle (eds.) Improving Life at Work. Santa Monica, CA: Goodyear.

Alderfer, Clayton P. (1980) "Consulting to underbounded systems," pp. 267-295 in C. P. Alderfer and C. L. Cooper (eds.) Advances in Experiential Social Processes, Vol. 2. New York: John Wiley.

Alderfer, Clayton P. and Kenwyn K. Smith (1982) "Studying intergroup relations embedded in organizations." Administrative Science Quarterly 27: 35-65.

Allen, Barbara and Lynwood Montell (1981) "Characteristics and settings of orally communicated history," pp. 25-46 in From Memory to History. Nashville, TN: American Association for State and Local History.

Allen, James B. and John B. Harris (1981) "What are you doing looking up here? Grafitti Mormon style." Sunstone 6(2): 27-40.

Allen, Robert F. (1980) Beat the System: A Way to Create More Human Environments. New York: McGraw-Hill.

Argyris, Chris and Donald A. Schoen (1978) Organizational Learning: A Theory of Action Perspective. Reading, MA: Addison-Wesley.

Armstrong, Robert Plant (1981) The Powers of Presence: Consciousness, Myth, and the Affecting Presence. Philadelphia: University of Pennsylvania Press.

Aronowitz, Stanley (1973) False Promises. New York: McGraw-Hill.

Babcock-Abrahams, Barbara (1974) "A tolerated margin of mess: the trickster and his tales reconsidered." Journal of the Folklore Institute 11: 147-186.

Babcock-Abrahams, Barbara (1975) "Why frogs are good to think and dirt is good to reflect on." Soundings 58: 167-181.

Baker, Edwin L. (1980) "Managing organizational culture." Management Review 69 (July): 8-13.

Bales, Robert Freed (1950) Interaction Process Analysis. Chicago: University of Chicago Press.

Bales, Robert Freed (1970) Personality and Interpersonal Behavior. New York: Holt, Rinehart & Winston.

Bandler, Richard and John Grinder (1982) Reframing: Neuro-Linguistic Programming and the Transformation of Meaning. Moat, UT: Real People.

Bandura, Albert (1969) Principles of Behavior Modification. New York: Holt, Rinehart & Winston.

Barley, S. F. and M. R. Louis (1983) "Many in one: organizations as multi-cultural entities." Presented at the 43rd Annual Meeting of the Academy of Management, Dallas, Texas.

Barnard, Chester I. (1938) The Functions of the Executive. Cambridge: Harvard University Press.

Barnett, Lynn (1976) "Play and intrinsic rewards: a reply to Csikszentmihalyi." Journal of Humanistic Psychology 16: 83-87.

Barzun, Jacques and Henry E. Graff (1977) The Modern Researcher (3rd ed.) New York: Harcourt Brace Jovanovich.

Bauman, Richard (1977) Verbal Art as Performance. Prospect Heights, IL: Waveland.

Beattie, John (1964) Other Cultures. London: Routledge and Kegan Paul.

Becker, H. S., B. Geor, E. C. Hughes, and A. L. Strauss (1961) Boys in White: Student Culture in Medical School. Chicago: University of Chicago Press.

Bell, Michael J. (1976) "Tending bar at Brown's: occupational role as artistic performance." Western Folklore 35: 93-107.

Bell, Michael J. (1984) "Making art work." Western Folklore 43: 211-221.

Bennis, Warren and Burt Nanus (1985) Leaders. New York: Harper & Row.

Bensman, Joseph and Israel Gerver (1963) "Crime and punishment in the factory: the function of deviancy in maintaining the social system." American Sociological Review 28 (August): 588-598.

Berger, Peter L., Brigitte Berger, and Hansfried Kellner (1973) The Home Mind: Modernization and Consciousness. New York: Vintage.

Berger, Peter L. and Thomas Luckmann (1966) The Social Construction of Reality: A Treatise in the Sociology of Knowledge. New York: Doubleday.

Berlyne, Daniel E. (1969) "Laughter, humor, and play," pp. 795-852 in Gardner Lindzey and Elliott Aronson (eds.) Handbook of Social Psychology, Vol. 3. Reading, MA: Addison-Wesley.

Berreman, Gerald (1968) "Ethnography: method and product," pp. 336-373 in James Clifton (ed.) Introduction to Cultural Anthropology. Boston: Houghton Mifflin.

Beyer, Janice M. and Harrison M. Trice (1987) "How an organization's rites reveal its culture." Organizational Dynamics 15: 4-25.

Blum, Albert A. (1961) "Collective bargaining: ritual or reality?" Harvard Business Review 39: 63-70.

Blumenreich, Beth and Bari Lynn Polanski (1974) "Re-evaluating the concept of group: ICEN as an alternative," pp. 12-18 in Gerald Cashion (ed.) Conceptual Problems in Contemporary Folklore Study. Bibliographic and Special Series 12. Bloomington, IN: Folklore Forum.

Blumer, Herbert (1969) Symbolic Interactionism: Perspective and Method. Englewood Cliffs, NJ: Prentice-Hall.

Boas, Franz (1955) Primitive Art (1927). New York: Dover.

Boatright, Mody C. (1961) Folk Laughter on the American Frontier. New York: Collier.

Boje, David M., Donald B. Fedor, and Kendrith M. Rowland (1982) "Myth making: a qualitative step in OD interventions." Journal of Applied Behavioral Science 18: 17-28.

Boland, Richard and Raymond Hoffman (1983) "Humor in a machine shop: an interpretation of symbolic action," pp. 187-198 in Louis Pondy et al. (eds.) Organizational Symbolism. Greenwich, CT: JAI.

Bolman, Lee G. and Terrence E. Deal (1984) Modern Approaches to Understanding and Managing Organizations. San Francisco: Jossey-Bass.

Bourne, P.G. (1967) "Some observations on the psycho-social phenomena seen in basic training." Psychiatry 30: 187-196.

Bradney, Pamela (1957) "The joking relationship in industry." Human Relations 10: 179-187.

Bronner, Simon (1984) "Folklore in the bureaucracy," pp. 45-57 in Frederick Richmond and Kathy Nazar (eds.) Tools for Management: A Symposium from the Pennsylvania Evaluation Network. Harrisburg, PA: PEN.

Brown, L. Dave (1980) "Planned change in underorganized systems," pp. 181-203 in T. G. Cummings (ed.) Systems Theory for Organizational Development. New York: John Wiley.

Brunvand, Jan Harold (1978) The Study of American Folklore: An Introduction (1968). New York: Norton.

Bryant, Clifton D. (1974a) "The violations of social norms at work," pp. 17-26 in Clifton D. Bryant (ed.) Deviant Behavior: Occupational and Organizational Bases. Chicago: Rand McNally.

Bryant, Clifton D. (1974b) "Work and deviant behavior: a conceptual introduction," pp. 3-14 in Clifton D. Bryant (ed.) Deviant Behavior: Occupational and Organizational Bases. Chicago: Rand McNally.

Burke, W. W. (1980) "Organizational development and bureaucracy in the 1980's." Journal of Applied Behavioral Science 16: 423-437.

Burke, W. W. (1982) Organization Development: Principles and Practices. Boston: Little, Brown.

Burrell, F. and G. Morgan (1979) Sociological Paradigms and Organizational Analysis: Elements of the Sociology of Corporate Life. New Hampshire: Hemeinann Educational Books.

Campbell, Donald T. and Julian C. Stanley (1963) Experimental and Quasi-Experimental Designs for Research. Chicago: Rand McNally.

Cash, Johnny (1976) One Piece at a Time. W. Kemp. CBS.

Celebration: A World of Art and Ritual (1982). Washington, DC: Smithsonian Institution Press.

Centers, Richard and Daphne E. Bugental (1966) "Intrinsic and extrinsic job motivations among different segments of the working population." Journal of Applied Psychology 50: 193-197.

Clark, Burton C. (1970) The Distinctive College: Antioch, Reed and Swarthmore. Chicago: Aldine.

Clark, Burton C. (1972) "The organization saga in higher education." Administrative Science Quarterly 17: 178-184.

Clegg, S. 1975. The Theory of Power and Organization. London: Routledge & Kegan Paul.

Cohen, M. D., J. G. March, and J. P. Olsen (1972) "A garbage can model of organizational choice." Administrative Science Quarterly 17: 1-25.

Collins, Camilla (1978) "Twenty-four to the dozen: occupational folklore in a hosiery mill." Ph.D. dissertation, Folklore Institute, Indiana University.

Conrad, Charles (1983) "Organizational power: faces and symbolic forms," in Linda L. Pacanowsky and Michael E. Pacanowsky (eds.) Communications and Organizations: An Interpretive Approach. Beverly Hills, CA: Sage.

Cooke, Robert A. and Denise M. Rousseau (1983) "The organizational culture inventory: a quantitative assessment of culture." Northwestern University (unpublished).

Coser, R. (1960) "Laughter among colleagues: a study of the social functions of humor among the staff of a mental hospital." Psychiatry 23: 81-95.

Csikszentmihalyi, Mihalyi (1975) Beyond Boredom and Anxiety. San Francisco: Jossey-Bass.

Culbert, Samuel A. and John J. McDonough (1980) The Invisible War: Pursuing Self-Interest at Work. New York: John Wiley.

Culbert, Samuel A. and John J. McDonough (1985) Radical Management: Power Politics and the Pursuit of Trust. New York: Free Press.

Cummings, Thomas G. (1984) "Transorganizational development," pp. 367-422 in B. M. Staw and L. L. Cummings (eds.) Research in Organizational Behavior. Greenwich, CT: JAI.

Cummings, Thomas G. and Kurt Motamedi (1982) Transorganization Development. Los Angeles: Graduate School of Business Administration, University of Southern California (mimeo).

Daft, Richard L. (1980) "The evolution of organizational analysis in ASQ, 1959-1979." Administrative Science Quarterly 25: 632-636.

Dandridge, Thomas C. (1976) "Symbols at work: the types and functions of symbols in selected organizations." Ph.D. dissertation, Graduate School of Management, University of California, Los Angeles.

Dandridge, Thomas C. (1983) "Ceremony as an integration of work and play." Presented at the conference on Myths, Symbols, and Folklore: Expanding the Analysis of Organizations, Santa Monica, CA.

Dandridge, Thomas C., Ian Mitroff, and William F. Joyce (1980) "Organizational symbolism: a topic to expand organizational analysis." Academy of Management Review 5: 77-82.

Davis, Stanley M. (1983) "Corporate culture and human resource management: two keys to implementing strategy." Human Resource Planning 6: 159-167.

Davis, Stanley M. (1984) Managing Corporate Culture. Cambridge, MA: Ballinger.

Deal, Terrence E. and Allan A. Kennedy (1982a) Corporate Cultures: The Rites and Rituals of Corporate Life. Reading, MA: Addison-Wesley.

Deal, Terrence E. and Allan A. Kennedy (1982b) "Who has the power in the corporate clan?" SAVVY (June): 40-44.

Deal, Terrence E. and Allan A. Kennedy (1984a) "How to create an outstanding hospital culture." Hospital Forum (January/February): 21-34.

Deal, Terrence E. and Allan A. Kennedy (1984b) "Tales from the trails: a journey into the existential underbelly of American business." Hospital Forum (May/June): 16-26.

Degh, Linda and Andrew Vazsonyi (1974) "The memorate and proto-memorate." Journal of American Folklore 87: 220-239.

DiMaggio, Paul and Paul Hirsch (1976) "Production organizations in the arts." American Behavioral Scientist 19 (July/August): 735-752.

Ditton, Jason (1979) "Baking time." Sociological Review 27: 157-167.

Dorson, Richard M. (1972) "Introduction: concepts of folklore and folklife," pp. 1-51 in Richard M. Dorson (ed.) Folklore and Folklife: An Introduction. Chicago: University of Chicago Press.

Dorson, Richard M. (1981) Land of the Millrats. Cambridge, MA: Harvard University Press.

Dreyfuss, Joel (1983) "Handing down the old hands' wisdom." Fortune (June 13): 97-98, 100, 104.

Dubin, Robert (1982) "Management: meanings, methods, and moxie." Academy of Management Review 7: 372-379.

Dundes, Alan and Carl Pagter (1978) Urban Folklore from the Paperwork Empire (1975) (1st ed. Austin: Unviersity of Texas). Bloomington: Indiana University Press.

Durkheim, Emile (1964) The Elementary Forms of the Religious Life (1915). London: George Allen and Unwin.

Edelman, M. (1964) The Symbolic Uses of Politics. Urbana: University of Illinois Press.

Edelman, M. (1977) Political Language. New York: Academic Press.

Emerson, Robert M. (1981) "Observational field work." American Review of Sociology 7: 351-378.

Emery, F. E. and E. L. Trist (1965) "The causal texture of organizational environments." Human Relations 18: 21-31.

Evered, Roger and Meryl Reis Louis (1981) "Alternative perspectives in the organizational sciences: 'inquiry from the inside' and 'inquiry from the outside.'" Academy of Management Review 6: 385-396.

Fairfield, Roy P. [ed.] (1974) Humanizing the Workplace. Buffalo, NY: Prometheus.

Feldman, M. S. and J. G. March (1981) "Information in organizations as signal and symbol." Administrative Science Quarterly 26: 171-184.

Fine, Gary Alan (1979) "Small groups and culture creation: the idioculture of Little League baseball teams." American Sociological Review 44: 733-745.

Fine, Gary Alan (1984) "Negotiated orders and organizational cultures: qualitative approaches to organizations." Annual Review of Sociology 10: 239-262.

Fine, Gary Alan (1985) "Occupational aesthetics: how trade school students learn to cook." Urban Life 14: 3-31.

Fordyce, Jack K. and Raymond Weil (1971) Managing with People: A Manager's Handbook of Organization Development Methods. Reading, MA: Addison-Wesley.

French, Wendell L. and Cecil H. Bell, Jr. (1973) Organizational Development: Behavioral Science Interventions for Organizational Improvement. Englewood Cliffs, NJ: Prentice-Hall.

Frith, Simon (1981) Sound Effects: Youth, Leisure and the Politics of Rock 'n' Roll. New York: Pantheon.

Frost, Peter J. (1982) "Changing organizational culture: the view from below." Presented at the annual meeting of the Academy of Management, New York.

Frost, Peter J. and Linda Krefting (1983) "Multiple metaphors: breaking out of the psychic prisons of organizational life." Presented at the conference Myth, Symbols & Folklore: Expanding the Analysis of Organizations, Santa Monica, CA.

Frost, Peter J., Larry F. Moore, Meryl Reis Louis, Craig C. Lundberg, and Joanne Martin (1985) Organizational Culture. Beverly Hills: Sage.

Furling, W. B. (1976) "The fun in fun." Psychology Today (June): 35ff.

Galbraith, Jay (1973) Designing Complex Organizations. Reading, MA: Addison-Wesley.

Gamst, Frederick C. and Edward Norbeck [eds.] (1976) Ideas of Culture: Sources and Uses. New York: Holt, Rinehart & Winston.

Geertz, Clifford (1971) "Deep play: notes on the Balinese cockfight," pp. 1-37 in Clifford Geertz (ed.) Myth, Symbol, and Culture. New York: Norton.

Geertz, Clifford (1973) The Interpretation of Cultures. New York: Basic Books.

George, Victoria and Alan Dundes (1978) "The Gomer: a figure of American hospital folk speech." Journal of American Folklore 91: 568-581.

Georges, Robert A. (1983) "Folklore," pp. 134-144 in David Lance (ed.) Sound Archives: A Guide to Their Establishment and Development. Milton Keynes, England: International Association of Sound Archives.

Georges, Robert A. and Michael Owen Jones (1980) People Studying People: The Human Element in Fieldwork. Berkeley and Los Angeles: University of California Press.

Gephart, Robert P. (1978) "Status degradation and organizational succession: an ethnomethodological approach." Administrative Science Quarterly 23: 553-581.

Gitlin, Todd (1983) Inside Prime Time. New York: Pantheon.

Glick, Paula Brown (1983) "Collective bargaining as a field for anthropological study." Anthropology of Work Review 4: 7-9.

Goffman, Erving (1959) The Presentation of Self in Everyday Life. New York: Doubleday.

Goffman, Erving (1963) Stigma. Englewood Cliffs, NJ: Prentice-Hall.

Graham, Allison (1971) Essence of Decision: Explaining the Cuban Missile Crisis. Boston: Little, Brown.

Green, Archie (1978) "Industrial lore: a bibliographic-semantic query." Western Folklore 37: 213-244.

Greer, Art (1976) No Grownups in Heaven: A T-A Primer for Christians and Others. New York: Hawthorne.

Gregory, K. (1983) "Native-view paradigms: multiple culture and culture conflicts in organizations." Administrative Science Quarterly 28: 359-376.

Greiner, Larry and Richard C. Snyder (1983) "The symbolic executive." Presented at the conference Mythology, Symbols & Folklore: Expanding the Analysis of Organizations, Santa Monica, CA.

Haas, Jack (1972) "Binging: educational control among high steel workers." American Behavioral Scientist 16: 27-34.

Hackman, J. Richard and Greg R. Oldham (1980) Work Redesign. Reading, MA: Addison-Wesley.

Handelman, Don (1977) Beyond Culture. Garden City, New York: Doubleday.

Handelman, Don (1982) "Reflexivity in festival and other cultural events," pp. 162-190 in Mary Douglas (ed.) Essays in the Sociology of Perception. London: Routledge & Kegan Paul.

Hans, James S. (1981) The Play of the World. Amherst: University of Massachusetts Press.

Harvard Business Review (1980) "It's not lonely upstairs: an interview with Renn Zaphiropoulos." Harvard Business Review 58 (November-December): 111-132

Heisley, Michael (1983) Coridistas de la Huelga: Singing and Song Making in the Lives of Two Individuals. Ph.D. dissertation, Folklore and Mythology Program, University of California, Los Angeles.

Hirsch, Paul (1969) The Structure of the Popular Music Industry. East Lansing: University of Michigan Survey Research Center.

Hirsch, Paul and John A. Y. Andrews (1983) "Ambushes, shootouts, and knights of the round table: the language of corporate takeovers," pp. 145-155 in Louis Pondy et al. (eds.) Organizational Symbolism. Greenwich, CT: JAI.

Hurst, David K. (1984) "Of boxes, bubbles, and effective management." Harvard Business Review (May/June): 78-88.

Huse, Edgar F. (1975) Organizational Development and Change. St. Paul, MN: West.

Iacocca, L. (1984) Iacocca: An Autobiography. New York: Bantam Books.

Ice, Joyce (1979) "Folklore among the employees at Grand Canyon National Park." Southwest Folklore 3: 18-30.

Jackson, Bruce (1987) Fieldwork. Urbana and Chicago: University of Illinois Press.

Jansen, Erik (1983) "Turning around plant 10 (A)." Research version. (unpublished)

Jansen, William Hugh (1965) "The esoteric-exoteric factor in folklore," pp. 43-51 in Alan Dundes (ed.) The Study of Folklore. Englewood Cliffs, NJ: Prentice-Hall.

Jelinek, Mariann, Linda Smircich, and Paul Hirsch [eds.] (1983) "Organizational culture." Administrative Science Quarterly 28: 331-502.

Jones, Michael Owen (1981) "A feeling for form . . . as illustrated by people at work," pp. 260-261 in Carl Lindahl and Nikolai Burlakoff (eds.) Folklore on Two Continents: Essays in Honor of Linda Degh. Bloomington, IN: Trickster.

Jones, Michael Owen (1982) "Another America: toward a behavioral history based on folkloristics." Western Folklore 41: 43-51.

Jones, Michael Owen (1983) "Organizational folklore conference." American Folklore Society Newsletter 12 (October): 6.

Jones, Michael Owen (1984a) "Corporate natives confer on culture." American Folklore Society Newsletter 13 (October): 6.

Jones, Michael Owen (1984b) "On mergers and managing: what every executive should know about corporate culture and organizational symbolism." California Folklore Newsletter 1 (Spring): 2.

Jones, Michael Owen., ed. (1984c) "Special section: works of art, art as work, and the arts of working—implications for improving organizational life." Western Folklore 43: 172-221.

Jones, Michael Owen (1985a) "Is ethics the issue?" pp. 235-252 in Peter J. Frost et al. (eds.) Organizational Culture. Beverly Hills, CA: Sage.

Jones, Michael Owen (1985b) "On folklorists studying organizations: a reply to Robert S. McCarl." American Folklore Society Newsletter (April): 5-6, 8.

Jones, Michael Owen (1987) Exploring Folk Art: Twenty Years of Thought on Craft, Work, and Aesthetics. Ann Arbor: UMI Research.

Kabanoff, Boris (1980) "Work and non-work: a review of models, methods, and findings." Psychological Bulletin 88: 60-77.

Kast, Fremont E. and James Rosenzweig (1970) Organization and Management: A Systems Approach. New York: McGraw-Hill.

Kidder, Tracy (1981) The Soul of a New Machine. Boston: Little, Brown.

Kiechel, Walter III (1979) "Playing by the rules of the corporate strategy game." Fortune (September 24): 110-115.

Kieschnick, William F. (1983) "A corporate culture for the competitive world." Bray Memorial Lecture, the Executive Forum, California Institute of Technology, Pasadena, CA.

Kilmann, Ralph H. and Mary J. Saxton (1983) Kilmann Saxton Culture Gap Survey. Organizational Design Consultants, Inc.

Kilmann, Ralph H., Mary J. Saxton, Roy Serpa, and Associates [eds.] (1985) Gaining Control of the Corporate Culture. San Francisco: Jossey-Bass.

Kluckhohn, Florence R. and Fred L. Stodtbeck (1961) Varieties in Value Orientation. Evanston, IL: Row Peterson.

Kreman, Bennett (1974) "Search for a better way of work: Lordstown, Ohio," pp. 141-150 in Roy P. Fairfield (ed.) Humanizing the Workplace. Buffalo, NY: Prometheus.

Lawler, Edward E. II and Allan M. M. Mohrman, Jr., Susan A. Mohrman, Gerald E. Ledford, Jr., Thomas C. Cummings, and Associates (1985) Doing Research That Is Useful for Theory and Practice. San Francisco: Jossey-Bass.

Lawrence, Elizabeth Atwood (1982) Rodeo: An Anthropologist Looks at the Wild and the Tame. Chicago: University of Chicago.

Lawrence, Paul and Jay Lorsch (1967) Organization and Environment: Managing Differentiation and Integration. Cambridge: Harvard University Press.

Leach, Edmund (1964) "Anthropological aspects of language: animal categories and verbal abuse," pp. 23-63 in Eric H. Lenneberg (ed.) New Directions in the Study of Language. Cambridge: MIT Press.

Legman, G. (1968) Rationale of the Dirty Joke: An Analysis of Sexual Humor. First Series. New York: Grove.

Lewin, Kurt (1947) "Group decision and social change," pp. 330-344 in T. M. Newcomb and E. L. Hartley (eds.) Readings in Social Psychology. New York: Holt, Rinehart & Winston.

Lewis, Grover (1979) "Farewell, my lovely gumshoe." New West 4: 16 (July 30): 34 ff.

Lorenz, Konrard (1952) King Solomon's Ring. New York: Time.

Louis, Meryl (1980) "Surprise and sense making: what newcomers experience in entering unfamiliar organization settings." Administrative Science Quarterly 25: 226-251.

Louis, Meryl (1983) "Organizations as culture bearing milieux," pp. 39-54 in Louis Pondy et al. (eds.) Organizational Symbolism. Greenwich, CT: JAI.

Lowry, Richard J. [ed.] (1973) Dominance, Self-Esteem, Self-Actualization: Germinal Papers of A. H. Maslow. Monterey, CA: Brooks/Cole.

Lupton, Thomas (1976) "Shop Floor Behavior," pp. 171-203 in Robert Dubin (ed.) Handbook of Work, Organization and Society. Chicago: Rand McNally.

March, James G. (1976) "The technology of foolishness," pp. 69-81 in J. G. March and J. P. Olsen (eds.) Ambiguity and Choice in Organizations. Oslo, Norway: Universitetsforlaget.

Martin, Joanne (1982) "Stories and scripts in organizational settings," pp. 255-303 in Albert H. Hastorf and Alice H. Isen (eds.) Cognitive Social Psychology. New York: Elsevier North-Holland.

Martin, Joanne and Melanie E. Powers (1983) "Truth or corporate propaganda: the value of a good war story," pp. 93-107 in Louis Pondy et al. (ed.) Orgnaizational Symbolism. Greenwich, CT: JAI..

Martin, Joanne and C. Siehl (1983) "Organizational culture and counterculture: an uneasy symbiosis." Organizational Dynamics 12: 52-64.

Martin, Joanne, Martha S. Feldman, Mary Jo Hatch, and Sim B. Sitkin (1983) "The uniqueness paradox in organizational stories." Administrative Science Quarterly 28: 438-453.

Martin, Joanne, Sim B. Sitkin, and Michael Boehm (1985) "Founders and the elusiveness of a cultural legacy," pp. 99-124 in Peter J. Frost et al. (eds.) Organizational Culture. Beverly Hills, CA: Sage.

McCarl, Robert S. (1974) "The production welder: product, process, and the industrial craftsman." New York Folklore Quarterly 30: 243-253.

McCarl, Robert S. (1976) "Smokejumper initiation: ritualized communication in a modern occupation." Journal of American Folklore 89: 46-67.

McCarl, Robert S. (1978) "Occupational folklife: a theoretical hypothesis." Western Folklore 37: 145-160.

McCarl, Robert S. (1979) "Describing the critical center: approaching work cultures from an applied ethnographic perspective." Presented at the Conference on Workers' Culture, Michigan State University.

McCarl, Robert S. (1984a) The District of Columbia Fire Fighters' Project: A Case Study in Occupational Folklife. Washington, DC: Smithsonian Institution Press.

McCarl, Robert S. (1984b). "You've come a long way—and now this is your retirement: an analysis of performance in fire fighting culture." Journal of American Folklore 97: 393-422.

McClelland, David C. (1972) "That urge to achieve," pp. 78-86 in David R. Hampton (ed.) Behavioral Concepts in Management. Encino, CA: Dickenson.

Meissner, Martin (1976) "The language of work," pp. 205-279 in Robert Dubin (ed.) Handbook of Work, Organization, and Society. Chicago: Rand McNally.

Mergen, Bernard (1978) "Work and play in an occupational subculture," in M. A. Salter (ed.) Play: Anthropological Perspectives. West Point, NY: Leisure.

Meyer, John and Brian Rowan (1977) "Institutionalized organizations: formal structure as myth and ceremony." American Journal of Sociology 83: 240-262.

Miller, Lawrence M. (1984) American Spirit: Visions of a New Corporate Culture. New York: William Morrow.

Mitroff, Ian (1985) Stakeholders of the Organizational Mind. San Francisco: Jossey-Bass.

Mitroff, Ian and Ralph Kilmann (1975) "Stories managers tell: a new tool for organizational problem solving." Management Review 64: 13-28.

Mitroff, Ian and Ralph Kilmann (1976) "On organizational stories: an approach to the design and analysis of organizations through myth and stories," pp. 189-207 in R. Kilmann, L. Pondy, and D. Sleven (eds.) The Management of Organizational Design. New York: North Holland.

Moberg, Dennis J. (1981) Job Enrichment Through Symbol Management. California Management Review 24: 24-30.

Moch, Michael and Anne S. Huff (1982) "Life on the line." Wharton Magazine 6 (Summer): 53-58.

Moch, Michael and Anne S. Huff (1983) "'Chewing ass out': the enactment of power relationships through language and ritual." Journal of Business Research 11: 293-316.

Montepio, Susan (1984) "Studying organizational culture through expressive behavior." Prepared for Folklore 259: Corporate Culture and Organizational Symbolism, University of California, Los Angeles. (unpublished)

Moore, Michael D. (1983) "Old People's Day: drama, celebration, and aging." Ph.D. dissertation, Folklore and Mythology Program and English Department, University of California, Los Angeles.

Moore, Sally F. and Barbara G. Myerhoff (1977) "Secular ritual: forms and meanings," pp. 3-24 in S. F. Moore and B. G. Myerhoff (eds.) Secular Ritual. Amsterdam: Van Gorcum, Assen.

Morgan, D.H.J. (1975) "Autonomy and negotiation in an industrial setting." Sociology of Work and Occupations 2 (August): 203-226.

Morgan, Gareth, Peter J. Frost and Louis R. Pondy (1983) "Organizational symbolism," pp. 3-35 in Pondy et al. (eds.) Organizational Symbolism. Greenwich, CT: JAI.

Morgan, Gareth and Linda Smircich (1980) "The case for qualitative research." Academy of Management Review 5: 491-500.

Moskowitz, Milton, Michael Katz, and Robert Levering (1980) Everybody's Business. New York: Harper & Row.

Mullen, Patrick B. (1972) "Modern legend and rumor theory." Journal of the Folklore Institute 9: 95-109.

Mullen, Patrick B. (1978) "'I heard the old fishmen say': folklore of the Texas Gulf Coast." Austin: University of Texas Press.

Myerhoff, Barbara (1978) Number Our Days. New York: Simon & Schuster.

Norman, Geoffrey (1972) "Blue collar saboteurs." Playboy (September): 86-98.

O'Day, Rory (1974) "Intimidation rituals: reactions to reform." Journal of Applied Behavioral Sciences 10: 373-386.

Oldenquist, Andrew (1982) "On belonging to tribes." Newsweek (April 5): 9.

Oldham, Greg R. and Daniel J. Brass (1979) "Employee reactions to an open-plan office: a naturally-occurring quasi-experiment." Administrative Science Quarterly 24: 267-284.

Oldsmobile Division (1971) Oldsmobile Action on Absenteeism and Turnover. General Motors Corporation.

O'Reilly, Brian (1984) "AT&T: what was it we were trying to fix?" Fortune (June 11): 30-36.

Oring, Elliott (1966) "The life history of Igor Slats." (unpublished)

Oring, Elliott (1984) "Dyadic traditions." Journal of Folklore Research 21: 19-28.

Oring, Elliott [ed.] (1986) Folk Groups and Folklore Genres. Logan: Utah State University Press.

Oshry, Barry (1976a) Notes on the Power and Systems Perspective. Boston: Power and Systems.

Oshry, Barry (1976b) Controlling the Contexts of Consciousness: The "I," the "We," the "All of Us." Boston: Power and Systems.

Oshry, Barry (1978) Organizational Spasms: When Healthy Organizations Meet Unhealthy Environments. Boston: Power and Systems.

O'Toole, James [ed.] (1974) Work in America. Cambridge: MIT Press.

O'Toole, James (1985) Vanguard Management. Garden City, NY: Doubleday.

Ouchi, William G (1980) "Markets, clans and hierarchies." Administrative Science Quarterly 25: 129-141.

Ouchi, William G. (1981) Theory Z: How American Business Can Meet the Japanese Challenge. Reading, MA: Addison-Wesley.

Ouchi, William G., and R. L. Price (1978) "Hierarchies, clans, and Theory Z: a new perspective on organizational development." Organizational Dynamics (Autumn): 25-44.

Ouchi, William G. and Alan L. Wilkins (1985) "Organizational culture." Annual Review of Sociology 11: 457-483.

Pacanowsky, Michael E. and Nick O'Donnell-Trujillo (1982) "Communication and organizational cultures." Western Journal of Speech Communication 46: 115-130.

Pascale, Richard Tanner and Anthony G. Athos (1981) The Art of Japanese Management: Applications for American Executives. New York: Warner.

Pauchant, Thierry (1985) "Review of *The Functions of the Executive,* by Chester I. Barnard." New Management: The Magazine of Innovative Management 2 (Winter): 60-61.

Perrow, Charles (1972) Complex Organizations. Glenview, IL: Scott, Foresman.

Peters, Thomas J. (1978) "Symbols, patterns and settings: an optimistic case for getting things done." Organizational Dynamics (Autumn): 3-27.

Peters, Thomas J. (1980) "Management systems: the language of organizational character and competence." Organizational Dynamics (Summer): 3-26.

Peters, Thomas J. and Nancy Austin (1985) A Passion for Excellence. New York: Random House.

Peters, Thomas J. and Robert H. Waterman, Jr. (1982) In Search of Excellence: Lessons from America's Best Run Companies. New York: Harper & Row.

Peterson, R. A. and D. G. Berger (1975) "Cycles in symbol production: the case of popular music." American Sociological Review 40 (April): 158-173.

Pettigrew, Andrew W. (1979) "On studying organization cultures." Administrative Science Quarterly 24: 570-581.

Pfeffer, Jeffrey (1981) "Management as symbolic action: the creation and maintenance of organizational paradigms," pp. 1-52 in L. Cummings and B. Staw (eds.) Research in Organizational Behavior, Vol. 3. Greenwich, CT: JAI.

Pondy, Louis R. (1978) "Leadership is a language game," pp. 87-99 in M. McCall and M. Lombardo (eds.) Leadership: Where Else Can We Go? Durham, NC: Duke University Press.

Pondy, Louis, Peter Frost, Gareth Morgan, and Thomas Dandridge [eds.] (1983) Organizational Symbolism. Greenwich, CT: JAI.

Pope, LeRoy (1979) "Americans spend 45 percent of work day doing nothing, consultant says." Journal of Commerce Review 66 (May 4): 1.

Powdermaker, Hortense (1950) Hollywood: The Dream Factory. Boston: Little, Brown.

Putnam, Linda L. and Michael E. Pacanowsky [eds.] (1983) Communications and Organizations. Beverly Hills, CA: Sage.

Radcliffe-Brown, A. R. (1952) Structure and Function in Primitive Society: Essays and Address. New York: Free Press.

Radcliffe-Brown, A. R. (1964) The Andaman Islanders. Glencoe, IL: Free Press.

Radest, Howard (1974) "The virtues of wastefulness: possibility or myth?" pp. 239-256 in Roy P. Fairfield (ed.) Humanizing the Workplace. Buffalo: Prometheus.

Read, Herbert (1964) "Civilization and the sense of quality," pp. 71-85 in To Hell with Culture. New York: Schoken.

Regan, Arthur (1983) "Myth, symbols & folklore: expanding the analysis of organizations." Folklore & Mythology 2 (December): 3-4.

Rice, A. K (1969) "Individual, group, and intergroup processes." Human Relations 22: 565-584.

Ritzer, George (1972) Man and His Work: Conflict and Change. New York: Appleton-Century Crofts.

Rohlen, T. P (1973) "'Spiritual education' in a Japanese bank." American Anthropologist 75: 1542-1562.

Rohlen, T. P. (1974) For Harmony and Strength: Japanese White Collar Organization in an Anthropological Perspective. Berkeley and Los Angeles: University of California Press.

Rowe, Alan J., Richard O. Mason, and Karl Dickel (1982) Strategic Management and Business Policy. Reading, MA: Addison-Wesley.

Roy, Donald (1959-1960) "'Banana time': job satisfaction and informal interaction." Human Organization 18: 158-168.

Roy, Donald (1974) "Sex in the factory: informal heterosexual relations between supervisors and work groups." pp. 44-46 in Clifton D. Bryant (ed.) Deviant Behavior: Occupational and Organizational Bases. Chicago: Rand McNally.

Rubin, Arnold (1979) "Anthropology and the study of art in contemporary western society: the Pasadena Tournament of Roses," pp. 669-715 in Justine M. Cordwell (ed.) The Visual Arts: Plastic and Graphic. The Hague: Mouton.

Runcie, John F. (1971) "Social group formation in an occupation: a case study of the truck driver." Ph.D. dissertation, Rutgers University.

Runcie, John F. (1980a) "By days I make the cars." Harvard Business Review 58: 3 (May/June): 106-115.

Runcie, John F. (1980b) "Dynamic systems and the quality of work life." Personnel 57 (November/December): 13-24.

Sahlins, Marshall (1976) Culture and Practical Reason. Chicago: University of Chicago Press.

Santino, Jack (1978) "The outlaw emotions: workers' narratives from three contemporary occupations." Ph.D. dissertation, Department of Folklore and Folklife, University of Pennsylvania.

Sashkin, Marshall (1984) "Participative management is an ethical imperative." Organizational Dynamics (Spring): 5-22.

Sathe, Vijay (1983) "Some action implications of corporate culture: a manager's guide to action." Organizational Dynamics (Autumn): 4-23.

Schein, Edgar H. (1978) Career Dynamics: Matching Individual and Organizational Needs. Reading, MA: Addison-Wesley.

Schein, Edgar H. (1981) "Does Japanese management style have a message for American managers?" Sloan Management Review 23: 55-58.

Schein, Edgar H. (1983a) "Organization culture: or, if organization development is culture change, is that possible and/or desirable?" Presented at annual meeting of Academy of Management, Dallas, Texas.

Schein, Edgar H. (1983b) "Corporate culture: what it is and how to change it." Presented at the convocation of the Society of Sloan Fellows, MIT.

Schein, Edgar H. (1983c) "The role of the founder in creating organization culture." Organizational Dynamics (Summer): 13-28.

Schein, Edgar H. (1985) Organizational Culture and Leadership: A Dynamic View. San Francisco: Jossey-Bass.

Schurr, Sam H., et al. (1960) Energy in the American Economy, 1850-1950. Baltimore, MD: Johns Hopkins Press.

Schwartz, H. and S. M. Davis (1981) "Matching corporate culture and business strategy." Organizational Dynamics (Summer) 10: 30-48.

Selznik, Philip (1957) Leadership and Administration. Evanston, IL: Row, Peterson.

Sergiovanni, Thomas J. and John E. Corbally [eds.] (1984) Leadership and Organizational Culture: New Perspectives on Administrative Theory and Practice. Urbana and Chicago: University of Illinois Press.

Shiota, Maruo (1982) "For the Japanese, there is no demarcation between work and play." Management Review 71 (March): 36.

Shuldiner, David (1980) "The art of the sheet metalworker." Southwest Folklore 4: 37-41.

Shure, Peter (1983) "Meeting News dollars and census." Meeting News (November).

Siehl, Caren (1985) "After the founder: an opportunity to manage culture," pp. 99-124 in Peter Frost et al. (eds.) Organizational Culture. Beverly Hills, CA: Sage.

Silverzweig, Stan and Robert F. Allen (1976) "Changing the corporate culture." Sloan Management Review 17: 33-49.

Singer, Milton B. (1984) Man's Glassy Essence: Explorations in Semiotic Anthropology. Bloomington: Indiana University Press.

Smircich, Linda (1983a) "Concepts of culture and orgnaizational analysis." Administrative Science Quarterly 28: 339-358.

Smircich, Linda (1983b) "Implications for management theory," in L. Putnam and M. Pacanowsky (eds.) Communication and Organizations: An Interpretive Approach. Beverly Hills, CA: Sage.

Smith, Kenwyn K. (1975) "The values and dangers of power conflict." Contemporary Australian Management 3: 19-23.

Smith, Kenwyn K. (1977) "An intergroup perspective on individual behavior," pp. 359-372 in J. R. Hackman et al. (eds.) Perspectives on Behavior in Organizations. New York: McGraw-Hill.

Smith, Kenwyn K. (1982) Groups in Conflict: Prisons in Disguise. Dubuque, IA: Kendall Hunt.

Smith, Lee (1984) "Cracks in the Japanese work ethic." Fortune (May 14): 162-168.

Smith, Robert J. (1972) "Festivals and celebrations," pp. 159-172 in Richard M. Dorson (ed.) Folklore and Folklife: An Introduction. Chicago: University of Chicago Press.

Snyder, Richard Christopher (1984) "Update on corporate culture." New Management: The Magazine of Innovate Management 1 (4): 55-56.

Snyder, Richard Christopher (1985) "To improve innovation, manage corporate culture," pp. 164-175 in Warren G. Bennis, Kenneth D. Benne, and Robert Chin (eds.) The Planning of Change. New York: Holt, Rinehart and Winston.

Snyder, Richard Christopher (1986a) Turning Around Plant 10 (B). Research version. (unpublished)

Snyder, Richard Christopher (1986b) Turning Around Plant 10 (C). Research version. (unpublished)

Sonduck, Michael M. and Barbara Perry (1983) "Anecdotal survey feedback: expanding the range of OD technology." Presented at the annual meeting of the OD Network, Pasadena, California.

Staw, B. M. (1980) "Rationality and justification in organizational life," in B. M. Staw and L. L. Cummings (eds.) Research in Organizational Behavior, Vol. 2. Greenwich, CT: JAI.

Stevens, Phillips (1980) "Play and work: a false dichotomy?" in H. B. Schwartzman (ed.) Play and Culture. West Point, New York: Leisure.

Stoeltje, Beverly J. (1979) "Rodeo as symbolic performance." Ph.D. dissertation, University of Texas.

Stoeltje, Beverly J. (1983) "Festival in America," pp. 239-246 in Richard M. Dorson (ed.) Handbook of American Folklore. Bloomington: Indiana University Press.

Strauss, George (1974a) "Is there a blue-collar revolt against work?" pp. 19-48 in Roy P. Fairfield (ed.) Humanizing the Workplace. Buffalo, NY: Prometheus.

Strauss, George (1974b) "Job satisfaction, motivation and job redesign," pp. 19-49 in George Straus et al. (eds.) Organizational Behavior: Research and Issues. Madison: Industrial Relations Research Association.

Susman, G. I., and R. D. Evered (1978) "An assessment of the scientific merits of action research." Administrative Science Quarterly 23: 532-603.

Swanson, Catherine and Philip Nusbaum [eds.] (1979) "Occupational folklore and the folklore of working." Folklore Forum 11: 1-65.

Tannenbaum, Robert, Newton Margulies, Fred Massarik, and Associates [eds.] (1985) Human Systems Development. San Francisco: Jossey-Bass.

Terkel, Studs (1974) Working (1972). New York: Avon.

Thomas, Kenneth W. and Walter G. Tymon, Jr. (1982) "Necessary properties of relevant research: lessons from recent criticism of the organizational sciences." Academy of Management Review 7: 345-352.

Thompson, James D. (1967) Organizations in Action. New York: McGraw-Hill.

Tichy, Noel M. (1983) Managing Organizational Transformations. Human Resource Management 22: 45-60.

Time (1983) "Hot 100." (July 4): 46.

Toelken, Barre (1976) "Seeing with a native eye: how many sheep will it hold?" pp. 9-25 in Walter H. Capps (ed.) Seeing With a Native Eye: Essays on Native American Religion. New York: Harper & Row.

Toelken, Barre (1979) The Dynamics of Folklore. Boston: Houghton Mifflin.

Trice, Harrison M. (1985a) "Rites and ceremonials in organizational culture," pp. 221-270 in S. B. Bacharach and S. M. Mitchell (eds.) Research on the Sociology of Organizations, Vol. 4. Greenwich, CT: JAI.

Trice, Harrison M. (1985b) "Studying troubled employees: gaining and keeping research access," pp. 109-132 in Donald F. Godwin et al. (eds.) The Business of Doing Worksite Research. Washington, DC: Department of Health and Human Services.

Trice, Harrison M. and Janice M. Beyer (1984a) "Employee assistance programs: blending performance-oriented and humanitarian ideologies to assist emotionally disturbed employees," pp. 245-297 in Research in Community and Mental Health, Vol. 4, Greenwich, CT: JAI.

Trice, Harrison M. and Janice M. Beyer (1984b) "Studying organizational cultures through rites and ceremonials." Academy of Management Review 9: 653-669.

Trice, Harrison M., James Belasco, and Joseph A. Alutto (1969) "The role of ceremonials in organizational behavior." Industrial and Labor Relations Review 23: 40-51.

Tunstall, W. Brooke (1983) "Cultural transition at AT&T." Sloan Management Review (Fall): 15-26.

Turner, Victor (1969) The Ritual Process: Structure and Anti-Structure. Ithaca, NY: Cornell University Press.

Turner, Victor (1974) Dramas, Fields, and Metaphors: Symbolic Action in Human Society. Ithaca, NY: Cornell University Press.

Ullian, Joseph Alan (1976) "Joking at work." Journal of Communication 26: 129-133.

Ulrich, Wendy L. (1984) "HRM and culture: history, ritual, and myth." Human Resource Management 23: 117-128.

Uttal, B. (1983) "The corporate culture vultures." Fortune (October 17): 66-72.

Van Gennep, Arnold (1960) Rites of Passage (1909). Chicago: University of Chicago Press.

Van Maanen, John (1973) "Observations on the making of policemen." Human Organization 32: 407-418.

Van Maanen, John (1978) "People processing: strategies of organizational socialization." Organizational Dynamics 7: 19-36.

Van Maanen, John. [ed.] (1979) "Qualitative methodology." Administrative Science Quarterly 24: 519-712.

Van Maanen, John and Stephen R. Barley (1984) "Occupational communities: culture and control in organizations." Research in Organizational Behavior 6: 287-365.

Van Maanen, John, James Dabbs, Jr., and Robert R. Faulkner (1982) Varieties of Qualitative Research. Beverly Hills, CA: Sage.

Van Maanen, John and Edgar Schein (1979) "Toward a theory of organizational socialization." Research in Organization Behavior 1: 209-264.

von Glassersfeld, Ernst (1984) "An introduction to radical constructivism," pp. 17-40 in Paul Watzlawick (ed.) The Invented Reality: How Do We Know What We Believe We Know. New York: Norton.

Walker, Ann (1983) "Davis' wealth of traditions." California Aggie (April 16): 1.

Walker, Charles W. and Robert H. Guest (1952) The Man on the Assembly Line. Cambridge, MA: Harvard University Press.

Walton, Richard (1972) "How to counter alienation in the plant." Harvard Business Review 50 (November): 70-81.

Warner, M. (1981) "Organizational experiments and social innovations," in P. C. Nystrom and W. H. Starbuck (eds.) Handbook of Organizational Design. New York: Oxford University Press.

Watzlawick, Paul (1978) The Language of Change. New York: Basic Books.

Watzlawick, Paul, John H. Weakland, and Richard Fische (1974) Change: Principles of Problem Formation and Problem Resolution. New York: Norton.

Weick, Karl (1969) The Social Psychology of Organizing (2nd ed.). Reading, MA: Addison-Wesley.

Weisbord, Marvin R. (1972) "What, not again! Manage people better?" pp. 3-15 in W. Warner Burke and Harvey A. Hornstein (eds.) The Social Technology of Organization Development. Fairfax, VA: Learning Resources.

Weiss, C. H. (1981) "Use of social science research in organizations: the constrained repertoire theory," pp. 180-204 in H. Stein (ed.) Organization and the Human Services. Philadelphia: Temple University Press.

Weisz, J. R., F. M. Rothbaum, and T. C. Blackburn (1984) "Standing out and standing in: the psychology of control in America and Japan." American Psychologist (September): 955-967.

Werner, Oswald and Joann Fenton (1973) "Method and theory in ethnoscience or ethnoepistemology," pp. 537-578 in R. Naroll and R. Cohen (eds.) A Handbook of Method in Cultural Anthropology. New York: Columbia University Press.

Westerlund, Gunnary and Sven-Eric Sjostrand (1979) Organizational Myths. New York: Harper & Row.

Whyte, William Foote (1960) "Interviewing in field research," pp. 352-374 in Richard N. Adams and Jack J. Preiss (eds.) Human Organization Research. Homewood, IL: Dorsey Press.

Whyte, William Foote (1961) Men at Work. Homewood, IL: Dorsey Press.

Widick, B. J. (1976) "Work in auto plants: then and now," pp. 6-17 in B. J. Widick (ed.) Auto Work and Its Discontents. Baltimore, MD: Johns Hopkins University Press.

Wilkins, Alan (1978) "Organizational stories as an expression of management philosophy: implications for social control in organizations." Ph.D. dissertation, Graduate School of Management, Stanford University.

Wilkins, Alan (1983a) "The culture audit: a tool for understanding organizations." Organizational Dynamics (Autumn): 24-38.

Wilkins, Alan (1983b) "Organizational stories as symbols which control the organization," pp. 81-92 in Louis R. Pondy et al. (eds.) Organizational Symbolism. Greenwich, CT: JAI.

Wilkins, Alan (1984) "The creation of company cultures: the role of stories and human resource systems." Human Resource Management 23: 41-60.

Wilkins, Alan L. and Nigel J. Bristow (1987) "You can't 'ape' excellence: why we need corporate statesmanship." Presented at the annual meeting of the Western Academy of Management, Hollywood, California.

Wilkins, Alan L. and William G. Ouchi (1983) "Efficient cultures: exploring the relationship between culture and organizational performance." Administrative Science Quarterly 28: 468-481.

Wilson, William A. (1981) "On being human: the folklore of Mormon missionaries, 64th Utah State University Faculty Honor Lecture." Logan: Utah State University Press.

Wolfe, William B. (1974) The Basic Barnard: An Introduction to Chester I. Barnard and His Theories of Organization and Management. Ithaca, NY: Cornell University.

Yankelovich, Daniel (1981) "New rules in American life: searching for self-fulfillment in a world turned upside down." Psychology Today (April): 35-91.

Yanow, Deborah J. (1982) "Toward a symbolic theory of policy implementation: an analysis of symbols, metaphors, and myths in organizations." Ph.D. dissertation, MIT.

Zemke, Ron and Thomas Kramlinger (1982) "Tell me a story: the critical incident technique," pp. 129-139 in Figuring Things Out: A Trainer's Guide to Needs and Task Analysis. Reading, MA: Addison-Wesley.

Zetterberg, Hans and Greta Frankel (1981) "Working less and enjoying it more in Sweden." Public Opinion 4 (August/September): 41-45.

About the Authors

Shirley L. Arora is a Professor of Spanish and Portuguese at the University of California, Los Angeles. She is the author of *Proverbial Comparisons and Related Expressions in Spanish* and articles on various aspects of proverb use as well as on oral narrative in Spanish.

Janice M. Beyer is Professor of Management at New York University. She is Past Chair of the Organization and Management Theory Division of the Academy of Management, and was editor of the *Academy of Management Journal* from 1985-1987. Among her publications are articles on ideologies and values in organizational decision making in the *Handbook of Organizational Design*, edited by Nystrom and Starbuck, and on changing organizational cultures in *Gaining Control of the Corporate Culture*, edited by Kilmann et al.

Don Christensen has an M.A. degree in History from the University of Illinois and an M.A. in Folklore from UCLA. His dissertation in progress at UCLA focuses on folklore in the diaries of Mormons in Utah. He resides in Valley Ford, Sonoma County, California, and teaches courses on varied topics, including organizational folklore.

Thomas C. Dandridge is an Associate Professor with joint appointments in the School of Business and the Rockefeller College of Public Affairs and Policy at the State University of New York, Albany. Among his writings on organizational symbolism are essays in *Academy of Management Review* (1981) and *Organizational Culture*, edited by Frost et al. (1985).

C. Kurt Dewhurst is Director of the Michigan State University Museum and Assistant Professor of English at Michigan State University. Some of his books are *Grand Ledge Folk Pottery: Traditions at Work* (1986), *Michigan Hmong Art* (1984), *Religious Folk Art in America* (1983), *Artists in Aprons* (1979), and *Rainbows in the Sky* (1978).

Roberta J. Evanchuk has a B.A. in Theater Arts and an M.A. in Folklore and Mythology from UCLA. A frequent guest choreographer for dance troups, she directed the Aman Dance Company's "California Heritage Suite" for the Olympic Arts Festival in 1984. Presently she is Administrative Assistant to the Folklore and Mythology Program at UCLA, where she has founded a dance group called Folklorismus.

Gary Alan Fine is Professor of Sociology at the University of Minnesota. He received his Ph.D. at Harvard in 1976 in Social Psychology with a minor in Folklore. He is the coauthor (with Ralph Rosnow) of *Rumor and Gossip: The Social Psychology of Hearsay* and the author of *Shared Fantasy: Role-Playing Games as Social Worlds*.

Rob Hanford earned his B.A. in History and M.A. in Folklore from the University of California, Berkeley, in 1969 and 1979. Since receiving his M.A. degree, he has worked for Pacific Gas and Electric as a service representative and meter reader, a job that afforded an unexpected opportunity to apply folklore research methods to the problem of energy distribution and consumption. Presently he is serving as a staff writer for a regional employee newspaper, *The De Salba Breeze*; articles include the oral history of retirees.

Michael Owen Jones is Professor of History and Folklore at UCLA and Director of the Folklore and Mythology Center, an organized research unit with library and archives. He was principal director of the international conference "Myths, Symbols & Folklore: Expanding the Analysis or Organizations" (1983). Among his publications are *People Studying People: The Human Element in Fieldwork* (co-authored with Georges) and *Exploring Folk Art: Twenty Years of Thought on Craft, Work, and Aesthetics*. His interests include the application of principles about traditions and symbolic interaction to leadership, human resources development and organizational change.

Joanne Martin is Associate Professor of Organizational Behavior in the Graduate School of Business and, by courtesy, the Department of Sociology, Stanford University. The author of numerous articles in major books and such journals as *Administrative Science Quarterly*, *Organizational Dynamics*, and *Journal of Experimental Social Psychology*, she has focused her research on three topics: organizational culture, distributive injustice, and research methods.

Jodi Martin is a graduate student in the Folklore and Mythology Program at UCLA. She has conducted field research on Christian testimonies, political organizations, and a law firm. In addition to being a student and a word processing specialist who has worked for several companies, she has written several children's books.

Peggy McDonald is a graphic designer and program coordinator with experience in arts administration and public management. She received her MBA degree from UCLA in 1984, with a specialty in marketing. Presently she is employed in the Company Clorox, Oakland, California.

Jay Mechling is Professor and Director of the American Studies Program at the University of California, Davis. He is editor of *Western Folklore*. His publications have appeared in such journals as *American Quarterly*, *Journal of Popular Culture*, *Journal of American Folklore*, *Journal of Social History*, *Central States Journal of Speech*, *Sociological Inquiry*, *Journal of Psychoanalytic Anthropology*, and *Human Organization*.

Ian Mitroff is the Harold Quinton Distinguished Professor of Business Policy in the Department of Management and Organization in the Graduate School of Business Administration, University of Southern California. He has authored more than 140 papers and 7 books on business policy, corporate culture, managerial psychology, strategic planning, and the philosophy and sociology of science. Some recent works include *Corporate Tragedies: Product Tampering, Sabotage, and Other Catastrophes* (with Kilmann) and *Stakeholders of the Organizational Mind*.

Michael Dane Moore earned his Ph.D. in English and Folklore at the University of California, Los Angeles; his dissertation is titled "Old People's Day: Drama, Celebration, and Aging." Currently he teaches business and technical communications at UCLA, along with courses in fieldwork and folklore. Cofounder of the UCLA Folklore and Mythology Center's Organization Studies Group, Dr. Moore has published articles both on American folklore and on business communications. He has worked as a consultant with organizations such as Honda, Glendale Federal Savings and Loan, and the RAND Corporation. Formerly he was Director of Public Relations for International Robotic Technologies, Inc. His research interests focus on rhetoric and ethnography.

John F. Runcie, the former Vice President of Human Resources, Doehler-Jarvis/Farley Industries, Inc., Toledo, Ohio, is now an independent consultant. His previous work includes organization development assignments with Anheuser-Busch, Inc., the St. Louis, Missouri, Police Department, and the Saline Water Conversion Corporation in Saudi Arabia. His publications include "Dynamic Systems and the Quality of Work Life," *Personnel* (1980), "By Day I Make the Cars," *Harvard Business Review* (1980), and *Experiencing Social Research* (1980).

Brian Rusted is the Director of the Centre for Canadian Studies at the University of Calgary, and coeditor of *Artifact: A Video Journal of the Expressive Arts*. He is a writer and filmmaker trained in communications research at the Annenberg School in Philadelphia and Northwestern University in Chicago. He is interested in the social classifications of taste and their role in the communication of cultural performances.

Caren Siehl is an Assistant Professor of Management and Organization at the School of Business Administration, University of Southern California. Before earning her Ph.D. in Organizational Behavior at the Graduate School of Business, Stanford University, she was employed by IBM in both marketing and customer support functions. Recent articles on organizational culture and symbolism have appeared in *Leaders and Managers: International Perspectives on Managerial Behavior and Leadership* (volume 7), and in *Organizational Dynamics*. Presently she is studying the impact of cultural differences on mergers and acquisitions, as well as the role of culture in the delivery of quality service.

Richard C. Snyder is a lecturer at the University of California at Berkeley, School of Business Administration, and is currently completing doctoral studies in Management and Organization at the University of Southern California. He was formerly Director of Planning for the Support Center, a national management consulting firm based in Washington, D.C., and is a cofounder of the Center for Nonprofit Management in Los Angeles. He has also worked as an adviser for McGraw-Hill management films and, before entering the management field, was a video cameraman and consulting media specialist. As an undergraduate, he studied Social Analysis and Communication at Antioch College, and first became involved in ethnographic work while traveling and studying in Latin America. His management writings have appeared in *New Management, The Planning of Change*, and various specialized publications.

Stephen Stern holds a joint appointment in the Folklore and Mythology Program and the Graduate School of Library and Information Science at the University of California, Los Angeles. A major focus of his research is a comparison between not-for-profit and for-profit organizations as revealed through the ways in which narrative, ritual, celebration, and symbolism shape these two modes of organizing work and leisure.

Peter Tommerup is a Ph.D. candidate in the Folklore and Mythology Program at the University of California, Los Angeles, with an allied concentration in Behavioral and Organization Science. His research focuses on the social creation and perpetuation of meaning systems in American organizations. Additional research interests include Appalachian culture and the performance of traditional American instrumental music in urban settings.

Harrison M. Trice is a Professor in the School of Industrial and Labor Relations at Cornell University. Among his many publications and papers are "Role of Ceremonials in Organizational Behavior" (with Belasco and Alutto), *Implementing Change* (with Beyer), and "Studying Organizational Cultures Through Rites and Ceremonials" (with Beyer), in *Academy of Management Review* (1984). He and Beyer are currently preparing a textbook on cultures in organizations.

Patricia Atkinson Wells, folklorist and arts administrator, is currently engaged in research on creativity, celebration and community identity. She has an M.A. in Folklore and Mythology, and presently is a Ph.D. candidate in the Folklore and Mythology Program at UCLA. She has served as consultant to the Tennessee Arts Commission, Tennessee Department of Education, Rutherford Council, National Association for the Preservation and Perpetuation of Storytelling, Hilltown Community Development Corporation, the California Sailing Academy, and the Girl Scouts of America.

David Scofield Wilson is Associate Professor of American Studies at the University of California, Davis. Among his many papers and publications are *In the Presence of Nature,* "Toward a 'Natural History' of People in Yosemite Park," "The Wolf Peach: An Essay in Thick Description Applied to Ethnobotanical Study," "Bricoleurs, Bureaucrats, and Big Farmers: Three Cultural Modes in Bringing Tomatoes and Technology Together," and "'Don't Tread on Me': The Rattlesnakes of American Culture."

William A. Wilson is Chair of the English Department at Brigham Young University; formerly he was Professor of English and History and Director of the Folklore Program at Utah State University. The recipient of many fellowships and honors, he has served as editor of *Western Folklore*, been a frequent contributor to *Utah Historical Quarterly*, and published *Folklore and Nationalism in Modern Finland*, "Folklore and History: Fact Amid the Legends," and many other works. The research on Mormon missionary lore that he describes in this book was conducted with John B. Harris, a colleague of his at BYU.

Terance J. Wolfe is a Ph.D. candidate in the Behavioral and Organization Science Group, Graduate School of Management, UCLA. For six years he taught management and organization behavior and psychology courses at the University of Maryland. The author of many papers at the meetings of such organizations as the American Psychological Association, the California Folklore Society, the OD Network, the American Folklore Society and the Western Psychological Association, he is currently conducting research on issues of power and political processes within organizations, especially regarding the implementation of information systems.